Socialism Its Theoretical Basis and Practical Application

AUTHOR'S PREFACE.

WITHIN the last few years socialism has spread to an
alarming extent. At the last general elections in Germany, June 16, 1903, it polled considerably above
three million votes. The jubilant exultation of socialists at this unparalleled success may easily be imagined. "Berlin the capital of socialism! Germany
the realm of social democracy!" Thus the *Vorwarts*
triumphantly exclaimed.

In view of this gigantic development of social democracy it certainly behooves every man of culture,
but above all the leaders in civil and social life, to
become familiar with socialist ideas, to make themselves acquainted with the scientific basis so much
vaunted by socialists, and to form an independent
judgment concerning them.

To oppose the spread of socialism by means of
police regulations, as was done by the famous Socialist
Law of Germany, must always prove utterly abortive;
in this struggle intellectual and moral weapons rather
will be used to advantage.

Modern socialism can and must be combated both
theoretically and *practically*. Practical endeavors are
of the first importance, and they above all will help
to check the further spread of social democracy,

3

and will erect a powerful dam to stem the tide of revolution. Social *reform* along reasonable lines will remove the grievances which now furnish ample material for the declamations of socialist agitators. For no one can deny that in our modern society many abuses call for correction; also we advocate social reform wherever needed.

However, reform is not the real aim of socialists; their purpose is the radical subversion of all existing social conditions and the reconstruction of society on an entirely new basis. That this their attempt is impracticable and fraught with disaster is to be seen in these pages. This *theoretical* exposition of socialism has become more important nowadays than ever before, nay, it is absolutely necessary.

From these remarks it is clear that our object is purely critical and negative; we do not make any proposals of practical reforms, not because we are opposed to them or deem them superfluous, but because they are beyond the scope of this work. Our views on this matter may be gathered from our "Moralphilosophie," vol. II. pp. 596 sqq.

In our refutation of socialists it has been our constant endeavor to enter into their ideas to the best of our power, to study their principles in their own writings, to inquire into the foundations upon which their system is based, to examine their principal demands and the relations they bear to each other. The task was by no means an easy one. Socialists themselves do not agree in the details of their demands, and within their system many different modifications are possible, all of which call for separate examination. Notwithstanding these difficulties our exposition of socialistic tenets has been acknowledged by prominent socialist leaders as substantially correct. Thus Kautsky in his *Neue Zeit* (1891, II. p. 637) remarks of our work: "Marx's theory has been rendered much better by Cathrein than by any of the liberalist 'socialist-killers.' The author has at least read the works which he discusses."

In this eighth [German] edition special attention has been bestowed on a more thorough exposition and refutation of the "materialistic conception of history" and its application to socialist ideals. Also the controversy between Bebel's orthodox party and the revisionists with Bernstein and von Vollmar at their head has received fuller treatment. The most recent literary productions for and against socialism have been pressed into service as far as possible. Besides, our account of the present state of socialism in different countries has been corrected according to the latest data available.

VICTOR CATHREIN, S.J.

VALKENBERG, HOLLAND, June, 1903.

PREFACE TO THE THIRD AMERICAN EDITION.

SINCE its first appearance in 1890 Father Cathrein's book has gone through eight large editions. It has been translated into Spanish, French, English, Italian, Polish, Flemish, Bohemian, and Hungarian. The Rt. Rev. Bishop of Muenster in a special rescript recommended the work to the serious consideration of his clergy. Liberal and Protestant papers, as, for instance, the *Deutsche Reichs- und Staatsanzeiger*, have referred to it in terms of the highest praise, calling special attention to its thorough presentation and striking refutation of socialism. Competent critics have declared the present volume to be the best refutation of socialism to be found in the German language. Thus in 1894 (No. 691) the Protestant *Reichsherold* avers: "Cathrein is the author of the best refutation of social democracy that has ever come to our knowledge." A critic in the *Kreuzzeitung* speaks of our author's presentation and criticism of socialist theories as "exceptionally thorough."

This generous praise bestowed from such different quarters gives proof that Father Cathrein's accuracy and thoroughness may be relied upon, and renders any commendation oh our part perfectly superfluous. However, a few words of explanation as to the making of the present edition may not be out of place.

The first and second American editions of this work

were prepared by Rev. James Conway, S.J. But, keeping pace with the increasing importance of the subject, the German original, from being merely an extract from the author's larger work on Moral Philosophy, has now far outgrown its initial proportions. It has been completely recast and expanded into a complete though succinct treatise on socialism in all its aspects. In view of the quickened activity and growing influence of socialists in the United States it became highly desirable to have an English version of this book in accordance with the latest German edition. As, however, Fr. Conway was prevented by other duties from taking the matter in hand, I resolved to take advantage of a stay in Europe to prepare a new translation in collaboration with the Reverend Author, who has aided me with many valuable suggestions and additions.

Besides comprising all of the matter contained in the eighth German edition, the present volume offers a reliable account of socialism in the United States compiled from authentic socialist sources. Also in other respects the book has been adapted throughout to American conditions. It has thus been increased to more than twice the size of the former American editions, and may rightly be styled an entirely new work. Of course, Fr. Conway's version was incorporated in the present text wherever possible. Fr. Conway has also kindly consented to see the book through the press, for which I beg to offer him my sincerest acknowledgments.

A copious alphabetical index will no doubt enhance the practical value of the work.

VICTOR F. GETTELMANN, S.J.

VALKENBERG, March 17. 1904.

CONTENTS.

9

CHAPTER II.

*EXAMINATION OF THE PRINCIPAL BASIS OF SOCIALISM:
THE MATERIALISTIC CONCEPTION OF HISTORY.*

SOCIALISM.

CHAPTER I.

NATURE AND DEVELOPMENT OF SOCIALISM.

Section I.

NATURE OF SOCIALISM. ITS RELATION TO COMMUNISM.

COMMUNISM has a wider signification than *socialism.* By *communism* in its wider sense we understand that system of economics which advocates the abolition of private property and the introduction of community of goods, at least as far as capital, or means of production, is concerned. *Communism* in this broad sense admits of various forms, the chief of which are the following:

1. *Negative communism* is restricted to the negation of private property. According to this form of communism all goods should equally be put at the disposal of all. This species of communism found a zealous apostle in the person of MOSES HESS, who flourished in the forties of the past century. Unrestricted right of enjoyment for every individual, no obligation of working, but active co-operation of all for the sake of the common interest, these were the fundamental dogmas of his gospel. This preposterous form of

13

communism is no longer advocated by any one, at least not to our knowledge; for it is evident that a system which does not exclude others from the use of those things which individuals have appropriated to themselves would ruin all industry and bring about a state of universal misery and utter disorder. For who would till a field, if others were permitted to come at will and to reap the harvest?

2. *Positive communism* demands the total or partial transfer of all property to the community, which is to be owner, administrator, and distributor of all the products. This communism may be of two or rather three different kinds:

(a) *Extreme positive communism* advocates the transfer of all goods without exception to one great common administration. All production and the use of all goods should be common—common meals, common dormitories, common hospitals, etc. This system was advocated by some of the earlier communists, and by some religious sects.

(b) *Moderate positive communism* advocates only the abolition of private property as far as capital, or the materials of labor, or productive goods in contradistinction to non-productive goods, is concerned. By productive goods are meant real estate, all kinds of raw material, factories, machines, tools, means of transportation, in fine, everything not intended for immediate consumption. These goods should be handed over to and be administrated by some sort of commonwealth. This moderate form of positive communism is at present the only one having adherents. They are divided into two large groups bitterly hostile to each other: *anarchism* and *socialism*.

(α) *Anarchism* (anarchist communism) demands

the transfer of productive property to independent *groups of workingmen* (communities). In these groups, united to each other by mere federation, each individual is to receive the entire product of his work. Moreover, all governmental functions are to cease. For, anarchists desire to realize absolute liberty and equality to their full extent. Nevertheless anarchism does not imply anarchy or disorder. If you ask, how can order be maintained without civil functionaries, without legislation, courts of justice, police administration, etc., anarchists will refer you to that highly modern theory of evolution, according to which mankind is supposed to ascend to higher and higher stages of perfection; after class differences and the domination of the rich are abolished, order will spring of its own accord from the lively sense of solidarity, which will then animate every human being. Every one will jealously safeguard the right of each one to do as he pleases as long as he does not inflict unwarranted injury on others. According to this doctrine *free contracts* are the only social bond, the compulsive power of the state being absolutely excluded.[1]

Unlike socialists, these anarchists eschew the use of so-called political means for obtaining their purpose; thus they disdain to take part in elections, parliamentary discussions, and the like. They appeal principally to violence and explosives, their aim being the quickest possible destruction of existing society. Their principles were formulated in great part already by PROUDHON († 1865),[2] and again by MAX STIRNER

---

[1] Cf. Jahrbücher für Nationalökonomie (1896), p 137 There are also anarchists who demand the abolition of government, but wish to maintain private property.

[2] Concerning Proudhon cf. *Menger* Das Recht auf den vollen Arbeitsertrag (1891), p. 73 sqq.

(*alias* Karl Schmidt, † 1857);[1] but the real founder of anarchism is to be sought in the Russian BAKUNIN († 1876). For the rest, the details of the anarchist theory have never been fully developed, and the views of different anarchists are widely divergent. Other anarchists of note besides those already mentioned are the Russian prince KRAPOTKIN, the geographer ELISÉE RECLUS, the former socialist JOHN MOST, and JOHN MACKAY.

In May, 1901, the German anarchists assembled in convention at Bietigheim near Stuttgart issued a manifesto, which contains the first official *programme* of their party.

"The present order of society [they maintain] is based on the system of oppression and exploitation and will never make any concessions to the working classes; social-reform laws are made merely for the purpose of cajoling workingmen into peace and contentment, but their effect is mostly hurtful. Therefore anarchists reject all participation in parliaments or other legislative bodies The revolutionary workingmen advocate the transfer to the community of all real estate, of the means of production, and of the public utilities of modern civilization. Their ideal is the free socialistic community, whose every member is at liberty to live and to act according to his own inclinations. In spite of persecutions on the part of the state and of capital, the revolutionary workingmen will pursue their goal undaunted. The 'Federation of Revolutionaries' promotes this purpose by enlightenment and culture, by revolutionary thought and senti-ment, by supporting the anarchist press and literature, by estab-lishing debating clubs, etc. Workingmen must be trained for the economic struggle, they must organize, found co-operative societies in order to obtain control of production and consump-tion and to hasten the socialization of the state. 'These are our doctrines, our goal, our methods. For this we combat with the conviction of final victory. This victory will be tanta-mount to liberty and prosperity for the entire nation.'"[2]

[1] Der Einzige und sein Eigentum (1844), published anew by Reclam.
[2] Cf *Germania* (1901), No 101, Supplement.

Besides these theoretical anarchists there are also practical anarchists who are perfectly unconcerned about speculative disquisitions. They aim at a radical destruction of civil organization and of all authority (*Ni Dieu, ni maître*); what is to happen thereafter they reck not. Such views are but the "phantoms of a heat-oppresséd brain."

Anarchists are not to be confounded with the French *communists*, who aimed at the political independence of the single communes without demanding a general abolition of private property.

By *communards*, on the other hand, are meant the supporters of the Paris Commune in 1871.

Nihilism is a peculiarly Russian phase of anarchism. Among its adherents are found a number of anarchists, but in itself it is a purely practical political party of revolutionary tendencies aiming at the destruction of the Czar's autocratic powers.

(*β*) *Socialistic communism*, or simply *socialism*, advocates the transformation of all capital, or means of production, into the common property of society, or of the state, and the administration of the produce and the distribution of the proceeds by the state. Since modern socialists, and chiefly the followers of Karl Marx, intend to realize this scheme entirely upon a democratic basis, they call themselves *social democrats*, and their system *social democracy*. Social democracy may be defined as that system of political economy which advocates the inalienable ownership on the part of the state of all capital, or materials of labor, as also the public administration of all economic goods and the distribution of all produce by the democratic state.[1]

[1] Many socialists protest against the expression "socialistic state;" whether they are right in doing so we shall see later on.

We call socialism a *system of political economy*, not as if it did not also lead to many political and social changes, but because the gist of socialism consists in the nationalization of property and in the public administration and distribution of all goods. Socialism, at least as it is conceived by its modern defenders, is in the first instance an *economical system*, and only secondarily and subordinately a political system affecting society, the state, the family, etc.

Socialism has been defined as the *political economy of the suffering classes*,[1] that is, "a philosophy which in its nature and in the sentiments of contemporaries is actually the economic philosophy of the suffering classes." This explanatory clause is, to say the least, superfluous; to our mind it is incorrect. It makes the nature of socialism dependent on an external factor, namely, the actual subjective conception of men. Even though all the socialists of to-day could be convinced of the impracticability of their system and made to abandon it, yet socialism would still remain the same system, though it no longer existed in the consciousness of contemporaries. On the other hand, the ideal state imagined by Plato is in truth socialistic, although his contemporaries looked upon his theory as an idle dream. Moreover, if such a definition were correct, the moderate economic system which is advocated by the German Centre party and other conservative politicians for the relief of the laborer and artisan would be socialistic, which we cannot grant to be the case.

The definition given by E. DE LAVELEYE [2] is equally vague and incorrect. By socialism he understands

[1] *Schönberg*, Handbuch der politischen Oekonomie, vol. i. p. 107 (2d ed.).
[2] Le socialisme contemporain, 6th ed., p. xii.

"every doctrine which aims first at greater equality
of social conditions, and secondly endeavors to obtain
this reform by means of the state or legislation." No
wonder, therefore, that he speaks of conservative,
Catholic, evangelical, and international socialism. It
is perfectly evident that such loose notions and comprehensive definitions cannot possibly form the basis
for a clear and thorough discussion of the nature of
socialism.

X EDWARD BERNSTEIN defines socialism as "the
movement toward, or the actual existence of, the
co-operative organization of society." [1]

From our own definition it is evident that every
socialist is a communist in the broader sense of the
term; but not every communist is a socialist. Positive communism is related to socialism as the genus
to the species. Every system advocating common
property or common ownership may be called *communistic*. But only that system can be termed *socialistic* which intends to organize the production and
distribution of goods by means of the entire society.
Of course, this organization presupposes the common
ownership of the means of production.

Karl Marx, the chief founder of modern socialism,
often spoke of himself as a communist; and rightly
so, since the general notion of communism is always
contained in the specific notion of socialism. Every
horse is an animal, but not every animal is a horse.
Thus every socialist is a communist, but not vice versa.
It is also manifest that neither in communism generally
nor in its special form called socialism is there any
question of a *distribution of property* either taking

---

[1] Die Voraussetzungen des Socialismus und die Aufgaben der Sozial-
demokratic (1899), p. 84.

place once for all or else recurring at stated periods. For the basic principle of communism is the absolute negation of private ownership in the means of production.

Moreover, it also follows that the so-called *agrarian socialists*, who deny only the right of private property in land, cannot simply be called socialists, although they defend many principles which would logically lead to the total abolition of private property.[1] Nor can those politicians and theorists who in principle admit the right of private property, but in their economical systems put the administration of private property almost entirely into the hands of the state, be confounded with true socialists.[2]

In the meaning which we have assigned to it the term *socialism* is current not only in German and English, but also in French, Italian, and Spanish, especially so in works of a scientific character. Also Pope Leo XIII. in his Encyclicals on the social question (*Quod Apostolici*, Dec. 28, 1878, and *Rerum Novarum*, May 15, 1891) employs the word socialism exactly as we do. Therefore we perfectly agree with Cardinal Manning in maintaining that to speak of Christian or Catholic socialism is a proof of vagueness of thought or at least of expression. It is our urgent desire that this term should retain its accustomed signification. Why breed confusion and obscurity by the ambiguous use of terms in discussions which stand most in need of clearness and of a well-defined terminology? However, we call attention to the fact that there is a great difference between *socialistic* and *social*. *Socialistic* or *socialist* is applied to everything referring to socialism, whilst *social* refers to life in human society. Every one may and should be an advocate of social reform, whilst combating strenuously all socialistic tendencies.

Wherever socialism exists at present it is also democratic,

---

[1] Concerning agrarian socialists cf our work The Champions of Agrarian Socialism (Buffalo, N. Y., Peter Paul & Bro.) and Moralphilosophie 4th ed , vol ii. p. 247 sqq.

[2] Cf our Moralphilosophie, vol. ii. p. 597. *Wagner*, Grundlegung der polit. Oekonomie, 3d ed , pt. I. § 18 sqq

aiming at the introduction of the greatest possible equality; therefore the terms *socialism* and *social democracy* may be regarded as synonymous. In French and English socialism is also often spoken of as *collectivism.*

SECTION II.

DEVELOPMENT OF SOCIALISM.

§ I. *Socialism of Antiquity and of the Middle Ages.*

From the most ancient times we meet with certain partially communistic systems and institutions. On the island of Crete we find a certain kind of communism introduced as early as 1300 B.C., which in later times Lycurgus took as his model for the constitution of Sparta. This constitution seems to have been Plato's ideal when he composed his work entitled "The Republic," as also, though in a more moderate form, in the work on "Laws;" for in these works he commends community of goods, community of education, and even community of meals. Aristotle,[1] who accurately describes these economic systems, has also clearly demonstrated their untenableness. While the communistic attempts of antiquity suppose a large portion of the population to be in the condition of slavery, there arose in the first Christian community in Jerusalem a higher kind of communism, based upon true charity and equality. Among the early Christians those who chose could retain their possessions; but most of them, of their own accord, sold all they possessed and gave the proceeds to the apostles for the common support of all.[2] In voluntary poverty the first Christians wished to devote themselves wholly to the service of God and of their neighbor. Such a

---

[1] Polit. u. 3.   [2] Acts v.

condition, however, in its very nature, considering men as they generally are, could not be obligatory, universal, permanent—a circumstance which was overlooked by the Apostolics, Albigenses, Anabaptists, and other sects which in the course of centuries fell off from the Church and clung to the principle of the unlawfulness of private property. Apart from these heresies and from some communistic political works of fiction based, as it seems, chiefly on the "Utopia" of Blessed Thomas More,[1] we may say that communism and socialism are essentially the growth of modern times. The reductions of Paraguay, which are frequently set up as models of communism, were not strictly communistic, and were destined only to be institutions of a transitory character.[2]

§ II. *The Pioneers of Modern Socialism.*

1. Modern socialism differs essentially from its precursors by the fact that it is a permanent phenomenon, to be met with in all civilized countries, wherever industry is highly developed. This latter circumstance by itself proves to evidence that there is question here not of a merely *external* appearance produced artificially by popular agitators and demagogues, but that we are confronted by a phenomenon rooted in, and nourished by, the soil of modern social conditions.

The roots of modern socialism are to be found first of all in the great development of industry and the

---

[1] On account of his Utopia Bl. Thomas More has often been numbered among socialists, but wrongly so, for, a distinction must be made between his criticism of the social conditions of his time and his descriptions of the Utopian state. The latter were intended merely to serve as a background for bringing the criticisms into brighter relief. At the close of the book he himself points out the absurdity of many Utopian institutions.
[2] Cf. *Stimmen aus Maria-Laach,* vol xxv p 455.

consequent modification of social conditions dating from the latter part of the eighteenth century. Since the French Revolution the unhampered development of industrial forces in unrestricted competition has undoubtedly brought about astounding results in the field of technical discoveries and their application to industry and commerce. But one of these results was also the great division of society into two hostile classes—a small number of wealthy capitalists, and an immense multitude of laborers—which classes are usually designated respectively as *capital* and *labor*. But above all, the *proletariat*, that homeless, floating population of our great cities which has already assumed gigantic proportions, is the almost inevitable result of modern industry, in as far as by its machinery it practically precludes the existence of independent tradesmen and promotes the concentration of great masses of factory laborers.

Side by side with this increasing proletariat the disruption of family life, drunkenness, and dissolute morals have been growing apace. Moreover, by the baneful influence of the higher classes gross materialism and an insatiable craving for enjoyment have penetrated the masses of the people, whilst numerous upstarts with their quickly amassed wealth openly revel in senseless luxury. Thus the smouldering fire of discontent needed but a breeze to fan the flames into a fierce conflagration.

The French Revolution of 1789 marked indeed a new epoch in the world's history. The third estate, the so-called bourgeoisie, raising the banner of liberty, equality, and fraternity, had come to power and influence. In opposition to them there was soon formed the fourth estate, consisting of penniless proletarians.

From the very beginning of the revolution "fraternity" was no more than an ornamental catch-word. Liberty and equality were indeed granted in political matters, but for a numerous class of the population they meant no more than the privilege of being free and equal in misery. It was then that unrestricted competition was let loose upon the world to strangle the unprotected artisans in ·its clutches. These victims are marshalled into line by modern socialism; they are to be emancipated by destroying the monopoly of capital in the hands of a few. No wonder, therefore, that already at the cradle of socialism was heard the cry: "La propriété, c'est le vol"—Property is theft [1]—the cry repeated later on by Proudhon and Lassalle, and hurled as a firebrand among an excitable populace.

2. The first to raise the standard of modern socialism was FRANCIS NOEL BABEUF, or, as he was pleased to style himself in revolutionary times, Gracchus Babeuf. The starting-point of his theory is the idea of equality. At the head of the Constitution of 1793 were displayed the words: "All men are equal by nature and by law;" and again: "The purpose of society is universal happiness." But for most people this declaration of equality and happiness remained mere waste paper, and the reason for this failure was imagined to be private ownership. To realize equality also on the field of economics Babeuf formulated the following demands: Every one is obliged to work; the time of work is to be determined by law; production is to be regulated by a supreme committee elected by the people; necessary work is to be allotted to the citizens; disagreeable jobs are performed in turn by every citizen; each

[1] *Brissot de Warville. Sur la propriété et le vol.* (1780).

citizen has a right to all commodities, which are to be distributed to each according to his needs.

At bottom Babeuf's demands are identical with those formulated by Bebel and other modern socialists. Foreshadowing, as it were also, the tactics of modern socialism, Babeuf promised his adherents a tremendous increase in production to follow from the adoption of his plans. To promote the execution of his ideas he founded a secret society, which was discovered by the police and brought him to the guillotine, May 27, 1797.

3. Whilst Babeuf took the idea of equality as the basis of his reforms Count HENRI DE SAINT-SIMON (1760–1825) built his plans on the foundation of *labor*. He was the first who endeavored to place modern socialism upon a systematic scientific basis, and at the same time he called into existence a school of scientific socialists. From him dates "scientific socialism" in the present acceptation of the term.

Liberal political economists had established the principle *that labor alone is the foundation and source of all value*, and, consequently, of all wealth. Socialism seized upon this principle and made it the basis of its operations against the modern conditions of property. Saint-Simon drew from this principle the conclusion that labor—industry in its wider sense— must be the standard of all social institutions; in other words, that the laborers should not as heretofore take the last but the first place in society; it was, therefore, the business of social science to restore the laborers to the position due to them.

Saint-Simon was only a theorist. He made no practical attempts to give effect to his views; nay, he did not even venture directly to question the right

of private property. From the principle that labor
alone is the source of value his disciple ENFANTIN
drew the conclusion that the unearned increment
obtained without working by landowners and capitalists
is unjust and therefore to be abolished. His conclusion is thereafter to be met with in socialistic literature
in endless variations. BAZARD, another disciple of
Saint-Simon, intending to remove the inequality and
seeming injustice of the existing conditions of property,
demanded a complete modification of the *rights of
inheritance.* In place of kindred he would make
merit the base of inheritance; or rather, the state
alone was to be the heir of all its children and distribute
the property of the deceased among the most worthy
of the living.

4. Almost contemporaneously with Saint - Simon,
CHARLES FOURIER (1772–1837) proposed his system of
socialism. Fourier proceeds from the supposition that
what is ordinarily called the will of God is nothing else
than the laws of universal attraction, which uphold the
universe and manifest themselves in the instincts and
tendencies of all things. Also in man these instincts
are revelations of the divine will. Therefore it is
unlawful to suppress them; they should be gratified;
from their gratification arises human happiness; but
the means to this gratification is the *organization of
labor.* For, as he claims, every man is entitled to his
share of labor, viz., he has the right to demand remunerative labor from the state, if he cannot obtain it elsewhere. As it seems, Fourier was the first to enunciate
this right in the sense in which it is accepted by socialists nowadays.[1]

---

[1] Especially in his books· Théorie des quatre mouvements (1808) and
Traité de l'association domestique-agricole (1822) Fourier's disciple

This organization of labor is to be brought about in this wise Proprietors, without losing the right of property, should contribute all their wealth to the common industry, in order that each individual in continued succession may be able to apply himself to that occupation to which his momentary instinct may incline him Such labor would be a delight. Fourier, moreover, makes the following propositions. On every square mile should dwell two thousand persons (a *phalanx*) in one large building (*phalanstère*) under the control of an overseer (*unarque*). The phalanxes, again, should be divided into series, the series into groups. Thus each one might at pleasure change his labor. From the proceeds of the labor four-twelfths goes to the capital as interest; three-twelfths is given to genius, and the rest, five-twelfths, is given to labor. Yet neither Saint-Simon nor Fourier ventured to suggest the abolition of private property For the rest, there is an intrinsic contradiction in the very fact that Fourier allows private property to exist and wishes to compel the proprietor to give all his capital for common use.

5. ROBERT OWEN (born 1771 at Newtown in Wales, died 1858) exercised a far-reaching influence upon the modern labor movement by being the first to introduce social reforms in his own spinning-factory at Lanark. By his benevolent institutions and his numerous writings he called the attention of the public to the wretched condition of factory hands.

His leading principle was: Man is but a chemical combination, the result of circumstances; every man may be trained to any kind of disposition and sentiments if he is but put into suitable surroundings. By careful organization the productiveness of labor might be raised to an incredible height, furnishing ample provision for everybody. Owen tried to put his ideas into practice by establishing a number of communistic colonies, the first and most important

CONSIDÉRANT developed his master's idea more fully and gained for it many adherents Cf *Menger,* Das Recht auf den vollen Arbeitsertrag p 16

of which was at New Harmony in Indiana. An
atheist himself, he decided to exclude God and religion
from his communistic establishments. But before long
all his experiments were doomed to dismal failure.

6. The example of Owen induced also ETIENNE
CABET (born 1788 at Dijon, died 1856) to draw up a
communistic programme. His plan was to change
France into a republic consisting of communist municipalities. His ideas he developed in the celebrated
novel, "Voyage en Icarie" (1840), which caused a great
stir among the laboring population of France.

In 1848 he founded his communist colony Icaria, at first in
Texas, and, after this attempt had failed, in the abandoned
Mormon city Nauvoo, Illinois [1] Slowly but steadily the colony
began to prosper, and at one time contained up to 500 colonists.
They succeeded in making their quarters comfortable, and their
cottages bore the stamp of neatness and cleanliness. Assiduous
work was required of all Icarians, but they were not wanting in
entertainments and enjoyments   A select library was free to
all; music, theatricals, and dances agreeably diversified the
monotony of the daily routine. Newspapers in several languages were issued at Icaria both for the instruction and amusement of the colonists and for advertising and money-making
purposes Cabet insisted on retaining family life; education,
however, was to belong to the community The instruction
imparted was very thorough and calculated to instil communist
principles Public worship was unknown; each one could choose
his belief as he pleased Financially the colony was at first
a marked success But, as prosperity increased, discord and
petty quarrels became rife, resulting finally in the expulsion
of Cabet and his partisans from Icaria, August 3, 1856 His
few faithful followers founded a new colony at Cheltenham
near St Louis; but notwithstanding the financial support obtained from France, internal strife caused its disruption within
a few years. Icaria, on the other hand, now established in
southern Iowa, began to prosper anew; toward 1875 it num

---

[1] Cf *Hillquit*, History of Socialism in the U S. (1903), p 129 sqq

bered about 70 members living in frugal contentment. But here also discord and disputes were unavoidable   The Icarian youth nurtured in communistic principles soon became unmanageable, fond of novelty, despising the experience of their elders. The year 1878 witnessed the complete rupture between the older and younger generation. The faction of the juniors remained at the old homestead, forming the so-called Icarian Community which in 1884 moved to California, where it was soon dissolved [1]

The "old party" were assigned the eastern part of their former domain and were incorporated as the New Icarian Community. With no accession from the outside they struggled on till their final dissolution.

On March 13, 1895, the Cincinnati *Wahrheitsfreund* had the following communication from Corning, Iowa: "After long but useless struggles the communistic settlement called Icaria Community, situated about three miles east of here, has finally been disrupted   A receiver is to be appointed and the existing property is to be distributed among the members or their heirs " [2]

7. Like Bazard, so also LOUIS BLANC (1813–1882) finds the root of all economic evils in free competition; and the only remedy, according to him, is in the public organization of labor. The state should undertake the part of the chief producer, and. gradually extend its production so as to make private production impossible. After the state has achieved this result it should regulate and control the entire industry of the nation. Louis Blanc was also the first who endeavored to bring the right to labor into action by erecting national workshops for laborers out of work.

8. In Germany KARL RODBERTUS (1805–1875) is considered the first representative and pioneer of "scientific" socialism. He developed his theories in his letters and essays on social questions and political

[1] Cf *Hillquit,* loc cit , p 137
[2] Cf. *A Shaw,* Icaria (New York, 1884).

economy.[1]   He himself characterizes his doctrine as the 'logical development of the principle introduced into political science by Adam Smith, and further developed by Ricardo, *that all goods, considered from an industrial standpoint, are only the product of labor, and cost nothing but labor.*"

If the division of the national produce is left to itself, says Rodbertus, the wages of the laborer become an ever smaller portion of the national produce the more production increases: and this gives rise to pauperism and to industrial crises   These evils can be remedied only by the gradual introduction of society into a condition in which neither real estate nor capital can further exist, but only wages or labor income

9. The great agitator FERDINAND LASSALLE (1825–1864) has exercised a more permanent influence upon the development of socialism, at least in Germany, than even Karl Marx, of whom there will be question anon.   Thousands of cheering workingmen surrounded the famous "labor king," as he passed his army in review or inflamed the passions of the multitude by his overmastering eloquence.   In blatant self-conceit he boasted that "every line he wrote was equipped with the culture of the century."   But for his theories the renowned demagogue was entirely dependent on Karl Marx.   As peculiarly his own we may in some respect designate what he called *the iron law of wages,* which, to avoid useless repetitions, will find an explanation later on.

Another idea original with Lassalle was his plan of establishing *co-operative associations* of workingmen.   These associations were to be subsidized by the state in order to overthrow the

[1] Soziale Briefe an v. Kirchmann (1850-51), Briefe und sozialpolitische Aufsätze (1882)   Lately there has been a good deal of controversy whether Rodbertus borrowed from Marx or vice versa.   Some are of opinion that both have "borrowed," Rodbertus from the Frenchman Proudhon, and Marx from the Englishman W. Thompson.

despotism of capitalists and gradually to lead over to complete socialism It appears that Lassalle intended to realize his plans of reform by lawful means and upon a national basis The followers of Lassalle forming the General Union of German Workingmen were fiercely antagonized by the adherents of international socialism, the so-called "Eisenacher," who, under the leadership of Bebel and Liebknecht, stood up for Marxian ideas The feud was finally patched up at the Gotha convention, 1875, by the adoption of a compromise platform

§ III. *The Chief Founder of Modern Socialism,* KARL MARX.

A HISTORICAL SKETCH

KARL MARX has been dubbed by the Berlin *Vorwarts* (1894, No. 62) "the greatest teacher of the socialist parties in the world," and "the giant pathfinder of socialism."

Marx was born of Jewish parents at Treves, May 5, 1818. In 1824 the whole family embraced Protestantism Young Marx completed his classical studies in his native town, and then took a course of law and later on of philosophy at Bonn and Berlin. In 1841 he was admitted as private professor at the University of Bonn, but already the following year he became editor of the democratic-liberal *Rhenish Gazette*, which was suppressed in 1843 on account of its opposition to the government. The same year he married Miss Jenny von Westphalen, with whom he moved to Paris, where he devoted himself assiduously to the study of political economy and of socialistic writings, and was soon gained over to socialist principles.

Here he also made the acquaintance of FREDERICK ENGELS,[1] who was henceforth his most intimate friend, his inseparable companion and collaborator As the first result of their united

[1] Born at Barmen, 1820, died in London, 1895 Principal writings Die Lage der arbeitenden Klassen in England (1845) Der Ursprung der Familie, des Privateigentums und des Staates (2d ed , 1886), Herrn Eugen Duhrings Umwalzung der Wissenschaft (2d ed , 1886) Die Entwicklung des Sozialismus von der Utopie zur Wissenschaft (4th ed , 1891).

efforts they published in 1845: "Die heilige Familie. Gegen
Bruno Bauer und Konsorten." Their inflammatory articles
against absolutism caused their expulsion from France, where-
upon they settled first at Brussels, and in 1848 published con-
jointly another book, "La misère de la philosophie, réponse
à la philosophie de la misère de M. Proudhon." The same year
witnessed the appearance of the "Manifesto of the Communist
Party" drawn up by Marx and Engels at the request of the
Communist Union   This manifesto contains the germs of all
the leading ideas developed by Marx later on, and closes with
the battle-cry of modern socialism: "Proletarians of all countries,
unite!" The following year we meet Marx at Cologne editing
the *New Rhenish Gazette,* which, however, enjoyed but a brief
existence.   Exiled also from Germany, Marx henceforth resided
permanently in London, devoting himself entirely to study and
literary occupations. The first important result of his studies
was his "Criticism of Political Economy," 1859, which was
followed in 1867 by the first volume of "Capital." The second
edition of this volume appeared in 1872, and the fourth revised
by Engels [1] in 1890. The second and third volumes were prepared by Engels from the literary remains of his friend.
The original plan called for a fourth volume, which, however,
has not been forthcoming

   To the year 1864 must be assigned the foundation of the
International Workingmen's Association, in which Marx played
a prominent part. At his instigation a great convention of
workingmen of different nations assembled in London to discuss
the project of an international organization of workingmen
and proletarians   A committee was appointed for drawing up
the statutes of this international organization and for preparing
the convention to be held the following year at Brussels. The
first resolution of this committee was the establishment of a general council consisting of a president and one corresponding

---

[1] Unless the contrary is expressly stated, our quotations from the first
volume of Capital are according to the fourth edition.
   Translator's Note —Of the first volume of Capital there exists an
English version published in London and also reprinted in America with
different pagination.   However, for the sake of greater accuracy and convenience the quotations also from the first volume are, as a rule, translated directly from the German original independently of the London
edition. The numbers, therefore, refer to the pages of the fourth German
edition

member for each of the nations concerned. Marx was chosen member for Germany. The address to the workingmen proposed by him and accepted by the general council concludes with the words of the communist manifesto: "Proletarians of all countries, unite!"

The statutes and the declaration of principles drafted by Marx were also adopted   The following characteristic passages may be cited here: "In consideration that the emancipation of the working class must be accomplished by the working class itself, that the struggle for the emancipation of the working class does not signify a struggle for class privileges and monopolies, but for *equal rights and duties*, and the *abolition of class rule;* that *the economic dependence of the workingman upon the owner of the tools of production,* the sources of life, *forms the basis of every kind of servitude; . . .* that therefore the economic emancipation of the working class is the great end to which every political movement must be subordinated; . . . that the emancipation of labor is not a local nor a national, but a social problem, which embraces all countries in which modern society exists, . . . the First International Labor Congress . . . regards it as the duty of man to demand the rights of a man and citizen not only for himself, but for every one who does his duty "[1]

This platform was ratified by the Geneva convention, 1866. Henceforth an International convention took place almost every year. The Brussels convention of 1868 resolved to replace the Bible and religion by the cult of those men who had gained distinction by increasing the material well-being of mankind. The Basle convention of 1869 decided that society has a right to change private property in landed estates into common ownership by the community.

But soon dissensions, owing in great part to national jealousies, sprang up principally concerning the powers of the general council   The federalists or anarchists under the leadership of Bakunin were loth to bear the dictatorship of the general council and felt jealous at the prominent position occupied by a German, K. Marx.

[1] *Hillquit,* History of Socialism in the U S, pp 177-180. (Here and throughout the book *italics are ours* —Tr) Cf. *Jager,* Der moderne Sozialismus (Berlin, 1873), p 56   This work is still one of the most reliable concerning Marx and the "International," it also contains copious extracts from Marx's Inaugural Address.

The latter's adherents, called centralists, were of opinion that only a strong general council vested with almost unlimited powers was able to lead the labor party to victory. This dispute between federalists and centralists had the effect that no more conventions were held after 1873 and that the general council, which had been transferred from London to New York, was soon dissolved. Although at present there exists no interna tional organization of workingmen, yet the ideas which gave it birth are still continually at work. It is also since 1864 that the division of the proletariat into anarchists and socialists has become distinctly marked.

After the disruption of the International Workingmen's Association, Marx never again appeared before the public, but devoted himself exclusively to literary work until his death, March 14, 1883.

B. THE SCIENTIFIC BASIS OF THE MARXIAN SYSTEM.

The foundations of modern socialism are partly historical, partly theoretical. It may be asked in the first place: What are the causes which occasioned and promoted the rise and spread of socialistic ideas? In the second place we may ask: What arguments are adduced by socialism to establish the theoretical justice or necessity of its demands? The answer to the first question will give us the material and historical foundations of socialism; the answer to the second will point out its theoretical basis.

The historical foundations of socialism have been briefly sketched above (p. 21). They are embedded in the conditions of modern civilization. Socialism had already penetrated far and wide before any scientific demonstration of its theories was attempted or even thought of. It is now almost universally acknowledged that it was Marx who placed socialism on a scientific basis, and therefore he is looked up to by socialists with a quasi-religious veneration.

But which are those *fundamental tenets* discovered and formulated by Marx, on account of which he is reputed to be the founder of "scientific" socialism? The answer to this question is given by Fr. Engels. "Two great discoveries, the *materialistic conception of history* and the revealing of the secret of capitalist production by means of *surplus-value;* these discoveries we owe to Marx. Through them socialism has become a science." [1]

What is meant by the materialistic conception of history on the part of socialists? It is briefly this: The entire history of mankind with its political, religious, and moral phenomena is but the grand process of evolution, wherein nothing is stable and immutable except the one constant law of perpetual change, and wherein all progress is accomplished only by the formation of economic contrasts and of the class wars resulting therefrom.

This is the Marxian system in a nutshell. In this system the most heterogeneous elements are cemented into unity. In the preface to the first edition of his work on the development of socialism (1882) Engels glories in the fact that German socialists are proud to be the descendants not only of Saint-Simon, Fourier, and Owen, but also of Kant, Fichte, and Hegel. Of Kant indeed there are but scanty traces, but of the others, all have furnished stones for the erection of the Marxian edifice.

In Marx's system three points must be distinguished, the *method*, the *contents*, and the *aim*, or in other words, the conclusions arrived at.

[1] *Engels*, Die Entwicklung des Sozialismus von der Utopie zur Wissenschaft (1891), p. 26.—In his preface to the second edition of Capital Engels seems to grant that the theory of surplus-value was advanced previous to Marx by some English socialists, notably William Godwin, Charles Hall, and William Thompson.

I.—*The Marxian Method.*

Marx's method, the so-called dialectic method, has been taken over from Fichte and Hegel. According to Hegel the absolute idea is developed in this order of succession: thesis, antithesis, synthesis. That which exists is annulled by something else the germ of which was contained in the first; this first negation is annulled again by a second negation—the so-called negation of negation—and thereby there is produced a more perfect form of that which was annulled at first.

An example will render more intelligible what is here expressed in characteristically Hegelian obscurity. A grain of barley falling "upon favorable soil will be affected and changed by the influence of heat and moisture; it sprouts; the grain as such disappears, it is annulled, in its stead there arises from it a plant which is the negation of the grain. What, however, is the normal life-history of this plant? It grows into flower, is fertilized and finally produces other grains of barley. As soon as these are ripe the plant withers and is annulled in its turn. The result of this negation of negation is again a grain of barley but multiplied twenty or thirty fold." [1]

The grain of barley, therefore, is the thesis, the resultant plant is the antithesis, the multiplied grains of barley the synthesis. But, you object, at the conclusion of the process this example shows but a multiplication of barleycorns, it is not a process of transformation. To this objection Engels replies by another example illustrating the transformation of the species. "Take some docile flowering plant, e.g., a dahlia or an orchid, treat its seed and the plant

---

[1] *Engels*, Herrn E. Duhrings Umwälzung der Wissenschaft, 2d ed., pp. 126, 127.

springing from it with the skill of an experienced gardener, and the result of this negation of negation will be not only a greater quantity of seed, but also an improved quality capable of producing more beautiful flowers, and every repetition of this process, every new negation of negation, will result in still greater improvement." [1]

A similar process is said to be observed in history. This Engels illustrates by another example. "Every civilized nation begins with public ownership of land (?). As soon as the nation has progressed beyond a certain stage, the development of agriculture causes this public ownership to be felt as shackling production. It is abolished, annulled, and after shorter or longer intermediate stages it is changed into private ownership. But, after private property in land has produced a higher degree of development, it becomes in its turn a shackle hampering production, as is the case at present not only on small but also on extensive estates. The necessity of abolishing it and of changing it back to public property has become imperative. But this necessity does not imply the restoration of public ownership as it existed originally; it means the establishment of a far higher and more perfect form of common ownership which, far from hindering production, will give it free scope and allow it to utilize to the full the chemical discoveries and mechanical appliances of modern times." [2]

Such is the Hegelian dialectic method adopted by Marx and Engels. It is "but the science of the general laws of motion and of development in nature, in human society, and in thought." [3]

[1] *Ibid*, p. 127   [2] *Ibid* p. 129.   [3] *Ibid.*, p 133.

Ancient philosophy—the *metaphysical* mode of thought, as Engels calls it—started from the supposition that there are a number of ideas and principles not subject to change or modification, independent of time or space and in thus far eternal. The new philosophy fathered by Hegel—the *dialectic* mode of thought—knows nothing of unchangeable concepts and principles except in the realm of mathematics. Not only the visible universe, but also mankind, its thought, volition, and action, are supposed to be in a continual process of development, wherein nothing is permanent except an eternal coming into existence (*das ewige Werden*).

The Hegelian system, Engels tells us, "was the first to interpret the whole of the material, historical, and intellectual world as a process of everlasting motion, change, transformation, and evolution, the first to make the attempt of pointing out the internal correlation of this motion and development. From this point of view the history of mankind no longer appeared as a senseless jumble of violence and bloodshed, . . . but as the natural evolution of the human race; and henceforth it became incumbent on the philosopher to trace this gradual development through all the mazes of error, and to prove that, in spite of external appearances pointing to its being the product of chance, it has followed certain well-defined laws." [1]

But Hegel failed to accomplish the task incumbent on him. He was an "idealist, i.e., the concepts of his brain were not regarded by him as the more or less abstract representations of external realities and occurrences; on the contrary, things and their development were for him but the materialized images of the

[1] *Engels*, Die Entwicklung des Sozialismus, p. 22.

'idea' existing somehow or other already before the world. Thereby everything was turned topsy-turvy and the actual condition of the world completely inverted. . . . The Hegelian system as such was a mis-begotten monster—but it was also the last of its kind." [1]

Moreover, this system was subject to an intrinsic contradiction. "On the one hand it necessarily pre-supposed that historical conception according to which the history of mankind is but a process of evolution which by its very nature cannot have its intellectual termination in the discovery of so-called absolute truth; and on the other hand it (Hegel's system) poses as the very cream of this same absolute truth. A comprehensive system of conceiving nature and history, which is to be complete once for all, is incompatible with the first principles of the dialectic mode of thought." [2]

This conviction on the part of Marx and Engels that German idealism is radically wrong led to the adoption of materialism.

II.—*The Contents of the Marxian System: Historical Materialism*

The idea of constant dialectic evolution was taken over from Hegel. But what is the thing evolved, and what determines the direction to be taken by the process of evolution? Convinced of the errors of Hegelian idealism, Marx and Engels became converts to FEUERBACH'S historical materialism. Feuerbach once for all did away with the "dualism" of spirit and matter and categorically proclaimed the sovereignty of materialism.

Engels thus speaks of his own "conversion": "Then

Ibid., p. 23.   [2] *Ibid* p 23.

came Feuerbach's 'Essence of Christianity.' At one blow it shattered the contradiction (of Hegelianism) by unceremoniously raising materialism to the throne again. Nature exists independently of philosophy; it is the basis upon which mankind, itself a product of nature, has grown up; *beyond nature and man there is nothing, and those higher beings created by our religious fancy are but the fantastic reflections of our own being.* The spell was broken; . . . only he who has experienced the liberating influence of this book can have any conception of it. Enthusiasm was catching; for the nonce all of us were disciples of Feuerbach. How Marx grew enthusiastic over this new idea, and how much he was influenced by it notwithstanding his critical demurs, may be seen by reading his 'Holy Family.' " [1]

According to Feuerbach "matter is not the creation of the spirit, but the spirit itself is but the highest product of matter. This, of course, is materialism pure and simple." [2] Feuerbach's materialism, however, was mechanical, anti-dialectic. It assumed that nature is in motion, but this motion was conceived to be going forever in a circle, "and therefore it never advanced, it always produced again the same results." [3] This view was wrong. "We are living not only in nature but also in human society, and society no less than nature has an evolution of its own with a corresponding science." [4]

There was now question of determining, on a materialistic basis of course, those laws of motion according to which the history of mankind has been evolved. Marx and Engels boast of having solved

[1] *Engels,* Ludwig Feuerbach, 2d ed., pp. 10, 11.   [3] *Ibid.,* p. 19.
[2] *Ibid.,* p. 18.   [4] *Ibid.,* p. 22.

this problem by their *materialistic conception of history.* It is not by abstract ideas, they say, that the process of evolution is started and directed in its course, but the decisive influence is exercised by the conditions of production.

Marx has presented the best summary of his materialistic theory of history in the preface to his "Criticism of Political Economy." Bernstein declares that this preface, together with the third chapter of Engels' "Socialism, Utopian and Scientific," [1] is the most remarkable presentation of historical materialism. Says Marx:

"In the social production of their means of subsistence men enter upon certain necessary relations independent of their will, relations of production corresponding to a certain stage of development in their material productive forces The sum total of these conditions of production forms the economic structure of society, the real basis upon which is raised an ethical and political superstructure, and to which correspond certain forms of social consciousness The method of production in our material life shapes and determines also our entire social, political, and intellectual process of life. It is not the mind of man which determines his life in society, but, on the contrary, it is this life which determines his mind In a certain stage of development the material productive forces come in conflict with the then existing conditions of production, or in other words, with the conditions of ownership, within which production had moved hitherto. From being forms of development these conditions change to shackles fettering the productive forces. Then there occurs an epoch of social revolution. With the transformation of its economic basis the whole gigantic superstructure is overturned more or less rapidly. In the consideration of such revolutions it is necessary to make a clear distinction between the revolution in the material economic con-

[1] *Engels'* Die Entwicklung des Sozialismus von der Utopie zur Wissenschaft, already repeatedly quoted, is published in English under the above title.

ditions of production, which is easily ascertained by science, and the ethical, political, religious, artistic, or philosophical, in brief the ideological forms, in which mankind becomes conscious of this conflict and fights it out. . . . No form of society will perish before all the productive forces for which it affords room are fully developed, no new conditions of production will take their place before the material conditions necessary for their existence have been hatched in the bosom of the society preceding them. . . . The bourgeois conditions of production are the last antagonistic form preceding the process of social production, antagonistic not in the sense of individual antagonism, but of an antagonism arising from the conditions of the social life of individuals; but the productive forces developing in the bosom of bourgeois society at the same time create the material conditions requisite for the final resolution of this antagonism. With this form of society we have reached the last stage antecedent to the ideal human society " [1]

Kautsky is pleased to call this Marxian summary " a classical production." Masaryk in his noteworthy criticism of Marxism [2] does not like this epithet, since the chief qualities of a classical production are wanting: precision and clearness. In fact, in Marx's way of putting things there is much to be criticised. Yet his main principle is clearly expressed. The whole of ideology, he wishes to tell us, i.e., the whole of our moral, religious, ethical, philosophical, and political ideas, is conditioned by the manner of production and of exchanging the products; as this manner changes, so also the ideology based upon it is changed. The latter has no independent existence, it is but the reflection in the human mind of the exterior conditions of production. Exactly the same idea we find expressed, e.g., in the following sentence

[1] Kritik der polit. Oekonomie, preface, pp. xi, xii.
[2] Die philosophischen und soziologischen Grundlagen des Marxismus (Vienna, 1899), p. 9.

of "Capital": [1] "Technology reveals the active relation of man to nature, the immediate process of production going on in his life and thereby also in his social conditions and *in the resulting intellectual concepts.*" [2]

The following is from the pen of Engels, the most authoritative exponent of Marxian ideas:

"At the root of the materialistic conception of history there is the proposition that production, and next to production the exchange of products, forms the base of social order; that in every society known to history the distribution of products and the corresponding social distinction of classes and states of life is conditioned by the objects and the manner of production Accordingly, the ultimate causes of social changes and of political revolutions are not to be looked for in the brains of men and in their growing comprehension of eternal truth and justice, but in the changes affecting the manner of production and exchange; they are to be looked for not in the philosophy but in the political economy of the epoch in question If at any time the conviction begins to be prevalent that existing social institutions are unreasonable and unjust, that reason has changed to nonsense, and benefit to annoyance, it is but an indication of the fact that the methods of production and exchange have been silently transformed so as no longer to tally with the social order which had been adapted to former economic conditions. This means at the same time that also the remedies for these discrepancies must be contained more or less perfectly developed in the changed conditions of production. These remedies, however, are not to be drawn from an imaginative brain, but by using our brains they are to be discovered in the existing material facts of production." [3]

Again, at the grave of his life-long friend Engels thus expounded Marx's leading idea: "Darwin discovered the law of evolution in organic nature, Marx in the history of mankind. He disclosed the simple fact hidden hitherto by ideological excres-

[1] Vol. 1. p 336
[2] Cf. also Capital, vol. III part II p 324
[3] E. Dührings Umwalzung der Wissenschaft, 2d ed., p 253, Entwicklung des Sozialismus 4th ed. p 27.

cences, the fact that above all else men stand in need of meat and drink, of shelter and clothing, before they can engage in politics, science, art, religion, etc , that therefore the production of the immediate material means of life and the corresponding stage of economic evolution of a nation or epoch forms the foundation from which the civil institutions of the people in question, their ideas of law, of art, of religion even, have been developed and according to which they are to be explained—and not the reverse, as has been done heretofore." [1]

These words are not to be taken in the sense that the production of the material necessaries of life is an indispensable prerequisite for a higher spiritual life, in this sense the "*primum vivere dein philosophari*" of the ancients is the merest truism having no need of being discovered by Marx What is meant is rather that the form of production generates and determines the higher social life of a nation in its entirety, its notions of law, morality, philosophy, religion, art, etc. That this is the only correct interpretation is sufficiently evident from the passages quoted above.

In some of his letters, written after the death of Marx, Engels has somewhat restricted the determining influence of the conditions of production upon the "ideological superstructure."

Thus in 1890 and again in 1895 he writes that the production and reproduction of real life is *ultimately* the determining factor of history, but it is *not the only one* The state of political economy is indeed the basis, but the different elements of the superstructure—the political, religious, and philosophical ideas of the people in question—also exercise their influence upon the course of development. "The political, ethical, philosophical, religious, literary, artistic, etc., development is based on the economic. But all of them react on one another and on their economic basis." [2]

It is beyond doubt that according to Marx and Engels a multiplicity of factors influence the development of society. But the *ultimate* source of all these factors is the method of *production*. Production, i.e., productive labor in its widest sense, determines the conditions of property, and from them results

[1] *Mehring*, Die Lessing Legende (1893), p 434.
[2] Cf *Bernstein*, Die Voraussetzungen des Sozialismus (1899), p. 7.

the moral, political, and philosophical superstructure. This superstructure, of course, is supposed to react again upon its foundations, i.e., the conditions of production.

According to this conception of history, political economy is the basis and starting-point of social science. The course of the world's history and the development of civilization is determined, not by moral or philosophical notions, but by economic conditions. Law, politics, religion are but the superstructure erected on this economic basis and partake in its gradual transformations. Each new economic era produces its corresponding superstructure of law and politics, and this it does—according to the dialectic method—by the *formation of contrasts*. The economic conditions are gradually modified, whilst the state of property and of the entire social superstructure remains as yet unchanged. Thus the conditions of production gradually come in conflict with the social and political institutions, especially with the conditions of property. The resultant class differences become more and more acute until a social revolution introduces a state of society in accordance with the new conditions of production.

III —*Aims and Conclusions.*

The theory of history which we have just now expounded serves Marx as an explanation of modern economic development, whereby he intends to show that *our modern capitalist society must needs bring forth as its natural result the socialistic order of society.* In order to grasp the force of his argument we must take a look at his second great "discovery," which, in the opinion of Engels, has effected the transition of socialism from the utopian to the scientific stage. This discovery is the doctrine of *surplus-value*, based on the Marxian doctrine of *value*.

1. *Value.*—In capitalistic society every kind of produce partakes of the character of merchandise. In every class of merchandise a twofold value may be distinguished, the *value in use* and the *value in exchange*. Bread may serve as food, there you have its value in use; it may also be sold or bartered for other goods, there you have its value in exchange. Marx defines *use-value* as the utility of an object in satisfying human wants, a utility derived from its chemical and physical properties; but *exchange-value*, he says, consists in the ratio according to which different kinds of use-values may be bartered for each other. If I know, e.g., that 20 lbs. of yarn may be bartered for two pair of shoes, both objects have for me the same exchange-value, however different their use-values may be. Exchange-value, however, accrues to merchandise only on account of the human labor expended on it, and the measure of labor embodied in the merchandise determines also its value in exchange. *Two kinds of merchandise embodying the same amount of necessary co-operative labor are also of the same exchange-value.* This is Marx's famous *law of value*. Goods are bartered for each other according to the ratio of the average necessary labor embodied in them. In a later chapter this theory will be examined and expounded more fully in the words of Marx himself. What has been said so far may suffice for the present.

2. *Surplus-value. The Secret of Surplus-making.*— From his doctrine of value Marx deduces his doctrine of surplus-value by applying what has been said in general about exchange-value also to man's *labor capacity*.

Modern conditions have reduced the labor capacity of workingmen to the rank of mere merchandise. The laborer is personally free, but, not possessing the means of production, he is forced to offer his labor capacity for sale. Thereby capitalists are enabled to get rich at the expense of their workingmen. But let Marx himself explain his ideas:

In every kind of merchandise, also in labor capacity, there is a distinction between use-value and exchange-value. The exchange-value of labor capacity is determined by the average quantity of labor it represents, or by the price of victuals ordinarily required for its sustenance[1] In labor capacity there is, however, also a certain use-value, a gift of nature, "without cost to the laborer, but very remunerative for the capitalist."

The value (exchange-value) of labor capacity is therefore quite a different thing from its exploitation in actual work (its use-value).

This difference in values is the object which the capitalist has in view when purchasing "labor capacity." The capitalist pays merely for the exchange-value of labor capacity, but what he aims at obtaining is its specific use-value, namely, its power of producing values exceeding its own. For this specific purpose it is employed by the capitalist, who acts therein according to the immutable laws of exchange. In fact, the seller of labor, as of any other commodity, realizes no more than its exchange-value, yet he disposes of its use-value—i e., he is paid for the exchange-value only of his labor, and yet surrenders its entire use-value to the purchasing capitalist. He cannot receive the price for the former without surrendering the latter. The use-value of his labor, namely, the work actually done, belongs to the seller no more than the use-value of oil sold belongs to the oil-dealer The capitalist pays for the daily value of labor capacity and then claims the use of it during the entire day, or the work of a whole day. *The fact that the daily sustenance of a*

[1] The value of labor capacity is similar to that of any other merchandise and is determined by the labor time required for the production or reproduction of the article in question . The value of labor capacity is equivalent to the value of a certain amount of victuals (Capital, vol I. pp. 133, 134.) Whenever Marx speaks simply of value he always means exchange-value.

man's labor capacity costs but half a day's work, whilst the man is able to work during the entire day, that therefore the value created by his labor in a day is twice as great as its own daily value, is, of course, very fortunate for the purchaser, but not at all unjust toward the seller. The capitalist has, of course, foreseen this enjoyable circumstance Therefore the workingman finds in the shop the means of production sufficient *not merely for six but for twelve hours' work.*[1]

Suppose the workingman needs three shillings for his ordinary daily support. This is the exchange-value of his labor and therefore also the wages he receives A part of his working time, let us say six hours, is expended in producing again in a different shape the value which he has received in money— three shillings This part of the working time is called by Marx the necessary time But the workingman is required to work beyond this time even up to twelve hours. If his activity did not extend beyond the necessary time there would be no surplus-value for the capitalist, who would but get back in a different shape what he paid as wages to his workingmen. Therefore, it is in the interest of capitalists to prolong the hours of work beyond the strictly necessary time This second working period, says Marx, in which the workingman is toiling beyond the requirements of strict necessity, implies indeed work and expenditure of strength, but it produces no value for him It forms the surplus-value which has for the capitalist all the attractiveness of a creation from nothing [2] This surplus-value is appropriated by the capitalist without expense and, according to the prevailing "bourgeois" standard of right and law, also without the appearance of injustice. For, labor is supposed to belong to the owner of the materials upon which it is expended, and in our present-day society this owner is not the producer (the workingman), but the capitalist.

3. *Transformation of the Surplus-value into Capital, the Accumulation of Capital and the Industrial Reserve Army.*—We have heard the Marxian explanation of the origin of surplus-value. In an order of society in which the means of production are monopolized by

[1] Capital, vol. I. pp. 156–157.   [2] *Ibid.*, p. 178.

a certain class, surplus-value can be created only by exploiting the labor of others. Surplus-value is essentially "a value acquired without compensation, the product . . . of the unremunerated labor of others." [1] The surplus-value thus acquired is employed in its turn to facilitate production and to obtain other and greater quantities of surplus-value and is thus transformed into *capital.* Capital is the sum total of all the means of production owned by private individuals and employed for the acquisition of surplus-value, i.e., for the exploitation of labor; it is simply value or money accumulating, or, as Marx terms it, "value hatching surplus-value."

The transformation of the means of production, and especially of money, into capital presupposes that "the owner of money finds free laborers for hire, free in the sense that as individuals they are at liberty to dispose of their labor," and that, on the other hand, they have no means of production of their own. [2]

The owners of these means will, of course, employ them for further production only with the supposition that from the process they may expect surplus-value, and thus effect a new appropriation of the work of others. "Value now becomes value in process, money in process, and, as such, capital. It comes out of circulation, enters into it again, preserves and multiplies itself within its circuit, comes back out of it with expanded bulk, and begins the same round ever afresh." [3]

The capitalist is forever forced to increase his business and to utilize every technical advance, else competition will push him to the wall. Enlarged business facilities involve more "surplus-value" but

[1] *Ibid.,* pp. 533, 179.   [2] *Ibid,* p. 131.   [3] *Ibid.*

also more misery among the proletariat. "He who was but the owner of money is now strutting about as capitalist, the possessor of labor capacity follows him as his hired laborer; the one with knowing smiles wreathing his face, full of bustle and business; the other shy and demurring, as if he had offered his skin for sale and now but expected to be flayed." [1]

4. *Amount of Surplus-value; its Relation to Profit.*— The total capital employed in the production of surplus-value may be divided into two parts, *constant* capital and *variable* capital.

Constant capital is the amount expended in the acquisition or improvement of raw materials, machines, buildings, etc., because of itself this property is not productive of surplus-value. For, exchange is always between equivalents, and the machines are not able to create surplus-values, since whatever they bestow on the manufactured products they lose themselves. Of course, all this is true only in the Marxian theory of values.

Variable capital, on the other hand, is that part which "is exchanged for labor capacity," in other words, the amount paid in wages to the workingmen. This amount changes its size, because it realizes not merely an equivalent but something beyond it, the so-called surplus-value. The relation of surplus-value to variable capital is called the *ratio of surplus-value* or of exploitation.[2] This ratio increases with the increas-

---

[1] Capital, vol I. p 139

[2] Marx is fond of clothing his ideas in a mathematical garb. Let the total capital advanced by the contractor be called C, its constant part c, the variable part v, then at the beginning of the job $C = c + v$. After the process of production is finished we have an amount of manufactured goods with a total value $C_1 = c + v + m$. In this equation m stands for the absolute surplus-value consisting of unpaid labor   To determine the ratio of increase in the capital it is necessary to abstract from c, or in other words to make $c = 0$, since it represents that part of the capital which is

ing number of wage-earners employed and with the excess of the daily working hours beyond the necessary working time (Capital, vol. I. p. 267).

The ratio of surplus-value is not the same as the *ratio of profit*. The latter is the proportion between the surplus-value and the total capital—variable and constant—being equal to $\frac{m}{c+v}$. If, e.g., the constant capital amounts to $4000, the variable capital to $1000, and the surplus-value to $1000, then the ratio of surplus-value is 100%, the ratio of profit only 20%. But the composition of different capitals is very different, and as the value of machines and raw materials, together with the quantity used on any working day, is very variable, Marx must needs concede that capitals having the same ratio of surplus-value may yet have different ratios of profit.

The capitalist looks principally to profit, therefore it must be his endeavor to attain the greatest surplus-value with as little capital as possible He will see to it that the workingmen are kept at work as long as possible beyond the necessary time; it will be in his interest to employ the cheaper labor of women and children; and finally his attention will be directed toward increasing the output by means of mechanical appliances.[1]

constantly recurring in the product, and to consider only the ratio between m and $v \left(\frac{m}{v} \right)$. This is the *ratio of surplus-value*

[1] By way of illustration a somewhat longer passage of Marx's Capital may be cited here *verbatim* "In as far as machinery renders muscular strength superfluous it renders possible the employment of laborers without muscular strength or full bodily development, but endowed with deftness and dexterity. The employment of women and children was therefore the first step of the capitalist after the introduction of machinery This powerful substitute for labor and laborers at once became a means of increasing the number of wage-earners by making every member of the workingman's family regardless of sex or age directly tributary to the dominion of capital. Forced labor on behalf of the capitalist usurped the place of childish games as well as of work performed in the domestic circle and within the limits of morality on behalf of the family Before this time the value of labor capacity was determined by the working time required for the sustenance of the individual adult laborer as well as for

This last circumstance, coupled with the increasing technical perfection of machinery, *is rendering the workingman more and more superfluous* In a former period organized industry dislodged the independent artisan, but on account of the imperfection of its machinery it required for its extensive operations the services of an increasing number of wage-earners; but in a more advanced stage the contrary takes place. Industry seeks to intensify production, to attain the greatest results with the least expense of labor, and wherever possible by mechanical appliances to supersede labor altogether. On account of technical improvements one mill-hand is at present enabled to perform with the same amount of labor one hundred times as much work as in the beginning of the nineteenth century. In this manner more and more laborers are superseded by machinery. There is formed an army of wage-earners exceeding the industrial demand for labor This is the so-called "industrial reserve army" always at the disposal of capital When industry is working at high pressure this army is called into action, at the succeeding crisis it is again "thrown on the streets."

This reserve army reduces wages to a level corresponding to the demands of capital. "The law," says Marx, " which keeps the relative excess of population or industrial reserve army in constant equilibrium with the extent and energy of the accumulation (of capital), rivets the laboring man closer to capital than Prometheus was riveted to the rock by Vulcan It necessitates an accumulation of misery corresponding to the accumulation of capital. The accumulation of wealth at one pole is at the same time an accumulation of misery, tortures, slavery, ignorance, bestialization, and moral degradation at the opposite pole, i.e.,

the sustenance of his family But in as far as machinery brings every member of the family upon the labor market, it distributes the value of the father's labor capacity over the whole family. Thus his own labor is depreciated To purchase a family comprising, let us say, four members capable of work is perhaps more expensive than it was formerly to purchas` the labor of its head but to make up for this four working days take the place of one and their price decreases in the same ratio as the excess of surplus work of four people exceeds the surplus work of one To sustain the family four of its members must not only work, but they must furnish surplus work on behalf of capital Thus from the very outset machinery not only widens the circle of human material to be exploited, but it also raises the degree of exploitation " (Capital, vol I. pp 358, 359)

This is a good sample of Marxian argumentation Statements without proof, arbitrary generalizations and exaggerations clothed in Hegelian phraseology.

on the part of that class of society which produces as [an increase of] capital [that which ought to be] its own product." [1]

Already in their communist manifesto Marx and Engels maintained: "Instead of rising with the advancing progress of industry, the modern laboring man sinks more and more below the condition of his own class. The laborer becomes a pauper, and pauperism develops much faster than population and wealth "

5. *The End of the Capitalist Method of Production.*— In keeping with his materialistic conception of history Marx finally explains the transformation of present society into the socialistic state of the future:

The same laws of evolution which at present enable the capitalist to oppress and exploit the laboring man will also cause him to be replaced by a higher order of society. The number of competitors is gradually narrowed down, "one capitalist kills a good many others," their power is becoming more and more oppressive, whilst on the other hand the disinherited are growing in numbers and wallowing deeper in misery Financial crises multiply and thus prove that the conditions of production have outgrown the present order of society. The concentration of manufacture, the formation of co-operative societies, and the training of organized labor will soon advance so far as to burst the shackles of monopolized capital Then "the expropriators shall be themselves expropriated," individual property shall be restored, but "on the basis of the attainments achieved during the capitalist era, namely, *the co-operation of independent workingmen and the common ownership in land and in the means of production acquired by their labor.*" [2] "The change from scattered private property based on the work of the individual to capitalist ownership is of course a tedious, cruel, and difficult process, by far more so than the transformation into social property of whatever is owned by private capitalists, whose wealth is already actually based on the co-operative exploitation of the instruments of production. In the former case, there is question of a few usurpers expropriating the mass of the people, in the latter case a small number of usurpers are expropriated by the mass of the people."

[1] Capital, vol 1 p. 611.   [2] *Ibid*, pp 728, 729.

6. *Future Society according to Marxian Ideals.*— The passage just quoted is of special importance in affording us a glimpse at the future socialistic order of society, as it existed in the mind of the "pathfinder of socialism." A comparison of this passage with others in his "Capital" will show that Marx advocated the following institutions in the socialistic order of society:

(*a*) *Collective ownership of all the means of production* brought about by the *expropriation* of the usurping capitalists, by means of democracy established *by the people.*

(*b*) *Common exploitation* of the productive forces on the basis of *free co-operative labor,* i.e , the official organization of labor on a democratic basis [1]

(*c*) The *output* will be considered as a common co-operative product. Part of it will serve as means for further production. The rest destined for consumption will be distributed and become private property. This is "the private property based on one's own labor" of which Marx speaks repeatedly.

(*d*) With regard to the *distribution* of the co-operative products Marx distinguishes two periods or phases of communism.

(*α*) In the *first period* of communist society, when it is but newly hatched from the egg of capitalist society and still bears

---

[1] Cf the following passage from Capital, p 45 "Let us imagine a union of free human beings working with their means of production owned collectively, and consciously expending their individual forces in co-operative labor. There will then be reproduced all the conditions in which Robinson Crusoe was working, only now the work will be social instead of individual. One other essential difference there will be. Robinson's products were exclusively his own and for his own immediate use. The total product of our union, on the other hand, would be a co-operative product. A certain part of it would have to serve again as means of production and would remain common property, The other part would be for the consumption of the members Therefore it would have to be distributed. The manner of distribution would vary according to the special organism of co-operative production and according to the corresponding degree of development in the producers Only as a parallel to the production of merchandise do we suppose that each producer's share will be determined by the time of his work The time of work will therefore play a double part. On the one hand its distribution on a co-operative plan will maintain the right proportion between the different functions of labor and the different requirements of the community. On the other hand the time of work will serve for measuring the share of the individual producer in the co-operative labor and in that part of the common product destined for individual consumption." Cf. also Capital, p. 493.

traces of the old shell, labor time must serve as a standard of distribution. "In accordance with this principle each producer (i.e., laborer, in contradistinction to capitalists who do not produce) will receive—after deduction has been made for the needs of the society—exactly what he has contributed to it. His contribution is his individual share of labor. The social working day consists of the total of the individual hours of labor; the individual labor time of each producer is the part of the social working day furnished by him; it constitutes his share. The society will give him a certificate that he has furnished a certain quantity of work—after deducting his work for the common fund—and by showing his certificate he will draw from the society's stores an amount of provisions equivalent in value to his work. The amount of work given to the society in one shape is received again in another."

"The ruling principle is here evidently the same as in the exchange of merchandise, in as far as it is an exchange of equivalents. Form and contents are indeed different, since under the then circumstances no one will be able to give anything except his work, and because nothing can become personal property except the articles intended for individual consumption. As to the distribution of the latter among the several producers the same principle will be applied as in the exchange of equivalent commodities, equal amounts of work in different shapes will be exchanged for each other." [1]

From all this Marx concludes that in the first communist period there will be no possibility of perfect equality. There will be indeed no class distinctions, because each one will be a workingman like all the rest; but "different individual talents and capacities will be acknowledged as privileges of nature." "In substance as well as in their nature rights will be unequal, . . . but these inconveniences are unavoidable during this first period of communist society which, after long travailing, is just then issuing forth from the womb of capitalist society. Right can never be superior to economic conditions and to the development of civilization determined by them " [2]

(β) In a later and *more perfect period* "individual labor will exist as an integral part of the total work," [3] i e , the individual

---

[1] *Marx* in the *Neue Zeit*, 9th year, I. pp. 566, 567.
[2] Capital, vol I p. 567.
[3] *Ibid* , p 566.

as such will have no special title to the products of co-operative labor, but each one will receive according to his needs. "In a higher phase of communist society, after the slavish subordination of the individual under the divisions of labor, and consequently the opposition between mental and bodily work has disappeared; after labor has ceased to be merely the means of sustaining life, but has become an urgent desire; after the individual has become more perfect in every respect, increasing thereby also the productive forces and giving full play to the fountains of co-operative wealth—then only the narrow ordinary barriers of right and justice can be demolished, and society may inscribe upon its banner: Each one according to his abilities, to each one according to his needs." [1]

The reader is requested to note this remarkable passage; we shall have occasion to revert to it in a later chapter.

§ IV. *The Present State of Socialism.*

I. SOCIALISM IN GERMANY.

1. After this brief sketch of the notion and history of scientific socialism it may be well to review its present condition first of all in the land of its birth, in Germany. The growth of German social democracy is sufficiently indicated by the following statistics:

In the elections for the Imperial Diet (Reichstag) there were polled for social democratic candidates:

in 1871 . .. ..   118,655 votes
" 1874.   340,078   "
" 1877.   481,008   "
" 1878.   420,662   " (in spite of the Reichstag's being dissolved)
" 1881.   335,307   " (in spite of the Socialist Law)
" 1884 . . .   507,798   "
" 1887.   673,283   "
" 1890. 1,323,300   "
" 1893. 1,786,738   "
" 1898. 2,107,076   "
" 1903. 3,010,771   "

[1] Capital, vol. I. p. 567.

Social democracy is therefore by far the most numerous party in the empire. In 1898 more than one fourth of a total of about 7,600,000 votes was polled for socialist candidates; and in 1903 they reached nearly one third of not quite 9,500,000 votes The Hanseatic towns, Hamburg, Bremen, and Lubeck; the capitals of the federated states, Berlin, Dresden, Karlsruhe, Stuttgart, etc, in fact almost all the large cities are represented in the Reichstag by socialists. Of cities with more than 100,000 inhabitants Crefeld and Aix-la-Chapelle alone carried a conservative candidate at the first ballot.

Of course, it must be taken into account that, as experience has proved, many give their votes for socialist candidates, not because they approve of their principles, but because they wish to give forcible expression to their dissatisfaction with certain conditions or with the candidates of the other parties. Moreover, social democrats more than any other party everywhere put up polling candidates, in order to brag about their number of votes. In the elections for the Reichstag in 1898, and again in 1903, they were running candidates in every one of the 397 election districts

In the elections of 1898 the number of socialist members of the Reichstag rose from 48 to 58, in 1903 from 58 to 81. According to the report of the executive party committee, July 1, 1902, the *party press* showed the following figures Besides the central organ, the Berlin *Vorwärts*, and the scientific weekly *Neue Zeit* the socialist press in Germany comprised:

54	papers published	daily
10	" "	three times a week
4	" "	twice a week
7	" "	once " "
1	" "	twice a month
2	" "	once " "

Moreover, two bi-weekly comic papers and two weekly illustrated journals besides the *Gleichheit*, a magazine devoted to the interests of workingwomen

The socialist trade-union press numbers

1	journal issued	three times a week
32	journals "	once a week
2	" "	three times a month
21	" "	twice a month
11	" "	once " "

Up to the present writing these figures have remained unchanged The *Neue Weltkalender*, the official party almanac,
had in 1901 a circulation of 140,000 copies. Numerous pamphlets are scattered broadcast through the land. Millions of
copies of an illustrated tract published by the executive committee were spread through the whole empire even in the mean-
est hamlets During the fiscal year July 1901–July 1902 the
party fund expended $80,843 00 for purposes of propaganda,
for the support of members of the Reichstag, etc.[1]

The chief representatives of German social democracy are at present A. Bebel, K. Kautsky, E. Bernstein, J. Auer, P. Singer, G. von Vollmar, W. Heine,
H. Molkenbuhr, A. Stadthagen, A. von Elm, etc.;
they as well as their whole party base their demands
on Marxian principles exclusively, at least ever since
1891. Formerly, from 1875 on, they upheld the so-
called *Gotha platform* or *programme,* as German socialists term it.

In that year the partisans of Marx—the so-called
Eisenacher under the leadership of Liebknecht and
Bebel—and those of Lassalle—the Lassalleans led
by von Schweitzer—assembled in convention at
Gotha and drew up a joint compromise platform.
Against the first draft of this document Marx raised
some objections and criticisms, which he handed in
writing to the leaders of the social democratic party.
His remarks were entitled "Marginal Notes on the
Platform of the German Labor Party." With regard
to some points the criticisms of Marx found favor
with the convention, not so with regard to others.
Owing to this circumstance Engels thought fit in 1891
to publish the "Marginal Notes" from the unpublished
papers of his friend, and thus they appeared in the

---

[1] Cf Report of the Transactions of the Social Democratic Party Convention of 1902, pp 25-31

Neue Zeit. It was a disagreeable surprise sprung on the socialist members of the Reichstag, but after all it compelled them to take the revision of their platform into serious consideration. The discussion took place in the party convention at Erfurt, Oct. 14–20, 1891, resulting in a new platform, the so-called Erfurt programme.

For the sake of comparison both platforms, the earlier Gotha programme and the present Erfurt programme, will be printed here *in extenso.*

A. *The Gotha Programme* (1875).

I. Labor is the source of all wealth [1] and culture; and since universally efficient labor is possible only through society, it follows that, the universal duty of labor being supposed, the entire product of labor belongs with equal right to the entire body of society—that is, to its individual members—each according to his individual wants

In the present state of society labor materials are monopolized by capitalists; and the dependence of the laboring class thence arising is the cause of misery and slavery in all its forms.

The liberation of labor requires the transformation of all labor materials into the common property of society, and the social control of all labor, together with the application and just distribution of the entire proceeds of labor, for the use of all.

---

[1] In his Kritik des sozialdemokratischen Programms Marx has declared this statement to be *false,* and so it is undoubtedly Hence some have concluded that Marx has abandoned his theory of all value being derived from labor This, however, is not the case According to Marx the national wealth consists of *use-values* which are due to nature at least as much as to labor Whether a land is rich or poor in wine, cereals, coal, etc , depends a good deal on the nature of the soil and on the geological formation and geographical position of the country, a fact which Marx noways denies But from this very dependence of labor on the means of production springs the servitude of workingmen in all social conditions where they are not themselves the owners of capital Marx's theory of value goes no further than to say that the *exchange-value* which gives to merchandise its distinctive character consists of the labor necessary for its production But from these premises he draws the conclusion that during the capitalist era the formation of *private* wealth—in opposition to *national* wealth—or, in other words, the accumulation of surplus-values in the hands of capitalists, is effected by the appropriation of the labor of others.

The liberation of labor must be the work of the laboring class, which is opposed by all the other classes as by reactionary masses

II. Proceeding from these principles, the socialistic labor party of Germany seeks by all means to bring about a free state and a socialistic organization, the abolition of the iron law of wages and of the system of wage-working, the removal of oppression of every form, and of all social and political inequality.

The socialist labor party of Germany, though operating within the confines of the nation, is conscious of the international character of the labor movement and is determined to discharge all the duties which this universality imposes upon the laborers to bring about the brotherhood of all men

The socialist party of Germany demands, in order to prepare the way for the solution of the social problem, the institution of socialistic industrial associations at the public expense under the democratic control of the laboring people. These associations are to be of such dimensions that from them the socialistic organization of the entire people may be developed.

This portion of the programme contains the economic aims and, consequently, the gist of the social democratic aspirations. It is followed by a second political programme which voices the political aims of the movement—in the first place, the final and permanent ends and, in the second place, the means which are gradually to transform our present society into a socialistic state.

The socialist labor party of Germany demands that the constitution of the state should rest upon the following principles: (1) Universal, equal, and direct suffrage with private ballot, and obligatory voting of all subjects of the state from the age of twenty upward, for all elections in state and municipality. The election-day is to be on a Sunday or a holiday. (2) Immediate legislation by the people Decisions regarding peace and war by the people. (3) Universal military service. Civil militia instead of standing armies (4) The abolition of all exceptional legislation, especially regarding the freedom of the press, of association, and of holding public meetings, and generally of all laws which in any way restrict the free expression of opinion, free thought and research. (5) Administration of justice by the people Administration of justice free of expense to all. (6) Universal and equal education of the people by the state; universal compulsory education; free instruction in all educational institutions. Religion to be declared a private matter.

The socialist labor party of Germany demands in the present existing social circumstances

(1) The greatest possible extent of political rights and franchises in conformity with the above demands (2) One only progressive income-tax for state and municipality in the place of all existing taxation—particularly in the place of the indirect taxation which weighs so heavily upon the people (3) Unlimited right of association (4) A normal working day suited to social circumstances[1] Prohibition of Sunday labor. (5) Prohibition of child labor, and of such labor for women as is injurious to health and morality (6) Laws protecting the life and health of the laborers Sanitary control of the workmen's dwellings. The supervision of mines, factories, workshops, and domestic industries by officers elected by the workmen Efficient employers' liability law (7) The regulation of prison labor. (8) Independent administration of all aid and benefit funds

B. *The Erfurt Programme* (1891).

I. The economical development of civil society necessarily leads to the destruction of small industries, the basis of which is private ownership of the laborer in the means of production.

---

1 By normal working day is meant *here* the maximum of working hours permitted by law in any given industry Others, again, understand by the normal working day the necessary social labor time of an individual, which varies in proportion to his natural wants and to the productiveness of his labor The length of this normal working day would be ascertained by figuring out the number of hours required for the manufacture of the entire national product, and how much of this time would fall to the share of each laborer This normal working day presupposes a collectivist organization of society, and seems to be what *Marx* understands by the term

Rodbertus and others understand by the normal working day the number of hours which a laborer of medium health and strength and of medium effort, under ordinary conditions, can work daily This time, of course, varies in each industry The more laborious and dangerous the work, the shorter also the working hours.

It divests the laborer of all means of production and transforms him into a penniless proletarian, while the means of production become the sole property of a comparatively small number of capitalists and real-estate owners.

Hand in hand with the monopoly of capital goes the abolition of the disorganized small industries by the formation of vast industrial organizations, the development of work-tools into machines, and a gigantic increase of the productiveness of human labor   But all the advantages of this change are monopolized by the capitalists and landowners. For the proletariat and the declining middle classes—common citizens and farmers—this social change is tantamount to a growing insecurity of existence, of misery, oppression, slavery, degradation, exploitation.

The number of proletarians increases, the army of superfluous laborers assumes greater dimensions from day to day the conflict between the oppressor and the oppressed is becoming more and more violent—that conflict between the bourgeoisie and the proletariat which divides modern society into two hostile camps and is the common characteristic of all industrial nations.

The chasm between rich and poor is widened by those financial *crises* which are grounded in the very nature of capitalistic production—crises which become ever more extensive and destructive, make universal insecurity the normal state of society, and give evidence that the productive forces of our age have become uncontrollable by society, and that private property in the means of production has become incompatible with their proper utilization and full development

Private property in the means of production, which formerly was a means of securing to the producer the ownership of his produce, has nowadays become a means of dispossessing farmers, laborers, and small merchants, and of making the non-laborers —capitalists and landowners—the possessors of the produce of labor   Only the transformation of private capitalistic property in the means of production—i e , land, mines and mining, raw materials, tools, machinery, and means of communication— into common property, and the change of private production into socialistic—i e , production for and through society—can effect that the extensive industry and the ever-increasing productiveness of social labor shall become for the exploited classes, instead of a source of misery and oppression, a source of the highest prosperity and of universal and harmonious perfection.

This social revolution implies the liberation, not only of the laboring class, but of the entire human race, which is suffering under our present condition. But this emancipation can only be the work of the laboring classes, since all other classes, notwithstanding their clashing interests, take their stand on the platform of private property in land and in the means of production, and make the preservation of modern society on its present basis their common object.

The struggle of labor against capitalistic oppression is necessarily a political one. The laboring class cannot carry on its industrial struggles and develop its economic organization without political rights It cannot effect the transfer of the means of production into the possession of the body social without possessing itself of political power

To give to this struggle of the laboring class spontaneous activity and unity, and to assign to it its natural direction—this is the end and aim of the social democratic party.

The interests of the laboring classes are the same in all countries where capitalistic industry exists Owing to the extent of international commerce and industry the condition of labor in every country becomes more and more dependent on the condition of labor in all other countries. The emancipation of the laboring classes is therefore a work in which the laborers of all civilized countries should take part In this conviction the social democratic party of Germany feels and declares itself to be at one with the intelligent organized laborers of all other countries.

The social democratic party of Germany does not contend for new rights or privileges for the laboring classes, but for the abolition of the rule of the classes and of the classes themselves, and for the equal rights and equal duties of all without distinction of sex or pedigree. Proceeding from these views social democracy in modern society opposes not only the exploitation and oppression of the laboring class, but every kind of exploitation and oppression, no matter against what class, party, race, or sex they may be brought to bear.

II. Proceeding from these principles, the social democratic party of Germany demands for the present.[1]

1 Universal, equal, direct suffrage by private ballot for all citizens over twenty years of age, without distinction of sex, in all elections and ballotings. Representation proportioned to the number of population, and meanwhile a redistribution of election districts after each census. Biennial elections. Elections and other ballotings to be held on a legal holiday. Compensation for representatives   Abolition of every restriction of political rights except in the case of legal disfranchisement.

2 Direct legislation by the people through the right of initiative and referendum. Self-rule and self-administration by the people in empire, state, province, and community. Election of magistrates by the people; their responsibility in solidarity to the people   Annual grant of taxation.

3 Education for universal military service. Popular militia instead of standing armies   Decisions regarding peace and war by the representatives of the people. International disputes to be settled by arbitration.

4 Abolition of all laws which restrict or suppress freedom in the expression of opinion; the right of forming associations and holding conventions.

5. Abolition of all laws which subordinate woman to man in public and private life

6 Religion is to be declared a private concern; the use of public funds for ecclesiastical and religious purposes to be abolished   Ecclesiastical and religious communities are to be regarded as private societies which are perfectly free to manage their own affairs.

7. Secularization of the schools[2]   Compulsory attendance at the public schools. Instruction, use of all the means of instruction (books, etc), and board free of charge in all public elementary schools, and in the higher institutions of learning

---

[1] Namely, as long as the present state of society with its private ownership of the means of production remains.

[2] The book of Kautsky and Schonlank, Grundsätze und Forderungen der Sozialdemokratie (Berlin, 1892), p 44, remarks on this passage "If religion is a private concern, .   then the school is in consequence a purely secular institution   . . To mix up the instruction of the children with religious affairs would be a fundamental error. Therefore the co-operation of ecclesiastical persons in the work of instruction is inadmissible."

for such pupils of both sexes as, on account of their talents, are judged fit for higher studies.

8. Gratuitous administration of justice and legal advice. Administration of justice by judges elected by the people. The right of appeal in criminal cases Indemnification of those who have been unjustly accused, arrested, or condemned. Abolition of capital punishment.

9. Free medical attendance, also in childbirth; free medicine. Free burial

10. Graded and progressive taxation on income and property to meet all public expenses which are to be defrayed by taxes Obligatory self-valuation Taxation on hereditary property, graded progressively according to the extent of the property and the degree of kindred of the heirs Abolition of all indirect taxes, customs, and other economical imposts, which subordinate the general interests to the interests of the few.

For the *protection of the laboring class* the social democratic party of Germany demands for the present:

1. National and international legislation for the protection of labor on the following basis: (*a*) The determination of a normal work-day not exceeding eight hours. (*b*) Prohibition of industrial labor by children under the age of fourteen years (*c*) Prohibition of night-work, except in those branches of industry which of their nature, for mechanical reasons or for the common welfare, require night-work. (*d*) An uninterrupted rest of at least thirty-six hours every week for each laborer. (*e*) Abolition of the force system.

2. Supervision of all industries Investigation and regulation of the condition of labor in town and country by means of imperial and provincial labor bureaus and labor councils. An effectual system of industrial hygiene.

3. Equality between agricultural laborers or servants and industrial laborers; abolition of the domestic relations between masters (or mistresses) and servants

4 Maintenance of the right of coalition.

5. Insurance of laborers to be regulated by the imperial government, with due co-operation of laborers in the administration.

The adoption of the Erfurt programme scored a decisive victory for the partisans of Marx as against those of Lassalle. The chief points of distinction between it and its predecessor are the following: The Erfurt programme lays far more stress on the so-called materialistic conception of history, which, according to Marxian ideas, is supposed to effect the transition from the capitalistic to the socialistic order of society by means of a natural, irresistible process, and especially by the monopolist concentration of the means of production. On the other hand, the assertion that labor creates all wealth and also the iron law of wages were cancelled. Nor is there any further mention of co-operative societies and of "reactionary masses" opposed to the workingmen. Besides the capitalists the new platform mentions also the landowners as monopolizing the means of production. Finally, the Erfurt platform takes a more decided stand on the woman question Equal rights with men are claimed for women in public as well as in private affairs.

2. As regards essentials German social democrats all take their stand on the above-mentioned platform; yet of late there have arisen *different factions* which are probably destined to wield a far-reaching influence on the further development of socialism.

The *young socialists*, led by Werner, Wildberger, Auerbach, and others, made their appearance in the early nineties and insisted on a "double-quick tempo" and a more open profession of revolutionary principles. They blamed the socialist leaders of laying too much stress on "parliamenting," a means to which they themselves assigned rather the rôle of an advertising medium. They evidently broached anarchistic principles à la Most and Hasselmann. Some of their number were excluded from the social democratic party and endeavored to form a new party, the "Union of independent socialists." Their attempt never became of any importance, yet it cannot be doubted that among social democrats there are still many adherents of principles similar to those of the "young socialists," clamoring for more vigorous manifestations of the revolutionary character of social democracy.

Of greater significance for the future of socialism is the division into *orthodox Marxists* and the so-called *revisionists* who are headed by G. von Vollmar and of late by E. Bernstein.

Already in the beginning of the nineties Vollmar protested energetically against proceeding too impetuously, and thereby caused a lively controversy among socialists. Vollmar wished to base his efforts upon the present state of society, to advance the betterment of the workingman by such reforms as are possible under existing circumstances, and thus step by step to effect the organic transition from the old order of society to the new. The party leaders, especially those of Northern Germany—Vollmar himself is a Bavarian —Bebel, Liebknecht, etc., attacked him in no measured terms, casting up to him that he is a "state socialist," endeavoring to form an opportunist national reform party, etc. Genuine socialism, however, Bebel remarked, "looks upon these proximate demands as accidental trifles and lays the principal stress upon the final aims, not vice versa, as Vollmar insists on doing."

The dispute between Vollmar and his opponents waxed warmest concerning the notion of "state socialism." Being charged with advocating state socialism, Vollmar published an essay bearing that title in the *Revue bleue*, in which he expresses his opinion as follows: State socialism, speaking generally, may be taken to mean that the existing state is not merely an organization for political purposes, but that its sovereignty embraces the entire field of economics, so that it belongs to its province not only to regulate all the relations between workingmen and employers but also to effect the transfer of any branch of production to the supervision or even into the immediate administration of the state. Vollmar sees no reason why this kind of state socialism should be so strenuously opposed; he rather thinks that social democracy might do well to approve and support a good many projects proposed by state socialism.

This opinion was fiercely assailed in the *Vorwarts* by Liebknecht, and in the *Neue Zeit* by Kautsky. There was talk of treason to party principles. But as Vollmar rightly remarked, there was in the whole controversy a good deal of beating about in the fog.

Indeed, Vollmar's definition is rather vague. It might be endorsed even by such as are not social democrats. Socialists can adopt it as their own, if they consider state socialism not as their ultimate goal, but only as a means or as the natural transition to their ulterior socialistic purpose. In this sense Vollmar had propounded his opinion, as is plain from the statements made in the above-mentioned article and from his later declarations. Therefore he did not hesitate to move in common with Liebknecht the following resolution, which was almost unanimously adopted by the Berlin party convention, 1892:

"The party convention declares· Social democracy has nothing in common with so-called state socialism This state socialism, in so far as it aims at state ownership for fiscal purposes, proposes to place the state in lieu of the private capitalist and to endow it with the power of putting upon the people the two-fold yoke of economic exploitation and political slavery

"This so-called state socialism, in so far as it is occupied in social reform or in improving the condition of the laboring classes, is a system of half-hearted measures, owing its existence to fear of social democracy By trifling concessions and all manner of palliatives it endeavors to alienate workingmen from social democracy and thereby to paralyze the latter.

" Social democracy has never disdained to demand such measures on the part of the state or to approve them when proposed by others, whenever they were calculated to effect an improvement in the condition of the laboring classes in the present economic system. But it considers such measures merely as some trifling part payment, which will in no wise influence our striving after the socialistic reorganization of state and society

" Social democracy is essentially revolutionary, state socialism is conservative Social democracy and state socialism are irreconcilable opposites "

The first part as well as the concluding sentence speak for Liebknecht, the second last paragraph for Vollmar. With the latter it was more a question of tactics than of principles; and since with regard to tactics his opinion had prevailed, he actually came out victorious despite the full-mouthed verbiage against state socialism.

The most interesting point of the whole discussion, however, is the fact that all parties appealed to the social democratic convention for an authentic declaration on state socialism, a declaration which should put a stop to the quarrel. Here then we have a supreme doctrinal authority in regular form, an *ex cathedra* decision of the party convention! Vollmar disputed the competence of the convention for any such declaration; the adoption of this resolution, he said, would transform the party convention into a "Church Council." Kautsky, on the other hand, was for the decision. There was not question, he thought, of the scientific value of state socialism, but of the attitude which social democracy as a political party should assume regarding it.[1] But the attitude of the party depended first of all on a correct definition of state socialism. If Vollmar's definition was correct and in harmony with socialist principles, then it was highly unjust and tyrannical to take him to task· or perhaps even to exclude him from the party on that account. But can the party convention, composed as it is for the most part of men without much higher education, be qualified to decide whether a given definition of state socialism is correct and in harmony with socialist principles? Most assuredly not. And in fact Kautsky, Liebknecht, and the rest, by appealing to the convention, wished but to force their own opinion on Vollmar.

3. The feud between orthodox Marxists and Vollmar's "moderates" entered upon a new stage when E. Bernstein began his incisive criticism on the foundations of Marxism. In the case of Vollmar it had remained doubtful whether it was a fight about principles or merely about tactics, but with Bernstein and his partisans no doubt was possible on that head. Here there was question of fundamental differences in principle, about the "to be or not to be" of Marxism. As long as the scientific foundations of socialism were criticised by avowed opponents, criticism could be set aside by some stock phrases about complete ignorance of socialism, malevolent misrepresentations, etc. This policy, of course, would not do against Bernstein, a trusty and prominent comrade.

Up to the repeal of the German Socialist Law in

[1] *Neue Zeit*, xi. pp 210 sqq.

1890 Bernstein was editor of the *Sozialdemokrat* of Zurich, the then principal organ of German socialists; after that he lived for a number of years in London in constant intercourse with Fr. Engels.

In a series of stirring articles he subjected the "scientific" part of the party platform to a searching criticism, trying especially to demonstrate that the conception of the materialistic theory of history contained in the party platform needed a thorough revision. Even Marx and Engels, he maintained, had not been always consistent in their views. Above all, Bernstein found fault with the so-called "theory of collapse." Marx and Engels started from the assumption that the development of capitalist society would soon bring about such a concentration of industries, such an accumulation of capital in the hands of a few, such an increase in numbers and in misery of the penniless proletariat, that a great social cataclysm, the universal collapse of society, would become inevitable. Among socialist leaders, Bebel, Liebknecht, Kautsky, etc., this assumption was held sacred as an infallible dogma. Consequently they took it to be their most urgent duty to foster and promote the capitalist evolution and thus to hasten the approach of the catastrophe. Engels himself and Bebel after him had already predicted the collapse of society— the great "Kladderadatsch"—as going to take place before the close of the nineteenth century. It stands to reason that such assumptions are not favorable to great activity in social reforms—rather the contrary. This explains the ill-concealed aversion of the socialist leaders for trades-unions, their predilection for arousing the discontent of workingmen and for fanning the flames of class hatred, their endless and excessive

complaints about the constant pauperization of laboring men, their ever-growing exploitation, and so on.

In the articles mentioned above Bernstein opposed
these views very energetically, and as the result of his
discussion he published a book entitled "Die Voraussetzungen des Sozialismus und die Aufgaben der Sozialdemokratie." [1]   The gist of this book lies in the
following statements.   The introductory theoretical
sentences of the Erfurt platform may be of immense
value in the hands of demagogues, but they are contradicted by facts.   Neither the small tradespeople
nor the peasantry are on the point of disappearing,
nor can it be maintained that in civilized countries there
is an increase of misery, servitude, and decadence.
Bernstein inveighs likewise against the orthodox
Marxian principle that socialism is an objective historical necessity.   If this were the case the exertions
of the socialist party would be mere waste of strength.
The life of modern nations is by far too complex to be
comprehended within the compass of one principle.

Bernstein's strictures provoked fierce attacks on
the part of the comrades, especially Kautsky, Bebel,
Plechanow, Fr. Mehring, and others who assailed him
in the *Neue Zeit* and the *Vorwärts*.   Bernstein was
not slow to answer, being supported by the *Sozialistische Monatshefte* and by not a few of the party members.

The faction of the "undaunted"—Bebel and his
followers—appealed to the party convention on the
plea that Bernstein was ruining socialism.   The
Stuttgart convention did not yet dare to decide for or

[1] Stuttgart, 1899.   The original articles were collected and published by
Bernstein with the title Zur Geschichte und Theorie des Sozialismus
(Berlin, 1901).

against the "heretic," but at Hanover, in 1899, the Bernstein affair was taken into serious consideration. However, it soon became apparent that the Bernstein partisans were more numerous than had at first been believed.* Only a few delegates, headed by Liebknecht, clamored for a downright repudiation of Bernstein for the sake of Marxian orthodoxy. Others, as David, von Vollmar, von Elm, and Fendrich, stood up for Bernstein. Auer tried to mediate, and jeered at the irreconcilable comrades à la Stadthagen "who were forever marching ahead, bearing aloft the standard of social revolution with the ultimate object dangling from the flagpole." Even Bebel, Bernstein's chief accuser, finally moved a resolution which the accused was ready to sign *cum grano salis*. It was as follows:

The past development of bourgeois society has given our party no occasion to relinquish or to change our fundamental views concerning it. In the future as in the past our party is in the field of class struggles, where the liberation of the working class must be its own achievement, and therefore we consider it the appointed task of the laboring class to gain political supremacy, and by its help to effect the common ownership of the means of production and the social organization of production and exchange, thereby to bring about the greatest possible happiness of all.

To reach this goal our party will use every means suitable to the purpose and compatible with our fundamental principles Without being deceived as to the nature and the character of the bourgeois parties, which are but representatives and champions of the existing order of state and society, our party does not refuse to go hand in hand with them in single cases, wherever there is question of strengthening our party at the elections, or of extending the political rights and franchises of the people, or of really improving the social conditions of the working classes and advancing civilization, or of combating tendencies hostile to the laborer and the common people However, our party in its entire activity retains complete autonomy and inde-

pendence and considers every successful achievement as merely
a step in the direction of the ultimate goal

Our party is neutral as regards the establishment of co-operative societies   Wherever the necessary preliminary conditions
are fulfilled the establishment of these societies is considered as
calculated to improve the social position of their members.   The
establishment of these societies as well as every kind of organization among workingmen for the safeguarding and promoting of
their interests is considered also as a proper means of educating the laboring classes in the management of their own affairs;
but these co-operative societies are not credited with any decisive influence in the liberation of the laboring classes from
the bondage of wage slavery.

In combating militarism in army and navy, and as to the
colonial policy, our party maintains its former position.   Likewise it keeps to its former international policy, aiming at a mutual
understanding and universal brotherhood of the nations, in the
first place of the laboring classes in civilized countries, in order
to effect by a general federation the accomplishment of the
tasks incumbent upon all.

Accordingly there is no reason for our party to change either
its principles or fundamental demands, or to adopt different
tactics or a different name, i e., to transform the social democratic party into a democratic socialist reform party; and we
decidedly repudiate every attempt at veiling or shifting our
position with regard to the existing order of state and society
and the bourgeois parties.[1]

To appreciate this resolution to its full value we
must remember that Bernstein's partisans also voted
for it, after their leader had declared his acceptation.
In any case it was a victory for the advocates of present
improvements as against the dreamers about future
prospects, because now for the first time the party
approved the trades-union movement and the formation of co-operative societies.

However, the politicians, i.e., the executive party

[1] Report of the Transactions of the Socialist Party Convention at Hanover
Oct 9-14, 1899, p 243

committee and the parliamentarians—Bebel, Lieb-knecht, etc.,—were not a little prejudiced against the trades-union movement. They were not wanting, indeed, in assurances of their platonic friendship for the unions, still they viewed the whole movement with a good 'deal of mistrust, and covertly expressed their apprehension lest it should drift social democracy into the wake of a bourgeois reform party. Already at the Cologne convention in 1893 the politicians and the union leaders—Legien, von Elm, etc.— had entered upon very spirited altercations, which have since been repeated from time to time. The apprehensions of the "politicians" were not altogether unfounded. For, the unions naturally direct their attention to what is at present practically obtainable and thus contribute in no slight degree to the improvement of their members' economic condition. Once the workingman has got a snug berth and finds that his own interests are connected in a hundred ways with the permanence of society, his revolutionary fervor, the leading motive of the genuine socialist, begins to cool. He is no longer conscious of belonging to the great order of "proletarians of all countries;" his zeal for contributing in hard cash to the international cause is perceptibly diminishing; he has other interests nearer and dearer to his heart. No doubt, therefore, that the development of the trades-unions is, to say the least, not favorable to the revolutionary tendencies of extremist social democracy. And it was at Hanover that the trades-union movement and in general the formation of co-operative societies was first acknowledged by the party as justifiable measures.

In reviewing the Hanover debates concerning the party platform in the November number of the *Sozialistische Monats-*

hefte, 1899, David remarks that three different reasons induced the Bernstein faction to vote for Bebel's resolution.

1 By its clause on election compromises and co-operative societies it embodied a good slice of Bernsteinism, so that for the sake of the practical concessions the theoretical gewgaws could be taken into the bargain. 2. Bebel had amended his motion so as to make it read, there is no reason to change the principles and fundamental demands, where at first it read *the platform* of the party. Thereby was acknowledged the undesirableness of being tied to certain statements of the Erfurt platform. The discussion also brought it home to the delegates that the theory of concentration is to be modified in so far as agriculture is to be exempted from it. The theory of pauperization made such a poor showing that no one is any longer inclined to admit it, the theory of crises is in a critical state, and finally the theory of collapse is highly compromised. On the whole, the first four paragraphs of the Erfurt programme are a "medley of truth and fiction, of facts and hypotheses, of problems and prophecies." 3 Bernstein's partisans were justified in voting for Bebel's motion by the fact that it indicates the only and final goal of socialism, "the greatest possible happiness of all." To this goal everything else is to be subordinated, even the social organization of production, nay, even the socialist principle itself. "Society is considered to be of more account than its exterior form—this is meant by Bebel's goal."

In this conception of socialism the fundamental ideas of Marxism have undoubtedly been abandoned

Bernstein continued his attacks on Marxism and propounded his diverging opinions even in a lecture before a "bourgeois" gathering. This brought on another heated discussion at the Lubeck convention, September, 1901. The clashing opinions were couched in two resolutions moved by Bebel and Heine respectively. In their preambles both resolutions acknowledged the necessity of self-criticism for the intellectual progress of the party. Heine's resolution then went on to say that there was no occasion for the party to recede from the principles of the resolution adopted at Hanover in 1899, and that thereby the motions against Bernstein were to be considered as settled: but Bebel's resolution declared that by his one-sided criticism, neglecting to criticise bourgeois society also, Bernstein had assumed an equivocal position and had aroused the displeasure of his comrades. In the expectation that Bernstein would be amenable to reason and act accordingly, the convention should pass over the motions against him and take up the order of the day. Heine's motion was dropped by 166 votes against 71, that of Bebel was carried by a majority of 203 against 31, four delegates having abstained from the ballot. Upon Bebel's assurance that the resolution did not imply a vote of distrust against Bernstein, the latter filed the following declaration:

Comrades· As I have already declared in my open letter to the Stuttgart convention, the votes of delegates cannot in any way make me waver in my convictions Yet on the other hand I have never been indifferent to the vote of the majority of my comrades It is my conviction that the resolution adopted by you is objectively wronging me, that it is based on false premises, as I have already explained to you But since comrade Bebel declared that it implied no vote of distrust, I also declare that I accept the vote of the majority as such, and that I shall treat it with that respect and consideration which is due to the decision of the convention

This meaningless declaration was received with "thunderous applause." The *Vorwarts* remarked triumphantly: "The conclusion of the Bernstein discussions implies the adjustment of differences and the assurance of future harmonious co-operation of the whole party; it indicates the firm purpose of burying the tomahawk of personal quarrels." But in view of Bernstein's declaration that he remained unshaken in his convictions there can hardly be question of an adjustment of differences.   Bernstein may have modified his tactics for the time being, in principle the gaping chasm remains, and sooner or later will assert itself with a vengeance.   Even Bebel had announced at Lubeck that a revision of the Erfurt platform could not be postponed very long.

However, at the Dresden convention of 1903 nothing was as yet decided.   Personal encounters took up most of the time; when, after a heated discussion, a resolution was adopted condemning the policy of the so-called revisionists, it amounted to very little, since it stigmatized those revisionists who renounce the ultimate goal and content themselves with obtaining reforms in the existing order of society.

4. In conclusion we may mention another source of antagonism within the party which is liable to cause many a squabble among the comrades.   We mean the antagonism between *college men and proletarians.*

Already in the beginning of 1901 Kautsky had pointed out this antagonism in his comments on the discussions of the socialist conference of Saxony. He noticed in those discussions "the symptoms of a wide-spread feeling against the academic element in our ranks" which had become manifest also on other occasions.   Toward the close of the same year the *Neue Zeit* had an article on the same subject from the pen of a "proletarian."   He says among other things that animosity against the college men has actually spread far and wide, and it is not confined to some of the college men, but is directed against "the whole academic tribe," and with many of the comrades it seems to be more or less of a principle.   It has certainly caused hard feeling that young men just fresh from the university, whose tendencies cannot be controlled, are preferred to old and tried laboring comrades. "We are a party of workingmen, and it does not look well that among our members in the Reichstag, in the editorial rooms of our press, and in the other offices of the party there should be so many 'doctors.' This sentiment has been expressed again and again. It is also quite certain that the expression in our platform, 'the emancipation of the laboring classes must be the work of the laboring classes themselves,' is often misunderstood and interpreted in the sense that no one can be a full-blood socialist unless he is a workingman."

Also the manner in which many college men are carrying on their superficial talk and supercilious airs have often roused the ire of the workingmen. But without college men there would be no socialist science or literature. Socialism cannot do without them, although their scientific productions find few readers among workingmen. The proletarian quoted above laments: "We know that during the last few years, though circumstances were comparatively favorable, not one of the works published by Dietz, Stuttgart, has been a profitable investment. Besides we must remember that not everything which is bought is also read, but often lies for years without being cut open. It is a general complaint that the 'free' singing, gymnastic, and bicycle societies, nay, even 'free' smoking clubs take up the entire leisure time of workingmen."

II. Socialism in the United States.

A. Historical Sketch.

Before entering upon a more detailed account of the present status of socialism in the United States it may not be out of place to take a glance at its historical development. In this inquiry we shall abstract from the utopian ideas and attempts of Owen, Cabet, Brisbane, and others of that ilk, and confine our attention to the manifestations of the international "scientific" socialism of which there has been question in the preceding pages, i.e., to the socialism based on Marxian principles.

Already before the Civil War Marxian ideas were disseminated principally by German immigrants in New York and the adjoining States. Thus, e.g., the General Labor Union founded in April, 1853, by Joseph Weydemeyer, a disciple of Marx, consisted exclusively of Germans. It advocated land reform and the organized union of all the different trades throughout the country "to obtain by legal means sufficient guarantees for the humane existence of laborers." In September of the same year, 1853, a number of English-speaking workingmen joined their German comrades to form the Amalgamated American Society of Workingmen. They demanded the abolition of all laws hostile to laboring men, compulsory attendance at school and gratuitous instruction, gratuitous administration of justice, immediate naturalization of immigrants, public ownership of public utilities and institutions, etc.[1]

But, without having exercised any far-reaching influence, the Amalgamated Society died soon after of inanition. The German labor unions, which for the greater part were infected with socialist principles,

---

[1] Jubilee number of *New-Yorker Volkszeitung*, Feb. 21, 1903, pp 9, 10 The *N Y Volkszeitung* is the principal German organ of the Socialist Party, and its jubilee edition contains several essays of an historical and retrospective character from the pens of socialist leaders, Jonas, Schlueter, Schewitch, Morgan, and others.

kept on agitating, but by 1860 even they had lost much of their former importance, which decreased still more during the war of secession.[1] In 1867 a number of Lassalleans called into existence a political party, the so-called SOCIAL PARTY, but its complete failure at the elections in 1868 caused its speedy disruption.[2]

At the same time the constant influx of immigrants belonging to the International Workingmen's Association, founded principally by Marx in 1864,[3] gradually changed the character of the German labor unions, and in the autumn of 1869 there was founded in New York the German Section of the International Workingmen's Association, which was based entirely on Marxian principles, and zealously propagated Marxian ideas. Other sections of the International composed of different nationalities soon followed. Some of them, together with different socialistic trades-unions in and about New York and Philadelphia, constituted the SOCIAL DEMOCRATIC WORKINGMEN'S PARTY OF NORTH AMERICA, July 4, 1874.[4] Its principal press organs were the German *Sozial Demokrat* and, since 1875, the *Socialist*.

In Chicago several sections of the International had been organized in the early seventies. The socialist elements of the middle West gradually developed into the Labor Party of Illinois, having its executive committee in Chicago.[5] At a convention in Philadelphia, July 19-22, 1876, the American Federation of the International Workingmen's Association,

---

[1] *Ibid.*, p. 10.
[2] Cf. *Morris Hillquit, History of Socialism in the United States* (1903. Funk & Wagnalls Co.), p. 195; Hillquit is a prominent member of the Socialist Party.
[3] Cf. above, p 18
[4] Cf. *Hillquit, History of Socialism,* pp 204, 207.
[5] *N. Y. Volkszeitung,* Jub Ed , p 25.

the Labor Party of Illinois, and the above-mentioned Social Democratic Workingmen's Party were amalgamated into the Workingmen's Party of the United States.[1] At the Newark convention of 1877 this name was changed to SOCIALIST LABOR PARTY OF NORTH AMERICA.[2]

This date is a landmark in the history of the present socialist parties. Up to this time the efforts of socialist organizations, especially in the political arena, had been scattered and intermittent. Henceforth Marxian socialism began to strive steadily for political power, and for the next twenty years the only political organization which advocated Marxian principles was the Socialist Labor Party. Already in the first year of its existence the elections showed remarkable results, e.g., 1800 votes in New York, 6238 in Buffalo, 9000 in Chicago; much of this success, however, was owing no doubt to the great labor troubles of that period. In 1879 the socialist votes of Chicago amounted to about 12,000. Their party organ, the *Arbeiter-Zeitung*, was now issued daily and a new one was published for a time in English. Their prosperity was checked, however, by the inroad of anarchist elements, who after the Greenback movement of 1880 captured the *Arbeiter-Zeitung* and also voiced their ultra-anarchistic ideas in a new English publication, the *Alarm*. Thus anarchists and socialists became associated and identified in the minds of the public. The Haymarket tragedy, May 4, 1886, retarded the socialist movement in Chicago for a number of years.

In the East the Socialist Labor Party was progressing slowly; its showing at the polls was not encouraging to the leaders. As the system of elec-

[1] *Hillquit*, p. 209.   [2] *Ibid.*, p. 210.

tions then in vogue required each party to print and distribute its own tickets, socialists were unable to cope with the powerful machinery of the old-line parties. Besides, the return of industrial prosperity cooled the socialist fervor of the laboring classes and greatly reduced the numerical strength of the Labor Party, which in 1883 dwindled to about 1500 members. Renewed activity, however, and in 1890 the introduction of the so-called Australian ballot system in New York State changed the face of affairs, and in the very same year the number of socialist votes in that state exceeded 13,000.[1] The same thing happened sooner or later in other states. At the presidential elections in 1892 the Socialist Labor Party polled a total vote of 21,512, distributed over six states, New York, New Jersey, Massachusetts, Connecticut, Illinois, Pennsylvania. From that time on new territory was gradually brought into the circle of socialist politics and the socialist vote rose slowly but steadily, as is shown by the following figures:

1893. 25,666
1894. 30,120
1895. 34,869

In the presidential elections of 1896 the socialist candidates carried a total of 36,275 votes in twenty states of the Union. In 1897 this vote rose to 55,550, and in 1898 to 82,204, the highest ever polled by the Socialist Labor Party as such [2]

After this cursory glance at the exterior origin and growth of the Socialist Labor Party we must direct our attention to its interior spirit and development, and to the causes which brought about the split into

---

[1] *N. Y. Volkszeitung,* Jub Ed , p. 27.
[2] *Hillquit,* History of Socialism, p. 283.

two political organizations. That the principles and aims of the Socialist Labor Party were from the first practically identical with those of its German proto-type is evident from the manifesto issued by its National Convention at Baltimore, 1883: [1]

Labor being the creator of all wealth and civilization, it rightfully follows that those who labor and create all wealth should enjoy the full result of their toil. Therefore we declare:

That a just and equitable distribution of the fruits of labor is utterly impossible under the present system of society. This fact is abundantly illustrated by the deplorable condition of the working classes, which are in a state of destitution and degrading dependence in the midst of their own productions. While the hardest and most disagreeable work brings to the worker only the bare necessaries of life, others, who labor not, riot in labor's production. We furthermore declare:

That the present industrial system of competition, based on rent, profit-taking, and interest, causes and intensifies this inequality, concentrating into the hands of a few all means of production, distribution, and the results of labor, thus creating gigantic monopolies, dangerous to the people's liberties; and we further declare:

That these monster monopolies and these consequent extremes of wealth and poverty supported by class legislation are subversive of all democracy, injurious to the national interests, and destructive of truth and morality. This state of affairs, continued and upheld by the ruling political parties, is against the welfare of the people.

To abolish this system, with a view to establish co-operative production, and to secure equitable distribution, *we demand that the resources of life, namely, land, the means of production, public transportation, and exchange, become, as fast as practicable, the property of the whole state.*

We have here the fundamental tenets of Marxian socialism as they are laid down in the Gotha programme (cf. p. 59). With regard to the doctrine of labor creat-

---

[1] *Richard T. Ely,* Labor Movement, pp. 269, 270.

ing all wealth and Marx's attitude toward it see the footnote on p. 59. Also the platform adopted in 1876 was, as Hillquit terms it,[1] "a scientific and somewhat abstract exposition of the cardinal points of Marxian socialism."

The socialist movement in the United States, founded and promoted, as it was, principally by foreigners insufficiently acquainted with the institutions and language of our country, could not prosper unless it appealed to the bulk of American-born workingmen by becoming "Americanized."

"The endeavor to 'Americanize' is the keynote to the activity of the Socialist Labor Party throughout its entire career." [2] One of the principal means of attaining this purpose was recognized to consist in gaining a foothold in the existing trades-unions and making them instruments of socialist propaganda. This was accomplished to a great extent in New York City, where the Central Labor Union, founded in 1882, adopted a platform containing the principal socialist demands.[3] The German trades-unions, organized 1885 under the name of United German Trades of the City of New York, rendered valuable services to the cause of socialism by promoting the circulation of the *New-Yorker Volkszeitung*, founded in 1878, which was then, as it is still, the principal champion of German-American socialists.

The example of New York was followed by Brooklyn, Philadelphia, Cleveland, Baltimore, Buffalo, and other cities, where central bodies of German trades-unions were affiliated to socialism.[4] Not satisfied,

[1] History of Socialism, p. 210.
[2] *Ibid*, p 214
[3] *Ibid*, p 284
[4] Cf. *Hillquit, ibid*, p. 287.

however, with the influence acquired in local organizations, the Socialist Labor Party strove to take root in the great national confederations of trades-unions, the Knights of Labor and the American Federation of Labor.

Ever since 1881 numerous socialists had joined the Knights of Labor, and in 1893 they succeeded in electing delegates to the General Assembly of the Order. But heated controversies about the editorship of the official organ of the Order caused a split, and in 1895 most of the socialists retired from the ranks of the Knights. A similar attempt to capture the American Federation of Labor by introducing socialist planks into the platform was defeated at the convention of the Federation in December, 1894. Now the officials of the Socialist Labor Party, headed by Daniel De Leon, who had been prominent in the affairs of the Knights of Labor, found themselves at loggerheads with both the principal labor organizations of the country.

To offset this disadvantage Daniel De Leon created a rival organization—THE SOCIALIST TRADE AND LABOR ALLIANCE. It was the ostensible aim of this Alliance to gather into its fold the army of unorganized laborers and thus to form a political ally of the Socialist Labor Party. But in reality its nucleus was formed of those trades-unions which at the instigation of De Leon had formerly joined the Knights of Labor, and now at his request seceded from that Order. Other trades-unions in sympathy with socialism followed their lead, whilst in the way of organizing non-union laborers hardly anything was accomplished.

The trades-unions "pure and simple" were fiercely antagonized by the socialist party leaders, who at the same time inaugurated a genuine reign of terror within the party limits. Heated and personal polemics were carried on in the *New-Yorker Volkszeitung* and *The People*, De Leon's official organ. In 1899 the faction opposed to the party administration broke out in open rebellion; at a convention held in Rochester they repudiated the Socialist Trade and Labor Alliance and resolved to join the Social Democratic Party, which had been organized quite independently in 1897 at Chicago, mainly through the efforts of Eugene V. Debs of American Railway Union fame. After prolonged negotiations the union was finally cemented at the convention of Indianapolis, July 1901.[1] The new party rapidly gained in strength, rising from 9545 votes in 1898 to 96,918 in 1900, whilst the Socialist Labor Party never recovered from the shock and seems to be decidedly on the wane.

B. The Present State of the Socialist Parties.

As was mentioned above, there are at present two socialist parties in the United States, the old Socialist Labor Party headed by Daniel De Leon, and the new Social Democratic Party which at the Indianapolis convention of 1901 adopted the name SOCIALIST PARTY, retaining, however, the former appellation in some states, notably New York and Wisconsin, in order to conform with the requirements of the election laws in those states. Each of the two parties poses as being alone genuinely socialistic, and decries the other as a "fake" or "bogus" socialist party. Thus, e.g., in a four-page leaflet published by the Socialist Labor Party[2] the rival Socialist Party is branded as

[1] Cf *Hillquit*, History of Socialism, pp 324–339.
[2] Labor Library, Feb. 1902

the production of capitalist politicians to fool the voters and to bring disunion into the socialist ranks. It is charged with co-operating with capitalists and the old-line parties and with running candidates on their tickets. The Socialist Party in retorting [1] stigmatizes its opponent as a party of "scabs," whose only purpose of existence is to antagonize the efforts of organized workingmen for the improvement of their situation. These few samples may suffice to show the amiability of present relations between the two parties. Both are in perfect accord, however, with regard to their ulterior political objects, both are equally based on the historical and economical theories of Karl Marx, as will be seen by a comparison of their respective platforms.

The present official platform of the Socialist Labor Party was adopted at the New York convention, June 2–8, 1900; it is, however, practically identical with the one drafted by Lucien Sanial and accepted by the Chicago convention of 1889. The tendency to "Americanize" the socialist movement is plainly traceable in the twofold reference to the "founders of this republic."

PLATFORM OF THE SOCIALIST LABOR PARTY.

The Socialist Labor Party of the United States, in convention assembled, re-asserts the inalienable right of all men to life, liberty, and the pursuit of happiness.

With the founders of the American republic we hold that the purpose of government is to secure every citizen in the enjoyment of this right, but in the light of our social conditions we hold, furthermore, that no such right can be exercised under a system of economic inequality, essentially destructive of life, of liberty, and of happiness

[1] Cf. *N. Y. Volkszeitung,* Oct 30, 1903.

With the founders of this republic we hold that the true theory of politics is that the machinery of government must be owned and controlled by the whole people; but in the light of our industrial development we hold, furthermore, that the true theory of economics is that the machinery of production must likewise belong to the people in common.

To the obvious fact that our despotic system of economics is the direct opposite of our democratic system of politics, can plainly be traced the existence of a privileged class, the corruption of government by that class, the alienation of public property, public franchises, and public functions to that class, and the abject dependence of the mightiest of nations upon that class.

Again, through the perversion of democracy to the ends of plutocracy, labor is robbed of the wealth which it alone produces, is denied the means of self-employment, and, by compulsory idleness in wage slavery, is even deprived of the necessaries of life.

, Human power and natural forces are thus wasted, that the plutocracy may rule

Ignorance and misery, with all their concomitant evils, are perpetuated, that the people may be kept in bondage

Science and invention are diverted from their humane purpose to the enslavement of women and children

Against such a system the Socialist Labor Party once more enters its protest   Once more it reiterates its *fundamental declaration that private property in the natural sources of production and in the instruments of labor is the obvious cause of all economic servitude and political dependence*

The time is fast coming when, in the natural course of social evolution, this system, through the destructive action of its failures and crises on the one hand, and the constructive tendencies of its trusts and other capitalistic combinations on the other hand, shall have worked out its own downfall.

We, therefore, call upon the wage-workers of the United States, and upon all other honest citizens, to organize under the banner of the Socialist Labor Party into a class-conscious body, aware of its rights and determined to conquer them by taking possession of the public powers, so that, held together by an indomitable spirit of solidarity under the most trying conditions of the present class struggle, we may put a summary end to that barbarous struggle by the *abolition of classes, the restoration of the land and of all the means of production, transportation, and distribution to the people as a collective body*, and the substitution of the Co-operative Commonwealth for the present state of planless production, industrial war, and social disorder; a commonwealth in which every worker shall have the free exercise and full benefit of his faculties, multiplied by all the modern factors of civilization.

The official platform of the Socialist (Social Democratic) Party was adopted at the Indianapolis convention, July 29-31, 1901, at which the union of the Rochester faction of· the Socialist Labor Party and of Debs' Social Democrats was finally effected. It indulges in a fuller exposition of Marxian principles and is also more explicit as to its immediate demands than the platform of the Socialist Labor Party.

NATIONAL PLATFORM OF THE SOCIALIST PARTY.

The Socialist Party, in national convention assembled, re affirms its adherence to the principles of International Socialism, and declares its aim to be the organization of the working class, and those in sympathy with it, into a political party, with the object of conquering the powers of government and using them for *the purpose of transforming the present system of private ownership of the means of production and distribution into collective ownership by the entire people.*

Formerly the tools of production were simple and owned by the individual worker To-day the machine, which is an improved and more developed tool of production, is owned by the capitalists and not by the workers This ownership enables the capitalists to control the product and keep the workers dependent upon them

Private ownership of the means of production and distribution *is responsible for the ever-increasing uncertainty of livelihood and poverty and misery of the working class,* and it divides society in two hostile classes—the capitalists and wage-workers The once powerful middle class is rapidly disappearing in the mill of competition. The struggle is now between the capitalist class and the working class The possession of the means of livelihood gives to the capitalists the control of the government, the press, the pulpit, and schools, and enables them to reduce the working-men to a state of intellectual, physical, and social inferiority, political subservience, and virtual slavery.

The economic interests of the capitalist class dominate our entire social system, the lives of the working class are recklessly sacrificed for profit, wars are fomented between nations, indiscriminate slaughter is encouraged, and the destruction of whole races is sanctioned in order that the capitalists may extend their commercial dominion abroad and enhance their supremacy at home

But the same economic causes which developed capitalism are leading to socialism, which will abolish both the capitalist class and the class of wage-workers And the active force in bringing about this new and higher order of society is the working class All other classes, despite their apparent or actual conflicts, are alike interested in the upholding of the system of private ownership of the instruments of wealth production The Democratic, Republican, the bourgeois public-ownership parties, and all other parties which do not stand for the complete overthrow of the capitalist system of production, are alike political representatives of the capitalist class

The workers can most effectively act as a class in their struggle against the collective powers of capitalism by constituting themselves into a political party, distinct from and opposed to all parties formed by the propertied classes

IMMEDIATE DEMANDS.

While we declare that the development of economic conditions tends to the overthrow of the capitalist system, we recognize that the time and manner of the transition to socialism also depend upon the stage of development reached by the proletariat. We therefore consider it of the utmost importance for the Socialist Party to support all active efforts of the working class to better its condition and to elect socialists to political offices, in order to facilitate the attainment of this end

As such means we advocate·

1. The public ownership of all means of transportation and communication and all other public utilities, as well as of all industries controlled by monopolies, trusts, and combines. No part of the revenue of such industries to be applied to the reduction of taxes on property of the capitalist class, but to be applied wholly to the increase of wages and shortening of the hours of labor of the employees, to the improvement of the service, and diminishing the rates to the consumers.

2. The progressive reduction of the hours of labor, and the increase of wages in order to decrease the share of the capitalist and increase the share of the worker in the product of labor.

3 State or national insurance of working people in case of accidents, lack of employment, sickness and want in old age; the funds for this purpose to be furnished by the Government, and to be administered under the control of the working class.

4 The inauguration of a system of public industries, public credit to be used for that purpose in order that the workers be secured the full product of their labor.

5. The education of all children up to the age of eighteen years, and state and municipal aid for books, clothing, and food.

6 Equal civil and political rights for men and women

7. The initiative and referendum, proportional representation and the right of recall of representatives by their constituents.

But in advocating these measures as steps in the overthrow of capitalism and the establishment of the Co-operative Commonwealth, we warn the working class against the so-called public-ownership movements as an attempt of the capitalist class to secure Governmental control of public utilities for the purpose of obtaining greater security in the exploitation of other industries and not for the amelioration of the conditions of the working class.

Quite in opposition to the Socialist Labor Party the Socialist Party claims the regular trades-unions as its legitimate field of agitation, and its ulterior purpose is to make them hotbeds of socialism and if possible to control the great labor organizations so as to use them as powerful allies in the political struggle. This tendency of the Socialist Party is clearly expressed in the following resolution on trades-unionism appended to the platform:

"We consider it the duty of socialists to join the unions of their respective trades . . We call the attention of trades-unionists to the fact that the class struggle so nobly waged by the trades-union forces to-day, whilst it may result in lessening the exploitation of labor, can never abolish that exploitation. . . It is the duty of every trades-unionist . . to join the Socialist Party and to assist in building up a strong political movement of the wage-working class ."

The relative *numerical strength* of the two socialist parties in various sections of the United States is best seen by a glance at the election returns of 1902.

States	Socialist Party	Socialist Labor Party
Alabama	2,312	. . .
Arizona	519	. . .
*Arkansas	27	. . . .
California	9,592	207
Colorado	7,431	1,349
Connecticut	2,857	669
*Delaware	57	. . . .
*Florida	603	. . .
Idaho	1,800	. . .
Illinois	20,167	8,235
Indiana	7,134	1,756
Iowa	6,360	. .
Kansas	4,078	. .
Kentucky	1,886	535
Maine	1,974	. .
*Maryland	908	
Massachusetts	33,629	6,079
Michigan	4,271	1,282
Minnesota	10,129	2,570
Missouri	5,335	969
Montana	3,131	. . .

States	Socialist Party.	Socialist Labor Party.
Nebraska	3,157	......
New Hampshire...	1,057	. .. .
*New Jersey	4,609	1,918
New York	23,400	15,886
North Dakota.	1,245	......
Ohio	14,270	2,983
Oklahoma	1,963	......
Oregon	3,532	. ...
Pennsylvania.	21,910	5,157
Rhode Island.	......	1,283
South Dakota.	2,738	......
*Tennessee	.410	......
Texas	3,513	120
Utah.	2,927	......
*Vermont...	371	......
*Virginia.	225	157
Washington	4,739	834
*West Virginia.	286	.... .
Wisconsin	15,957	791
Wyoming	552	... .
Total	231,061	52,767

* In these states no socialist ticket was run in the state elections of 1902, the figures given are those of the presidential election of 1900 [1]

The *Worker*, a socialist paper published by the
same company as the *N. Y. Volkszeitung*, in its issue
of March 29, 1903, gives a slightly different total for
the Socialist Party, namely, 227,024. At the present
writing no reliable data concerning the elections of
1903 are as yet available. The *N. Y. Volkszeitung*
of Dec. 16, 1903, credits the Socialist Party in the
state of New York with 33,399 votes and the Socialist
Labor Party with 10,677. This means a loss of

[1] *N. Y. Volkszeitung,* Jub Ed , Feb 21, 1903, p. 11.

5209 for the Socialist Labor Party and a gain of
9999 for the Socialist Party. In other places, however, this party seems to have lost; thus in Massachusetts it failed to re-elect two of its three representatives in the state legislature. The number of
registered and paying members of the Socialist Party
is given at 21,277.[1]

But in order to appreciate the full strength of the socialist
movement we must cast a glance at the active propaganda carried on in the *party press*. The Socialist Labor Party publishes
an English daily in New York, *The People*, and several weekly
papers in foreign languages [2]

The Socialist Party on the other hand is represented [3] by four
monthly magazines: *The International Socialist Review*, Chi-
cago; *Wilshire's Magazine* and *The Comrade*, New York, *The
Southern Socialist;* and by some twenty-four English weeklies·
The Worker, New York; *Chicago Socialist*, Chicago; *The
Social Democratic Herald*, Milwaukee; *Labor*, St Louis; *Iowa
Socialist*, Dubuque; *The Oklahoma Socialist*, Guthrie; *The
Appeal to Reason*, Girard, Kas , *The Coming Nation*, Rich Hill,
Mo.; *The Idaho Socialist*, Idaho Falls, *The Utah Socialist*,
Salt Lake City, *The New Times*, Spokane, Wash , *The Social-
ist*, Seattle, Wash , *The People's Press*, Albany, Ore ; *The
Advance*, San Francisco, *The California Socialist*, San Francis-
co; *The Los Angeles Socialist*, Los Angeles; *The People's Paper*,
Santa Barbara, Cal ; *The Alliance of the Rockies*, Colorado;
The Toiler, Terre Haute, Ind ; *The Newport Socialist*, New-
port, Ky.; *The Referendum*, Minnesota; *The Erie People*, Erie,
Pa.; *The Ohio Socialist*, and a few others

Of these *The Appeal to Reason* alone is reputed to have a circulation of more than 250,000 copies.

In the German language there are three dailies· *New-Yorker
Volkszeitung*, *Philadelphia Tageblatt*, and *Cincinnatier Arbeiter-
Zeitung;* seven weeklies· *Vorwärts*, New York; *Wahrheit*, Mil-
waukee; *Arbeiterzeitung*, St Louis, *Sheboygan Volksblatt*, She-

---

[1] *N Y Volkszeitung*, Jan 10, 1904
[2] *Hillquit*, History of Socialism, p 340
[3] *Ibid.*, p 345, *N. Y. Volkszeitung*, Jub. Ed., p. 32.

boygan; *San Francisco Tageblatt; Neues Leben,* Chicago; *Arbeiterzeilung,* Buffalo.

There is also one weekly paper each in the following languages: French, *L'Union des Travailleurs,* Charleroi, Pa.; Polish, *Robotnik,* Chicago; Bohemian, *Spravedlnost,* Chicago; Italian, *Lo Scalpellino,* Barre, Vt.; Swedish, *Arbetarn,* New York; Hungarian, *Nepszava,* Cleveland, O.; and Jewish, *Forward,* New York.

Of trades-union journals which have decided socialistic leanings and more or less openly defend socialism we may mention one monthly, *The Miner's Magazine,* Denver; a number of weeklies, as, e g , *The Workers' Gazette,* Omaha, Neb ; *The Union Picket,* Dayton, O.; *The Citizen,* Cleveland, O.; and several others, especially those appearing in languages other than English.

In concluding this sketch we must revert once more to the connection between the Socialist Party and the trades-unions, and more especially the American Federation of Labor. True to its settled policy laid down in the resolution on trades-unionism quoted above, the Socialist Party has striven with might and main to obtain control of the great labor federations. And in fact, in June 1902, the Western Labor Union, with a total membership of about 150,000, the Western Federation of Miners, and the United Association of Hotel and Restaurant Employees, all assembled in convention at Denver, indorsed the Socialist Party in politics and adopted its platform. In November of the same year an attempt was made at the New Orleans convention of the American Federation of Labor to introduce a socialist resolution, which was rejected after a prolonged debate by a vote of 3744 to 3344.[1] The attempt was to be renewed at the Boston convention, Nov. 16–21, 1903. But the twenty-eight socialist resolutions submitted to the convention were defeated by a vote of 11,282 against 2185, and when

---

[1] *Hillquit,* History of Socialism, pp. 343, 344.

in revenge a socialist candidate for president of the Federation was run against Gompers, who is far too conservative for socialist reformers, the result of the ballot was 12,254 votes for Gompers and only 1134 for "Comrade" Kreft.

From the foregoing account the observant reader will easily draw the conclusion that the Socialist Labor Party is becoming comparatively insignificant, whilst the Social Democratic or Socialist Party must be styled the true representative in the United States of *International* socialism. Whether its future development will keep pace with its increase during the last few years, whether it will persevere undaunted in its struggle for collectivist ownership, or whether it will gradually become a "revisionist" reform party, experience alone can show. This much is certain, that it deserves the most serious consideration on the part of both clergy and laity.

The preceding pages had been sent to the printer before the National Convention of the Socialist Party was held at Chicago, May 1–6 (1904). The transactions of that convention, especially the adoption of a new national platform, necessarily call for some additions to this chapter.

Contrary to the expectations of socialists themselves, the convention proved remarkably harmonious. It adopted a new constitution with a strong tendency towards centralization, together with a programme of municipal reforms, both of which, however, are still to be submitted to the referendum of the party members, and thus it were useless to enter upon them here.

What Hillquit terms the keynote in the activity

of the former Socialist Labor Party, namely, the desire of "Americanizing" the collectivist movement in the United States, seems to have been realized at last. E. Untermann, one of the chief luminaries of the convention, with evident pleasure reports to the German weekly, *Die Neue Zeit* (No. 35, p. 275), that of the 183 delegates representing 36 states and territories 120 were native-born Americans. The introductory paragraph of the platform adopted by the convention represents socialism as the highest embodiment of American ideals, and Eugene V. Debs, the nominee for the presidency, in his speech of acceptance, emphatically declares: "The platform upon which we stand is the first American utterance upon the subject of international socialism. Hitherto we have repeated, we have reiterated, we have followed. For the first time in the history of the American movement we have realized the American expression of that movement. There is not a line, not a word in that platform which is not revolutionary, which is not clear, which does not state precisely and properly the position of the American movement."

We shall not withhold from our readers this remarkable *American utterance* of the principles of international socialism. However, as Untermann remarks in the article quoted above, not too much importance is to be attached to the wording of the platform. Socialist theorists may find it unsatisfactory in more than one respect. To our mind the new platform is eminently a campaign document. It is bold and scathing in its condemnation of existing institutions, and gives in popular form the gist of the specious arguments which are most likely to make socialism acceptable to the unsophisticated. As an interesting specimen of socialist rhetoric it shall be reprinted here in full without further comment:

NATIONAL PLATFORM OF THE SOCIALIST PARTY.
ADOPTED MAY 5, 1904

I.

The Socialist Party, in convention assembled, makes its appeal to the American people as the defender and preserver of the idea of liberty and self-government, in which the nation was born; as the only political movement standing for the programme and principles by which the liberty of the individual may become a fact; as the only political organization that is democratic; and that has for its purpose the democratizing of the whole of society

To this idea of liberty the Republican and Democratic parties are equally false They alike struggle for power to maintain and profit by an industrial system which can be preserved only by the complete overthrow of such liberties as we already have, and by the still further enslavement and degradation of labor.

Our American institutions came into the world in the name of freedom. They have been seized upon by the capitalist class as the means of rooting out the idea of freedom from among the people Our state and national legislatures have become the mere agencies of great propertied interests. These interests control the appointments and decisions of the judges of our courts They have come into what is practically a private ownership of all the functions and forces of government. They are using these to betray and conquer foreign and weaker peoples, in order to establish new markets for the surplus goods which the people make, but are too poor to buy They are gradually so invading and restricting the right of suffrage as to take away unawares the right of the worker to a vote or voice in public affairs By enacting new and misinterpreting old laws, they are preparing to attack the liberty of the individual even to speak or think for himself, or for the common good

By controlling all the sources of social revenue, the possessing class is able to silence what might be the voice of protest against the passing of liberty and the coming of tyranny It completely controls the university and public school, the pulpit and the press, and the arts and literatures By making these economically dependent upon itself, it has brought all the forms of public teaching into servile submission to its own interests.

Our political institutions are also being used as the destroyers of that individual property upon which all liberty and opportunity depend The promise of economic independence to each man was one of the faiths upon which our institutions were founded But, under the guise of defending private property, capitalism is using our political institutions to make it impossible for the vast majority of human beings ever to become possessors of private property in the means of life.

Capitalism is the enemy and destroyer of essential private property Its development is through the legalized confiscation of all that the labor of the working class produces, above its subsistence-wage. The private ownership of the means of employment grounds society in an economic slavery which renders intellectual and political tyranny inevitable.

Socialism comes so to organize industry and society that every individual shall be secure in that private property in the means of life upon which his liberty of being, thought, and action depend It comes to rescue the people from the fast increasing and successful assault of capitalism upon the liberty of the individual

II.

As an American Socialist Party, we pledge our fidelity to the principles of international socialism, as embodied in the united thought and action of the socialists of all nations In the industrial development already accomplished, the interests of the world's workers are separated by no national boundaries. The condition of the most exploited and oppressed workers, in the most remote places of the earth, inevitably tends to drag down all the workers of the world to the same level The tendency of the competitive wage system is to make labor's lowest condition the measure or rule of its universal condition Industry and finance are no longer national but international, in both organization and results The chief significance of national boundaries, and of the so-called patriotisms which the ruling class of each nation is seeking to revive, is the power which these give to capitalism to keep the workers of the world from uniting, and to throw them against each other in the struggles of contending capitalist interests for the control of the yet unexploited markets of the world, or the remaining sources of profit

The socialist movement therefore is a world-movement. It knows of no conflicts of interest between the workers of one nation and the workers of another It stands for the freedom of the workers of all nations; and, in so standing, it makes for the full freedom of all humanity.

III.

The socialist movement owes its birth and growth to that economic development or world-process which is rapidly separating a working or producing class from a possessing or capitalist class The class that produces nothing possesses labor's fruits, and the opportunities and enjoyments these fruits afford, while the class that does the world's real work has increasing economic uncertainty, and physical and intellectual misery, for its portion

The fact that these two classes have not yet become fully conscious of their distinction from each other, the fact that the lines of division and interest may not yet be clearly drawn, does not change the fact of the class conflict

This class struggle is due to the private ownership of the means of employment, or the tools of production Wherever and whenever man owned his own land and tools, and by them produced only the things which he used, economic independence was possible. But production, or the making of goods, has long ceased to be individual The labor of scores, or even thousands, enters into almost every article produced Production is now social or collective Practically everything is made or done by many men—sometimes separated by seas or continents—working together for the same end But this cooperation in production is not for the direct use of the things made by the workers who make them, but for the profit of the owners of the tools and means of production, and to this is due the present division of society into two classes, and from it have sprung all the miseries, inharmonies, and contradictions of our civilization.

Between these two classes there can be no possible compromise or identity of interests, any more than there can be
peace in the midst of war, or light in the midst of darkness. A
society based upon this class division carries in itself the seeds
of its own destruction. Such a society is founded in fundamental injustice. There can be no possible basis for social
peace, for individual freedom, for mental and moral harmony,
except in the conscious and complete triumph of the working
class as the ônly class that has the right or power to be.

IV.

The socialist programme is not a theory imposed upon society
for its acceptance or rejection It is but the interpretation of
what is, sooner or later, inevitable. Capitalism is already struggling to its destruction. It is no longer competent to organize
or administer the work of the world, or even to preserve itself.
The captains of industry are appalled at their own inability
to control or direct the rapidly socializing forces of industry.
The so-called trust is but a sign and form of the developing
socialization of the world's work. The universal increase
of the uncertainty of employment, the universal capitalist
determination to break down the unity of labor in the trades-
unions, the widespread apprehensions of impending change,
reveal that the institutions of capitalist society are passing
under the power of inhering forces that will soon destroy them.

Into the midst of the strain and crisis of civilization, the
socialist movement comes as the only conservative force. If
the world is to be saved from chaos, from universal disorder and
misery, it must be by the union of the workers of all nations in
the socialist movement The Socialist Party comes with the
only proposition or programme for intelligently and deliberately
organizing the nation for the common good of all its citizens.
It is the first time that the mind of man has ever been directed
toward the conscious organization of society.

Socialism means that all those things upon which the people in
common depend shall by the people in common be owned and
administered. It means that the tools of employment shall
belong to their creators and users; that all production shall
be for the direct use of the producers; that the making of goods

for profit shall come to an end, that we shall all be workers together; and that all opportunities shall be open and equal to all men.

V.

To the end that the workers may seize every possible advantage that may strengthen them to gain complete control of the powers of government, and thereby the sooner establish the co-operative commonwealth, the Socialist Party pledges itself to watch and work in both the economic and the political struggle for each successive immediate interest of the working class; for shortened days of labor and increases of wages; for the insurance of the workers against accident, sickness, and lack of employment; for pensions for aged and exhausted workers; for the public ownership of the means of transportation, communication and exchange; for the graduated taxation of incomes, inheritances, franchises and land values, the proceeds to be applied to the public employment and improvement of the conditions of the workers; for the complete education of children, and their freedom from the workshop; for the prevention of the use of the military against labor in the settlement of strikes; for the free administration of justice; for popular government, including initiative, referendum, proportional representation, equal suffrage for men and women and municipal home rule, and the recall of officers by their constituents; and for every gain or advantage for the workers that may be wrested from the capitalist system, and that may relieve the suffering and strengthen the hands of labor. We lay upon every man elected to any executive or legislative office the first duty of striving to procure whatever is for the workers' most immediate interest, and for whatever will lessen the economic and political powers of the capitalist, and increase the like powers of the worker.

But in so doing, we are using these remedial measures as means to the one great end of the co-operative commonwealth Such measures of relief as we may be able to force from capitalism are but a preparation of the workers to seize the whole powers of government, in order that they may thereby lay hold of the whole system of industry, and thus come into their rightful inheritance.

To this end we pledge ourselves, as the party of the working class, to use all political power, as fast as it shall be entrusted to us by our fellow-workers, both for their immediate interests and for their ultimate and complete emancipation. To this end we appeal to all the workers of America, and to all who will lend their lives to the service of the workers in their struggle to gain their own, and to all who will nobly and disinterestedly give their days and energies unto the workers' cause, to cast in their lot and faith with the Socialist Party. Our appeal for the trust and suffrages of our fellow-workers is at once an appeal for their common good and freedom, and for the freedom and blossoming of our common humanity. In pledging ourselves, and those we represent, to be faithful to the appeal which we make, we believe we are but preparing the soil of that economic freedom from which will spring the freedom of the whole man.

That the attitude of the Socialist Party in reference to the trades-unions remains unchanged is proved by the following resolution adopted after a prolonged discussion by a vote of 107 to 52:

The trades-union struggle requires the political activity of the working class The workers must assist and permanently secure by their political power what they have wrung from their exploiters in the economic struggle. In accordance with the decisions of the International Socialist Congresses in Brussels, Zurich, and London, this convention reaffirms the declarations that the trades and labor unions are a necessity in the struggle to aid in emancipating the working class, and we consider it the duty of all wage-workers to affiliate with this movement.

Political differences of opinion do not and should not justify the division of the forces of labor in the industrial movement. The interests of the working class make it imperative that the labor organizations equip their members for the great work of the abolition of wage slavery by educating them in socialist principles.

III. Socialism in Other Countries

1. *France.*—In Germany socialism radiated as it were from one common centre under the almost exclusive sovereignty of Marxism; in France, on the contrary, there were formed numerous socialist groups arising independently of each other. To this day many of them have not been affiliated to any comprehensive federation; others have been aggregated during the last few years into departmental or regional unions; still others have lately united to form the "Fédération des socialistes indépendants de France." These latter number among their ranks several deserters from the radicalist bourgeoisie, e.g., Millerand, Jaurès, Viviani; but they lack a well-defined platform, the only unifying element being on the one hand a rather platonic affection for socialistic ideals and on the other their opposition to the extreme socialists.

There exist moreover three socialist organizations of some importance. In the first place the so-called "*parti socialiste révolutionnaire*" under the leadership of Vaillant and Sembat. (Being adherents of Blanqui they also go by the name of Blanquists.) They are firm believers in revolution and in forcibly taking possession of the political power instead of conquering it slowly by the ballot. The "parti ouvrier français" under the leadership of Jules Guesde is practically identical in spirit and principles with German social democracy, and is perhaps the best organized division of French socialists. Its partisans are frequently referred to as *Marxists*. Jules Guesde has outlined the platform of his party in the following statements:

1 Society at large takes possession of the means of production, factories and workshops become common property,

capitalists disappear and involve in their own ruin the whole
army of moneyed gentlemen, brokers, middlemen, intriguers,
etc 2 Competition and over-production will cease; no labor
is wasted, statistics will indicate the exact amount of productions needful to the community. 3. At first the workingman
will work three hours a day, the unlimited perfectibility of
machinery will reduce the necessary working time to one hour
daily (¹) 4 Individual property will not be abolished, but limited to what is strictly personal. Those capitalists who quietly
submit to their being dispossessed of the means of production
shall be indemnified in money or labor-certificates, but in such a
manner that the present system cannot possibly be perpetuated.[1]

From the Marxists have branched off the so-called
possibilists. They are moderate socialists endeavoring
to attain their end in the regular course of legislation
by introducing gradual reforms wherever they are at
present possible; hence their name   The possibilists
are split into two different organizations with diverging
tendencies. They are the "Fédération des travailleurs
socialistes de France," under the leadership of *Brousse*,
hence also called Broussists, and the "Parti ouvrier
socialiste révolutionnaire," or Allemanists. The latter
in opposition to the former look upon parliamentary
activity merely as an instrument of propagandism;
they have no pretensions to gaining political power,
but devote their energies to agitation in the field of
economics.

At the elections in April, 1898, the different factions
mentioned above polled at the first ballot:

Guesdists (Marxists)	350,000	votes
Blanquists	32,000	"
Allemanists	42,000	"
Broussists and independent voters.	516,000	"
Total	940,000	votes

[1] Cf *Antoine*, Cours d'economie sociale, p 204

Since the elections of May, 1898, there are in the Chamber 46 socialist deputies of various factions. They have entered upon a compact to form a parliamentary party with the following three principles as their base of union: "1. The fundamental principle of the socialist party is the attainment of political power by means of the organized proletariat. 2. We wish to prepare the transformation into social property of all the means of production, transportation, and credit, which capitalist feudalism has already snatched from the hands of the individual owners. 3 To the historical right which has created power and transfers power into other hands without modifying it—to this right we oppose the right of the nations based on fraternal peace among peoples freely shaping their own destinies. To capitalism with its international organization for controlling the world's markets it is necessary to oppose the international harmony of workingmen."

French socialism entered upon a new stage by the admission of Millerand into the ministerial cabinet of Waldeck-Rousseau. Both Blanquists and Guesdists remonstrated energetically against the step taken by Millerand and branded the participation in bourgeois government as incompatible with socialist principles. Millerand's friends appealed to a general convention of French socialists. They met in Paris in December 1899. The right of sending delegates had been granted to all organizations existing prior to Jan. 1, 1899, and agreeing to the minimum programme drawn up by Millerand, namely, socialization of the means of production, conquest of the political power by means of the organized proletariat, and international harmony. In this convention the Blanquists and Guesdists with 818 votes against 634 Allemanists and Broussists decided that the occupancy of a seat in a bourgeois ministry is incompatible with socialist principles.

But to forefend a complete rupture a compromise resolution was adopted by 1140 against 245 votes. It was conceded that in extraordinary circumstances the entrance of a socialist into a bourgeois ministry might be taken into consideration, yet it should be the aim of the party to conquer only the elective public offices, "since they depend on the organized proletariat, which thereby lawfully and peacefully initiates the political expropriation of the capitalist classes to complete it by revolution." [1]

Hereby the quarrel was not settled, but merely smoothed over. The convention unanimously resolved a uniform party organization to be known as the "Socialist Party of France." A permanent executive board consisting of delegates from the different organizations is to nominate the party candidates for the elections, and the socialist press is to obey the resolutions of the party convention. It is easily perceived that this union is rather loosely cemented and does not do away with the opposition in fundamental principles. The socialist convention of Bordeaux, 1902, did not yet dare to expel Millerand from the party ranks.

The fifth international socialist convention of Paris, Sept. 1900, decided the institution of a permanent international committee and secretary, with the duty of collecting and arranging the decisions of former international conventions, of demanding accounts concerning the state of the political and economic movement in the several countries, and of drawing up

[1] Cf. Soziale Praxis, ix. p 293.

a general report, of preparing the international conventions and their daily schedule, and finally of issuing manifestoes concerning the great questions of
the day in as far as they affect the interests of the
proletariat.[1]

This international socialist bureau has been established at Brussels; the present secretary is Victor
Serwy. Its first session took place Dec. 30, 1901,
and according to its first report 22 countries are
represented by delegates, namely, all European
countries with the exception of Portugal, Roumania,
and Turkey; besides there are Japan, the United
States, the Argentine Republic, and Australia.

2. *Austria.*—Austrian social democracy is moulded
after the pattern of German socialism. This is proved
to evidence by its party platform adopted unanimously
at the Vienna convention, Nov. 2–6, 1901. This platform is practically a counterpart of its German prototype. Its statement of principles and demands may
find a place here.

The social democratic labor party of Austria strives to obtain
for the people at large without distinction of nationality, race, or
sex the liberation from the fetters of economic dependence, of
political oppression, and of intellectual decadence The cause
of these intolerable conditions is to be sought not in single political institutions, but in that all-powerful fact which shapes and
dominates the present state of society, the fact that the means of
production are monopolized in the hands of a few proprietors
The possessors of labor capacity, the laboring classes, are thereby
reduced to a most galling dependence on the owners of the means
of production including the soil, namely, on the class of landowners and capitalists whose political and economic supremacy
is embodied in the modern state

Technical progress, the increasing concentration of produc-

[1] *Ibid.*, x. p. 6.

tion and property, the absorption of all economic power by capitalists and trusts, has the effect of despoiling a growing percentage of formerly independent tradesmen and farmers of their means of production, and of bringing them directly or indirectly in the bondage of the capitalists as wage-earners, employees, or debtors The proletariat is increasing in numbers, and corresponding to this increase exploitation rises to a higher degree.   Thereby the standard of living of the laboring classes contrasts more and more with the rapidly growing productive capacity of their labor and with the resultant accumulation of wealth

But the more the ranks of the proletariat are swelled by the development of capitalism, the more also the former is forced and also enabled to take up the struggle against the latter.   More and more the dislodgment of private production renders private property unnecessary and even harmful, whilst in the mean time the necessary intellectual and material prerequisites for new forms of co-operative production based on common ownership in the means of production are evolving.   At the same time the proletariat becomes conscious of its duty to foster and to hasten this development.   It recognizes the fact that the *transfer of the means of production into common ownership by the people at large is the goal,* whilst the conquest of political power is but a means in the struggle for the emancipation of the laboring classes.   Only the proletariat, conscious of its existence as a class, and organized for the combat can be the promoter of this necessary development.   *To organize the proletariat, to inspire it with the consciousness of its condition and of its duty, to prepare it intellectually and physically for the struggle and to keep it thus prepared, this is the programme of the social democratic labor party of Austria*   For the achievement of this purpose it will employ every means which is appropriate and in conformity with the people's natural standard of right and wrong.

In every question of politics or economics the social democratic labor party of Austria will contend for the class interests of the proletariat and will strenuously oppose the palliating or glossing over of class differences, as well as the exploitation of laborers in favor of the bourgeois parties

The social democratic labor party of Austria is international.   It repudiates the privileges of nationality as well as those of birth and pedigree, of property and descent, and declares that the struggle against exploitation must be as international as exploitation itself. It condemns and combats every restriction of the liberty of speech and every kind of tutelage on the part of the state and the Church It strives for legal protection of the working classes and struggles to obtain the greatest possible influence of the proletariat in all public affairs.

Proceeding from these principles the social democratic labor party of Austria demands for the present:

1. Universal, equal, direct suffrage by private ballot, in the empire, province, and commune, for all citizens over twenty years of age without distinction of sex Elections proportional to the population Elections to be held on a legal holiday Triennial periods of legislatures Compensation for representatives.

2. Direct legislation by the people through the right of initiative and referendum. Home-rule and administration by the people in the empire, province, and commune

3 Abolition of laws restricting the freedom of speech; perfect liberty of the press by the repeal of the objective procedure[1] and of the restrictions on the peddling of printed matter. Abolition of all laws restricting the right of association and convention

4. Abolition of all restrictions on the liberty of motion, especially of all vagrancy laws

5. A law to be made and enforced providing for the severe punishment of officials meddling with the political rights of individuals or of societies

6. Guaranteed independence of the judiciary Gratuitous administration of justice and legal advice Indemnification of those unjustly arrested or condemned Election of the juries by universal and equal suffrage by private ballot Subjection of all the citizens of the state to the ordinary laws and courts. Abolition of capital punishment

7. Organization of the sanitary service by the state and the commune Free medical attendance and medicines

8. Religion to be declared a private concern Separation of

---

[1] A kind of press censorship by which a publication may be suppressed as dangerous without any specific inactment.

Church and state and the establishment of ecclesiastical and religious communities as private associations perfectly free to manage their own affairs   Obligatory civil marriage

9 Obligatory, gratuitous, and secularized schools perfectly adapted to the needs and the development of the several nationalities   Means of instruction and board to be free for all pupils in the elementary schools and in the higher institutions for those pupils who are capable of further development.

10 All indirect taxes and imposts to be replaced by graded and progressive taxation on income, property, and inheritance

11 Popular militia instead of standing armies. Education for universal military service. Arming of the entire people. Decisions regarding peace and war by the representatives of the people

12 Abolition of all laws subordinating woman to man in public or private life

13 Co-operative societies of workingmen to be freed of all the burdens and limitations which restrict their activity.

The platform then details the minimum demands in the matter of protection for laborers within the present order of society, namely, entire freedom of coalition, a maximum working day of eight hours, without restrictions or exceptions, an uninterrupted rest over Sunday of at least thirty-six hours, a thorough reform of workingmen's insurance, etc.

From the wording of the platform it is apparent that the theory of the increasing, absolute pauperization of workingmen has been abandoned. Dr. V. Adler, the author of the new platform, openly acknowledges the failure of the pauperization theory. "Engels himself," he remarks, "writes in his published criticism on the Erfurt platform: 'It is not correct to say that the misery of the proletariat is increasing. The growth of organization will perhaps restrain the growth of misery; one thing is certainly growing, the insecurity of the proletarians' existence.' " [1] Another avowal of Adler is equally remarkable. "To the best of our power," he says, " we oppose the politics of the middle classes and we oppose the bourgeoisie, and we ought to do so much more. Thereby we promote the conditions of development and the prerequisites of the new order of society." [2]

Another prominent Austrian socialist, Pernerstorfer,[3] rails at those who still ascribe to the theories of pauperization, of collapse and dictatorship, the significance which they had thirty years ago.

Information concerning the present status of Austrian socialism is contained in the report of the general executive board. At the last elections for the Reichsrat the socialist party polled 799,462 votes. It is therefore numerically the strongest party in Austria, exclusive of Hungary; yet it numbers but ten representatives in the House.

In the matter of newspapers the whole party controls forty-eight political journals Of these, eight are daily papers—three in German, two in Czech, two in Italian, and one in Polish—two papers appear three times a week, five twice a week, twenty-six are weeklies, six are semi-monthlies, besides one monthly. There are, moreover, fifty socialist trades journals, twenty-six of which are in German, twenty in Czech, three in Polish, and one in Italian There is furthermore the *Arbeiterschutz*, representing the sick-benefit associations, and three comic papers, two German and one Czech.

3. *Belgium.*—The strength of Belgian socialism, which is based entirely on Marxian principles, is apparent in the election returns. In the general

[1] Cf Transactions of the Vienna Convention of Nov. 2-6, 1901, p 101.
[2] *Ibid* , p 105.
[3] *Ibid.* p. 119.

elections for the legislature, May, 1898, the official reports registered 329,332 socialist votes; in 1900 they had gone up to 463,529, and in 1902 to 476,862 votes, so that they are at present represented by 34 deputies. However, it must be remembered that in Belgium the system of plural votes is in force, so that the number of voters cannot be ascertained exactly. The socialist party displays great activity. It controls a great number of political dailies and a still greater number of weeklies and trades journals.

4. *England.*—Up to the present time socialism has made scant progress in England, although a great number of German and French socialists enjoyed unlimited freedom of propagating their ideas. In 1895 Engels remarked: "I have finally come to the conviction that English workingmen entertain no thought of putting an end to capitalist production, their only endeavor being to make the most of their actual situation." Bernstein, also well acquainted from personal observation with the conditions of British workingmen, is of the same opinion.[1] The English mind is too practical to take stock in utopian dreams. The powerful trades-unions contend for what is immediately attainable without pursuing nebulous phantoms. Hyndman, a prominent English socialist, is forced to acknowledge this fact. Socialism, he wrathfully declares, is in no better condition to-day than it was fifty years ago. English workingmen are moderate, gentle, long-suffering wage-slaves, who have no thought of actually injuring their employers or of touching the sacred rights of private property. This would mean revolution, and English workingmen are not revolutionaries.[2]

---

[1] Cf. Soziale Praxis, ix. p 1288.
[2] *Ibid.*, p 1287.

The comparative insignificance of the socialist movement in England may be gathered from the fact that in the elections of 1900 but thirteen of the 670 members of Parliament were chosen as the representatives of labor, and even these were fusion candidates of the Liberals, Radicals, or Irish. But one member, Keir Hardie, owes his seat to the workingmen exclusively.

5. With regard to *Switzerland* we may repeat what we have written over twenty years ago.[1] Despite the hospitality accorded to foreign socialists, and despite the greatest freedom of expansion, indigenous socialism has never come to be of any importance. In 1879, the socialist ranks numbered up to 15,000; at present the whole party as such amounts at most to 6,000 members. The *Grütliverein*, an association closely allied to socialism, consisting exclusively of native Swiss, has a membership of 16,000. At the elections for the National Council, 1902, the socialists returned seven candidates. The total of socialistic votes is estimated at 63,000,[2] but many of them were polled by workingmen who are not socialists. The reasons for the slow development of Swiss socialism are enumerated by G. Adler as being "first, the obstacles in the way of propagandism owing to the want of industrial concentration; secondly, the steadiness of the country's political and social development; finally, the sober and practical character of the nation, which shows great resemblance to the sound and healthy English type." [3]

England and Switzerland afford, therefore, very instructive object lessons. They prove to evidence that

---

[1] *Stimmen aus Maria-Laach*, xxi p. 67.
[2] *Neue Zeit*, 21st year, I p 250
[3] Handwörterbuch der Staatswissenschaften, 2d ed., article *Sozial demokratie.*

wherever socialism is untrammelled by restrictions, and must needs take part in practical social reforms, its revolutionary edge is soon blunted.

6. *Italy* has long been the classic land of anarchists and conspirators. But it was only within the last few years that a strictly socialist party has been formed. The parliamentary elections show the following figures in the socialist ballot: 26,000 votes in 1892; 78,000 in 1895; 135,000 in 1897; and 170,000 in 1900. The fact, however, is to be taken into account that the election laws tend to debar the poorer classes from the polls.

For some time two diverging tendencies have been noticeable within the ranks of the Italian socialist party, and an open rupture seemed inevitable. The "revolutionaries" or semi-anarchists, with Ferri and Labriola at their head, rebelled against the general executive committee, lost as it was in the swamp of compromises with the bourgeois classes. The revolutionaries clamored for radical proceedings against the government and demanded above all that their deputies in parliament be subjected to the control of the party convention. The more moderate faction, the so-called reform party of Turati, Chiesa, and Bonomi, rejected these revolutionary demands, and insisted on participating energetically in social reform.

At the party convention of Imola, Sept. 1902, the quarrel was adjusted. A compromise resolution moved by Bonomi was carried by 456 against 279 votes. It was as follows:

The goal of socialism is the emancipation of humanity from the yoke of capitalist exploitation, an emancipation to be attained by means of collectivism The road to this emancipation is the class struggle of the awakened proletariat against the eco-

nomic and political organization of the class of monopolists and
owners of production Since all reforms intending the economic, political, and moral improvement of the proletariat contribute at the same time toward hastening the social revolution,
the convention declares the existence of two different tendencies
to be perfectly compatible The convention decides that the
policy of the party is reformatory because it is revolutionary,
and revolutionary because it is reformatory—in other words
that it is simply (*semplicemente*) socialistic

Furthermore this resolution grants to the deputies in parliament the power of forming independent decisions, but requires
them to keep in touch with the opinions and desires of the proletariat at large.[1]

7. The "social democratic union" of *Denmark* celebrated its twenty-fifth anniversary on Feb 12, 1903.
At the elections for the Folkething it obtained the following results:

In 1887. . . . . 8,408 votes
" 1898. . . . . 25 019 "
" 1901. . . . . 41,955 "

At present, the party holds fifteen seats in the Folkething and nineteen in the town council of Kopenhagen.
In the different parts of the country there are 200
organized sections, and 22 daily or weekly papers.[2]
Danish social democracy is intimately connected and
in touch with German Marxism.

8. In *Sweden* the socialist unions numbered in the
beginning of 1900 about 40,000 members. In the Diet
of Stockholm they are represented by but one deputy,
since only the well-to-do have the right of suffrage.
The trades-unions comprise up to 60,000 members. In
1899 they joined the social democratic party, which
now controls three dailies with 20,500 subscribers.

[1] *Vorwärts*, Sept. 10, 1902   [2] *Ibid* , 1903, No 40

In *Norway* the political unions of socialists have a total membership of 11,600. The trades organizations comprise 260 unions with a total of 20,730 members, many of whom, however, are not socialists.

9. In *Spain* organized laborers in great part still adhere to the anarchist principles of the Bakunin school. The social democratic party with a Marxian platform, founded at the close of the seventies by Iglesias and Mesa, developed very slowly. In Spain as well as in Germany there are two socialist organizations supplementing each other· one political, the other one trades-unionist. In March, 1902, the political organization consisted of 70 societies with a total of over 8,000 members. The trade organization, the so-called *Union général de Trabajadores*, was composed at the same period of 226 sections, numbering altogether 32,778 members.[1] But by no means all of these union men are socialists. It is said that at the elections of 1898 about 20,000 socialist votes were cast.

Besides the *Socialista*, edited by Iglesias in Madrid, eight other papers are controlled by the party.

10. *Holland.*—At the general elections of 1901 the social democratic votes amounted to 38,279; in 1897 there had been 13,035. The socialist party is represented in the Chamber by seven deputies. The party platform is in strict accordance with that of German socialists.

11. The *Australian Socialist Union* was formed in October 1890, chiefly at Sydney, New South Wales. Its official platform remarks, among other things: "The time of senseless production, of competition and private undertakings is past, the sources and means

[1] Cf. *Neue Zeit*, 20th year, vol II, p 16.

of production and distribution of wealth must be declared and treated as common property; i.e., land, mines, factories and machines, raw material, shipping, wharves and elevators, and all concurrent factors serving for the production and distribution of goods must become the property of the state." [1]

[1] *Berliner Volksblatt,* 1890, No. 301.

CHAPTER II.

EXAMINATION OF THE PRINCIPAL BASIS OF SOCIALISM: THE MATERIALISTIC CONCEPTION OF HISTORY.

THE "materialistic conception of history" is the fundamental dogma of Marxian socialism. This is at present generally acknowledged. In the opinion of Fr. Engels it was by this conception of history that socialism advanced to the rank of science.[1] In this conception of history two elements are to be distinguished: first, the general theory and, secondly, its application in behalf of socialism. Every Marxian socialist must needs adopt the materialistic conception of history as the foundation of his edifice, but not every one who accepts that theory must also necessarily draw from it the conclusions arrived at by Marx and his followers.

SECTION I.

THE MATERIALISTIC CONCEPTION OF HISTORY AS A GENERAL THEORY.

By their materialistic conception Marx and Engels intended to establish an entirely new method of his-

---

[1] Cf. above, p. 35 Bernstein in his Voraussetzungen des Sozialismus und die Aufgaben der Sozialdemokratie, p. 4, writes· "It is incontrovertible that the most important part in the foundation of Marxism, so to say the fundamental law which permeates the whole system, is his specific theory of history, which goes by the name of materialistic conception of history. With this theory stands or falls the principle of the whole system, its every modification involves a corresponding change in the other parts of the system "

torical research and interpretation. Their whole theory may be reduced to the following four simple statements:

1. There is no dualism of spirit and matter.

2. In the social relations and institutions of man there is nothing immutable; everything is subject to a constant process of change.

3. In this constant change production and the exchange of products are the determining and decisive factors.

4. Social development is effected by the formation of economic contrasts and class struggles.

These statements will be examined in turn.[1]

§ I. *Materialistic Monism.*

The first postulate of the materialistic conception of history is: There is no dualism of spirit and matter. This means that nothing exists beyond matter, that everything is either matter or some form of development caused by the motion of matter. Says Engels:[2] "The real unity of the world is its materiality." "Every form of being is matter." "Motion is the mode of being of matter."[3] "Beyond nature and man there exists nothing."[4] "Motion as well as matter can neither be created nor destroyed."[5] This implies the other assertion that there is no personal God, the Creator of the world,[6] no Providence watching over the destinies

---

[1] Cf. *Masaryk*, Die Grundlagen des Marxismus (Vienna, 1899); *Stammler*, Wirtschaft und Recht (Leipzig, 1896); *Woltmann*, Der historische Materialismus (Düsseldorf, 1900); *Friedländer*, Die vier Hauptrichtungen der modernen sozialen Bewegung, P. I. Marxismus und Anarchismus (Berlin, 1901), etc.

[2] E. Dührings Umwälzung der Wissenschaft, 2d ed. p. 28.

[3] *Ibid.*, p. 45; L. Feuerbach, 2d ed., p. 10.

[4] *Ibid.*, p. 11.

[5] *Ibid.*, p. 45.

[6] According to Engels the relation of thought and being, of intellect and nature, constitutes the profoundest philosophical problem. "Those

of mankind, no spiritual, immortal soul, no retribution in a life to come, that man is but an animal further advanced in evolution. "Life is the mode of being of the albuminoids." [1] Marx, as well as Engels, Bebel, Liebknecht, etc., never tires of repeating that man very gradually developed from the brute—in Marx's opinion from the ape. It need not be mentioned that thereby Christianity, its doctrines of paradise, of original sin, of redemption by means of the incarnation and death of Jesus Christ, of heaven and hell, are thrown overboard. Socialist leaders are fully aware of these consequences and make them their own. No occasion is allowed to pass without giving free vent to their hatred of Christianity.

It cannot be expected of us to refute here all the errors indicated above, together with countless others, necessarily connected with them. This would require not merely a treatise on apologetics, but also an entire course of philosophy. Besides, socialists are too self-confident to offer any proofs for their assertions; at most they are content with revamping the stale objec-

who maintained a spirit pre-existing nature and thus in the last instance some kind of creation—and with some philosophers, e g , Hegel, creation is far more intricate and impossible than in the Christian system—those, I say, formed the camp of idealists Those others who looked upon nature as the first being belonged to the various materialist schools " (L Feuerbach, p 14)

[1] Dührings Umwälzung, p 68 It has been objected by certain socialist critics that historical materialism does not necessarily imply philosophical materialism, that a socialist may be an adherent of the materialistic conception of history without denying the dualism of spirit and matter. We reply that historical materialism is evidently to be taken in the sense in which its originators, Marx and Engels, understood it They certainly looked upon historical materialism as intimately connected with and based upon philosophical materialism Engels, e g , narrating his "conversion" from Hegel's idealism to Feuerbach's materialism, tells us that now there was question of "*harmonizing with and of building up upon this materialistic basis* the science of society, i e , the substance of the so-called historical and philosophical sciences " (L Feuerbach, 2d ed , p 22)

Also E Dietzgen (*Neue Zeit*, 22d year, 1. p 238) confesses openly: "Because our materialism is based upon the unity of spirit and matter, it is quite correctly called dialectic materialism "

tions of Feuerbach, Strauss, Darwin, and others of that ilk. We address ourselves to readers who have still some regard for their dignity as human beings.

§ II. *The Constant Process of Evolution.*

The second postulate of the materialistic conception of history is: Nothing is immutable, everything is subject to a constant, never-ending process of change. This is the Hegelian process of formation, applied on the basis of materialism. "Every form of being is matter, and motion is the mode of being of matter." Accordingly there are no unchangeable concepts and principles in the domain of politics, economics, law, morality, and religion. In the realm of mathematics alone Marx and Engels are willing to admit immutable principles, although even here the "eternal truths" are said to be rather few and far between.

It is plain that such views are the outcome of the grossest materialism, that they are of account only in so far as they are connected with materialism, and that they will necessarily share its fate. Just as God is the Eternal and Immutable in whom there is no shadow of change, no past or future, but an eternal present, thus also it will remain true forever that He is the Creator, the supreme Lord and final Goal of all things. It will remain true forever that man is created to serve God and thereby to attain eternal salvation, that in the life to come there is an eternal retribution for good and bad. True forever will be every word spoken by the infallible Truth, by the mouth of the prophets, and lastly by His only Son: "My words shall not pass." In brief, every iota of revealed truth will remain true forever, just as the so-called materialistic conception of history is a pernicious error, pernicious most of all to those who endeavor to use it as a bulwark against Christianity and its doctrines and sacraments.

If the truths of the Christian revelation are immutable and eternal, the same must be said no less of the fundamental concepts and principles of the natural order. They are the natural revelation of the thoughts of the Eternal, who is the source and fountain-head of all truth. Moreover, they are in manifold and necessary connection with divine revelation. In the course of centuries the notions of circle and square have not changed; nor will they ever change, just as little as the general notions of the religious and moral order and the principles derived therefrom shall ever become different. Our ideas are not vacant forms, but the intellectual images of the essence of things which ever remains the same throughout the changes of the physical world. The nature and destination of the first man did not differ from ours, and will be found to be the same in the last human being treading the earth.

The negation of eternal and immutable concepts and principles makes knowledge and science impossible and involves hopeless contradictions. Science deals with what is necessary and immutable. It is not satisfied with registering exterior phenomena, it tries to penetrate to and to lay bare the hidden causes and governing laws and thence to draw its conclusions; it endeavors to ascend to general and necessary principles. But how can this be done if no general, necessary, and immutable notions exist? If there are no immutable concepts, there is also no intellectual communication between different generations. It is impossible to enter upon the mode of thought of times gone by or to foresee in aught the destinies of future ages. The identity of concepts is completely lacking. How can we know whether Plato or Aristotle have reasoned correctly, how can we at all fathom their meaning, if their concepts and opinions were quite different from ours? In fact, we are completely at a loss to know whether they had ideas and opinions at all, because what we understand by these terms is mayhap a product of modern economic conditions unknown to the ancients. The most gruesome scepticism is the only logical consequence of the "materialistic conception of history."

And thus naturally enough socialists are not lacking in contradictions They are explicit to a fault in detailing the development of society in the past and the future But how can they be sure that there was development in the past and that there will be development in the future? For, the notion of development has perhaps never been realized or will soon cease to be realized How do they make out that religion, that private property in the means of production, that marriage "in the present acceptation of the term" shall vanish, if we cannot know whether there will be men in the future, and if there will be, whether they will have the same concepts or not ? How do they know that in every period new political, religious, and moral ideas are the result of the economic conditions ? Whence this general law, equally applicable to all times ?

Probably in order to escape these difficulties and contradictions Marx and Engels concede the existence of immutable and eternal truths in the mathematical sciences, i.e., in the sciences capable of mathematical treatment—mathematics, astronomy, mechanics, physics, and chemistry, and perhaps also biology.[1] By this concession they quite unconsciously overturn their entire evolutionary theory. For the above-mentioned mathematical sciences presuppose a great number of concepts and principles which they have in

---

[1] Cf *Engels*, Dührings Umwalzung, 2d ed , p. 74 sqq.

common with all other sciences, and which are properly
the subject of philosophy.

The notions of being, substance, essence, quality,
quantity; motion, force, cause, effect, law, necessity,
time, eternity, relation, equality, knowledge, cognition,
will, evolution, and countless others are the common
property of all the sciences, not excluding the mathematical. They are the subject-matter of philosophy,
whose duty it is to elucidate them in every respect and
to arrange them in systematic order. From these
immutable concepts, independent of time or space,
there arise immutable principles which form the basis of
correct thought and which are taken over from philosophy by the mathematical sciences. Among them we
find, e.g., the principle of contradiction that nothing
can be and not be at the same time in the same respect;
the principle that two things which are equal to a
third are also equal to each other; the principle that
every effect must have a cause, that the effect cannot be greater than its cause, that a constant and
permanent effect must be owing to a constant and
permanent cause; the principle that the whole is
greater than its part, that everything acts according
to its nature, and that in nature there are unchangeable
laws which can be discovered by observation, etc. Whatever we know scientifically about the certitude of our
cognition, about the trustworthiness of our senses and
of our consciousness, about the existence of things outside of ourselves, about the certainty derived from the
testimony of others, all this and much more must be
presupposed by the exact sciences as irrefragable and
immutable truth. To deny or doubt these principles
is to render science impossible; to accept them is to
establish a firm foundation, whence we may safely rise

to the knowledge of the highest and final cause of all things, the Creator of heaven and earth. But thereby we shall have reached also the indestructible sanctuary of religion and morality.

There are, therefore, eternal concepts and truths; there are principles as unchangeable and eternal as the eternal Truth itself from which they are derived. It is consequently evident fraud or naive self-delusion, if socialists imagine they cannot be refuted by religious and philosophical arguments, because, forsooth, religious and philosophical notions have been changed in the course of ages according to the state of economic conditions. If this socialist assumption were correct, there would, of course, be an end of religion and philosophy, but there would also be an end of "scientific" socialism, in fact of every science.

More especially it is entirely wrong to say that no valid inferences as to social institutions can be derived from the nature of man. Man is indeed capable of development and increasing perfection, but he ever retains essentially the same nature and the same propensities. He will ever remain a being composed of body and soul inclined to enjoyment and violence, to self-seeking, ambition, and anger, and only by overcoming himself can he obtain and preserve the mastery of reason over the lower appetites. And, as we shall show hereafter, it is also a constant law that the propensities and talents of men, however similar in their general nature, are nevertheless variously manifested in different individuals and therefore necessarily entail inequalities in social life.

§ III.   *Evolution and Economics.*

We have arrived at the third postulate of the materialistic conception of history: In the process of evolution the economic conditions are the determining and decisive factors. The production and exchange of articles of consumption are the foundation of social order. If production is modified the change entails a gradual transformation of the entire superstructure, society, politics, law, morals, and religion. Some characteristic passages of Marx and Engels, in which this view is formulated, have been quoted above (pp. 41–43). In consequence, "the ultimate causes of all social changes and political revolutions" . . . are to be looked for "in the modifications affecting production and exchange."

Here is laid bare the very marrow of the materialistic conception of history. The first two postulates discussed above, Marx and Engels have taken over ready made from the schools of Feuerbach and Hegel; the one now under discussion is entirely of their own manufacture.

But by it they are haplessly involved in flagrant contradictions. Their thesis is supposed, of course, to be of general and permanent value and to be equally true throughout every epoch of human history. However, it forms no part of the mathematical sciences. Therefore Marx and Engels must needs concede that there are immutable concepts and principles outside of the exact sciences.

Moreover, it is plain that this postulate has no meaning or value except from the point of view of downright materialism. To him who knows that God has infused into man a spiritual soul according to His own image and likeness, that He has implanted in this soul a yearning after the full possession of truth and goodness, to him, I say, it is perfectly evident that economic conditions cannot be "the ultimate cause of all social changes." In man there are not only sensual appetites and propensities to be satisfied in the domain of economics, but there are also higher aspirations which wield a decisive influence upon his volition and action and thereby upon the development of social institutions.

It is to be granted, indeed, that before everything else man must live, that he must find nourishment, clothing, and comfortable shelter, and therefore economic activity will ever be of paramount importance in human life. "*Primum vivere, dein philosophari.*" This truism had no need of being discovered by the giant intellect of Marx. But man does not live by bread alone. His spiritual, immortal soul craves nobler food. He longs to expand the domain of his power and knowledge; he desires to know not only what exists and is done, but also the how and the wherefore. Thus he advances along every line to the first cause of all things, to God, the Fountainhead and ultimate Goal of all being. Here we have the basis and root of religion. Man enters upon an intimate intercourse with the invisible Lord of all things, who is also the Lord and Guide of mankind. Death, moreover, snatches us away after a short span of life, and yet there is within us a yearning after complete happiness, an .rresistible longing for immortality.

Thus by thought and reflection every human being, however different the economic conditions of each one may be, will arrive at the belief in a life to come for

which our present life is but a time of trial and preparation, a life of eternal retribution for good or evil. Can
it be doubted that these thoughts and hopes of immortality are fraught with great influence upon the actions
of mankind independently of economic conditions?
For, economic conditions are widely different in different places; religion and morality on the other hand are
the common heirloom of the human race. To deny
all this, to explain religion and morality, law and
politics, as the result of economic conditions, to look
upon religion, as is done by Marx and Engels, as
"the fantastic reflection in the brains of men of the
exterior powers which dominate men's daily existence,"
is the grossest materialism.

More especially, the derivation of social and ethical
institutions from economic conditions is altogether
unwarranted, because every well-ordered system of
economics presupposes some kind of social organization, however primitive. To maintain, therefore, that
law and order are the product of economic conditions is
evidently to put the cart before the horse.

But what is the verdict of history as to the function
in the development of mankind ascribed by socialists
to the economic conditions? The honest and straight-
forward inquirer will find that religious and moral
concepts have much oftener been the cause of far-
reaching economic revolutions than the reverse. The
economic and social life of the Israelitic people was
surely in great part conditioned by its religious
faith. Christianity likewise is forsooth not the product
of economic conditions in the Roman empire during
the rule of Augustus. Christian dogmas were diametrically opposed to the opinions then prevailing, and yet
they gradually remodelled society, also in the matter

of economics. We need but call to mind the doctrine concerning the duty and the value of labor, the abolition of slavery, the lifting up of woman from the slough of degradation, the reorganization of the family, the creation of countless institutions of Christian charity and mercy.

Kautsky, indeed, is confident of his ability to derive the origin of Christianity from the economic conditions of imperial Rome. According to him "the aversion from earthly things, the death-longing of Christianity" is to be explained "from the material conditions of Rome under the emperors." [1] But how does this agree with the fact that Christianity did not originate on Roman soil but in the country of the despised Jews, where it had been foretold during twenty centuries in types and prophecies, and whence it spread throughout the world by the preaching of Jewish apostles? And besides, is the longing for death, the aversion from earthly things to be found at all in Christianity or perhaps even something peculiar to it? Only ignorance of the true nature of Christianity can prompt such assertions. Christianity teaches that this life is a preparation for the life to come, and that on the threshold of eternity every man will be confronted by a severe judgment, which will decide his eternal bliss or his eternal misery. But is this peculiar to Christianity? Is not the same doctrine to be found with the ancient Egyptians, Babylonians, Assyrians, Greeks, and Romans?

But the most significant point is the fact that Christianity is firmly based not on abstract ideas and opinions but on undoubted historical occurrences. During the reign of Augustus there appeared in Judæa the Messias

[1] *Neue Zeit,* 1896–1897, vol. I. p. 215.

expected by the chosen people for more than two thousand years. By countless miracles and prophecies, more especially by His glorious Resurrection, He proved Himself to be the Son of God sent by the Father. Already St. Paul strongly insists on this fact as upon the foundation of our belief; and many who were witnesses of the fact have sealed their testimony with their blood. Are these facts to be explained as the result of the then-existing economic conditions? Will the method of production and exchange prevalent at that time afford us any light on the question why Christ, without having pursued any course of studies, was enabled to proclaim a wonderful and exalted doctrine, which as a leaven has transformed the world; why at His command poor and ignorant fishermen were capable of preaching successfully the mystery of the cross, a stumbling-block to the Jews and a folly to the Gentiles, and of spreading the fame of their miracles and doctrines throughout the world?

The futility of any such explanation is evident to every one whose mind and heart have not yet drifted away from Christianity and common sense and landed on the shallows of materialism pure and simple. But, if the origin of Christianity cannot be derived from economic conditions, it is labor lost to account for the development of western civilization since the time of Christ by appealing to the methods of production and exchange. If every religion is but the "intellectual reflex in men's brains of their economic position," how could the Catholic Church throughout all times and in all places remain essentially the same in spite of different economic conditions from country to country and from century to century?

What we have said of Christianity in general may
be illustrated by many particular instances. Consider, e.g., the powerful influence of the crusades
upon western civilization. Were they perhaps owing
to economic conditions and not rather the outcome of
Christian faith? Also Mohammedanism, the Renais-
sance, and the Reformation have introduced sweep-
ing changes and have directed the course of social
development into different orbits. The English and
French Revolution can be traced back ultimately to
religious ideas, the latter more especially to the moral
and religious frivolity prevalent at the court and disseminated by the encyclopedists. And as regards our
present social evolution, also in the line of economics,
is it not due for the greater part to the false ideas of
modern liberalism?

Thus we might pass in review the whole of history, everywhere the fact would be apparent that the
course of civilization has been shaped by religious and
moral ideas at least as much as by economic conditions.
"The profoundest problem of the world's history to
which all others are subordinate," thus Goethe remarks,
" is the conflict between belief and unbelief." But to
one more point we must call attention, a point which
brings the untenability of the socialistic conception of
history into the strongest relief. Who can calculate
the influence brought to bear on their contemporaries
and on posterity by great men—statesmen, generals,
artists, scientists, saints? We need but call to mind a
Cyrus, an Alexander the Great, a Pericles, Constantine,
Clovis of France, Charlemagne, Alfred the Great,
Stephen I. of Hungary, Henry VIII. of England, Peter
the Great, and countless others. Let us suppose
Alexander the Great had been in the place of the Em-

peror Charles V., or Napoleon in that of Louis XVI., modern history would probably have taken a different course. Are men of genius the outgrowth of the economic conditions of their time and country? Of course, the great deeds of great men presuppose certain social conditions; but under the very same circumstances there are a thousand different possibilities as to the course of development, all of which very often depend on the character, talent, and energy of one man.

This weak point in the materialistic conception of history has not been left unchallenged by socialists themselves. We refer here in the first place to the interesting controversy in the *Neue Zeit*[1] between Kautsky and the English socialist Belfort-Bax.

The latter was of opinion that the Marxian historical theory, at least in the form in which it is advocated by Mehring, Plechanow, and Kautsky, stands in need of correction. He himself distinguished two parallel factors in evolution, one internal and the other external. The external factor consists of the economic conditions, the internal is in the "psychic impulse," in the ideas and opinions which dominate the doings of men. Both factors are at work simultaneously, but to a certain degree they are independent of each other.

Kautsky, on his part, spurned the imputation of holding views different from those of Marx and Engels Also in his opinion, he said, mind is a factor in evolution, but in a subordinate not in a ruling position He granted, too, that there are other interests besides those of economics, but he maintained that the state of production by creating conditions which present new problems to the intellect determines the direction of evolution

Both disputants are right, in as far as they assign to the intellect an important part in the evolutionary process; but they blunder egregiously if they imagine that from the materialistic point of view any independent activity can be ascribed to the intellect Kautsky, indeed, tries to reduce this activity to a minimum. He assigns a task to the mind, but it is the task of

[1] *Neue Zeit,* 1895-96, vol II pp 652 sqq , and 1896-97, vol I. p 231.

the servant. "Mind," he says, in the passage referred to above, " puts society in motion, not however as master of the economic conditions, but as their servant. They assign to it the tasks to be accomplished. And therefore they also determine the results which the mind can and must obtain in the given circumstances "

How can the mind be an independent factor over and above the economic conditions, if there exists nothing besides matter and motion, and if the mind itself, as Kautsky confesses, is but "a function of the brain"? Marx and Engels certainly entertained no such views They looked upon society, politics, law, and religion as the "superstructure" reared upon the economic conditions and subject to the same changes as the latter In a much-quoted passage Marx tells us: "Certain forms of social consciousness correspond to the sum total of production conditions in any given society." Again he says "The ideological world is nothing else than material substance transformed in the brains of men; man's mode of existence determines his thoughts " Engels glories in the fact of having proved, together with Marx, that "the whole of history hitherto is a history of class struggles, that the classes warring against each other are the inevitable results of the economic conditions prevalent at that epoch, that the economic structure of society always forms the objective basis which affords the ultimate explanation for the entire superstructure of ethical and political institutions and of religious and political thought in any given period of history. Hereby idealism was driven from its last stronghold, from its conception of history, the materialistic conception of history was firmly established and a way was found of explaining man's consciousness from his mode of existence instead of the reverse, as had been done heretofore." [1]

It is, therefore, quite against the spirit of Marx to derive the origin of economic conditions also from religious ideas. Marx as well as Engels maintains that religion is but "the fantastic reflection in the brains of men of those exterior powers which rule their daily life " But the reflection is determined by the reflected object, not the object by the reflection.[2]

[1] *Engels*, E Dührings Umwälzung der Wissenschaft, p 11.
[2] Also Professor Sombart, an ardent admirer and disciple of Marx, offers an explanation of historical development according to which "all the beliefs, ideals, philosophical views of men are the product of circumstances " Sozialismus und soziale Bewegung, p 52.

Bernstein is much more radical than Belfort-Bax in his criticism of the materialistic conception of history. He confronts the theory with the fact that the course of history is influenced not only by economic conditions, but also by local and national peculiarities, by political, religious, and moral facts and ideas. To his mind it is preposterous to apply the economic conditions as a uniform and automatic explanation of complicated historical phenomena Historical materialism will never do away with the fact "that men make their own history, that men have brains, and that the disposition of men's brains is not so entirely a mechanical matter as to be governed solely by the state of economics Why are workingmen, who as a class are in exactly identical situations, often diametrically opposed in their line of action? Their proceedings are influenced not only by various modes of thought, but also by historical reminiscences and traditions. Signal defeats are felt for many years in their demoralizing and disorganizing influence on the vanquished class." [1]

According to Bernstein the materialistic conception of history furthermore forces its adherents to the conclusion that the decisions and actions of men are after all but the necessary result of the material conditions of production The fact is, however, that men manifest an ever-increasing ability of directing the economic evolution and of making it subservient to their own interests. The economic forces no longer exercise their unlimited sway. "Individuals and nations withdraw more and more of their existence from the influence of a necessity which asserts itself without or even against their will " [2]

In this matter Bernstein's position is unexceptionable. Furthermore he tries to show that in later life Marx and Engels abandoned part of their former views and assigned a greater sphere of action to non-economic factors Also this may be admitted. The question now is, whether, after all these concessions to "ideological" factors, historical materialism still remains intact We think not. Materialism to be true to its principles can never acknowledge "mind" as an independent factor in history.

[1] *Bernstein*, Zur Geschichte und Theorie des Sozialismus (1901), p. 245.
[2] *Bernstein*, Die Voraussetzungen des Sozialismus, p. 10.

§ IV. *Evolution and Class Distinctions.*

It but remains now to examine the fourth and last postulate of the materialistic conception of history. It is: *The evolution of history is effected by economic contrasts and class struggles.*

"The history of society heretofore," thus we read in the communist manifesto,[1] "is a history of class struggles." According to Marx the conditions of production are changing slowly but steadily. Whilst this process is going on, the social order established during a former period remains, though at variance with the new conditions of production. Gradually the antagonism between the existing social order and the new economic relations asserts itself. "The awakening conviction," Engels tells us, "that existing social institutions are unreasonable and unjust, that reason has changed into unreason and benefit into injury, is but an indication of the fact that the methods of production and exchange have been silently transformed so as no longer to tally with the social order which had been adapted to former economic conditions. This means at the same time that also the remedies for these discrepancies must be contained—more or less perfectly developed—in the changed conditions of production. These remedies, however, are not to be drawn from an imaginative brain, but by using our brains they are to be discovered in the existing material facts of production."[2]

The meaning of this labored declaration can only be the following. Economics and vested rights come into conflict. It becomes evident that the traditional

[1] Manifesto of the Communist Party, Reissued (Berlin, 1891), p 9.
[2] *Engels,* E. Dührings Umwälzung der Wissenschaft, p. 253.

and vested rights are at variance with the new economic conditions and must needs be modified. But now the question arises, by what criterion can we judge and decide whether and wherein there is harmony or discord between economics and vested rights? This criterion must be some superior and immutable standard according to which we judge of vested rights existing at any given time. And this standard can be no other than the unchanging principles of natural law and the ultimate purpose to ,which all human institutions must be directed. The principles of natural law, however, are not within the ken of historical materialism, and can therefore not be used by it to evince the pretended conflict between right and economics.

Again, it cannot be denied that class struggles play an important part in the history of mankind; but to maintain that "the whole of history heretofore was the history of class struggles," [1] is but a sample of the one-sided exaggerations so common among socialists. Is there any record of class struggles in the whole of Oriental history? There are many accounts of national wars between Assyrians, Babylonians, Egyptians, Medes, Persians, etc. We read of great generals and conquerors who introduced radical changes in the political and social order; but of class struggles there is scarcely a trace. The great masses of the people were and remained oppressed, bearing their yoke in mute resignation. And yet these nations reached a marvellous degree of civilization. Later on, the main factors in social evolution were the national struggles between Greeks and Persians, the internecine wars of Greeks against Greeks, the hostilities of Greeks and Macedonians, of Greeks and Romans, of the Romans

[1] *Engels*, E. Dührings Umwälzung der Wissenschaft, p. 253.

and their neighbors, especially the Carthaginians. The influence of Greece and Rome upon the civilization of the entire Occident is incalculable, and it is in vain to explain it by a reference to class struggles.

Still later we meet with the wars of the Romans against the northern barbarians. Then took place that fusion of races from which sprang new and vigorous nations. Was it, perhaps, by class struggles that the Teutonic tribes were gained over to Christianity, and raised to a degree of civilization which elicits the admiration of unprejudiced historians? Again, what is the verdict of the history of India, where the very same classes of society, the so-called castes, have been existing for more than 3000 years, and are so firmly rooted as to defy every attempt at modification? In fine, were science and the arts and thereby the development of civilization ever influenced in any marked degree by class struggles? Are our modern inventions, especially those of printing and gunpowder, are steam-engines and electric motors, are steamboats, railways, factories, telegraphs, etc., to be looked upon as the products of class struggles? And yet they are the real revolutionaries, they are the creators of a new world.

Within the pale of the single nations class struggles have indeed taken place, as we know from the history of Greece and Rome. But these class struggles were, practically speaking, confined to a few cities, and had by no means as much influence on their development as was exercised by external relations and by the activity of great statesmen and generals.

Let us suppose, however, that history is a succession of class struggles. Will it then not follow as a necessary deduction from the materialistic conception of history that with every nation there must be found two antagonistic sets of principles in matters of religion, morality, law, and politics? Yet there is no trace of any such thing, neither among the ancient Oriental nations, the Egyptians, Chinese, Hindus, Assyrians, Persians, nor among the Greeks, Romans, Gauls, etc. The Roman plebeians did not differ from the patricians in their views on religion, morality, and law. Throughout the Middle Ages there was no diversity of opinion in religious, moral, and social matters despite the great struggles between different classes. In spite of their antagonism in the field of politics and economics, pope and emperor, knight and peasant, rich and poor, all firmly upheld the same principles of religion and morality. Look at the transformations which Italy and Spain have undergone since the downfall of the Western Empire, and yet in matters of religion, morality, and vested rights they have suffered no change. If in modern times these countries have been infected by unbelief, the poison is spreading not so much among those classes who suffer most from the new economic conditions, but among the so-called better class of people, who imbibe the venom of infidelity at the universities, just as they do also in other countries.

Section II.

APPLICATION OF THE MATERIAL CONCEPTION OF HISTORY AS THE BASIS OF SOCIALISM.

The general theory discussed in the preceding section forms the foundation upon which Marx and Engels have reared their socialistic edifice. Their theory of history was intended to show *why and how the modern capitalist order of society must needs develop into socialism.*

At the outset of the argumentation we find the doctrine of *surplus-value.* Surplus-value is said to be the labor of others appropriated free of expense. Urged on by an insatiable desire of gain the capitalist strives to increase the surplus-value in every possible manner. The first means to this end is to multiply the hours of work to a maximum, whilst reducing wages to a minimum; the second means is to render labor more productive by the perfection of technical appliances. Thus the contrast between "socialized production and capitalist appropriation" [1] becomes more and more accentuated. Industries on a large scale, in which there is a concentration of forces according to a uniform plan, are gradually ousting the industries on a small scale. At the same time the means of production are monopolized more and more in the hands of a few capitalists. "The antagonism between socialized production and capitalist appropriation becomes manifest in the form of an opposition between proletariat and bourgeoisie." [2]

But whilst within the single factories production approaches more and more to socialized organization, society without is in a state of complete anarchy. [3] A fierce anarchistic struggle for existence is raging among capitalists, every one of whom is manufacturing ahead for dear life regardless of the state of the market. This senseless struggle culminates "on the average every tenth year in an *economic crisis* which convulses society to its very foundation." Over-production, business embarrassments and failures, bankruptcies

---

[1] *Engels*, Entwicklung des Sozialismus, p. 31.
[2] *Ibid.*
[3] *Ibid.*, p. 33.

and compulsory sales, cause general disorder. The consequence of these crises is on the one hand the growing accumulation of capital in the hands of a few, and on the other the growing number of proletarian laborers and their increasing misery. There is formed an *industrial reserve army*, i.e., "a number of wage-earners at the disposal of capital, but in excess of its average demand, . . . to be called into activity when industry is working at high pressure, to be bundled out on the street after the inevitable catastrophe has set in, at all times like an iron ball chained to the feet of the laboring classes in their life-struggle against capital."

But, whilst on the one hand the proletariat is growing and its misery is heightened, the number of capitalists on the other is diminishing and their property swells to an alarming size. Finally, the antagonism between the small coterie of capitalists and the immense number of proletarians becomes so acute that "the state is forced to assume the direction of production." [1] "Instead of anarchy in social production there will then be production according to a uniform plan to meet the requirements of the community as well as of individuals. The proletariat takes the reins of government and first of all transforms the means of production into state property." But this first act, in which the state is the representative of society at large, will also be its last; the state is abrogated, class differences are abolished.[2] The socialist order of society reigns supreme.

This whole argumentation consists, therefore, of four essential points: 1. The doctrine of *surplus-value* based on Marx's theory of value; 2. The asser-

<hr/>

[1] *Engels*, Entwicklung des Sozialismus, p. 37.   [2] *Ibid.*, pp. 40, 41.

tion concerning the *concentration of industries* and the *accumulation of capital;* 3. The doctrine of the increasing number and destructiveness of *industrial crises;* 4. The assumption that with the accumulation of capital an increasing number of wage-earners are thrown out of work, thus forming an army of *superfluous laborers* who are plunged deeper and deeper in misery (pauperization theory). These four points are now to be discussed in turn.

§ I. *Marx's Theory of Value and Surplus-value.*

Capital, according to Karl Marx, comes to the world "dripping from every pore from head to foot with blood and dirt."[1] It is, according to its very nature, nothing else than the unpaid-for, stolen labor of the workman; or, as Lassalle calls it, "the property of others" (Fremdtum). In order to substantiate this death-verdict on capital, Marx avails himself of his peculiar theory of value which we have discussed in detail in an earlier chapter (p. 46 sqq.).[2] He distinguishes two kinds of value—value in use and value in exchange. *Value in use* consists in the utility of an object to satisfy human wants; *value in ex-*

---

[1] Capital, vol. I. p. 726.

[2] There are some who wish to retain the materialistic conception of history without accepting Marx's theory of value. But then they cease to be adherents of Marxian socialism. It is indeed inadmissible to represent the matter as if Marx had argued thus: Surplus-value is unjust, therefore capitalist society must be abolished. This is not Marx's view of the matter. His real argumentation is rather as follows: Surplus-value is essentially based on exploitation, and by its very nature tends to an increase of exploitation by which society will finally be divided into a mere handful of billionaire capitalists and a countless herd of proletarians, and then the collapse will ensue. In this sense Marx undoubtedly considered his theory of surplus-value as a fundamental tenet of his system. His conception of capital, capitalism, accumulation of products, is based entirely on the doctrine of surplus-value, which in turn necessarily presupposes his theory of value. Also Engels, as we have seen above (p. 35), plainly tells us that by the materialistic conception of history and by the doctrine of surplus-value, socialism has received its scientific character.

change consists in the ratio in which commodities are exchangeable for one another. Value in use, it is true, forms the basis of value in exchange, in so far as only useful things can have exchange-value. But in other respects *value in exchange is entirely independent of value in use.* The exchange-value is determined by the labor embodied in an object.

Let Marx explain his idea himself.[1] He says: " Let us take two kinds of merchandise, e g., wheat and iron. Whatever may be their ratio of exchange, it can always be expressed by an equation in which a certain quantity of wheat equals a certain quantity of iron, e g, one bushel of wheat $= x$ pounds of iron What is the meaning of this equation? It means that an equal amount of something common to both is contained in two different things Both are equal to some third quantity, which in itself is neither the one nor the other. But each of the two, in as far as it is value in exchange, must be resolvable into this third element "

But what is this third element common to both? "This common element cannot be any geometrical, physical, chemical, or other natural quality of the merchandise Its material qualities come into consideration only in so far as they contribute to its utility On the other hand, precisely the abstraction from the value in use evidently characterizes the ratio of exchange of different commodities Within the limits of this ratio one kind of use-value is worth as much as any other provided it is present in the right proportion." What then is that remaining element? "If we abstract from the use-value of merchandise, it retains but one quality, the quality of being the product of labor. But also the labor product has been changed in our hands. If we abstract from its use-value, we abstract also from its material composition and form by which it is useful. It is no longer a table, or a house, or yarn, or any other useful object. All its external qualities are, as it were, blotted out It is also no longer the product of the work of the joiner, or carpenter, or spinner, or of any definite productive labor." "Nothing has remained but the same ghostlike actuality, a mere crystallization of human

[1] Capital, vol I. p. 3

labor without distinction, i.e., of the expenditure of human labor capacity without regard to the manner of expending it. These objects now represent only the fact that in their production human labor has been expended, human labor has been stored up." [1]

"A value in use or an object has value only because human labor considered in the abstract is embodied or materialized in it. But how are we to measure the amount of its value? By the amount of 'value-creating substance,' i e., labor, contained in it The quantity of labor itself is determined by the time employed, and the labor-time again is measured by the unit of certain periods, as hours, days, etc."

"Now it might seem that if the value of any commodity is determined by the amount of labor expended in producing it, this commodity would be the more valuable the lazier and clumsier its producer, because he would need more time to produce it. The labor, however, which forms the substance of value must be equal human labor, an expenditure of equal labor capacity. The sum total of labor capacity in the whole society . . . is taken here as one and the same human labor capacity, although it consists of countless individual labor capacities. Each one of these individual capacities is the same as any other in so far as it has the character of average labor capacity and as such produces an average amount of social labor and needs therefore in the production of any commodity only the average labor-time or ·the *socially necessary labor-time* Socially necessary labor-time is the time required to produce a certain value with given normal social conditions of production, and with the average social degree of skill and intensity of labor." [2]

How Marx has utilized the principle that exchange-value is something intrinsically independent of use-value and consists only in "crystallized labor-time" for the explanation of capitalistic "surplus-making," we have already shown (p. 46 sqq.). The Marxian doctrine of surplus-value and of the process of accumulation is inseparably connected with his theory of value If the latter is false, then all the consequences deduced from it are null and void. Therefore we must examine this theory more closely.

[1] Capital, vol 1. p. 4.
[2] *Ibid* , p 5.

For his fundamental principle that the exchange-value of an object is not determined by its use-value, but exclusively by the labor expended upon it, Marx can appeal to the authority of the greatest political economists, Adam Smith, Ricardo, and others. Socialism in this as in many other regards, is only the lineal descendant of liberalism; it only draws the logical inferences from the principles of liberalism. Not until Marx, Lassalle, and other socialists had taken hold of this principle to use it as a deft weapon against private capital did any misgiving arise concerning it; then authors began to abandon it or at least to restrict it very materially.

In reality this principle is untenable. To understand this we need but inquire into the notion of *value*. It is one of those simple and primitive notions which are evident to every man and become obscured only when we attempt to analyze them. An object is said to be of value to us if it in any way appears desirable. Value therefore includes an objective and a subjective element. In order to be of value to us an object must be good in itself or at least it must appear to us as such, and moreover it must have some relation of adaptation to us, i.e., it must appear as in some way conducive to our preservation and perfection. In other words, value is the capacity of any thing to serve . the needs and desires of man and therefore to be estimated as desirable.[1]

Also purely spiritual goods are of value. The kingdom of heaven is far more valuable than any earthly goods, and therefore the prudent man is like unto a merchant who sacrifices all his earthly possessions to acquire the pearl of great price spoken of in

[1] Cf *Devas*, Political Economy, p. 4.

the Gospel. In a similar manner life and health are more valuable than money and estates.

Of *economic value* we speak in a more restricted sense. It is the business of economics to provide those material goods which are needed for the support, continuance, or enjoyment of man's material and intellectual life on earth. Therefore the economic value of these goods is the capacity they are estimated to possess of satisfying the above-mentioned needs.[1] Our striving after well-being impels us to aim at increasing the values at our disposal and to prevent their decrease.

In economic goods a twofold value may be distinguished: *value in use* and *value in exchange*. Also Marx rightly makes use of this distinction which we find already adopted by Aristotle and his commentators. Aristotle [2] distinguishes a twofold *use* of earthly goods: the one is proper to an object according to its peculiar character (χρῆσις οἰκεία); the other is common to it with all other objects (χρῆσις οὐκ οἰκεία). The philosopher illustrates this distinction by the example of a shoe. A shoe has a twofold use: the first is peculiar to it in contradistinction to other objects, and consists in this, that it can be used for the protection of the foot; the second consists in this, that it may be exchanged for other goods. This second use is common to the shoe with all other objects of merchandise. It may therefore be called common use or secondary use.[3] Value in use is therefore a

[1] *Ibid*, p 5 Cf. also *Philippovich*, Grundriss der polit. Oekonomie (1901), p 6

[2] Polit. I, 9 St Thom in I, Pol l 7. Silv Maurus in I. Polit. c. 6, n. 2.

[3] This distinction of use-value is much clearer, simpler, and more objective than those which we generally meet with in the works of modern political economists Many call use-value the fitness of an object for the use of the possessor himself, and exchange-value the fitness of the object to be

far more comprehensive notion than value in exchange. Exchange-value is also a kind of use-value, but not every value in use constitutes an exchange-value. Air and light are of continual value in use, but they are of no value in exchange.

What constitutes value in exchange? or in other words, what is required to make any object of value in exchange? First of all it must be capable of becoming private property. Exchange or barter is a kind of contract whereby one man yields up to another some economic good and receives some equivalent in its stead. This contract presupposes private property in some form or other.

Moreover, in order to be of value in exchange an object cannot be at the disposal of everybody in any desired quantity. Thus water is of great value in use, but in ordinary circumstances it is of no value in exchange, because it is free to all and because it is therefore useless to appropriate it, since no one will barter anything for water. But within the restrictions here mentioned every object which is of value in use is also of value in exchange. But how is this exchange-value to be determined? This can be done by comparing different objects with regard to the utility derived from them. The greater and more urgent the need which is relieved by some object in use, the smaller the quantity in which it is found, and the greater the trouble to be undergone in obtaining it, the greater also the value which we attribute to it.

given in exchange. But exchange itself is a use of the object by the possessor. Consequently the first member of the definition contains also the second. Others call use-value immediate value, and exchange-value mediate value. Others again reject this distinction altogether, and divide value into subjective and objective. As often as we shall, according to the ruling custom, distinguish between use-value and exchange-value, we shall understand by use-value the fitness of an article for all kinds of use, the use of exchange alone excepted.

But in most cases this determination of value does
not depend on the judgment of the individual, but on
the general estimate formed by society. This estimate
is not immutable, it changes according to time and
place. African negroes attach great value to many
things which Europeans look upon as trifles, whilst
some things which are of the utmost value to civilized
man are of no importance to savages.

If Marx had confined himself to the distinction
of these two kinds of value, no serious objection
could be raised against him; *but he has completely
rent them asunder.* Value in use, according to him,
is no factor in the determination of value in exchange.
He asks, why can I exchange, e.g., a bushel of wheat
for *x* boxes of shoe-blacking or *y* pounds of silk or
z ounces of gold, or why can I consider these quantities of the substances indicated as being of equal value?
And he answers: "In the ratio of exchange the exchange-value of different objects [appears] as something entirely independent of their values in use." [1]
Therefore, according to Marx, value in use has no
determining influence on value in exchange. But
this assertion of his is unproved and incorrect, and
involves him in contradictions.

1. It is *unproved*. The chief argument which
Marx adduces for his opinion is the following: Value
in exchange must be something *common* to all merchandise; but this common element cannot be anything else than the human labor embodied in it,
taken in the abstract. Therefore the labor contained in an object forms its exchange-value.

We grant that exchange-value is something common to all merchandise, because the various objects

[1] Capital, vol. 1 p 4.

of merchandise may be compared with each other according to their value in exchange. But we deny that this common element consists only in the labor contained in them. Marx does not produce any arguments for this opinion, but only mere assertions.

"The common element in all kinds of commodities cannot be a geometrical, physical, chemical, or any other natural quality of the goods themselves. Their physical properties come into consideration only in as far as they go to constitute their utility, or use-value. On the other hand, the exchangeableness of commodities is evidently characterized by abstracting from their usefulness. In regard to exchange the use-value of one object is just as much as the use-value of another, provided it be forthcoming in due proportion. As to their use-value, goods, in the first instance, differ in quality; but as to their exchange-value they differ only in quantity, and contain not a particle of use-value." [1]

This passage contains only assertions in lieu of arguments; nay, false statements presented to us as "evident." And yet upon these statements depend all the subsequent conclusions. We are surprised, in fact, that Marx so confidently affirms without proof that apart from labor there is no common element in different goods. Aristotle, to whom he repeatedly appeals, could have taught him better. This great philosopher teaches expressly that there is a common element in all commodities, according to which they can be compared with one another and estimated. This common measure or standard of exchangeable goods, according to the philosopher,[2] is usefulness, that is, their fitness for supplying the wants of mankind.

The commodities to be exchanged may be ever so

[1] Capital, vol. 1 p 12.
[2] Δεῖ ἄρα ἑνί τινι πάντα μετρεῖσθαι . . τοῦτο δ'ἐστὶ τῇ μὲν ἀληθείᾳ ἡ χρεία, ἢ πάντα συνέχει —Ethic v. 8.

different in other respects, they all agree in this one point that they satisfy some human need, that in some way or other they are useful and desirable. This furnishes a point of comparison and a standard of measurement.[1]

2. But the assertion of Marx that labor alone constitutes exchange-value is not only gratuitous: it is also *untrue*. Unwittingly Marx himself has penned his own refutation. He says: "Within the same ratio of exchange-value, the use-value of one object is as great as that of another, if it is only forthcoming in the same proportion." Why must the use-value be forthcoming in the same proportion? Evidently because in the determination of the exchange-value the usefulness of an object is by no means indifferent, but a decisive element. Moreover, how is it that, even according to the concessions of Marx himself, *useful objects only* can have exchange-value for society? Certainly because use-value or utility is an essential element in exchange-value. If one, for instance, with the greatest expenditure of labor manufactured boots from pasteboard, he yet could not find customers to buy them; they would have no exchange-value, because they would be useless; in other words, *because they would have no use-value*. Use-value is, therefore, an essential element of exchange-value.

But there are objects of use-value which have no exchange-value. Air and light, for instance, are

[1] *Hohoff* (Warenwert und Kapitalprofit, p 5) writes as follows "Commodities become commensurable only by abstracting from their use-value Linen, iron, wheat, the Iliad, illuminating-gas, arsenic, Eau de Cologne, and *Asafœtida*, etc , cannot be compared to another and measured by one another regarding their utility or use-value " And why not? In their specific use-value they differ indeed, yet they all agree in this, that they are useful to man, that they supply some human demand, in this respect they can be compared, estimated, and measured according to a fixed standard

useful though not exchangeable commodities. Very
true; but what follows from this fact? Only this,
that mere usefulness does not suffice to constitute
exchange-value; that other conditions must be added;
but it by no means follows that those things which
have exchange-value do not owe this value at least
in part to their usefulness. What would Marx say
to the following argument? There are men who are
not artists; therefore the notion of man does not
belong to the notion of an artist. The conclusion
drawn by Marx is not more logical. In order that
a useful object may have exchange-value it must be
fit to pass into the exclusive possession of an individual,
and must not be forthcoming in such quantities that
all can have of it whenever they please. But this
supposed, the exchange-value of an object depends
chiefly upon its use-value, or utility. In the primeval
forests of South America wood has no exchange-value,
either because there is no one to use it, or because every
one can have it for nothing, like air and water. But
suppose a merchant brings several shiploads of different kinds of wood to a European harbor, what will
then be the standard of its value? Is it the amount of
labor, the amount of expense and time, which the
transportation has cost? Certainly not; otherwise
all different species of wood conveyed from South
America would sell at the same price, which is not
the case. The better and more durable material will
sell at a higher rate. Fine cedar or mahogany,
abstracting altogether from the labor expended on it,
has a much greater exchange-value than pine or
birch.

By a thousand such instances we might show that
the value or price of an article is determined in the

first place by the general estimate of its usefulness. Good wine sells at a higher rate than bad wine, although the vintner may have expended the same amount of labor on the preparation of both. Why do our mine-owners sell coal from the same mine at different prices? Because the quality is different. In short, it is the quality, or the different degrees of objective goodness, that generally determines the exchange-value of objects independently of the amount of labor consumed upon them.

It would be carrying coal to Newcastle to attempt any further proofs of this truth. Nor can it be objected against the examples alleged that in all cases labor is necessary to give the object real value, for we do not deny that labor has a certain influence upon the exchange-value; but we do say that labor alone does not constitute exchange-value. For the rest, labor generally comes into account only in so far as it tends to give greater usefulness to a thing. Besides, there are in nature also objects which require no labor in order to be made useful, but which may be directly appropriated and exchanged for other commodities. Such are, for instance, coal-oil, wild fruits, etc.[1] Thus also in the products of human labor the exchange-value is determined in the first place not by the "socially necessary labor-time," but by their artistic qualities or other intrinsic perfections. If two authors, after an equal amount of labor and

[1] Cf Von Hammerstein, S J Stimmen aus Maria-Laach, vol x. p 426, *Hitze*, Kapital und Arbeit (1880), p 9 sqq. According to St Alphonsus Liguori (Theol. moral 1 3, n 801 sqq) it is the common doctrine of Catholic theologians that the price or exchange-value of an object depends not only on the labor expended in its production, but also on many other circumstances, on the utility of the commodity, on supply and demand, etc Thus St Thomas (S theol 2 2 q 77, a 2 ad 3) declares that the price of an article of merchandise is determined not by the degree of perfection of its nature, because sometimes a horse is dearer than a slave, but by the utility which man derives from the object in question.

preparation, publish their works, which of the two will have the larger sale? His, no doubt, which appears to the public more perfect in contents and expression. What determines the value and price of paintings at an exposition? Surely not the "socially necessary labor-time," but their intrinsic perfection, the fruit of genius rather than of labor. Why will a painting or even a pencil-sketch of Raphael or Dürer fetch such fabulous prices? Why are old manuscripts, rare prints, ancient medals and coins, and other things of that kind paid for so lavishly? Is it on account of the labor represented in them? Is it not rather their rarity, their perfection, their importance for the history of civilization, or something of that sort?

3. *Marx involves himself in contradictions.* According to Marx's theory of value the rate of profit, i.e., the relation of surplus-value to the total capital invested in any enterprise, must needs vary according to the "organic composition of the capitals." The value of raw materials and machines, the amount of materials used, and the wear on the machines differ considerably in different undertakings.[1] It is therefore to be expected that at the same rate of surplus-value every branch of industry should show a different rate of profit. But what is the case in reality? Here we find it to be a general law that capitals of equal magnitude yield equal profits regardless of their composition. Marx himself concedes the fact and acknowledges that it appears to be in flagrant contradiction to his law of value. But now how does he set about harmonizing facts and theory? Spirited controversies were carried on for years, within and without

[1] Capital, vol III. part I. p. 132.

socialist circles, as to how Marx would unravel this Gordian knot, a feat which he had reserved for the third volume of his "Capital." The volume has finally been published by Engels, and lo! Marx simply abandons his law of value. He confesses quite candidly that the rate of profit is independent of the composition of capitals, and that mercantile commodities are sold not according to their value—i.e., the labor contained in them—but partly below, partly above their value.[1]

Therefore Marx in the first instance bases his law of value upon experience, and acknowledges finally that his law is contradicted by experience. Of course, he endeavors to prop up his tottering law of value by the assertion that the sum total of prices paid corresponds to the sum total of values.[2] This contention is ably refuted by Boehm-Bawerk, who remarks that the purpose of the law of value can be no other than to formulate and explain the actual ratio of exchange of the various commodities. We wish to know why, e.g., a coat has as much value in exchange as twenty yards of linen, and according to what standard the exchange is effected. This is the purpose assigned to the law of value by Marx himself. But the ratio of exchange comes into question only in reference to single commodities.[3] But if it is granted that the ratio of exchange of single commodities is not determined by their value (the labor contained in them), then also the law of value is abandoned, and it is an arbitrary and useless assertion to maintain that the law of value remains in force for the sum total of commodities exchanged.

[1] *Ibid.*
[2] *Ibid*, p 140.
[3] *Boehm-Bawerk*, Zum Abschluss des Marxschen Systems, p 116 sqq.

4. If, therefore, the exchange-value of commodities is not determined exclusively by labor, but, above all, by their utility and applicability in the satisfaction of human needs, then also the entire theory of surplus-value, of the nature of capital, of the accumulation of capital, etc., must needs collapse, for all these are but deductions from the theory of value. We agree with Marx when he says: "The wages of labor are not what they seem to be [to many], namely, the value or price of labor itself; they are but the value or price of labor capacity." For, the contract between employer and laborer is ordinarily no more than a contract of hire. The laborer hires out his labor capacity, and in return receives the price of hire, in other words, the price for his hired-out labor capacity. But when Marx maintains that the exchange-value or the value of hire of human-labor capacity is determined by the cost of its production, he is but drawing a false conclusion from his theory of value. For, even supposing that two laborers need equally as much for their own support and for their families, still their labor capacities may differ widely as to their exchange-value, in so far as one man is more experienced, talented, skilful, and reliable than the other. A skilled worker will find employment sooner and receive better pay than the raw novice. As in all commodities, so also in labor capacity the value in exchange is determined in the first place by utility and practical applicability.

Just this very example, the difference in exchange-value of different labor capacities according to the utility of each, deals the death-blow to the Marxian theory of value. In accordance with this theory the exchange-value of labor capacity should be regulated by the cost of producing and sustaining it. This, however, is not the case. Why is a higher salary awarded to a capable, experienced, reliable manager, engineer, physician, or foreman than to an ordinary workman? Why do the perquisites of "star" actors, musicians, and singers often reach such enormous figures, whilst others in the same walk of life must be satisfied with a mere pittance despite their painstaking labor? Does the "star" actress, perhaps, need so much more for her sustenance than another? Or can talent, genius, beauty of voice and action, and similar qualities be reduced to the standard of "average labor-time," so that their cost may be figured out?

The collapse of Marx's theory of value necessarily implies also that of his other assertion, that the laborer needs but a part of his actual labor-time in order to produce an equivalent for the price of his labor capacity—the necessary labor-time—and that during the rest of the time he is doing "surplus work" for the benefit of the capitalist. The untenability of this assertion becomes still more evident, if we consider that according to Marx "the value of labor is determined not only by the labor-time necessary for the sustenance of the individual laborer, but also by that required for the sustenance of his family." [1] Who on earth has told Marx that *every* wage-earner imparts to the manufactured commodities not only as much exchange-value as is required for his own support and that of his family, but also something over and above, which is freely appropriated by the capitalist as surplus-value?

In fine, the entire socialist theory of value is so absurd that we are forced to ask ourselves, how could a man of Marx's talent and capacity hit upon such a

[1] Capital, vol 1 p. 359.

theory and make it the foundation of his whole system? The only explanation to be found in this is that in a very one-sided manner he took into consideration only the condition of industrial wage-earners, generalized that which is applicable to them under certain circumstances, and by purely ideological processes developed it into a comprehensive theory, into a so-called "scientific" system.

To meet a possible objection we would here remark that even in the socialist state the exchange-value of goods would still remain, and could not, even in socialistic circumstances, be determined by the labor spent in its production, for not only in commerce with foreign nations, but also in the division of produce among individuals, the exchange-value of goods would have to be taken into account, and even in this case it would be determined chiefly by the standard of usefulness. If two laborers in the socialist state would perform the same amount of work, it would be unjust to give to one as a remuneration a case of Johannisberger or Rudesheimer, and to the other the same amount of bad Mosel wine, or cider, on the plea that both the productions cost the same amount of labor. So also in the socialist state more labor could be procured for a bushel of good wheat than for the same amount of bad wheat, although the expenditure of labor upon the bad wheat may be just the same as upon the good. The same may be said of all similar commodities.

§ II.   *Concentration of Industries.*

Another fundamental tenet of the Marxian system is the assertion that the present capitalist order of production *necessarily leads to an increasing concentration of all industries, so that at last all industries on a small or medium scale are absorbed by a few industries on a colossal scale.*

Marx evidently reached this conclusion by arbitrarily generalizing certain phenomena to be met with in industry properly so called.

1. In the industries carried on by machinery and on a large scale there seems to be a certain tendency toward centralization and toward the crowding out of establishments on a small or medium scale.

In the MINING INDUSTRY of Germany the number of establishments has decreased since 1872, whilst their size increased. The following table shows the average change:

Average Time.	Number of Establishments.	Average Number of Wage-earners (in the Principal Establishments).	Sum of the Products in Thousands of Tons.
1871–1875	4,218	277,878	51,056
1881–1885	2,804	329,092	80,230
1891–1895	2,325	423,275	112,634
1896–1898	2,153	471,197	140,062
1900	2,470	573,078	174,666

The number, therefore, of establishments is decreasing, whilst the number of laborers and still more so the sum total of products is growing; only during the very latest years the number of establishments has been increased by new enterprises. Also in the SMELTING INDUSTRY the principal establishments have gone down from 241 in 1891 to 237 in 1895, but rose again to 241 in 1900, whilst the average number of wage-earners was 47,627 in 1891, 47,201 in 1895, and 59,664 in 1900, and the sum total of products rose from 4,148,000 tons in 1886 to 6,323,000 tons in 1895, and to 9,732,000 in 1900.[1]

The number of active *Breweries* decreased from 12,535 in 1877 to 7847 in 1895, and to 6903 in 1900, whilst on the other hand the total output rose from 20,360 million hectolitres (1 hectolitre = about 24 gallons) in 1877 to 37,733 million in 1895, and to 44,734 million in 1900.[2]

If we compare the productive establishments in general, excluding agriculture and forestry, we learn from the statistics of the German Empire that industries on a small or medium scale are growing more numerous rather than the reverse, though not increasing at the same rate as industries on a large scale. Thus there are enumerated:

[1] Statistisches Jahrbuch für das Deutsche Reich, 1902, p. 32.
[2] *Ibid.*, p. 36.

	In 1882.	In 1895.
Industries on a small scale (1–5 persons)	2,882,768	2,934,723
" " medium " (6–50 ")	112,715	191,301
" " large " (51 and over)	9,974	18,953

Therefore from 1882 to 1895 industries on a small scale increased 1.8%, those on a medium scale 69.7%, those on a large scale increased 90 per cent.[1]

From the statistics thus far available we cannot, indeed, as yet arrive at any final and conclusive judgment regarding industries. It is evidently still open to question whether this tendency toward centralization is altogether general and unlimited, though the great trusts in the United States are a mighty step in that direction. In any case it is unwarranted to conclude from the centralization of industries to the centralization of property, because industries on a large scale are owned for the most part by joint-stock companies. Very often, therefore, the amalgamation of several establishments into one or the expansion of one which is now owned by a stock company, implies the transfer of property from a few persons to a great many.

2. In industrial establishments therefore a certain centralizing tendency cannot be denied, but in AGRICULTURE there is noticeable a marked tendency favoring the growth of establishments on a small or medium scale.

In the *German Empire* the census of 1882 and that of 1895 show the following figures:[2]

	Below 2 ha.*	Below 2–5 ha.	Below 5–20 ha.
In the year 1882:			
Number of holdings.........	3,061,831	981,407	926,605
Total area in *ha*.	2,159,358	3,832,902	11,492,017
Average area in *ha*..........	0.71	3.91	12.40
In the year 1895:			
Number of holdings.........	3,236,367	1,016,318	998,804
Total area in *ha*.	2,415,914	4,142,071	12,537,660
Average area in *ha*..........	0.75	4.08	12.55

* *ha* = 2.47 acres.

[1] Statistisches Jahrbuch für das Deutsche Reich, 1902, p. 24.
[2] Statistik des Deutschen Reiches, Neue Folge, cxii. p. 11*.

	Below 20—100 *ha.*	Above 100 *ha.*	Total.
In the year 1882:			
Number of holdings.........	281,510	24,991	5,276,344
Total area in *ha.*...........	12,415,463	10,278,941	40,178,681
Average area in *ha.*.........	44.10	411.31	7.61
In the year 1895:			
Number of holdings.........	281,767	25,061	5,558,317
Total area in *ha.*...........	13,157,201	11,031,896	43,284,742
Average area in *ha.*.........	46.70	440.26	7.79

If we classify holdings of an area less than 5 acres as dwarf farms, those from 5 to 12.5 acres as small farms, those from 12.5 to 50 acres as medium, those from 50 to 250 acres as large farms and the rest as *latifundia,* then we find

	In 1895.	In 1882.
The number of dwarf farms.............	3,236,367	3,061,831
" " " small "	1,016,318	981,407
" " " medium "	998,804	926,605
" " " large "	281,767	281,510
" " " *latifundia*................	25,061	24,991

Therefore, the number of *latifundia* and large farms remained practically unchanged, whilst the medium farms increased by 72,100, the small farms by 34,832, and the dwarf farms by 173,338.

The distribution of the total agricultural area among the different classes of holdings is shown by the following table:

	Total Agricultural Area in Different Classes of Holdings.		Percentage of the Agricultural Area Occupied by the Different Holdings.	
	In 1895, *ha.*	In 1882, *ha.*	In 1895, Per Cent.	In 1882, Per Cent.
Dwarf farms.........	2,415,914	2,159,358	5.56	5.73
Small "	4,142,071	3,832,902	10.11	10.01
Medium "	12,537,660	11,492,017	29.90	28.74
Large "	13,157,201	12,415,463	30.35	31.09
Latifundia.............	11,031,896	10,278,941	24.08	24.43
Total............	43,284,742	40,178,681	100.00	100.00

This shows that from 1882 to 1895 "the intermediate farms have grown in number and size at the expense of the dwarf farms and the *latifundia.*" [1]

In *France* the agricultural holdings classified according to size were as follows:

Size of Holdings.	In 1882.		In 1892.	
	Number of Holdings.	Percentage.	Number of Holdings.	Percentage.
Less than 1 *ha.*	2,167,667	38.22	2,235,405	39.20
Between 1 and 10 *ha.*	2,635,030	46.46	2,617,558	45.90
" 10 " 40 "	727,222	12.82	711,118	12.47
More than 40 *ha.*	142,088	2.50	138,671	2.43
Total	5,672,007	100.00	5,702,752	100.00

If we compare the number of holdings and the area occupied by them in 1882 and 1892, excluding the area contained in the state forests, we get the following results:

Size of Holdings.	In 1882.			
	Number of Holdings.	Area in *ha.*	Percentage of Total Area.	Average Area of Holdings in *ha.*
Less than 1 *ha.*	2,167,667	1,083,833	2.18	0.50
Between 1 and 10 *ha.*	2,635,030	11,366,274	22.92	4.31
" 10 " 40 "	727,222	14,845,650	29.94	20.41
More than 40 *ha.*	142,088	22,296,104	44.96	156.71
Total	5,672,007	49,591,861	100.00	8.74

Size of Holdings.	In 1892.			
	Number of Holdings.	Area in *ha.*	Percentage of Total Area.	Average Area of Holdings in *ha.*
Less than 1 *ha.*	2,235,405	1,327,253	2.69	0.59
Between 1 and 10 *ha.*	2,617,558	11,244,750	22.77	4.29
" 10 " 40 "	711,118	14,313,417	28.99	20.13
More than 40 *ha.*	138,671	22,493,393	45.55	162.21
Total	5,702,752	49,378,813	100.00	8.65

[1] Statistik des Deutschen Reiches, Neue Folge. cxii. p. 11*.

There were therefore but slight changes during the period from 1882 to 1892. The holdings exceeding 40 *ha* decreased by 3,417, but the area occupied by them increased by 197,288 *ha* or merely 0.60% of the total agricultural area. The dwarf farms increased by 67,738 and their area by 243,420 *ha*. The holdings between 1 and 40 *ha* decreased by 33,632 and their total area by 653,807 *ha*. Unlike Germany, France shows a tendency of increasing the number of dwarf farms. But even according to the statistics of 1892 the small farms (3–100 acres) make up more than half the number (58.37%) of all the holdings and occupy more than half the total area (51.76%). The total number of agricultural holdings in France in 1892—excluding Algiers and the colonies—was 5,702,752.[1]

The state of agricultural holdings in the *United States* is shown by the following tables:[2]

Year.	Number of Farms.	Number of Farms Operated by—		
		Owners.*	Cash Tenants.	Share Tenants.
1900......	5,737,372	3,712,408	751,665	1,273,299
1890†....	4,564,641	3,269,728	454,659	840,254
1880†....	4,008,907	2,984,306	322,357	702,244

* Includes farms operated by owners, part owners and tenants, and managers.
† Not including farms with an area less than 3 acres.

The total number of farms increased therefore by 555,734 from 1880 to 1890, and by 1,172,731 from 1890 to 1900.

With regard to the size of the farms there were in

	10 and under 20 Acres.	20 and under 50 Acres.	50 and under 100 Acres.	100 and under 500 Acres.	500 and under 1,000 Acres.	1,000 Acres and over.
1900.....	406,641	1,257,496	1,366,038	2,290,282	102,526	47,160
1890.....	265,550	902,777	1,121,485	2,008,694	84,395	31,546
1880.....	254,749	781,574	1,032,810	1,695,983	75,972	28,578

From this table it is evident that all classes of farms increased in absolute numbers, most of all those from 10 to 500 acres. In

[1] *Ibid.*, pp. 58*-59*.
[2] Twelfth census, vol. v. pp. 688–690.

the percentage of total number of farms those above 1000 acres rose from 0.7% in 1880 to 0.8% in 1900, whilst those from 10 to 20 acres rose from 6.3% in 1880 to 7.1% in 1900, and those from 20 to 50 acres rose from 19.5% in 1880 to 21.9% in 1900; farms of other areas have slightly decreased in percentage.

If we turn our attention to *Holland* we find also there an increase in the number of agricultural holdings, as is proved by the following statistics:[1]

Size of Holdings.	Number.		Percentage.	
	In 1895.	In 1885.	In 1895.	In 1885.
1 to 5 ha.	78,277	70,132	46.70	44.85
5 " 10 "	34,360	32,227	20.50	20.61
10 " 20 "	29,708	28,629	17.72	18.31
20 " 50 "	21,810	21,776	13.01	13.93
50 " 100 "	3,282	3,355	1.96	2.14
100 " 150 "	135	170	0.08	0.11
150 and over.	41	80	0.03	0.05
Total.	167,613	156,369	100.00	100.00

In the classes ranging from 1 to 50 *ha* the holdings have increased in number, in those ranging above 50 *ha* they have decreased. The decrease is most striking in the *latifundia*. It is to be regretted that in the above statistics the holdings under 1 *ha* (garden-plots) have not been considered. In any case the above numbers prove that Holland possesses a goodly number of small farmers owning from 5 to 10 *ha* each.

Great Britain, the classic land of industrial enterprises, deserves our special attention. If anywhere, it was here that capitalism ought to produce the fruits prophesied by Marx. But what do we learn from the official statistics?[2] The agricultural holdings were as follows:

The totals of 1885 and 1895 cannot be compared, since in 1895 the holdings under one acre were not counted. But a comparison of the holdings exceeding one acre will show results similar to those noticed in Germany. Also in Great

---

[1] Statistik des Deutschen Reiches, cxii. p. 61*.
[2] Cf. *ibid.*, pp. 62*–63*.

Britain the areas of 1885 and 1895 prove that the intermediate farms have increased, whilst the *latifundia* have gone back somewhat.

Size of Holdings.	In 1885.		In 1895.	
	Number.	Area.	Number.	Area.
Less than 1 acre........	23,512	11,195	?	?
From 1 to 5 acres..	135,736	389,677	117,968	366,792
" 5 " 20 " ..	148,806	1,656,827	149,818	1,667,647
" ' 20 " 50 " ..	84,149	2,824,527	85,663	2,864,976
" 50 " 100 " ..	64,715	4,746,520	66,625	4,885,203
" 100 " 300 " ..	79,573	13,658,495	81,245	13,875,914
" 300 " 500 " ..	13,875	5,241,168	13,568	5,113,945
" 500 " 1,000 " ..	4,826	3,147,228	4,616	3,001,184
Over 1,000 acres........	663	882,615	603	801,852
Total.............	555,855	32,558,252	520,106	32,577,513

That there is no danger of the gradual absorption of small establishments by production on a large scale—especially not in agriculture—is evident from what political economists call the *law of increasing and diminishing returns.* In certain kinds of business the returns increase in proportion to their magnitude, i.e., in proportion to the capital and labor expended. The increasing size of the business reduces the relative cost of many items, as raw materials, machines, transportation, management, etc. This is the case, however, only in certain purely industrial enterprises. But there are other branches of business where the extension of production beyond a certain limit is attended by more loss than profit, and where, therefore, the rate of profit diminishes in proportion to the size. Experience so far seems to point to the fact that agricultural production is subject to this law of diminishing returns, at least on estates which go beyond a certain area. The reason for this is the fact that the growth of population renders necessary a more intensive culti-vation of the soil, a thing which is possible only in establishments on a small or intermediate scale. Only perfect knowledge and mastery of the soil will enable the owner of land to use it to the best advantage. Only the small or medium farmer will give equally to every part of his property the greatest amount of care, and will employ on it even his leisure hours, if perchance he

should have some other occupation. Also in the matter of fer-
tilizing and irrigation he can achieve much more than the owner
of extensive tracts of land.

A Schaffle remarks very correctly:[1] "The denser the population, the more its sustenance is to be secured by production
on a small or medium scale, which may be aided, not supplanted,
by co-operative institutions. The results of Bernhardi's classical work on 'Landed Estates, Great and Small,' concerning
gross and net returns, will not be shaken by the trumpet-blasts
of socialist world-reformers" In the same strain A. Wagner
avers with regard to agricultural production: "Where no special
causes of a political or legal nature are at work, there can be no
question of an economic and technical superiority of production
on a large over production on a small scale, at least not of a
general superiority. The inference that production and property
on a small scale will necessarily be supplanted by large estates
is just as false as that other one, that for the sake of better cultivation the change into large estates is desirable in the interests
of agricultural production and the labor forces engaged in it;
. . but least of all is the prognostication so generally unfavorable to production and property on a small scale, as modern
socialism would have it. Rather the reverse is the case, if we
consider the law of intensive cultivation which is developing in
proportion to the increase in numbers and wealth of the population, in proportion to the growing size of cities, and the wider
market open to agricultural products "[2] Buchenberger is of
exactly the same opinion.[3] Sering[4] remarks: "All the latest
investigations go to prove that public opinion prevalent heretofore has largely undervalued the technical productive capacity
of the small farmer   The net profits of large landed estates no
longer surpass those of intermediate farms."

This state of the case is so evident that even a number of socialists have been constrained to admit it   As early as the social-
democratic convention at Frankfort in 1894, Vollmar declared
in his report on the agrarian question: "In modern agriculture ·
production on a large scale proves to be not at all so very
superior in competition—unless under very special conditions—

[1] Die Aussichtslosigkeit der Sozialdemokratie (1885), p. 26
[2] Grundlegung der polit Oekonomie, 3d ed , II § 169
[3] Agrarwesen und Agrarpolitik, I. § 40, n 4
[4] Die innere Kolonisation im östlichen Deutschland (1893).

despite the many advantages it enjoys to the detriment of the community. This is the case not only in the raising of cereals, but much more so in the rearing of cattle, which latter is naturally on the increase since the world's market is open to it, whilst grain-raising has become unprofitable   Against this contention examples have been adduced from North America—monster ranches, hog-raising by steam, etc.   But such scattered instances, the results of which are not altogether beyond doubt, must be viewed rather sceptically, and least of all can they be generalized.   It may be stated as a general rule that if cattle-raising is carried on intensively and if there is a true care of cattle, the herds should not exceed a certain number, 60 to 70 head is about the limit.   In this manner cattle-raising is best adapted to establishments on a small or medium scale   The same may be said in general concerning the growing of fruit, grapes, vegetables, and other commercial plants   In the explanation of these circumstances so much at variance with our experiences in the field of industry we must consider in the first place that the tiller of the soil is not merely producing merchandise, but uses much of his produce for his own consumption . . From all this not a few agrarians draw the conclusion that in agriculture production on a large scale is superior only as long as cultivation is extensive, and that the economic development with its increasing intensity of production tends toward smaller establishments." [1]

Bernstein,[2] referring to a vast mass of statistics, remarks: "It is, therefore, beyond a doubt that in western Europe as well as in the eastern United States the small and intermediate agricultural establishments are increasing, whilst the large or monster farms are going back "   And in the *Vorwarts* (1899, n. 60) David writes· "After looking at the statistics of 1895 no one can seriously maintain that the farming class is tending toward economic ruin."

3. The middle classes find a safe refuge not only in agriculture, but also in the *mechanical trades* if they are

[1] Cf. the Transactions of the Social Democratic Party Convention (1894), p 147.
[2] Die Voraussetzungen des Sozialismus, p 65.

afforded the proper protection.   Recent investigations [1]
have proved to our mind that manual trades are not
doomed to destruction—at least not in the near future.
The one fact alone that, in spite of unlimited competition and great industrial development, German artisans and their families number more than six millions
is sufficient to prove that the mechanical trades are as
yet firmly established.

Certain lines of production, of course, have been monopolized
by factories; this fact cannot be controverted. People will
never forego the great reduction in point of cost and time of
production afforded by nail-factories, in order to resuscitate the
defunct trade of nailer.   Not only the nailer's trade, also those
of the cutler, dyer, weaver, spinner, have practically disappeared.
Also the shoemakers, joiners, tinsmiths, and locksmiths, at least
in the larger cities, barely maintain their ground and eke out a
scanty living.   On the other hand those engaged in certain por-
tions of the building trades—in roofing, painting, decorating,
paper-hanging, etc.—and also the bakers, butchers, upholsterers,
have not only held their own, but have even gained considerably.
Besides, a great number of artisans have started production on a
somewhat larger scale by the employment of journeymen helpers.
These trades will hardly ever be supplanted by factories.   In
fact, in many trades factory work is out of the question in so
far as they require the material to be fitted and fastened in place.
Such is the case in brick-laying, painting, paper-hanging, roofing,
plumbing, etc   Moreover, a good deal of new territory has been
opened to the artisan, as in gas and electric fixtures, in bicycle
and automobile repairs, in photographic work, and the like.

It should also not be overlooked that artisans heretofore were
unorganized and totally void of protection against unfair competition   And if they weathered the storm under such adverse
circumstances, they will do still better if they are protected by
organization.   Then, again, the distribution of the population
over the entire territory contributes to maintain the small trades.
If the people were massed together in large cities, there would be

[1] Untersuchungen über die Lage des Handwerks, published by the
"Verein für Sozialpolitik" (Leipsic, 1895 sqq.).

danger of an increasing concentration of production.   But in reality a great many people are scattered throughout the country in small towns, villages, and hamlets.   All these localities need their own establishments to provide their local needs This applies especially to the production of foodstuffs required in daily use—as bread and meat, which cannot easily be transported and preserved without danger of spoiling.

But above all in the *artistic trades* the handicraftsman will not easily be superseded.   Production by machinery and on a large scale provides for the general market· it cannot take regard of individual needs, desires, and tastes.   And yet individual needs and desires will always assert themselves   There is even reason enough to assume that the development of culture and education will intensify individual needs and tastes in matters of clothing, nourishment, upholstering, and decoration, and will consequently enhance the importance of the corresponding trades

Among the middle classes whose permanency is assured must finally be numbered those who are engaged in the liberal arts, in science, and literature. Society will always stand in need of physicians, druggists, surgeons, teachers, professors, editors, librarians, artists (painters, architects, sculptors, musicians, actors, etc.), engineers, judges, public functionaries in state and commune.   And yet none of these can be regarded as proletarians; the same must be said of commercial establishments on a small or medium scale which will not disappear—at least not in the country districts.

§ III.   *Concentration of Capital.   Theory of Pauperization.*

Socialists are masters in the art of repudiating or modifying former theories, as soon as they are shown to be in conflict with existing facts.   An instance in point is the theory of the progressive concentration of capital and of the concomitant "pauperization" of the proletariat. Liebknecht is reported by the *Vorwarts* to have said in a party meeting on April 25, 1900: "Bernstein also inveighs against the so-called pauperization theory. This theory has never been understood in the sense that the entire proletariat would first be buried in misery. Neither did Marx take it in that sense. *It is certainly true that the standard of living among workingmen has been improved as against formerly.* But none the less the workingman remains a proletarian. By this designation we do not mean a man plunged in misery, but one who has no chance of acquiring economic independence. It would be wilful blindness to deny that bourgeois society must finally collapse."

We are very thankful to Liebknecht for his admission that the economic situation of workingmen has been improved. But it is perfectly incorrect that Marx understood the pauperization theory in the sense indicated above. At least in their first period Marx and Engels spoke of a progressive pauperization of the proletariat. Their declarations on this point do not admit of any other explanation. We need but refer the reader to the passages quoted in a former chapter (p. 53): "One capitalist kills a good many others." "The concentration of the instruments of production and the socialization of labor reach a point where they become incompatible with their capitalist surroundings" In the Erfurt platform we read: "For the proletariat and the declining middle classes this social change is tantamount to a *growing* insecurity of existence, to *misery*, oppression, slavery, degradation, exploitation."

To bolster up the pauperization theory after some fashion or other many socialists speak now of *relative* pauperization. Absolutely speaking, they say, the situation of laborers is improving, but still the chasm between them and capitalists is widened, because the increase of wealth is proportionately greater with the latter than with the workingmen. A queer kind of pauperization! If my own position is improving, must I complain of an increase of misery, because my neighbor is improving more and acquiring wealth faster than I am? Besides, even this relative change of wealth cannot be universally maintained, as we shall see anon.

Till very recent times, however, socialists have described the condition of society in a way to make one believe that at present there exist only a small number of billionaires and a countless horde of pauperized proletarians. Already from the preceding paragraph it is evident that such descriptions are fraudulent exaggerations intended to rouse the passions of the poorer classes. Also the numerous establishments on a small or intermediate scale, whose permanence is beyond a doubt, necessarily imply the possession of capital in smaller quantities.

Moreover, the latest statistical returns go to prove that on the whole the income of the lower classes has been increasing. The distribution of wealth is indeed much too unequal, this we readily grant, but nevertheless we contend that the condition of the lower classes, more especially of the industrial laborers, has not become worse but better, and that therefore there can be no question of a progressive pauperization of workingmen.

In Saxony, e g , the individual persons whose income in 1879 was valued at less than 300 marks constituted 7 11% of the total population; in 1894, however, they had gone down to 5 61% At the same time the percentage of those whose income was less than 800 marks was reduced from 69.28% to 59.69%. On the other hand the percentage of incomes ranging between 800 and 950 marks rose from 5.27% to 8.96%, and that of the incomes between 900 and 1100 marks rose from 3.66% to 5.83%. Also the percentage of incomes from 1100 to 2800 marks has gone up. From 1894 to 1900 the number of persons whose income was less than 400 marks and who consequently were not taxed went down from 17.76% to 10.82%; the percentage of persons whose income did not reach 800 marks was reduced from 65.28% to 55.69%; the incomes of from 800 to 1600 marks rose from 24.02% to 31.34%, and those of from 1600 to 3300 marks rose from 7.12% to 8.07%.[1]

In the Grand Duchy of Baden 24.78% of the inhabitants were taxpayers in 1899, as against 19.73% in 1886. The percentage of taxpayers classified according to income is shown by the following table:

Income.	1886.	1899.
From 500 to 900 marks...............	63.7%	56.75%
" 1000 " 1400 "	16.9	21.73
" 1500 " 2900 "	13.3	14.86

In Prussia the number of taxpayers (whose income exceeds 900 marks) rose from 2,440,000 in 1892 to 3,380,000 in 1899, or from 8.15% of all the inhabitants to 10.09%. If the members of their several households are also taken into consideration, then 32.8% of the total population were valued at 900 marks and over in 1896, and 37.59% in 1899.

Income.	Taxpayers among 10,000 Inhabitants.	
	1892.	1899.
From 900 to 1200 marks................	367	440
" 1200 " 1500 "	143	160
" 1500 " 2100 "	124	133
" 2100 " 3000 "	75	88
Over 3000 marks.......................	106	119

[1] Cf. *Philippovich*, Grundriss der politischen Oekonomie, vol. I. p. 320. Handwörterbuch der Staatswissenschaften: Einkommen.

The growing number of taxpayers is shown by the preceding table, which indicates how many taxpayers of each class there are among 10,000 inhabitants.

In Great Britain and Ireland the total income of the people in 1851 was valued at £600,000,000, of which 260 million belonged to the class of those having an income exceeding £150. For the year 1881 the average calculation of the best statisticians showed a total income of more than 1200 million pounds, 540 million of which were assigned to the class with incomes above £150. In 1881, with an increase in population of 26%, there was, therefore, more money in the hands of non-taxpayers than among the whole nation in 1851, and almost twice as much as the same classes had in the last-mentioned year The increase in population was chiefly in the middle classes. The number of persons having an income of between £150 and £1000 increased from 300,000 to 990,000, the greatest advance being in those whose income ranges from £150 to £600. The average wealth of the United Kingdom has certainly gone up in the period of 1851 to 1881.[1]

That the laboring classes also had their share in the growing wealth is proved by the statistics of wages

The average yearly wages of an English mill-hand amounted

> from 1829–1831 to 546 shillings
>   "   1844–1846 " 564   "
>   "   1859–1861 " 670   "
>   "   1880–1882 " 844   "

Moreover, the price of ordinary provisions has not gone up for a very long time, but has rather been reduced The painstaking investigations of Samuel Andrews, secretary of the Oldham Master Cotton-spinners and Manufacturers, concerning the development of English cotton-mills from 1837 till 1887, proved

---

[1] Cf. Soziale Praxis, 6th year, p 948 — In his Voraussetzungen des Sozialismus, p 50, Bernstein concludes his proof for the fact that the number of property owners is not decreasing with the following peremptory remark "It is totally false to maintain that the present stage of evolution shows a relative, much less an absolute decrease of property owners The number of owners is growing not 'more or less,' but simply more, i e , absolutely and relatively more If the activity and prospects of social democracy depended on the decrease in number of property owners, socialism could indeed 'go to bed '" This is tantamount to a first-class funeral of orthodox Marxism

that in England in the year 1839–40 for a family of two adults and three children the average weekly expenses for food, heating, rent, clothing, etc., amounted to 34 s.; but in 1887 to 28 s. only. The receipts on the other hand—i.e., the wages of two adults—were only 21 s. in 1839–40 and 41 s. in 1887. Wages have advanced at a similar rate in other branches of industry.[1]

The change in wages from 1893 to 1900 is shown by the following table published by the *Labour Gazette* :[2]

Year.	Laborers Whose Wages Were Changed.		Net Results of the Changes per Week.	
	Number of Individuals.	Percentage of all the Laborers.	Total Amount in Pounds.	Average Amount for Each Person.
1893......	549,977	7	+ 12,425	+ 0 s. 5½ d.
1894......	670,386	8.5	− 45,091	− 1 " 4½ "
1895......	436,718	5.6	− 28,211	− 1 " 3½ "
1896......	607,654	7.7	+ 26,592	+ 0 " 10½ "
1897......	597,444	7.6	+ 31,507	+ 1 " 0¾ "
1898......	1,015,169	12.9	+ 80,815	+ 1 " 7 "
1899......	1,175,576	14.9	+ 92,905	+ 1 " 6½ "
1900......	1,088,300	13.8	+ 203,240	+ 3 " 8½ "

These figures prove that after a period of stagnation or even of retrogression, from 1893 to 1897, there were great advances in wages during the last three years, both as regards the number of laborers concerned and the amount of the increase. In fact, in 1900, more than one million laborers—14% of the total number—received a weekly advance in wages amounting to more than 2½ million dollars.

The general improvement in the situation of workingmen may also be concluded from the fact that the lower classes invest in stock companies and deposit their savings in banks and fraternal societies.

In England the cash assets of mutual benefit and savings associations consisting of or patronized chiefly by working people amount to 280 million pounds. Of these 100 million pounds are invested in stock.[3] Also in France, Belgium, etc., the working classes have large deposits in the savings-banks and mutuals.

The economic advancement of the laboring classes is proved

[1] Cf. Handbuch der Staatswissenschaften, article Arbeitslohn.
[2] Quoted by Soziale Praxis, 10th year, p. 416.
[3] Cf. *Local Government Journal*, quoted by Soziale Praxis (1897), p. 949.

to evidence by the report of the *Royal Commission on Labour* appointed by the English government to investigate labor conditions in England and Scotland. The majority report of this commission, published in 1894, speaks as follows: "Our investigations have confirmed the general impression that during the **last** fifty years wages have advanced considerably both as regards the nominal value and—with the exception of house-rent in large cities—as regards the buying power for the purchase of the respective necessaries With regard to sanitation the condition of labor is much improved If the general advance in wages of the year 1872, its subsequent permanence or even increase on the one hand, the reduction in price of the working people's articles of consumption on the other hand are admitted as undisputed facts, then the remark is justifiable that on the whole the condition of the laboring classes has made great advances during the last fifty years " This report was signed by Th. Burt, Ed Trow, and J. Burnett, three of the most prominent English labor leaders A minority of the commission consisting of four socialistic laborers, though reporting less favorably on the situation of the working classes, still admitted unreservedly that there is no question of its having become worse "On the contrary, we believe that by the legal and other reforms of the last sixty years the average condition of wage-earners has been steadily improving " [1]

The condition of laborers may not be everywhere as favorable as in England, but in almost all countries, especially in France and Belgium, the continual improvement of their position is undeniable.

With regard to Belgium Dr. F. Waxweiler, professor of political economy at the University of Brussels and chief of the Labor Bureau, has published very interesting investigations [2] By a detailed and accurate comparison of wages in 1896 and 1900, based on the official statistics of the Belgian coal-mining industry, he arrives at the following conclusions:

1. There has been a general advance in wages This general advance was very noticeable from 1896 to 1900. 2 Wages under two francs a day have disappeared altogether. 3 Daily wages have in many new instances been advanced beyond 7 50 francs.

---

[1] Cf. *Herkner*, Die Arbeiterfrage, 2d ed , p. 312 sqq
[2] Jahrbücher für Nationalökonomie und Statistik, 3d series, xxii p. 161 sqq.

The average yearly receipts of mine-workers in the kingdom of Saxony were 744 marks in 1869, 876 marks in 1872, 942 marks in 1875, 829 marks in 1878, 821 marks in 1881, 854 marks in 1884, 870 marks in 1885. In figuring out these average wages also women and children are taken into account. The average wages of pitmen were 855 marks in 1869, 956 marks in 1872, 1100 marks in 1875, 956 marks in 1878, the same in 1881, 961 marks in 1884, 995 marks in 1885.[1]

Prussia has furnished us with very instructive statistics of the five principal coal-mining districts. If we designate the underground miners as class A, other workingmen occupied underground as class B, and all other male adults working during the day as class C, we get the following tables showing the average yearly wages.[2]

Upper Silesia.				Ruhr District.			
Year.	Class A Marks.	Class B Marks.	Class C Marks.	Year.	Class A Marks.	Class B Marks.	Class C Marks.
1889	638	614	539	1889	1028	817	857
1891	774	728	649	1891	1217	925	950
1893	727	704	639	1893	1084	791	878
1895	740	713	634	1895	1114	816	893
1896	768	731	640	1896	1203	862	934
1897	794	765	648	1897	1328	926	993
Lower Silesia.				Saar District.			
1889	728	727	634	1889	913	773	692
1891	824	779	690	1891	1212	1018	908
1893	775	762	687	1893	1021	794	812
1895	796	765	669	1895	1030	796	826
1896	814	793	685	1896	1079	821	826
1897	849	820	709	1897	1101	838	820
Aix-la-Chapelle District.							
1889	913	773	692				
1891	1062	877	807				
1893	920	764	795				
1895	951	788	806				
1896	991	806	834				
1897	1068	850	852				

[1] Cf. Handwörterbuch der Staatswissenschaften, article Arbeitslohn.
[2] Cf. Jahresbericht des Vereins für bergbauliche Interessen im Oberbergbezirk Dortmund (1897), p. 57.

For the years 1899 and 1900 the *Reichsanzeiger* published the following average wages of Prussian mine-workers without regard to occupation:

	1899	1900
Anthracite coal mining in Upper Silesia.....	M. 801	M. 877
In Lower Silesia.....................	" 846	" 910
In the northern district of Dortmund.	" 1265	" 1348
" " southern " " "	" 1233	" 1296
In the districts of Dortmund and Osna-brück combined....................	" 1255	" 1332
Near Saarbrücken (state mines).........	" 1019	" 1044
Near Aix-la-Chapelle.	" 1069	" 1194
Bituminous coal mining, district of Halle....	" 871	" 931
Salt mining, district of Halle..............	" 1100	" 1142

The so-called "law" of the increasing pauperization of laborers is thus proved to be a fiction in flagrant contradiction with reality. No wonder that nowadays thoughtful socialists generally admit quite freely that in the face of facts this "law" has become untenable.[1] In connection herewith it is worthy of note that Marx himself already in the first edition of "Capital" (1867),[2] trying to prove progressive pauperization, acknowledges that since legal protection has been granted to workingmen there has begun "a physical and moral regeneration of factory laborers which must have struck the dullest eye." Also Engels, in prefacing the second edition (1887) of his work, "Die Lage der arbeitenden Klassen in England," which first appeared in 1845, remarks that its descriptions in many points no longer applied to present conditions.

[1] Cf. *Vorwärts*, 1897, n. 106 and 141.
[2] P. 273; 4th ed., p. 259.

§ IV. *Theory of Collapse and Crisis.*

The demolished dogma of the progressive pauperization of laborers involves in its ruin all the inferences derived from it. Marx and Engels had proclaimed that on the average every tenth year there would occur stupendous economical and financial crises which would shake society to its very foundations. According to the Erfurt platform "the chasm between rich and poor is widened by those financial *crises* which are grounded in the very nature of capitalistic production—crises which become ever more extensive and destructive, make universal insecurity the normal state of society, and give evidence that the productive forces of our age have become uncontrollable by society."

But where are the crises which ever become more extensive and destructive? In comparison with former times the number and extent of financial crises has rather diminished.[1] For the most part they were restricted to certain districts or branches of industry, and least of all must we look for their causes in the "very nature of capitalistic production," but in the artful manœuvres and unprincipled knaveries of cunning intriguers. We need but call to mind the Panama Canal swindle, the Banca Romana affair,

---

[1] A socialist writer in the *Vorwärts*, 1898 (n. 43, 2. supplement), Konrad Schmidt, criticises Marx's contention of the development of capitalist society toward a "collapse and catastrophe" which will necessitate armed interference and the proclamation of a dictatorship on the part of the proletariat. Says Schmidt: "The last fifty years of social evolution have not as yet borne out the prognostication. *The catastrophies have not materialized . . . the financial crises . . . have lost in acuteness and extent.* And however terribly large masses of the proletariat may suffer by the most shameful exploitation, *the prediction that the laborer will sink deeper as industry progresses, that the fate of his class under the capitalist system will be increasing pauperization, this prediction has not been fulfilled.* In the very mother-country of capitalism, in England, the situation of large numbers of workingmen . . . has been greatly improved."

and other frauds of a like nature. If the several governments had done their duty many of these crises could have been avoided.

The introduction of machinery in different lines of business within a very short time caused such a revolution of industrial conditions, that it took some time to realize the situation and to legislate accordingly. Indications, however, seem to point to a more peaceful and better regulated future also in the field of economics. Crises are not multiplying, but diminishing. Therefore also on this head the socialist theory of history has proved to be an enormous exaggeration contradicted by the actual facts.

§ V. *The Industrial Reserve Army.*

What are we to think, finally, of the increasing number of "discarded" laborers, of the steadily growing "army of supernumerary workingmen"? They exist only in socialist writings. Yet we are far from denying that nowadays men are out of work often enough, and that it must be one of the first cares of social reformers to remedy this evil. But we absolutely deny that this evil is a necessary consequence of private ownership in the means of production, or that it cannot be eliminated in the existing order of society.

As a matter of fact want of employment has not increased since the middle of last century In this respect England furnishes us very accurate information The number of able-bodied paupers in England and Wales has decreased almost continually since 1849, with the exception of 1863 and 1864, which show unusually high figures.

Relief was granted to the following numbers of adult able-bodied laborers:

In 1849 to 228,823, or 13 2 in every 1000 of the average population
" 1859 " 135,784, "   7 0 "   "   "   "   "   "
" 1869 " 170,710, "   8 8 "   "   "   "   "   "
" 1879 " 104,970, "   4 2 "   "   "   "   "   "
" 1889 "   98,817, "   3 4 "   "   "   "   "   "
" 1890 "   92,118, "   3 2 "   "   "   "   "   "

From 1891 to 1895 there seems to have been a slight increase in the number of the relieved   Of course, not all who were out of employment were the recipients of official relief.   Nevertheless, it is fair to conclude from the number of one category to that of the other.   Moreover, it should not be overlooked that at present the working class is far more numerous than formerly.

Also in the German Empire the last few years have shown that the number of the unemployed is not at all as formidable as people were formerly inclined to believe.   According to a census taken on December 2, 1895, there were on that day, at the worst season of the year, in the whole of Germany 553,640 unemployed, i e, able-bodied laborers out of work, a percentage of 3 43% of the whole number of workingmen.[1]   Even G Adler, who certainly cannot be accused of extreme antisocialist bias, is of opinion that according to modern statistics we are justified in not making too high an estimate of the number of the unemployed.[2]

Modern methods of production, far from rendering the workingman superfluous, have procured employment for an ever-growing number of men   The English cotton industry employed 259,336 hands in 1839; 330,924 in 1850; 450,087 in 1870; 492,903 in 1879; 528,795 in 1890. This does not look like rendering the workingman superfluous.   In Germany the official statistics mark an increase in the number of employees in manufactures, mining, smelting, and the building trades from 6,699,026 in 1882 to 8,601,354 in 1895.[3]   The average number of wage-earners in the mining industry rose from 273,930 in 1872 to 337,193 in 1886, to 430,155 in 1895, and to 573,078 in 1900.[4]   Also in the smelting industry the average number of wage-

[1] Cf Statistik des Deutschen Reiches, New Series, cu p 301.   On June 14, 1895, the number of unemployed laborers was 179,004 (p. 300).
[2] Handwörterbuch der Staatswissenschaften, article Arbeitslosigkeit.
[3] Cf Jahrbücher fur Nationalökonomie und Statistik, 3d series, xv. p. 87.
[4] Cf Statistisches Jahrbuch fur das Deutsche Reich, 1888, p 29, 1897, p. 35 1902, p 31

earners rose from 38,489 in 1872 to 42,402 in 1886, to 47,201 in 1895 and to 59 664 in 1900

The intrinsic reason why the workingman has not been superseded by machinery is not difficult to grasp. Machines, of course, are labor-saving devices and replace a good many workingmen, but on the other hand they widen existing fields of production and open up new ones. Moreover, machines must be constructed, tended, and repaired. To provide for the increased amount of raw material, to transport the finished products calls for additional forces. The hand of man is required to put the last finishing touch to the products of machinery. The invention of new machines as a rule also discloses new sources of revenue and employment. It may suffice to call to mind the telegraph and telephone service, the new photographic and printing processes, the plastic and ceramic industries, etc.

Thus we come to the undoubted conclusion: Both the materialistic conception of history and its application as the basis of socialism are huge fallacies. Out of certain abuses and drawbacks, which undoubtedly existed in industrial circles during the middle of the past century, and by means of unwarrantable exaggerations, arbitrary generalizations, and deductions, there has been concocted a general theory made to order as the "scientific" basis of socialism.

It is rather queer that the so-called "revisionists," headed by Bernstein—and their number among prominent socialists is very considerable—discard these fundamental tenets and still profess to be adherents of socialism. Bernstein himself went so far as to put up the paradoxical assertion: "The prospects of socialism depend, not on the decrease, but on the growth of social wealth. Socialism, or rather the socialist movement of modern times, has outlived many a superstition; it will outlive also the superstition that its future depends on the concentration of property, or, if you prefer, on the absorption of surplus-value by a diminishing number of capitalist mammoths. To the nine or ten million fathers of families who are despoiled by the transaction, it makes no difference in principle whether the social surplus-value is monopolized by ten thousand persons or whether it is distributed according to a graduated scale among half a million. The struggle for greater equalization of distribution and for an organization which will insure a more equal distribution is, on that account, not less justified and necessary." [1]

These words are self-contradictory. Bernstein admits that the condition of the lower classes is improving, both in an absolute and a relative sense, and yet he expatiates on the monopolizing of surplus-value in the hands of half a million as against the nine or ten million who are despoiled. Even an acute critic is thus misled by his socialist shibboleths. But is the struggle of the lower classes for a juster distribution not perfectly warranted? We ask in return: On what does Bernstein base his assertion that the present distribution is unjust? Marx used his theory of surplus-value to demonstrate the injustice of the capitalist system, but this theory Bernstein repudiates. How then will he make good his contention that the present distribution of wealth is unjust? At most we may concede that the present altogether too unequal distribution of property smacks of unfairness, and that the endeavor to procure greater equalization is

[1] Die Voraussetzungen des Sozialismus, p. 51.

justifiable. But this endeavor alone does not suffice to stamp one as a socialist, otherwise most men would nowadays be socialists.

Why then does Bernstein not confess fairly and squarely that he and his partisans constitute a reform party? He writes indeed: "The influence of social democracy would reach much farther than it does to-day, if it were bold enough to emancipate itself from a phraseology which is actually superannuated, and if it would wish to appear what it nowadays is in reality, namely, a democratic socialist reform party." [1]

"A democratic socialist reform party!" What is that supposed to be? Does Bernstein mean by it the "socialization of all the means of production"? On this point we are completely left in the dark. He is of opinion that from the spread of "socialist thought" we may conclude that we are rapidly approaching a time when social democracy is forced to make positive proposals of reform. The aim of these reforms would be the "general application of the principle of trades-unionism." This again is rather ambiguous. Trades-unionism is far from being a transition to socialism. In the mediæval cities the guilds and corporations were highly developed. Were they, on that account, approaching the socialist society of the future? Not in the least. In fact, strongly organized and exclusive trades-unions would be the safest bulwark against socialism and its levelling, equalizing tendencies.

[1] *Ibid.*, p. 165.

CHAPTER III.

THE OTHER FUNDAMENTAL TENETS OF SOCIALISM.

§ I. *Equal Rights of All Men.*

Equality of rights among men is another of the fundamental tenets and postulates of socialism. The socialist demand for equality assumes a twofold aspect, one *moderate* and the other *extreme*.

I. The moderate view is that of Marx and Engels. These two luminaries of "scientific" socialism describe the equality aimed at by socialists for the present as the abolition of all class distinctions: every one is to be a laborer like all the rest and to get his share of the social product according to the measure of his labor.

During the first stage of socialist co-operation Marx supposes "the right of the producers [to be] proportional to their output. Equality," he says, "consists in the fact that the same standard of measurement, labor, is applied to all. But one man may be physically or intellectually superior to another, he may furnish more work during the same time, or may be able to work longer; and if labor is to be used as a standard, it must be determined as to its duration and intensity, else it ceases to be a standard. Equal rights are thus unequal rights on account of unequal amounts of work. No class distinctions will be acknowledged, because each one is but a laborer like all the rest; but unequal individual talents and capacities are tacitly acknowledged as

184

privileges of nature. There are therefore unequal rights both as to their substance and to their nature."[1]

Similarly Fr. Engels maintains: "The real substance of the proletarian demand for equality is the demand for the abolition of class distinctions. The demand for any further equality inevitably leads to absurdities."[2]

On what grounds are we to acknowledge this moderate demand for equality as justifiable? Marx as well as Engels derives this demand from the theory of surplus-value. This, again, is but a deduction from the theory of value originated by Ricardo and more fully developed by Marx, according to which labor is the only "value-producing substance," and no commodity can have any exchange-value beyond the socially necessary labor-time contained in it.

From this theory, however, which, by the way, has already been shown to be untenable, it is impossible to infer the demand for equality even in the above restricted sense. At the utmost we may conclude from it that each one's share of the collective product will be equal to the work furnished by him, or as Marx has it: "The amount of work given to society in one shape is received again in another."

Let us assume that a workingman of great skill and assiduity in a short time earns enough not only to indulge personally in a *dolce far niente*, but even to hire one or more servants—who shall prevent him from doing so? And if, to boot, he were to receive some donations, or by inheritance, gambling, or otherwise obtain a share of other workingmen's product and live high in consequence, who shall prevent him? In this manner there would soon again be masters and ser-

[1] Zur Kritik des sozialdemokratischen Parteiprogramms. (*Neue Zeit*, 1890–1891, n. 2, p 567)
[2] *Engels*, H. Duhrings Umwälzung der Wissenschaft, p 96.

vants, rich and poor, laborers and idle drones, in brief, there would be class distinctions. Some men, preferring to keep bachelor's hall, could live in plenty and comfort, whilst others of less strength and fewer talents, but encumbered by a wife and children, would continually find the wolf at the door.

Moreover, what is to become of "organized social production," if each one is at liberty to stop or to take up work whenever he pleases, or whenever he thinks that he is no longer in need of work? Perhaps you answer that each one will be forced to work as long as the community or its representatives demand it. But this demand can surely not be inferred from the theory of value. Other more fundamental doctrines would have to be applied. Finally, if the amount of labor performed is to be the only standard of distribution, what is to become of those unable to work—the sick, insane, decrepit, orphans, etc.?

Besides we shall show further on that it is quite impossible to apply labor as a standard of distribution. For, who can pronounce a fair and satisfactory judgment on the skill of each laborer and on the intensity of his application, and thus determine quite exactly how much of the total product will constitute his share?

Marx seems to have been well aware of the undesirability of applying labor as an exclusive standard of distribution. He grants that there will be certain inequalities which are "inconveniences unavoidable during the first period of communist society, which, after long travail, is just then issuing forth from the womb of capitalist society. Rights can never be superior to economic conditions and to the development of civilization determined by them."

"In a *higher phase* of communist society, *after the*

*slavish subordination of the individual under the divi-
sions of labor and consequently the opposition between
mental and bodily work* has disappeared, . . . after
the individual has become *more perfect in every respect,*
increasing thereby also the productive forces, . . .
then only . . . society may inscribe upon its banner:
Each one according to his faculties, to each one
according to his needs."

In connection with what Marx has said concerning
the first period of communist society his last remarks
cannot be construed otherwise than to mean that only
in the second stage perfect equality will reign. Therefore also he is constrained to hold up before workingmen the picture of perfect equality as the ultimate goal
of social evolution; yet, wary man that he is, he shrouds
his goal in nebulous obscurity in the distance.

"Distance lends enchantment to the view."

In the above extract Marx barely hints at the reasons
supporting his hope for "a higher phase of communist
society." Economic evolution is expected to plane
down individual differences more and more. This
assumption, however, is contradicted by the testimony
of past historical development. It may even be put
down as a general experience that the specific variety
of social organisms and personal characteristics keeps
pace with the progress of civilization. Among savage
tribes we find the nearest approach to uniformity and
general equality of rights. The greater the advance in
social evolution, the greater also the distance from uniformity and equality. This was the case in the past
and will be such in the future. Not even the transfer
of private property in the means of production to col-

lective ownership would make the least difference in this respect, provided that civilization is retained at its present height and no recourse is had to brute force.

II. The demand for equality in its *extreme* form is the demand for perfect or absolute *equality of rights*. It acknowledges no diversity of rights and duties. It is in this sense that the demand for equality is taken by the great majority of socialists.

1. The Gotha platform calls for the "removal of all social and political inequality." The drafts for an "amended" platform proposed at the Erfurt convention all contained the same demand, and in its final wording we read that the social democratic party contends for "the abolition of the rule of classes and of the classes themselves, and for *the equal rights and equal duties of all* without distinction of sex or pedigree. Bebel,[1] Stern,[2] Kautsky,[3] and others demand equality for all in the conditions of existence. According to Liebknecht [4] there shall exist in the state of the future *absolute equality of rights*, and this equality is to be the only limit to freedom.

By such absolute equality of rights we cannot understand merely equality before the law; for such equality already exists in certain countries, as in the United States. The socialist demand is rather for *actual and universal equality of rights in actual social life.* And to leave no doubt as to the extent of this

---

[1] *Bebel*, Die Frau, p 265. we quote from the 18th edition.

[2] Thesen über den Sozialismus, p 19

[3] Das Erfurter Programm in seinem grundsätzlichen Teile erläutert, 1892 p 160

[4] *Berliner Volksblatt*, 1890, n 253   In his speech anent the Erfurt platform Liebknecht pathetically exclaims "Exploitation in every form shall cease, men shall be *free and equal, not masters and servants, but comrades, brothers and sisters* " Again, in a meeting Jan 12, 1892, he maintained: "We shall abolish supremacy in its every form and establish *equality in every direction.*"

demand the disregard of sex or pedigree finds special mention in the Erfurt platform.[1]

It has been asserted by some people that by rights socialism must assume the character "not of the party of *equality* but of the party of *justice;* not of the party of false democracy, but of the party of moral and intellectual—that is natural—aristocracy." [2] However, this seems to be an entire misconception of the very essence of socialism as a labor party, as the party of the fourth estate, of the proletariat. True, socialists pose as the party of justice. But whence have they the right to set themselves up as the vindicators of justice by claiming perfect equality of rights for all, and to brand modern society wholesale as unjust? If they wish to answer this question they can only point to the *equality* of all men, from which equality equal rights would follow. By substituting for the existing aristocracy a nondescript natural aristocracy, the laboring classes would profit nothing at all. Besides socialist leaders will not easily relinquish a catchword as efficacious as that of "perfect equality" with its magic influence in stirring up the downtrodden classes.

Finally, the demand for equality of rights is necessarily connected with the fundamental tendencies of socialism. The means of production are to become the collective property of the whole community. But every one is equally a member of the community,

[1] *Kautsky* (Das Erfurter Programm, etc , p 16) seems to hold that the principle of equality amounts only to equality of income, and he does not hesitate to remark that if the principle of equality really brought about any of the consequences pointed out by adversaries of socialism, it would be simply "cast overboard." This is the much-vaunted socialist science For all it cares, the principles now serving as bait for the proletariat may in future be cast overboard!

[2] *Paulsen*, System der Ethik, II p 424.

therefore every one must have the same rights to the common property. To introduce collective owner-ship and then to debar certain classes from disposing freely of the common goods would be self-contradic-tory. It would renew slavery and class supremacy in its most odious form. Let us, therefore, examine this assumption of equality itself.

2. True it is that all men have a like nature—that all men are perfectly equal, if considered in the ab-stract, according to their nature, apart from all concrete circumstances which must necessarily accompany actual existence. All have the same Creator, the same aim and end, the same natural moral law; all are members of one great family. Hence follows also that there are essential rights and duties which are, so to speak, necessarily engrafted on human nature and are the same with .all men. Every individual human being has, therefore, at all times and in all places, the right to be treated as a man. Every individual has also the right to the strictly necessary conditions of existence. But that all men must enjoy the same conditions of existence cannot be proved from the equality of men in the abstract.

3. As soon as we consider men as they really are we are confronted with the greatest possible variety from which necessarily arises a diversity of rights and duties. Some are in helpless infancy or tender youth; others are in the strength of manhood; others again are declin-ing to their graves in decrepit old age. From this variety necessarily follows a diversity of rights and duties. Or should helpless children and decrepit old men and women possess the same rights and duties as men in the prime of life? Should the infirm have the same rights and duties as the healthy, women the same

rights as men? We are aware that many socialists advocate such equality, particularly the absolute equality between man and woman. The marriage-union, according to them, is "a private contract without the intervention of a public functionary." Woman may, according to their tenets, love whom she pleases and as long as she pleases. If she is not satisfied with one alliance, she may loose the knot and bless some one else with her love. Married or unmarried, she is to enjoy perfect equality with the sterner sex.[1]

Bebel, however, may permit us to ask him: Must, then, men in turn with their wives rock the cradle, cook, knit, and darn, and attend to all womanly household duties? And, again, must women as well as men descend into the mines, perform the duties of coachmen, draymen, sailors, etc.? Must they gird on the sword, take up the knapsack and rifle, and march to the field of battle? In order to effect such equality we would have to go back to the most barbarous times, and even then this equality would be frustrated by the weakness of the female sex For why did nature bestow on woman so totally different an organization—talents, inclinations, and characteristics so different from those of man? Is not this intellectual, moral, and physical diversity an evident indication that the Creator of both natures has set for them a totally different task in society?

Bebel, it is true, thinks that the difference of endowments and inclinations in the two sexes is only the result of education—or rather of that "slavery" to which woman has been thus far subjected, and that with the change of education and social standing this difference would altogether disappear. This assertion

[1] Bebel, Die Frau, p. 192

is untrue. It is sufficiently refuted by the fact that this difference between man and woman confronts us everywhere, among all nations, even of the most diverse customs. It follows also of necessity from the physical organization of woman and from the duties and cares which are inseparably connected with motherhood.

Apart from the diversity of age and sex, even though we could picture to ourselves men and women in equal circumstances, such equality in the conditions of existence of all is unnatural. We have only to recall to mind how different men are in regard to inclinations, talents, characters, health, physical strength, natural wants—to say nothing of the moral differences in regard to prudence, temperance, industry, economy—to see the utter impossibility of this supposed equality. From this variety follows also diversity in regard to honors, influence, property, social standing, which could be prevented only by continued violence.

To bring home to ourselves with evidence the utter impossibility of such absolute equality, let us suppose, for instance, four brothers who bear the greatest resemblance to one another. Three of them get married; the fourth prefers to remain unmarried His rights and duties are quite different from those of the other three. Of these we shall suppose that one remains childless, the second has three children, and the third has eight. Their duties and rights have varied still more. Though we have admitted that all four brothers were, in the beginning, equally situated in regard to home, property, and business relations, yet, after some ten years have passed, the conditions of their existence have become very different The first has to provide for himself only The second has to provide for himself and his wife, the third has to provide for five persons, and the fourth for ten If now we take into account the difference in regard to talent, industry, etc., it becomes manifest that in less than half a generation the circumstances of the four brothers have changed in many regards. And if, moreover, sickness, misfortune, persecutions have exercised a disturbing influence upon the relations, may it not easily happen that within one generation the equality has altogether disappeared? And what differences will set in during the following generation which has already begun under such unequal conditions?

Socialists may object that in the preceding example we suppose the now existing conditions of society, but in the socialistic state of society such a development would be altogether impossible, as the care of children, of the sick, etc, would be in the hands of the community, woman would take the same part in labor as man; and each one would live upon the produce of his own labor. Very true; but we maintain only that inequality is the necessary outcome of the natural development of man, and that socialism could not without external violence prevent such inequality. A gardener may effect that all the trees of a park are equally high, or rather equally low; but only by continued and violent pruning. Such an unnatural condition, however, cannot be lasting.

4. So far we have taken only the family into consideration. But beyond the boundaries of the family, owing to the countless shades of inclinations and wants, various social gradations are formed. It is only by an extensive division of labor that men can satisfy their wants and propensities and arrive at a higher degree of culture. But the division of labor again produces as a necessary result the division of society into various ranks and professions, which have for their basis the different inclinations and talents of men, and afford to each individual the opportunity of choosing a suitable vocation.

However we may conceive of an advanced state of society, there will always be ignorant people, and, consequently, always teachers. Have the pupil and the teacher the same rights and duties? There will always be apprentices and masters. Can the master and the apprentice have the same rights and duties?

There will always be sick persons and persons decrepit with old age; and, consequently, there will be physicians and surgeons and nurses. Can these have exactly the same rights and duties as those intrusted to their charge? There will always be agriculture, commerce, industry, science, and art. Shall those who devote themselves to these various pursuits have exactly the same conditions of life? Shall all men and women, in the same way, be trained to the profession and practice of all these various avocations?

The more moderate class of socialists, it is true, are inclined to admit different vocations with different emoluments in "the state of the future." On the other hand, the extremists—to whom Bebel belongs —would do away with all inequality in the different vocations. By education and culture, according to Bebel, it is possible to make all men fit for all professions, so that each one "in his turn" is fit to discharge all the various functions of social life. Also Marx speaks of a general adaptability of workingmen in a higher stage of development. This assumption, however, is absurd, and is based on an incredible exaggeration of human abilities, as we shall have occasion to show hereafter; but it is quite logical, for it follows with rigid necessity from the principles of socialism. He who has once undertaken, on the ground of the equality of all men, to upset the existing order of society, and to create equal conditions of life for all, cannot permit that society freely adopts professions or callings which, in regard to emolument, labor, and dangers, are so widely different from one another—as are, for instance, the professions of an author or an artist, and the employment of a miner, a fireman, a stable-boy, a hod-carrier, a laborer in a chemical factory or spinning-mill.

We conclude with the beautiful words of Aristotle. "The lawgiver must be more intent on equalizing the desires of men than their property." [1]

§ II. *The Iron Law of Wages.*

1. *The iron law of wages* was the chief weapon used by Lassalle against existing capitalism. Herein liberal social economists, Adam Smith, Ricardo,[2] J. B. Say, and others, had prepared the way for him. Lassalle [3] appeals with evident comfort to these great authorities in establishing his iron law.

With Marx himself the law of wages never found recognition, and it has also been expunged from the present official platform of German socialism. Yet Lassalle numbers still many adherents among socialists, and his writings have been republished as a means of propagandism. It is therefore not out of place to bestow some attention on his "iron law of wages." The meaning of this law is gathered best from Lassalle's own explanations:

"The iron economic law, which in our day, under the rule of supply and demand, determines the wages of the laborer, is the following: The average wages are always confined to the neces-

---

[1] *Aristotle*, Polit II c 7

[2] According to the teaching of Ricardo, the average wages will always, in the long run, coincide with the cost of production Ricardo distinguishes between the natural price and the market price of labor The natural price is that which is necessary generally to make existence and propagation possible The market price, on the other hand, is that which under the law of supply and demand is actually paid for labor The latter may sometimes exceed the natural price, and sometimes fall below it, but it will always fall back to the natural price It may be conceded that Lassalle has expressed this law in more odious terms than did Ricardo, but in substance their teaching exactly coincides

[3] Especially in his Arbeiter-Lesebuch and Offenes Antwortschreiben In the latter Lassalle cites for his opinion besides Ricardo, Adam Smith, and Say, also Malthus, Bastiat, and John Stuart Mill.

sary sustenance which, according to the custom of a given nation, is necessary to insure the possibility of existence and propagation. This is the point around which actual wages oscillate like the swing of a pendulum, without ever remaining long either above or below this standard. Wages cannot permanently rise over this average; otherwise there would result from the easier and better condition of the laborers an increase of the laboring population and a supply of hands which would again reduce the wages to, or even below, the average point.

"Nor can wages permanently fall below the average of the necessary sustenance of life; for this would give rise to emigration, celibacy, prevention of propagation, and finally the diminution of the laboring population by want, which consequently would reduce the supply of hands and again raise wages to their former or even a higher rate. The actual average wages consist, therefore, in a constant oscillation about this centre of gravity, to which they must always return, around which they must revolve, standing sometimes above and sometimes below." [1]

"That laborers and wages continually revolve in a circle, the circumference of which can at most reach the margin of what is barely sufficient to satisfy the necessary wants of human sustenance . . . is a circumstance which never changes." [2]

Lassalle, it is true, admits that these customary necessities of life are greater in our day than in former times; but notwithstanding all this the laboring classes are, in given social circumstances, always confined to what is barely necessary for the continuance of existence and of propagation. Therefore, according to Lassalle, the laborer has no prospect of bettering his condition. [3]

2. This is the dreadful law of which socialists have made use until the most recent times to discredit the institution of private property. [4] But their appeal to this law is without foundation.

---

[1] Offenes Antwortschreiben, p. 10.   Arbeiter-Lesebuch, p. 5.
[2] Offenes Antwortschreiben, p. 12.
[3] Arbeiter-Lesebuch, p. 27.
[4] Cf. the Gotha platform.   As we have remarked above, the law of wages is expunged from the present platform.   Nay, more: Liebknecht and others have since maintained that they had always rejected it.   And yet they supported the Gotha platform for fifteen years.   And yet, for a quarter of a century, workingmen were assured on the strength of that law that

a. If by the iron law Lassalle would only assert that under the rule of supply and demand and as long as workingmen are unorganized and unprotected a certain tendency exists to confine wages generally to what is barely necessary for the support of life, we would have no quarrel with him. For this tendency is a natural result of the selfishness of the rich, who are at the same time the mightier class. The average man is naturally inclined to purchase at a low and to sell at a high rate. As the laborer wishes to sell his labor power at the highest possible rate, so also the employer will endeavor to purchase labor at the lowest possible figure. But the rich employer is commonly ˏthe mightier, and will therefore succeed oftener in reducing wages below the normal figure than the laborer will succeed in raising them above the normal standard. Yet this universal tendency, which is the result of human selfishness, is by no means an economic law; else it might be also regarded as an economic law that dealers adulterate goods and that men grow rich by idleness.

But this state of things may be remedied by wise protective legislation in behalf of workingmen and by the organization of strong labor unions.

b. That Lassalle's principle can be regarded as an economic law lacks every semblance of proof. In order that an economic law, in the proper sense of the word, may be established, we must have a fact which from certain permanent causes necessarily exists in all places and at all times. This, however, is not the case with the supposed law of Lassalle; or, if it is, it has not thus far been proved. Let us

every effort at bettering their situation in the present order of society was useless. Is this not the height of frivolity?

examine the arguments which Lassalle, and before him Ricardo, adduce.

Wages, he says, cannot permanently rise beyond· the average of what is barely necessary, according to custom, for the support of life; for else there would result an increase of the laboring population, and consequently of the supply of labor hands, which would again reduce wages to the former standard. But is it true, let us ask, that the laboring population will increase in the same proportion as the comforts of life? Such a statement cannot be borne out; experience rather teaches the contrary. He who would find large families in England, say, must not look for them in the dwellings of the better-to-do laborers, or wealthier classes, but in the poorest tenements of the Irish laborers. In like manner, in America large families are to be found generally among the poorer classes of immigrants, while the birth-rate among the wealthier classes is notoriously low. Again, there is no land whose population generally is better off than France, and in no land is the rate of increase of population so low. And the reason is evident, even though we abstract altogether from religious influence. The better off a laboring family is the more it is concerned, as a rule, to maintain its social standing and to rise to a still higher rank. Rash marriages are more rarely entered upon in such circles than in the lower ranks of society. It does not follow, however, that morals are purer in the higher than in the lower strata of society. There is another feature of the question, however, which Lassalle overlooks. Granted that better circumstances would produce an increase of population, yet it does not thence follow that the competition of the laborers would increase in like manner, for it would take a period of from sixteen to twenty years at least to produce any marked effect of such increase. Children are not from their very birth capable of competition. Consequently, even according to the supposition of Lassalle, a laborer could for well-nigh a generation receive more wages than would be "necessary, according to existing customs, for the support of life and for propagation."

It may also happen that, despite the increase in the supply of labor, wages do not diminish, as with the supply also the demand may increase. If the demand for labor increases in the same proportion as the supply, wages remain the same; but it may easily happen that in many places, owing to new enterprises, the demand for labor may steadily increase for years, so that the increase of the number of laborers does not necessarily entail the diminution of wages.

We have no proof, therefore, that wages cannot for a considerable time exceed what is necessary for the maintenance of life. Nor has Lassalle proved that wages may not in some cases remain permanently below this standard. In that case he thinks emigration, celibacy, restriction of propagation, and finally a decrease of the laboring population resulting from misery would ensue, which would lessen the supply of labor hands and would bring wages back again to their former standard.

But, as we have already remarked, poverty does not lessen the birth-rate unless in that extreme case in which the laborers are literally starved. It can easily happen, and has happened, sad to say, that in many places the laboring classes have for a long time led a wretched life in the sense of Lassalle, without any perceptible diminution in the birth-rate. Poverty does not prevent marriages among the poor, nor does it prevent propagation. The poor are precisely in this respect often much more conscientious than those who call themselves the cultured classes. For the rest, even though poverty might produce a decrease in the birth-rate among the laborers, yet the effects of this diminution would be noticeable in the labor market only after the lapse of many years. In the mean time the gaps would be filled up by new laborers coming from surrounding districts. Marx has established, on the data of inquiries made by physicians and inspectors of factories, that in many manufacturing districts the laborers had lived for many years in the most wretched misery without experiencing any increase of wages. Lassalle's law, therefore, whether we consider it from its favorable or unfavorable aspect, remains unproved.

But it is not only *unproved:* it is simply *false.* The principal touchstone of economic laws are facts. Now what are the facts in regard to Lassalle's law? The statistics quoted above (p. 165 sqq.) are proof sufficient that long since the position of laborers, especially in England, has been improved, and that above all, in the matter of wages, there has been constant progress. We trust to God that a wise social policy to be pursued in the future will make the improvement permanent.[1]

---

[1] Karl Marx from the outset rejected Lassalle's iron law of wages. Nay, in his Criticism of the Social Democratic Programme he characterizes the insertion of this law in the platform as a "revolting retrogression"; and rightly so, from his own standpoint. According to Lassalle, the injustice of the wage system consists only in this, that the laborer's wages can never go beyond a low maximum, and thus the wage-worker is doomed to a miserable existence. According to Marx, the wage system in the capitalistic order of things is absolutely unjust and intolerable, because it makes the laborer the slave of the capitalist, and permits the workman to labor for his sustenance only, with the obligation to work a certain

§ III. *Undue Emphasis of Industrial Life.*

Socialists demand that all, without exception, take an active part in the system of social production. The "universal duty of labor" insisted on by the Gotha platform is, indeed, no longer mentioned expressly in the Erfurt platform, but in the election proclamation of April 30, 1903, it is emphasized anew by the social democratic party of Germany, and it is, moreover, a necessary inference from the demand of "equal rights and equal duties" and from the systematic organization of labor.

Every individual must enter the service of the community, and receive his portion of the common labor dealt out to him. No one is allowed to possess any productive property of his own, or to produce anything on his own account. For the satisfaction of all his wants he is directed to the state magazines. The education and instruction of youth are to be the business of the state, as is also the care of the sick. In short, every one is to have just so much freedom and so much right as the community concedes to him. We shall have occasion to discuss this point more at length hereafter. Suffice it here to say that this socialistic theory tacitly presupposes that society or the state has the *unlimited right of disposal over every individual;* that every one is destined in the first instance for the ser-

portion of the time for nothing, merely to produce "surplus-value" for the capitalist. For "surplus-value" is always effected at the cost of the laborer, and as the capitalist is then only willing to carry on industry when his money is likely to produce "surplus-value," capital is of its very nature calculated for oppression It is a "pitiless beast of prey" Hence he was forced to consider the adoption of Lassalle's iron law in the socialist programme as a step backwards Nay, the adoption of this law was diametrically opposed to, and an abandonment of, Marx's theory of "surplus-value." Hence we can easily understand his indignation at finding the *iron law* on the socialist platform.

vice of the community, and that for the mere purpose of industrial production.

This is the pagan idea of the state as we find it in Plato and other heathen writers. It does not tolerate any personal rights as against the community; it also virtually denies that the first and highest end of man upon earth is the service of God and the attainment of perfect happiness after death. As a logical consequence of this pagan view of the state and of the individual, socialism *unduly exaggerates the importance of industrial life* or the production of wealth. As in the life of the individual the pursuit of earthly goods, if estimated according to its true importance, occupies the last place in human activity, so also it should be in the life of human society at large. The acquirement of the means of subsistence is subordinate to the higher intellectual aspirations of man. The end of earthly goods is only to prepare the ground upon which higher and more ideal goods are produced.

Now, since it is impossible that all in the same way devote themselves to such various occupations, there must be different callings and states in life, which require long-continued preparation, and which do not all occupy the same place, but form a certain hierarchical order, consisting of various grades subordinate to one another. By their very nature the various classes employed in the production of the necessaries of life (laborers, artisans, husbandmen, etc.) occupy the lowest grade, while the different professions naturally take a higher place on the social scale. We do not mean to imply, however, that the former are not worthy of all consideration and honor, or that those who are employed in procuring the daily necessaries of life have less merit before God: we would only say that the

higher professions, considered in themselves, secure a
higher rank in society, that they require higher endowments and greater culture, and, consequently, may
claim greater consideration.

Now, what is the design of socialism? Socialism
will make the laboring class the ruling one, and make
the results of labor (the production of values) the
standard of the social organization itself and of the
social position of each member of society. Society is
to become one great productive union. No one may
withdraw himself from the duty of production. Unproductive, useless individuals shall not be tolerated.
That in such an organization, in which all members
are forced to be productive, there is no room for higher
callings—e.g., for a priesthood consecrated to the
divine service, for religious orders, for those who devote
themselves to arts and sciences for their own sake—
goes without saying.

Socialism turns away man's thoughts and desires
from lofty ideals and debases them to the level of material enjoyments. Elevation of heart and mind is an
unknown quantity in the socialist philosophy. But no!
we are deceived. Also socialism lays claim to *ideals*.
But of what kind are they? The socialist Stern [1] enu-
merates them in the words which Heine, the poet of
cynicism, addressed to the Saint-Simonians: "You
demand simplicity of apparel, chasteness of life, in-
sipid enjoyments; we, on the contrary, demand nectar
and ambrosia, garments of purple, and fragrant per-
fumes, luxury and magnificence, dancing nymphs,
music, and comedy;" but this, the same socialist adds,
we demand for all and we shall grant it to all.

Thus it seems that the mire of Epicureanism, exem-

[1] *Stern*, Thesen über den Sozialismus, p. 34

plified in the life of Heine, constitutes the socialist heaven. This brings us to another fundamental tenet of socialism.

§ IV. *Socialism and Religion.*

I. Principal Tenets of Socialism Incompatible with Religion

After what has been said above (p. 120 sqq.) anent the materialistic conception of history there can be no doubt that "scientific" socialism is essentially irreligious or even openly hostile to religion. The socialist theory implies first of all the negation of any dualism of spirit and matter. "The real unity of the world," Engels tells us, "is in its materiality." According to socialist doctrine there is no spirit, there is but matter and motion. Consequently there can be neither God nor divine Providence; man is devoid of an immortal soul no less than the brute animal from which he has been evolved; all hope for a better future in a life to come is idle folly.

1. Whatever heretofore was looked upon as belonging to the ideal, intellectual order is set down by Marx and Engels as the product of economic conditions in any given epoch. "The economic structure of society always forms the real foundation, according to which the whole superstructure of ethical and political institutions as well as the religious, philosophical, and other views of every historical period are ultimately to be explained."[1] "Religion is nothing but the fantastic reflection in the brains of men of those powers by whom their daily existence is dominated, a reflection in which natural forces assume

---

[1] *Engels*, Dühring's Umwälzung der Wissenschaft, p. 11

supernatural forms." [1] Religion is a "costume" [2] or
a "mask." [3] On that account it need not be abolished
by force, it will "die off" and disappear, as soon
as there are no more objects to be reflected. [4] Also
Kautsky informs us that in the ranks of the socialist
party there is growing up a new system of morals
and philosophy. He does not speak of a new religion,
because forsooth there will be no more fantastic
reflections.

Socialist leaders never tire of repeating that the
materialistic conception of history is the foundation
principle of modern "scientific" socialism; it is called
by an American socialist [5] "the central thing in socialism." He says, "it is to history and social science
what the law of gravitation is to physics." Now, if
all this is true, and if on the other hand the very
essence of this historical materialism is incompatible
with, or rather subversive of all true religion, then
the attitude of socialism toward religion is sufficiently
characterized.

To a socialist conscious of his aims and purpose
and fully imbued with the doctrine he is propagating
it must seem ridiculous to see any one trying to prove
that socialism and religion are incompatible. As a
faithful adept of historical materialism, he knows
that he cannot have any religion; and if all men
were to turn socialists, religion would indeed disappear without the application of violent measures.

2. The hostile attitude of socialism toward religion
is shown further in its purely natural, earthly con-

[1] *Ibid*, p 304
[2] *Engels* Feuerbach, p 65
[3] *Neue Zeit*, 1894, p 5
[4] *Engels*, Feuerbach, p 305
[5] *Charles H. Kerr*, What to Read on Socialism, p. 1.

ception of human life. Or could, perhaps, a system which proceeds from the supposition that man is created by God for eternity, and is placed here on earth to merit heaven by the fulfilment of the divine will—could such a system set up material production as the highest standard of society, and allow a share of earthly goods only to those who take an actual part in production? Could such a system regard religion as a matter of indifference or put it aside as a thing not worth caring for? Thus we see that the fundamental idea of socialism is in contradiction not only with Christianity, but with every form of religion. The decalogue of socialism are the supposed rights of men; its god is the democratic, socialistic state; its last end is earthly enjoyment for all; the object of its worship is production.

3. Also the *first demand* of socialism is tacitly based upon *atheism.* It demands perfect equality of rights and of the conditions of life for all, and that in every regard, but chiefly in social life. Every inequality in social life is characterized by socialism as an unbearable fraud and oppression. Although reason and revelation teach that the servant should be subject to his master, the inferior to his superior, the wife to her husband, and the child to the parent, and that for conscience' sake, because it is the will of God, yet socialism considers all this as a violation of the equal rights and duties of all According to socialistic views, each one has the right to submit only to those laws and that authority which he himself has acknowledged and approved. Thus the *principle of authority*, as coming from God and requiring obedience for conscience' sake, is subverted. That socialism dissolves the marriage union, not only in the

Christian sense, but also in the juridical sense, we shall have occasion to see when we treat of the relation of socialism to the family.

4. Socialism is no less in contradiction with Christian teaching on the rights of property. Christ no more emphatically condemns the immoderate quest of riches, and no more forcibly recommends poverty of spirit as a higher degree of perfection, than He clearly acknowledges the justice of private property, also in the materials of labor, and that not only for His own times and nation but for all places and all ages to come. He has not abolished the moral precepts of the Old Law as laid down in the Decalogue: nay, He has enforced them anew. In the New Testament as well as in the Old, it is a breach of the divine law even to covet our neighbor's field, house, or oxen. To the rich youth who asked to be instructed on the way to salvation Christ answered that he should keep the commandments of the Decalogue; and He added the counsel: "If thou wilt be perfect, sell what thou hast and give to the poor, . . . and come, follow Me." Could Christ speak thus if He considered private property, to which certainly belong houses and lands, as unjust? To Ananias St. Peter answered he might have kept his land if he chose. Among the first followers of Christ and the apostles there were many who possessed private property (e.g., Martha, Joseph of Arimathea, Philemon). Like Christ Himself and His apostles, the Church at all times acknowledged the right of private property in the materials of labor (lands, tenements, produce, etc.). It is therefore contrary to the teaching of Christianity to condemn all such private property as unjust or to brand it as "theft," as socialism actually does.

5. Christianity forbids *revolution*—that is, a violent subversion of the lawfully existing social order. But socialism is, according to the acknowledgment of its own leaders and representatives, an essentially revolutionary movement. True, when this reproach is made to social democrats they take refuge in the ambiguity of the word "revolution;" they say that there are also peaceful and constitutional revolutions. However, this answer is but beating about the bush. Of course, we do not assert that socialists engage in secret conspiracies, in deep-laid plots and schemes, in placing mines and throwing bombs in true anarchist style. Their ringleaders have sense enough to understand that nowadays attempts of this nature must necessarily prove abortive, and end with a fearful massacre of the insurgents.

Socialists are rather intent on spreading their ideas, thus preparing the ground and gaining possession of political power. But when their strength has reached ample proportions and the time seems to be ripe for the execution of their plans, they will not shrink from resorting to brute force. A revolutionary dictatorship will crush with its iron heel whoso dares to resist, and with fire and sword it will usher in the dawn of the communist order of society.

Or are, perhaps, the learned and cultured leaders of the social democratic party so simple as to believe that all private owners would freely surrender their possessions to the community, that the Church would freely renounce its institutions and its possessions, that monarchs would freely descend from their thrones, that the nobility would readily sacrifice their inherited rights, and the peasantry abandon the lands tilled by their forefathers?

Fortunately for ourselves we need not be content with general speculations on this point. The leading champions of socialism have time and again revealed their heart of hearts with most commendable sincerity.

Already in the Communist Manifesto Marx and Engels declare "that their purposes can be attained only by a violent subversion of the existing order   Let the ruling classes tremble at the communist revolution." Not less openly Marx declared at the congress of The Hague in 1872: "In most countries of Europe *violence* must be the lever of our social reform. *We must finally have recourse to violence in order to establish the rule of labor.* . . . The revolution must be universal, and we find a conspicuous example in the Commune of Paris, which has failed because in other capitals—Berlin and Madrid—a simultaneous revolutionary movement did not break out in connection with this mighty upheaval of the proletariat in Paris." These words require no comment.

Also in his "Kritik des sozialdemokratischen Programms" he confesses openly that the transition from capitalist to communist society can be effected only under the rule of a revolutionary dictatorship of the proletariat.

Bebel, commenting in the German Reichstag upon occurrences in Paris, says: "These events are but a slight skirmish in the war which the proletariat is prepared to wage against all palaces." On another occasion he declared that this reform cannot be brought about by sprinkling rose-water. In one of his works, "Unsere Ziele," p 44, he writes as follows on the application of violence: "We must not shudder at the thought of the possible employment of violence; we must not raise an alarm-cry at the suppression of 'existing rights,' at violent expropriation, etc. History teaches that at all times new ideas, as a rule, were realized by a violent conflict with the defenders of the past, and that the combatants for new ideas struck blows as deadly as possible at the defenders of antiquity. Not without reason does Karl Marx, in his work on ' Capital,' exclaim: Violence is the obstetrician that waits on every ancient society which is about to give birth to a new one; violence is in itself a social factor."

At the socialist convention of Ghent (1877) Liebknecht exclaimed: "The army will after all consist of sons of the people
whom we are gaining over by our revolutionary propaganda.
. . . When the day shall have arrived, rifles and cannons will of
their own accord face about to prostrate the foes of the socialist
people "

After Hirsch Lekuch, convicted of a murderous attempt on
the governor of Vilna, had been executed June 10, 1902, the
Vorwarts (n. 28), under the heading: *A Martyr of Oppression,*
remarks: "The executed man has been enrolled forever in the
history of the downtrodden Russian people, which is a history
of dreadful sufferings no less than a history of dauntless heroism." Is this not open commendation of political murder?

From all this it appears to evidence that socialism
and Christianity are no less opposed to each other than
darkness and light, and that whoever knows what
socialism is, and what it aims at, can join its ranks
only at the sacrifice of Christianity and religion in
general.

II Socialism Explicitly Hostile to Religion.

A. Testimonies of German Socialists.

It was hardly necessary to labor so much to show
the conflict between socialism and Christianity, since we
have the *express official testimony* of the socialists
themselves upon the fact. The German social democracy in its official platform declares religion to be a
"private matter." Thus the socialist state, at least,
is altogether divorced from religion,—non-religious
and atheistic. To put more stress upon this point,
the Erfurt platform, besides declaring religion to be a
private concern, also demands that "the use of public
funds for ecclesiastical and religious purposes be
abolished."

This doctrine is directly antagonistic to the teaching of the Catholic Church, which has always condemned as untenable and injurious the principle of absolute separation of Church and state.[1] It is contradicted also by right reason. The state owes to God, to itself, and to its subjects the duty of supporting and encouraging to the best of its power the true religion instituted by God. In the present order of things this religion is that of Christ and none other. And since, moreover, the entire education of youth, according to socialists, is the business of the state, it follows that education should take no cognizance of religion; in other words, that it should be non-religious and godless. The community as such should not concern itself with God and religion, but must consider both as equally indifferent. The Erfurt platform explicitly demands secularization of the schools, i.e., godless education.

This view of the matter must needs be the outcome of contempt for religion and is the first step toward a persecution of the Church. Let us suppose that the Church wishes to erect bishoprics and parishes, to entrust priests with the care of souls, to take in hand the religious instruction of the young, to regulate marriage and public holydays, etc.—would, in that case, the socialistic state leave the Church at perfect liberty? Would it be possible for Church and state, which are both concerned with the same human beings, to avoid a conflict? And if the socialistic state would force priests and religious, nay, even bishops, to abandon their vocations and to contribute their share to the public production of wealth—would not that be an

---

[1] Cf. Syllabus thes. 55; also the Encyclical of Pope Leo XIII, Immortale Dei.

open violation of the Church's rights? Would it not lead to perpetual conflicts, which would finally develop into downright persecution?[1] And what would be the result if the Church would claim a right to at least so much ground as would suffice for its churches, convents, parsonages, hospitals, seminaries, etc., and, moreover, if it should demand labor power and materials for the erection of such institutions? Would not the socialistic state, from its standpoint, be forced, in that case, flatly to refuse such demands on the part of the Church, and thus violate the Church's most sacred rights, and take away, as it were, the ground from beneath her feet?

The apparent toleration of religion in the socialist state as a private affair, is, therefore, merely a sop for simple souls. Socialists are not prepared to give offence to those who still maintain in their hearts some attachment to religion by demanding from them all at once the surrender of religion. But of its very nature socialism is the enemy of every religion which undertakes to raise the aspirations of men from earth to heaven, and to preach to man that he does not live on bread alone.[2] It is not by mere chance that the most noted socialists are so outspoken in their hatred

---

[1] Bebel (Die Frau, p 320) says anent the future order of society "If any one has still any religious propensities he may satisfy them in company with his congeners   Society will not care about it.   To make his living the priest will be obliged to work, and learning thereby he will finally come to the conviction that *to be the highest is to be a man*   Morality has nothing to do with religion, the contrary is asserted by simpletons and hypocrites . . . Moral concepts as well as religion are the results of the economic condition of mankind."

[2] The construction which socialists often put upon the expression. Religion is a private concern, is well illustrated by the remarks of the German trades-union journal *Der Zimmerer* (cf. *Cologne Volkszeitung*, 1902, n 230): "The expression in the socialist platform   Religion is a private concern, is often taken to mean that socialists should abstain from religious questions, that to do otherwise is an infraction of the party platform.   This, of course, is not and cannot be its meaning   Upon closer inspection it will

of religion, and that they generally indulge in the most irreligious and blasphemous language.

The expression "draft on eternity" (*Wechsel auf das Jenseits*), the trite blasphemy with which they characterize the Christian efforts of social reform, is well known. The *Social Demokrat*, the former official organ of the German socialists, had almost on every page the most virulent abuse of what is called "clerical ascendency," and was generally bristling with the most shocking blasphemies And its successor, the Berlin *Vorwarts*, the present official party organ, yields in naught to its predecessor. In a Christmas reflection (No. 301) it accuses Christianity of fulfilling none of its promises. "We know," it says, "that Christianity has not brought redemption. We believe in no Redeemer; but we believe in redemption. No man, no God in human form, no Saviour, can redeem humanity. Only humanity itself—only laboring humanity—can save humanity." In 1891 (No 261) we read in the same paper: "The fear and anger of Protestants as well as Catholic clericals is

appear that the demand for declaring religion a private matter is in the second part of the platform which contains the principal demands made for the present. The meaning is, therefore, that the *present state should look upon religion as a private concern*, that the state should in consequence make no appropriations for any religious purpose nor discriminate in favor of or against any denomination The above expression does not manifest the attitude of socialism toward religion, it merely declares the attitude toward religion to be assumed by the existing governments. This demand is directed against the arrogance and encroachments of the Church, which should be regarded and treated by the state as a mere private association. If our demand, however, is interpreted to mean that socialists have no right to bother about questions of religion, it is thereby made a bulwark for the Church The modern labor movement would suffer a thorn to remain in its flesh if it allowed any obscurity to subsist concerning its attitude toward religious belief. *Social democracy as a philosophical system can have no other relation to the Church than to reject its soporifics and to wage relentless war on by far the greater part of its doctrines.* This attitude is postulated already by the very fact that the Church demands faith in a God of infinite goodness, wisdom, and justice against whose will not even a sparrow falls from the roof. Well then. If such a God exists, it were unheard of temerity, yea, blasphemy on the part of the laborer, to organize in trades and political unions for improving his situation "

It is scarcely necessary to point out that the last sentence is blooming nonsense. We might as well maintain, that for a Christian it is a sin to work because he must trust in God for assistance. Christianity knows no such nonsensical doctrines Yet the very same argumentation is applied by the *N. Y. Volkszeitung* of Nov 1, 1902, in an article declaring that socialists cannot adhere to any religion, because religion forbids self-help.

proof that socialism threatens their innermost substance. We are sure of success. The priesthood may cling ever so closely to the policeman and the money-bag; this will at most hasten its downfall." In an article for Pentecost (1893, No. 118) the same journal tells us: "The founders of the Christian Church grafted Christian myths, feasts, and institutions upon pagan myths. . . According to the Christian myth the Holy Ghost came down on the first Pentecost. . . Socialism is also a new doctrine, and proclaims the joyful gospel of redemption, but not of redemption through a Messias. May the disciples to-day and to-morrow pour out the spirit of socialism upon thousands of unbelievers This is our 'Pentecost.'" Another time it says (1894, No. 70, 1 suppl): "Good Friday was celebrated by a good many Berlin proletarians by a pilgrimage to the German Golgotha, the graves of the March victims (revolutionaries)" On Easter, 1896, we read: "About 1863 years ago, according to the Christian legend, the founder of Christianity died on the cross, because He had advocated equality among men. On the day when international socialism shall cast off the twofold yoke of mammon . . . the million-headed son of man—the laboring populace—will celebrate his resurrection. The celebration of that resurrection is our Easter-day, the Easter-day of humanity."

That the same anti-Christian spirit is still rife in the editorial sanctum of the *Vorwarts* is proved by the article entitled "Pfingstgeist" (spirit of Pentecost) in No 21, 1901. "We celebrate a feast of nature and of intellect. Our celebration is not meant for the blind sway of brutish lust, but also not for the supernatural manifestations of a fancied supersensual world. The Holy Spirit of our times does not proclaim humanity and self-denial, as Christianity has done at a period of general decadence. The Holy Spirit of our times preaches humanity, etc."

The *Neue Welt* the illustrated supplement of the *Vorwarts* (1896, No. 47), characterizes the story of Adam and Eve as a "foolish dream " Another time (1898, No. 6) it says: "The threats of hell in a future life are to be laughed at, drafts on heaven are to be despised. The former are fanaticism, the latter are speculation."

In November, 1897, the Charlottenburg local of the social-

democratic union of masons passed the following resolution:
"If a member of the union dies and a clergyman accompanies
the funeral, no floral offerings will be made for the deceased "

Karl Marx allows no opportunity to pass without an open
or covert thrust at Christianity. According to him, religion is
an "absurd popular sentiment," a "fantastic degradation of
human nature." "Man makes religion," he says, "not religion
man." Then, again, religion is "the sentiment of a heartless
world, as it is the spirit of spiritless conditions. It is the opium
of the people." "The abolition of religion as the deceptive
happiness of the people is a necessary condition for their true
happiness " "Religion is only an illusory sun, which revolves
around man as long as man fails to revolve around himself " [1]

"As man is dominated in religion by the creations of his
imagination, thus he is dominated in the capitalist system by
the product of his own hand " [2] "Man becomes a savage after
ceasing to be an ape." [3] Marx had resolved to prepare a
German edition of Lewis Morgan's notorious book, which tries
to derive the origin of the family from a perfectly bestial state
of man. Unable to execute his plan he intrusted it to his friend
Engels, who accomplished his task in "The Origin of the
Family," which was subsequently retranslated into English.
In his criticism of the socialist platform [4] Marx demanded
that the labor party declare its intention "of delivering men's
consciences from the spectre of religion."

Engel's views on religion are sufficiently manifested by his
utterances quoted above (p. 121 sqq.). In his work on Feuerbach (p. 52) he says: "Religion had its origin in a very primeval
period, from ambiguous and rather primitive views of men concerning their own nature and their surroundings But ideology,
wherever it exists, is developed in accordance with the given
subject-matter; otherwise it is no ideology, i e., an occupation
with thoughts as though they were independent, self-developed
beings subject to no other laws than their own That the course
of this process is determined by the economic conditions of the
men in whose minds it takes place, is necessarily hidden from

---

[1] *Deutsch-Franzòs Jahrbücher*, Paris, 1844 p 71. *Cf. Volksblatt*, No.
281; Capital, vol. I. pp 19, 39.
[2] Capital, vol I p 585.
[3] Zur Kritik des sozialdemokrat Parteiprogramms, p 564
[4] *Ibid.*, 575

those men, else there would be an end of all ideology." Religion, therefore, is naught but hallucination!

Bebel, in the words of the frivolous poet Heine, leaves "heaven to the angels and the sparrows."[1] If we are to believe him, "theology is in contradiction with natural science and will disappear in the society of the future."[2] Again: "The conviction that heaven is on this earth," and that "to die is to end all here," will impel every one to lead a natural life.[3] "The gods do not create men, but men create gods and God." "Natural science has shown 'creation' to be a myth, astronomy and physics prove that 'heaven' is a phantom."[4] In the Reichstag session of December 31, 1881, the present leader of German socialism declared: "In politics we profess republicanism, in economics socialism, in religion atheism "

Liebknecht confessed at the Halle convention: "As regards my own self I had done with religion at an early age. . . . I am an atheist; I do not believe in God. . . . Science is hostile to religion. . . . Science provides for good schools; they are the best means against religion." He is of opinion that the dependence of the forms of religion upon economic conditions is so evident that there is no need of a conflict with religion. "We may peacefully take our stand upon the ground of socialism, and thus conquer the stupidity of the masses in so far as this stupidity reveals itself in religious forms and dogmas."[5]

Dietzgen, in his blasphemous sermons on "Religion and Social Democracy,"[6] surpasses all others in his savage onslaught against religion. As characteristic of his style we quote the following: "If religion is to be understood as a belief in supersensible, immaterial substances and forces, if it consists in a belief in higher gods and spirits, [social] *democracy has no religion.* In the place of religion it sets up the consciousness of the insufficiency of the individual, who for his perfection requires to be supplemented, and, consequently, subordinated to the entire body social. *A cultured human society is the supreme good in which we believe.* Our *hope* rests upon the organization of

---

[1] Unsere Ziele, p 38.
[2] Die Frau, p. 319
[3] Ibid , p. 337.
[4] Ibid , p 320. Bebel's Die mohammedanisch-arabische Kultur-periode is a mean and venomous attack on Christianity.
[5] Berlin *Volksblatt*, 1890, n 281.
[6] Fifth ed., Berlin, 1891, pp. 16, 17.

social democracy This organization shall make that *love* a reality for which religious fanatics have displayed such irrational enthusiasm " [1]

In the *Neue Zeit* [2] Kautsky lately expressed his dissatisfaction at the French socialists, especially Jaurès, for not being radical enough in their onslaught on the *congregations*. "I prefer the German method (of waging war on the Church) to the French, not because it renounces war, but wages it much more effectively. The one-sided attack on the congregations . . . is merely like lopping off the branches of the tree, thereby causing it to grow more vigorously. *The ax must be laid at the root of the tree*, but this can be effected only by withdrawing the state subsidy from the secular clergy."

In the party convention at Hamburg a Mrs. Steinbach spoke in defence of the editor of the *Neue Zeit*. "An editor," she said, "who is supposed to write a paper for a million of readers and to please them all would have to be God, and in Him we do not believe " According to the *Vorwarts* this sentence was received with great applause and merriment. Nevertheless the same woman boldly declared that she looked upon it as barbarous "to deprive those of religion to whom we cannot as yet give a new religion. Religion should remain a private concern "

This anti-religious tendency recurs in countless variations in the so-called socialist "poetry," a favorite occupation of which is to parody whatever is Christian. There are socialist songs for Christmas, Easter, and Pentecost, full of mockery and blasphemy. In the "Christmas Marseillaise" [3] we read, for instance:

> Oh, hope no more in ancient guise
> To see a wondrous star arise
> To lead thee to the Saviour's stable,
> 'Tis not the meaning of the fable.
> Look up, a star is shining bright,
> 'Tis socialism's beacon light,
> And thou thyself redeemer art, etc.

[1] The real opinions of socialists concerning religion are revealed in the following pamphlets recently published and widely circulated also in the United States by the Socialist Literature Co of New York *Bebel*, Glossen zu Guyot's Die wahre Gestalt des Christentums, *Stern*, Die Religion der Zukunft, *Lommel*, Jesus von Nazareth, *Adolf Douai*, Wider Gottesund Bibelglauben, *Losinsky*, War Jesus Gott, Mensch oder Uebermensch? and countless others of the same calibre

[2] Twenty-first year, vol 1, p 506

[3] *Max Kegel*, Sozialistisches Liederbuch.

For the day on which Christendom celebrates the death of the Redeemer on the cross the socialist song-book offers the following blasphemous skit:

> Woe, woe to that pale Nazarene!
> As well as He I am, I ween,
> The Godhead's own incarnate son.

The believer in immortality is thus derided by a socialist versifier:[1]

> And if I die, what shall to me
> Hereafter then be shown?
> Thou fool! Thy question has no sense;
> *Hereafter is on earth alone.*

The Christmas number (1897) of the socialist *Wahre Jakob* was headed by a poem entitled: "We also celebrate Christmas" One stanza is as follows:

> And though we are of faith devoid
> In the Christ of our childhood days,
> And though from clashing fables dark
> We strive to reach the blesséd light,
> And though our faith has disappeared
> That us from bondage to redeem
> A Saviour came in heavenly light—
> Yet Christmas still we celebrate,
> Because in firmest faith we trust
> That tyranny will disappear, etc.

The socialist poet Levy thus mocks those who believe in a life to come:

> Ha! your virtue we deride,
> For joys hereafter you may wait;
> With golden youth we will abide
> With light and love in earthly state.[2]

B. Testimonies of Socialists Outside Germany.

A few testimonies from socialists outside of Germany will show that socialism is everywhere alike in its anti-religious trend.

[1] *Neue Zeit*, 1894, n. 2.   [2] *Neue Welt*, 1903, n. 5.

B. Malon, a ringleader of French socialism and translator of Marx's "Capital," said on his deathbed: "I die in my pantheistic, evolutionistic, socialist faith."[1]

Similarly Leo Franckel, the intimate friend of Marx and Engels, declares in his last will: "No priest shall attend my deathbed or my funeral, in order to save my soul. I believe neither in heaven nor in hell." His testament was read at his grave in the Paris cemetery of Père Lachaise before a large concourse of socialists of all countries, who were "deeply impressed by the solemnity of the funeral celebration"[2]

In an article by the French socialist, Paul Lafargue, translated and published in the International Socialist Review (Nov. 1903), by Charles H. Kerr of the Chicago socialist publishing firm of the same name, we find the following passage (p 293): "*The victory of the proletariat will deliver humanity from the nightmare of religion.* The belief in superior beings to explain the natural world and the social inequalities, and to prolong the dominion of the ruling class, and the belief in the posthumous existence of the soul to recompense the inequalities of fate will have no more justification when once man . . . shall live in a communist society from whence shall have disappeared the inequalities and the injustice of capitalist societies."

But the hatred of French socialists for everything religious is plainly manifested by their late doings in the Chamber of Deputies. The socialist deputies clamored most for the suppression and expulsion of the congregations. Over 20,000 innocent nuns were driven from their institutions of charity and even from their country, mainly at the instigation and compulsion of socialists "Comrade" Jaurès, one of their principal leaders, was almost ostracized and had to eat humble pie for having allowed his daughter to be educated and to make her first communion in a convent academy. Thus French socialists understand the phrase: "Religion is a private concern."

The *Austrian socialists* adopted, May 30, 1898, a resolution proposed by Pernerstorfer, which contains the following expressions: "*Socialism is directly contradictory to Roman clericalism,* which is enslaved to unyielding authority, immutable dogmas, and absolute intellectual thraldom. We doubt all authority,

---

[1] Cf *L Say*, Contre le socialisme (1896), p. 82.
[2] *Vorwärts*, 1896, n 81

we know of no immutable dogma, we are the champions of
right, liberty, and conscience (!) . . . Besides the struggle for
the economic demands of the working class we also combat for
the highest spiritual possessions And this ancient struggle
between light and darkness will be decided in favor of light,
in favor of socialism."

This resolution was passed "with thunderous applause," as
the *Vorwärts* reports.[1]   At the convention of Austrian socialists at Graz, September 2, 1900, Ellenbogen urged upon socialism the duty of "waging war against clericalism, which is stultify-
ing the people." (*Cologne Volkszeitung*, 1900, n 810). On
April 23, 1901, Pernerstorfer declared in the Austrian Reichsrat. "Roman fetishism is no religion."

At the convention of *Spanish socialists* in Madrid, September
21, 1899, it was resolved "to expel any 'comrade' who supported positive religion."   The Berlin *Vorwärts* (1899, n. 225)
characterized this resolution as "an answer to the mediæval
zelotism of Spanish clericals "

C. Testimonies of American Socialists.

Also in the United States the chief socialist organs have time
and again voiced their anti-religious and atheistic sentiments.
A few choice specimens may be quoted here. The *New Yorker
Volkszeitung*, the principal representative of scientific socialism
in New York State, writes under date of October 9, 1901:[2]
"Socialism and belief in God as it is taught by Christianity and
its adherents are incompatible *Socialism has no meaning
unless it is atheistic*, unless it declares that we do not need so-
called divine help, because we are able to help ourselves. Only
the man who ceases to believe begins to feel that he can act. The
laborer who relies on God, who in the piety of his heart assumes
that all that God does is well done—how can that same laborer
develop revolutionary forces for the overthrow of authority and
social order, both of which, according to his faith, are instituted
by God?"[3]

For Christmas of the same year the above-mentioned paper
regales its readers with an "historical" account of the origin of

---

[1] *Vorwärts*, 1896, n 126, suppl.
[2] The following three extracts are quoted by the *Buffalo Volksfreund*,
weekly ed., Dec. 25, 1903.
[3] Cf. note on p. 212.

this feast which is said to be taken from "Egyptian and Grecian myths." Christmas is said to be "a feast of love," a feast "in honor of the growing light of day." "*We do not believe in the Saviour of the Christians*," our Saviour will come "in the shape of the world-redeeming principle of socialism."

The foul and blackguard manner in which certain socialist publications wage war against Christianity is exemplified by the report concerning Archbishop Corrigan's death contained in the *Vorwarts*, a weekly supplement of the *New Yorker Volkszeitung*. It is from the issue of May 10, 1902.

"New York, May 6 Archbishop Corrigan died last night after a protracted illness Preparations are going on for a grand funeral with the usual paraphernalia. The 'soul' of the prelate whizzed out of his mortal remains straight up into the seventh heaven, and now the Bishop is staying there with lovely little angels and other beautiful beings hovering about him. Let him who is fool enough, believe it "

For Comrade Buck [1] it is a self-evident proposition that "proud man himself must see in the *Pithecanthropus Erectus*, or extinct Ape-man of Malaysia, the link of kinship that binds him to the rest of the animal kingdom," and that there was a "development of the human race from animality, and through savagery to civilization." We need not point out that this is an implicit denial of Christian revelation Charles H. Kerr plainly tells us that the main principle of socialist philosophy is "*historical materialism*," i.e, atheism [2] Walt Whitman, the "poet of wider selfhood," the favorite bard of American socialists, thus voices his mission: "I only am he who places over you no master, owner, better, God, beyond what waits intrinsically in yourself " [3]

How atheism and irreligion are propagated among socialist and union laborers in the United States is well illustrated by the following notice in the Buffalo *Arbeiterzeitung*, March 10, 1901 "Dr. Titus Voelkel, the well-known free-thought agitator of North America, will soon arrive in Buffalo and present two or three of his lectures His subjects will be. 'The Blessings of Infidelity;' 'Christianity and Socialism,' and 'Immortality ' Certainly most interesting questions for thoughtful and pro-

[1] *International Socialist Review*, Chicago, Sept. 1903, p. 153.
[2] What to Read on Socialism, p. 1.
[3] *Ibid*, p 27.

gressive people   The comrades, male and female, should see to it that the meetings are well attended, *and especially that such of the union laborers be induced to come who are as yet entirely in the bondage of religious superstitions.* . . .

"He (Voelkel) will hold up a lighted torch before the minds of reactionaries in political, religious, and social matters, and *will furnish the irrefutable proof that belief in dogmas and a Church is the bane of humanity.*"

These utterances might perhaps be repudiated by native-born American socialists as being the exaggerations of a German agitator   But how could the antagonism between genuine Christianity and thorough-going socialism be more forcibly stated than in the following passage culled from an article by George D. Herron,[1] erstwhile Congregationalist minister at Burlington, Iowa, later on professor of "Applied Christianity" at Grinnell University, but now one of the intellectual chiefs of the Socialist Party and secretary for the United States in the International Socialist Bureau? Says Mr. Herron: "Every appeal to men to become socialists in the name of Christianity will result in the corruption and betrayal of socialism in the end, and in the use of the movement for private ends.   People cannot separate Christ from Christianity.   And Christianity to-day stands for what is lowest and basest in life.   The Church of to-day sounds the lowest note in human life   It is the most degrading of all our institutions, and the most brutalizing in its effects on the common life   The Church is simply organized Christianity.   For socialism to use it, to make terms with it, or to let it make approaches to the socialist movement, is for socialism *to take Judas to its bosom.* . . .   Official religion and militarism are the two guardians of capitalism, and the subtle methods of the Church, in destroying the manhood of the soul and keeping it servile, are infinitely more to be dreaded by the socialist movement than the world's standing armies."

And yet a Chicago socialist publishing-house, to whose periodicals Mr. Herron is a frequent contributor, advertises a pamphlet by C W Woolridge, "The Kingdom of Heaven is at Hand," as "an excellent book *to give to a minister or a church member*   It shows how the teachings of Jesus lead directly to

[1] Quoted by *Goldstein*, Socialism The Nation of Fatherless Children, p. 93   Other utterances of American socialists concerning religion may be found on p 85 sqq.

socialism." [1] This looks pretty much like trying to catch a gudgeon, if he is simple enough to take the bait.

§ V. *The Root of Socialism. Relationship of Socialism to Liberalism.*

From our whole exposition of socialism it is evident that only a very superficial observer could possibly consider it the invention of some designing trickster or the artificial product of political adventurers. We have pointed repeatedly to the remoter origin and deeper sources of socialism. Yet it will be worth our while to review the actual causes of the socialist movement and to present them here arranged in proper order. We are the more willing to undertake this duty, since it will give us the opportunity to shed more light, not only upon the real significance of socialism, but also upon its intimate connection with *liberalism.*

Socialists themselves acknowledge that they have only drawn the logical conclusions from principles set up by liberals; and liberalism is accused by Catholics generally of having given birth to socialism. The liberals, on their part, with horror and indignation disclaim all connection with socialism. Liberalism does not profess, so say its defenders, to abolish private property: it only makes ownership free. Nor does it profess to advocate a servile industrial organization: it only advocates unrestricted freedom for all.

Notwithstanding all the protestations of the liberals, we cannot but consider socialism as the lineal descendant of liberalism, however much the parent may try to disown its offspring. The question is this, whether the principles set up and defended by liberals logically

---

[1] What to Read on Socialism (Kerr & Co), p 29.

lead to socialism or not; and this question we believe must be answered in the affirmative.

1. The deepest roots of socialism are *atheism* and *materialism.* If it is once admitted that all ends with this life, that man has no higher destiny than the lower animals which wallow in the mud, who, then, can require of the poor and oppressed, whose life is a continued struggle for existence, that they bear their hard lot with patience and resignation, and look on with indifference while their neighbors are clad in purple and fine linen, and daily revel at sumptuous banquets?

Is not the inextinguishable yearning for perfect happiness implanted also in the breast of the workingman? If you despoil him of every hope of a better life to come, what right have you to prevent him from striving to obtain happiness on earth as best he can, and therefore to make imperative demands for his share of earthly goods? [1] Is he not a man as well as his employer, who thrives on the laborer's exertions? Who can prove to workingmen from the standpoint of atheism that it is meet and just that one should pine in poverty and want, while another enjoys abundance of all things, since all have the same nature, and no reason can be given on atheistic grounds why the goods of this world should belong to one rather than to another? If the atheistic and materialistic theory is true, the demands of socialism are certainly just—that all the goods and enjoy-

[1] On Feb 23, 1890, *Bebel* said in the Reichstag "You know as well as we that *the more faith in a life to come disappears from among the people, the more the people will clamor for having their heaven on earth.*" This thought is not quite original with Bebel. Heine had said the same fifty years before Remarking on the subversive influence of German philosophy on religion he continues· "The overthrow of the old beliefs has also uprooted the former morality. . . . The destruction of a belief in heaven is of consequence not only in morals but also in politics The common people chafe at their earthly misery and yearn for happiness on earth. Communism is the natural outcome of these changed views, and it is spreading all over Germany. (Heine's Works, vol. III. Hamburg, 1876, pp. 113-115.)

ments of this life should be equally divided among all; that it is, therefore, unjust that one should live in a magnificent palace and enjoy all pleasures without labor, while another is living in a squalid cellar or cold garret, and cannot, even with the greatest effort, obtain enough bread to appease his hunger.

Already in 1847, in a speech before the Prussian Diet, BISMARCK expressed this same idea in the following words: "I do not understand how in those states (which are not based on religion) the ideas of the communists, for instance, concerning the immorality of private ownership and the high moral value of theft as of an attempt to restore the inborn rights of men, can rightfully be prevented from asserting themselves if they have the power to do so. For, also these ideas are looked upon by their originators as very humanistic, yea, as the prime flower of humanism. Therefore, gentlemen, let us not curtail the Christian sentiments of our people." [1]

Now, who is it that has preached and propagated atheism in all its forms? Who has sought by all ways and means to restrict the influence of Christianity in the school and in public life? Who is it that proclaimed extreme Darwinism as a dogma and popularized it for the ignorant masses? Who is it that even in our own day, in speech and in writing, in the chairs of universities and in public assemblies, preaches the grossest atheism? It is the representatives of *liberalism*, beginning with the French Encyclopedists down to our own university professors, who combat and decry the faith in God and in Christ the Saviour as stupidity and superstition. More especially Hegel and Feuerbach are the intellectual progenitors of the socialist heroes Marx and Engels (cf. above, p. 37 sqq.). Hence Marx himself utters the sarcastic taunt against the liberals, that athe-

[1] Cf. *Busch*, Bismarck und seine Leute während des Krieges mit Frankreich, vol. I, p 210.

ism seems to them a venial fault compared with the crime of criticising the traditional conditions of property.[1] Wherein they have sinned therein they are punished.

It is especially by its baneful influence on the *schools* that liberalism has disseminated unbelief in the great mass of the people. For the last century already the universities have been hotbeds of infidelity. A pitifully small minority of university professors still make open profession of Christianity. By far the greater number is indifferent if not hostile to the Christian religion, or at most professes some milk-and-water kind of Christianity.

From the universities the streamlets of infidelity are trickling farther and farther. Wherever liberalism dares to show its true nature it endeavors to banish religious influences from the elementary schools, and, as it is called, to secularize them. And in doing so liberalism is but consistent with its principles.

Lately a liberal university professor—Dodel-Port—published a book which permits us to look behind the scenes perhaps more than is agreeable to some of the professor's associates. His work is entitled, "Moses and Darwin." What, the author asks, is taught at our universities? *Darwin* and always Darwin. The doctrines of creation, of paradise, of the fall of the first man, the narration of miracles, he tells us, have been cast aside by modern science and relegated into the realm of fables. The representative "scientists" teach that there is no personal God, that man was developed from animality, that there is no immortal soul

---

[1] Capital, Introduction, p ix. *Virchow*, one of the chief luminaries of liberalism, publicly maintained in the Prussian Diet, May 8, 1891, that he could not understand how a reasonable man could imagine that men are on earth in order to prepare for heaven.

and no free will, and that in the history of mankind everything is determined by mechanical laws as in the rest
of nature, etc.   This is the teaching of the universities.

But what is taught in the (German) elementary
schools? The very reverse. There the children are
imbued with a belief in *Moses*, in the existence of God,
the creation of the world, the fall of man, miracles, etc.

Is this contradiction to go on forever? No, is the
verdict of our author. Off with the customary mask
of hypocrisy! Let us show our true colors. Eject
Moses and his miracles from the elementary school,
that not every student of the higher branches may be
forced to fight out the hard struggle between two systems which are diametrically opposed.

From the liberal point of view this demand is
perfectly justified; but from it we can also perceive
to whom is due that infidelity which is infecting all
classes of the population and has blessed us with
modern socialism and its revolutionary ideas.[1]

Socialists are fully aware that their atheism is based on
modern infidel science   Engels terms "the German labor
movement the inheritor of classical German philosophy."
Bebel has repeatedly acknowledged his indebtedness to modern
scientists   On September 16, 1878, he said in the Reichstag
"Gentlemen, you attack our views on religion because they

---

[1] In the session of the Reichstag of May 23, 1878, Dr Jörg remarked
very aptly "The most urgent necessity is the *regeneration of the school*
Personally I fear less the socialism of the present than the socialism of the
future which is growing up among our young people   Owing to mistaken
political calculations the schools have more and more been withdrawn
from religious influences and thereby their doors have unwittingly been
opened to socialism   Modern pedagogy, or, I might say, the modern school-
craze, has become a seminary of socialism   Willy nilly, the effect is to
raise the children above their level and thus to sow dissatisfaction broadcast among the people.   Thus I wish to be understood, if I tell you openly
that a wretched, burdened laborer who does not pray, who has forgotten or
never learned it, will fall an easy prey to socialism as soon as it comes to
fetch him "
If this be true of German elementary schools, what shall we say of our
American public schools with their fads and pretensions?

are atheistic and materialistic. I acknowledge the correctness
of the impeachment. . . I am firmly convinced that socialism finally leads to atheism. But who has established the
scientific and philosophical foundations of those atheistic doctrines which cause you so much anxiety and displeasure? Was
that done by socialists? Edgar and Bruno Bauer, Feuerbach,
David Strauss, Ernest Renan—were they socialists? They were
men of science . . . We have adopted our atheistic tenets in
accordance with our scientific convictions, and we feel obliged
in conscience to spread them among the masses. Why should
that be forbidden to one party which is allowed to the other?"
The spokesmen of modern science will be at a loss to find
a suitable reply; for, even if they do not make open profession
of infidelity, they are, at least for the most part, infected with
the principles of Strauss and Renan.

2. The second great principle of the revolutionary
party is *equality.* Here again socialism takes the
same stand as liberalism, and draws the last consequence from its principles. Who invented the watch-
word *liberty, equality,* and *fraternity,* and thus gave
an appearance of right and even of duty to the bloody
French Revolution? It was the representatives of
liberalism. The worthies of the Revolution—the
Jacobins and Girondists—were the true forefathers
of the modern liberals, who delight in their principles
and phraseology, and continually spout liberty and
equality. In virtue of this liberty and equality the
ancient order of things was subverted; the privileges
of the nobility and the prerogatives of the Church
were abolished; every memory of ancient institutions
was effaced; the people were declared sovereign;
and, finally, the "citizen Capet" was brought to
the scaffold. True, when the liberal bourgeoisie
had once taken hold of the reins of government, they
were eager to put a stop to the further development
of their principles. After the Church had been

persecuted and, as far as this was possible to human power, suppressed, the heroes of the Revolution—Robespierre at their head—were eager to introduce the worship of a Supreme Being in order to check the masses. After the property of the Church and of the nobility had been seized upon, and individuals had enriched themselves from the wealth of the nation, it was declared in the constitution that private property was sacred and inviolable. After the aristocracy had been removed and the hierarchy of the Church had been suppressed, they determined to establish an aristocracy of genius and wealth. Was such a step consistent? Had they any right to demand of the people to be satisfied with that equality which conferred upon it a semblance of freedom, but left it totally bereft of protection, and finally surrendered it to the power of the capitalists? Was the people not entitled to require that they should redeem their promises, and finally establish perfect equality in real earnest? We consider that demand as logical and just, according to the principles of liberalism.

3. The close relation of socialism to liberalism may be still more clearly shown in reference to the adopted *theory of value.* He who accepts this modern socialistic theory of value—that the exchange-value of all productions is only the *result of labor*, or accumulated labor—cannot possibly consider as just the conditions of modern production in which the laborer is always at a disadvantage, but must logically come to the principles of socialism. But who first established the socialistic theory of value? Is this theory the invention of socialism? By no means; it is the traditional doctrine of liberalism. Adam Smith, Ricardo, Say, and all the so-called classical political

economists belong to the liberal school; and they have almost without exception laid down the principle that all value is to be credited to labor.   Lassalle, as we have already shown, in establishing his theory of value could point to a stately line of liberal social economists.   In recent times this theory, however, is either wholly abandoned, or at least essentially modified by liberals.   They soon discovered what a dangerous weapon they put into the hands of socialism. But it was too late.   The fact cannot be concealed from the world that liberalism forged the most dangerous weapon which socialism is using for the subversion of the existing social order.

4. Not only theoretically, but also practically, did liberalism pave the way for socialism.   The way was smoothed chiefly by the introduction and enforcement of *unlimited industrial competition*, with all the liberties and privileges which it brings in its train. All protecting organizations which, in the course of time, had arisen to counteract unlimited competition, whether in theory or in practice, were, in the name of freedom, violently suppressed.   Even the laws against usury were abolished in the interest of freedom.   Thus society was disintegrated, the weaker industries were isolated and, owing to unlimited competition, fell victims to the superior power of capital.   Moreover, since modern discoveries were made to serve rather the interests of a few capitalists, the solid middle class, which formed the strongest support of the existing social order, began more and more to disappear, and society was divided into two hostile classes—the wealthier bourgeoisie, on the one hand, with their inveterate hatred of the Church and the nobility, with their insatiable avarice and

reckless oppression of the laborers as of an inferior race; on the other hand, the huge masses of the poor, particularly laborers in factories, filled with hatred and revenge against their capitalist oppressors. Thus a fertile soil was prepared for social democracy. It needed only agitators to make the "disinherited" acquainted with the results of agnostic science, and to fling the firebrand of rebellion into the masses of the laborers—and there stood social democracy full-fledged.

5. Moreover, liberalism endeavored to bring about a *centralization* in all departments of social economy, not only by utilizing modern discoveries in the field of industry, but still more by its control of education, and even of science, religion, and politics. Now, socialism, according to its very nature, aims at the greatest possible centralization. The means of production, the organization of labor, the distribution of produce, education, instruction—all is to be controlled by the state. The state takes upon itself the duties of the separate community, of the family, and of the individual. Hence Schäffle [1] logically concludes that "all centralization of the liberal state advances the cause of socialism and harmonizes with its principle."

But who has employed all means to centralize education, Church government, marriage discipline, the care of the poor? Who has abolished the independence of municipalities, churches, and religious orders, and given all into the hands of the state? This is the work of liberalism. Socialism is, therefore, nothing else than the logical development of the liberal idea of

[1] Quintessence of Socialism. English version edited by B. Bosanquet, London, p. 52.

the state. The state is the source of all right, say the liberals; to this principle socialism can rightfully appeal against liberalism and in favor of its own entire programme.

Thus it is beyond a doubt that liberalism and socialism are closely related to each other, and that there is, therefore, no possibility of an efficient stand against socialism from the side of liberalism. Liberalism has but one means against socialism—the police. As soon as it tries other remedies its inconsistency and inefficiency against socialism become lamentably evident.

CHAPTER IV.

SOCIALISM IMPRACTICABLE.

SECTION I.

STATE OF THE QUESTION.

§ I. *Socialistic Evasions.*

SOCIALISTS are adepts in the art of criticising modern
social conditions. Every grievance that is cropping
up, be it large or small, must furnish the text for a
homily on the oppressiveness, injustice, maladminis-
tration, and bankruptcy of the present social system.
In social democracy alone all hope is centred, it
alone is the redeemer of suffering humanity. Tirades
of this kind may be found almost every day in the *Vorwarts* and other socialist publications.

Fault-finding and criticising are easy. But if we
venture a modest inquiry as to what the socialist gentlemen propose to establish in lieu of the existing social
order, they suddenly become wonderfully reticent. Instead of detailing their plans for the future, they have
recourse to obscure and meaningless phrases, they
make pitiable efforts to evade the question, or even
shower down upon the unlucky questioner a flood of
invectives, calling him a dogmatizing blockhead, a
man devoid of science or power of thought, affected
with incurable stupidity, and such like pleasantries.

233

Whence these tactics? The answer is plain. Socialism, especially in Germany, has become a powerful political party. Political parties, however, are easily kept together as long as their platform is highly aggressive and critical and as negative as possible in its demands; and the more so the more wide-spread the dissatisfaction with other parties. But if the socialist leaders were to draw up a positive programme of practical measures, the party would soon disrupt entirely, or at least split into different factions. Also here the old adage would be verified: *Quot capita, tot sensus.*

Again, there is reluctance on the part of socialists to reveal their ideas on the future state of society for fear of criticism and ridicule. From the times of Minos to those of Cabet's Icaria, every attempt of practical communism has been doomed to dismal failure.[1] It needed no excessive penetration to foretell as much. And if now socialists were to come down from the clouds and to unfold their plans of the future, it would soon be evident that they are but revamping ancient, unpractical utopias. Therefore they wisely remember that silence is gold.

That in reality there are no other motives for this socialist game of hide-and-seek is made evident by a glance at the pitiable subterfuges by which socialist

---

[1] Concerning the communistic settlements made principally in the United States during the last century, cf *Stimmen aus Maria-Laach*, vol. XLIX. p. 284 sqq, *H. Noyes*, History of American Socialism, *Nordhoff*, Communistic Societies of the United States, *Morris Hillquit*, History of Socialism in the U. S., part I. Of about one hundred communist experiments practically all have been failures. Most of them did not even reach the first anniversary of their foundation. Only those which were based on religious tenets have been more or less successful, but without attaining to any importance. (One of this kind, the Amana community in Iowa, is still in existence.) It is self-evident that communities based on religious enthusiasm cannot be introduced generally, and that their temporary success furnishes no argument for the practicability of the socialist scheme

leaders try to evade curious questions concerning the future state of society. We shall present to the reader an assortment of their current excuses, that he may judge for himself of the much-vaunted "scientific methods" and the "consciousness of purpose" of socialists.

1. "*What we think of future society does not concern you.* Therefore you need not bother our heads about it." A truly wonderful reply! Socialists are about to tear down the house in which we have lived peacefully hitherto; they want to make us emigrate, willy nilly, into a new abode, and yet we are denied the right to inquire into the condition of this new dwelling! Or are socialists inclined to throw all their opponents overboard before the shore of the promised land is reached?

2. "*Well, how do the other parties imagine that future society will be?*" How can such a question be addressed in full earnest to those who do not advocate any radical change of social conditions, but who rather endeavor to retain existing society at least as to its main features? A man who intends to preserve his house and to repair it as far as circumstances require, has no need of drawing up a plan for a new dwelling. But we are quite justified in demanding such a plan from him who is about to destroy the old house and to erect a new one.

Only a madman will tear down his house without knowing whether he will be able to replace it by a better one. Now, socialists are clamoring for "a radical abolition of the present social order" (Liebknecht), they intend to "make a clean sweep" of modern society (Bebel). They pursue their aim by all possible means, by arousing the passions of the poorer classes against the rich, by conjuring up before the eyes of the working population deceitful visions of a future reign of justice and prosperity. We are, therefore, perfectly justified in insisting that socialists should state their aims and purposes clearly and unmistakably.

3. "*What is to be done after the death of present society, events will show.*" This is unpardonable frivolity toward the whole of society. A system of organization for a society numbering tens of millions cannot be fetched from the pantry like a meat pie; it must be prepared long beforehand and introduced by gradual transitions. In fact, in all great changes, notably in the French Revolutions of 1789, 1830, and 1848, there were but enacted plans and measures which had been considered in detail many years before. The actual Revolution merely put into practice the plans long before matured in theory. Only raving maniacs destroy regardless of the future.

4. "*Idyllic pictures of the future are unscientific and utopian.*" So they are, in sooth; but to advance this excuse is rather strange for socialists who are hoodwinking the people with visions of future bliss. It is rank rascality to inveigh in unmeasured terms against existing society and to arouse the most ardent hopes in the hearts of workingmen by picturing to them their future paradise, but when it comes to give detailed information about it, to beg to be excused, because, forsooth, idyllic pictures of the future are unscientific and utopian.

The inquiry into the practicability of the future state can be called unscientific only if we are prepared to assume that in future men will be quite different and actuated by other motives than at present. Many socialists, indeed, favor this assumption, which, however, is undoubtedly false. Man may become more perfect, but at bottom he will remain essentially the same and be actuated by the same propensities and impulses.

We do not require of socialists to detail the future organization of society to the very last item, but we must demand of them to point out at least the principal features of their future building, the foundations, the main walls and pillars, the different floors and compartments, that we may know whether we can live there or not. No sensible man will expect the human race to take a leap in the dark with the chance of landing in chaos. Not unfrequently socialists demand that their schemes for the future be shown to be impracticable. This is shifting the burden of proof to the wrong shoulders. By their reorganization of society socialists intend to remove the existing misery and to inaugurate a reign of freedom and happiness. They have, therefore, the burden of proof; they must demonstrate the possibility of the proposed social system.

5. So far we have spoken of the future *state*. This word also serves socialists as a loophole to escape unwelcome questions. "In the future we do not want any state at all," Bebel exclaimed when hard pressed by his opponents in the Reichstag on the score of his schemes for the future. Mere tomfoolery! Socialists must also admit that in future there will be required some sort of regular community life, they must advocate what Engels and Bebel call "creating an organization of the administration which is to take charge of production and exchange," in order that collective industry "may become a source of the greatest prosperity and of universal harmonious

perfection." [1]   In a society of this kind there must be
laws, therefore also legislative and judicial powers.
What else is needed to constitute a state?   That the
people itself is supreme lawgiver and judge leaves
untouched the essence of the state.   It is useless
cavilling for socialists to maintain that they want no
state in the future.   In his speech anent the Erfurt
platform Liebknecht himself characterized the question whether the socialist system was to be called a
state or not as a "war about words."

Of course, if Engels' definition of the state as "an
organization of the exploiting class for the maintenance
of the conditions of production and thus especially
for the heavy-handed oppression of the exploited
classes" [2] is accepted as true, then it is evident why
socialists advocate the abolition of the state.   But
this definition is not only arbitrary, but manifestly
incorrect, since it makes of an accidental abuse the
very essence of the state.

Moreover, by advancing excuses of this kind,
socialists forget to act their part.   They pretend
to eschew visions of the future and yet they predict
that in future there will be a social and economic
system without a state.   It might perhaps be objected
that a state necessarily presupposes authority, whilst
socialists intend to abolish every artificial and trumped-
up authority.   "We are opposed to every authority,"
Bebel exclaimed in the Reichstag (Feb. 3, 1893),
"to that of heaven as well as to those of earth with

---

[1] Marx illustrates his idea of the future state by referring to a society of
free laborers, "who work with instruments of production owned in common,
and who consciously expend their many individual labor capacities as *one
social labor power*"   The "systematic social distribution of labor. . . .
regulates the proportion of the different functions to the different needs."
(Capital, p 45)

[2] Entwicklung des Sozialismus, p. 40.

which you confront us." Only that authority Bebel
is willing to tolerate which each one has acquired for
himself.

If this tirade is to be taken literally, it is tantamount
to the hare-brained anarchist motto *Ni Dieu, ni
maître.* Imagine a community numbered by millions
carrying on production and exchange according to a
uniform plan, but without any regulating authority!
It is probable, therefore, that Bebel rejected authority
only in so far as it is based on class supremacy and
special privileges. But that socialists should have
recourse to such ambiguities in order to ward off
their assailants is an indication of the little confidence
they have in the firmness of their own position.

6. The inquiry concerning the future state is "*a
question which only fools will answer.*" Thus Liebknecht replied to Dr. Bachem (Feb. 7, 1893), and he
added: "The state of the future is a matter of imagination; . . . it is in certain respects an ideal, but science
was never concerned about it. Our party has . . .
never admitted into its platform the Utopia of a
future state; . . . our party has never spoken to
the workingmen about the future state, except as about
a Utopia."

Liebknecht could have pronounced no more scathing condemnation of himself and his whole party
than is contained in these words. If only fools
answer questions concerning the future state, and if
socialists, notably Liebknecht, have answered such
questions, among which category of men shall we
class him and his "comrades"?

In the official platform, indeed, there are only a
few, but comprehensive, indications concerning the
system planned for the future. The party leaders,

however, from the first to the last, have given very
detailed answers to questions to which, as Liebknecht
tells us, only fools would reply. Detailed descriptions
of the future are furnished by Liebknecht himself
in his book: "Die Grund und Bodenfrage," which,
though published in 1876, is still offered for sale by
the *Vorwärts*. Also in his other work, "Was die So-
zialdermokraten sind und was sie wollen,[1] he indulges
in copious descriptions of the future.

The writings of Bebel abound still more in graphic
accounts of the future, e.g., his book " Unsere Ziele"[2]
and especially his famous work " Der Frau," which is
teeming with vivid pictures of the coming paradise.
Last year (1903) the thirty-fourth edition of this book
was published, but not one of the glowing descriptions
has been curtailed. Bebel himself declared in the
Reichstag (Feb. 6, 1893) that he abides fully and
squarely by whatever he had laid down in his last-
mentioned book. On the same occasion he repeated
twice that the aims of socialism can be ascertained
as to their main features in the existing socialist
literature. Thus, almost in the same breath Liebknecht proclaims that only fools can answer questions
concerning the future state, and Bebel refers to his
book "Die Frau," which by a remarkable coincidence
was just then published in its fourteenth edition, and
to socialist literature in general for the required
answer. And at the very same time Liebknecht
avers that his party never speaks to the workingmen
about the future state! What opinion can be enter-

[1] Second ed (Berlin, 1891). Also published in English by Kerr & Co.,
Chicago

[2] Sixth ed , 1886. In his preface Bebel remarks that he no longer agrees
with all the positive statements made in the book, yet he reissues it again
"because it is still of some value for *agitating.*" This is evidently the
main point.

tained of men entangled in such contradictions and talking at random, just as momentary necessity requires?

The example of Liebknecht and Bebel induced other partisans of socialism to furnish graphic accounts of how things will be managed in future and thus to answer questions which no reasonable man is supposed to answer. We may mention, e. g., J. Stern,[1] O. Köhler,[2] Bruno Geiser,[3] G. P. Weilgert,[4] Atlanticus.[5]

It cannot be objected by socialists that these predictions are merely private opinions, for, the opinions of so many prominent "comrades," who are looked up to by their followers as leaders in Israel, may certainly be taken as the general view of the party. And if the leaders are so ready with their answers, what visions of a future paradise will be conjured up by the fertile imagination of the masses?

7. There remains yet one excuse used by socialists to get rid of importunate questioners: We need not make any plans for the future, because *the existing social system of its own accord develops into socialism.* No one can predict what the future will be like, therefore

---

[1] Thesen über den Sozialismus, 1891.

[2] Der sozialdemokratische Staat, 1891.

[3] Die Forderungen des Sozialismus an Zukunft und Gegenwart, 1876.

[4] Die positiven Ziele der Sozialdemokratie, 1890

[5] Ein Blick in den Zukunftsstaat, 1898 This book has a preface by Kautsky, who remarks, that the socialist party is not tied down to any fixed plans for the future, but also that it does not taboo schemes of future social construction. Ideals of the future are to his mind the firmest bond of union between the different classes of workingmen "Take away from the struggling proletariat its socialist aims, and you deprive it of its enthusiasm and solidarity" Besides, socialism hasn eed of practised thinkers from the bourgeois ranks, but these "intellectuals" will not be attracted to socialism if its revolutionary aims are obscured The greatest champions of the proletariat—Marx, Lassalle, etc —were idealists and revolutionaries, not merely advocates of paltry labor reforms "If theoretical reasons forbid the movement to become more important than our aims the same is the case also for practical reasons of propaganda." Propaganda, as it seems, always takes the leading part. Quite recently Kautsky himself attempted to sketch visions of the future in a book entitled "Am Tage nacht der sozialen Revelution," 1903

all descriptions of the future are utopian dreams long
since discarded by "scientific" socialism. Socialists do
not clamor for the future society, they await its coming.

Such language may befit orthodox socialists who
cling convulsively to their theories of concentration, of
pauperization and collapse. The real worth of these
theories, however, has been exposed above (p. 158 sqq.),
and the revisionists who join us in rejecting them as at
variance with reality are entirely unjustified in offer-
ing similar excuses.

But the assertion that we do not know in the least
what the future will be like is utterly false. Man
remains essentially the same everywhere and at all
times, a being composed of body and soul, with the
same inclinations and aversions, the same leaning
toward enjoyment, idleness, liberty, and independence, etc.

Moreover, Bebel and the rest have not always spoken
as they do now. In his book "Unsere Ziele," the
eleventh edition of which appeared last year (1903),
Bebel avers: "When the time of action has arrived it
will be too late for theoretical discussions. The plans
for our future state must be worked out in every detail
before the great event."

When his contradictions were cast up to him in the
Reichstag by the deputies Richter and Bachem, Bebel
replied that his views had been modified, that since the
time of the pronouncement quoted above he had "developed" further. On the same occasion he made
the important confession that his party is "*continually
moulting*"

This is the much-vaunted "science" which socialists
never tire of extolling. In every edition Bebel's work
"Die Frau" has the following boastful conclusion:

"*Socialism is science* applied with full consciousness and clear knowledge to every function of human activity." Yet at the same time he endeavors to protect himself and his partisans by referring to their "continual moulting." Can we really speak of science if the most deep-rooted convictions of to-day are rejected as false to-morrow? Genuine science rears blocks of granite for an indestructible edifice. As long as there is reason to fear that our theory may be exploded some fine morning, it is anything but an immutable verdict of science. If socialism is indeed "continually moulting," a little more modesty would certainly not come amiss, but alas! genuine science and swaggering bravado are not usually found together.

Besides, the appeal to the "moulting" process will not avail Bebel very much. For the predictions of the future contained in his former works are repeated again and again in every new edition of "Die Frau." Why does he regale his readers anew with the selfsame visions, although his own views have been modified? although present society is developing of its own accord into the future system? although no one can know how things will look after twenty or thirty years? Is it perhaps because these predictions "are of some value in agitating"?

There is yet another circumstance liable to arouse serious doubts as to whether Bebel himself believes in the inevitable development of the socialist system. Both he and Engels had prophesied the great *Kladderadatsch* (the social revolution) to take place before the close of the nineteenth century. At the Erfurt convention Bebel declared: "I make no secret of it, it rejoiced my heart when my friend Engels in his well-known letter in the *Sozialist* predicted a radical change for the year 1898. Vollmar was pleased to poke fun at it, but I wrote to Engels: 'Old man, you and I are the only "juniors" of our party.'" [1]

Was Bebel, indeed, of such astounding simplicity as to believe that in the brief period of seven years till 1898 existing society would "develop" into collectivism? Meanwhile, 1898 has come and gone. Where is the great *Kladderadatsch*, the collectivist society? We are inclined to suppose that Bebel merely employs these catchwords as bait for the impatient rabble who cannot brook the slowness of parliamentary activity and therefore threaten to join the anarchist ranks. In fact, he acknowledged as much when, in his reply to Vollmar, who urged measures of present reform, he said that present reform tactics would ruin the party; the "comrades" would lose their enthusiasm if they were told that the ultimate purpose can be attained only in the remote future.

What we have said so far may suffice to characterize the present tactics of socialists. In view of their hole-and-corner politics and the screening of their ulterior projects it looks like a farce to see the *Vorwärts* [2] proclaiming in bold words: "We have nothing to conceal and our banner is waving in bold defiance." And again: [3] "In reality, our party is the only one that shows and can show to the people its purposes undisguised."

§ II. *Main Features of the Socialist Commonwealth.*

Despite their evasions socialists have time and again laid down and officially proclaimed certain funda-

---

[1] Report of the Transactions, pp. 282, 283 During the same Erfurt convention Bebel also said "I am sure the realization of our ultimate purpose is so near at hand that but few in this hall will not live to see the day" (Report, p 172.)

[2] Vorwärts, 1892, n. 275.

[3] *Ibid,* 1893, n. 138.

mental tenets concerning the future organization of society, from which it is possible to sketch the general features of the future collectivist system. "As to their main features, our projects for the future may be ascertained at any time in our existing literature." [1] And in fact the principal characteristics of future collectivism are indicated clearly enough for a reasonable verdict about its practicability.

1. *The Erfurt platform* says that the growing number of crises gives proof "that private property in the means of production has become incompatible with their proper utilization and full development. . . . *Only the transformation of private capitalistic property in the means of production*—i.e., land, mines and mining, raw material, tools, machinery, means of communication—*into common property and the change of private production into socialistic*—i.e., production for and through society—can effect that the extensive industry and ever-increasing productiveness of social labor shall become for the exploited classes, instead of a source of misery and oppression, a source of the highest prosperity and of universal and harmonious perfection."

Thereby the foundations of existing society are overthrown, class supremacy and the classes themselves are abolished, consequently also "the exploitation and oppression of the laboring class," in fact "every kind of exploitation and oppression, no matter against what class, party, race, or sex," are removed.

In the above sentences are contained the following demands:

(*a*) Transfer of the means of production into

---

[1] Bebel in the Reichstag, Jan. 31, 1893.

collective ownership, therefore abolition of private property in all the means of production.[1]

Whether the change to collective ownership is to be brought about suddenly or gradually, by peaceful means or by violence, with or without compensation to the expropriated, is beside the question   We insist on this purposely, because in his notes on the Erfurt platform Kautsky[2] maintains "The transition to the socialist system does not at all imply the expropriation of artisans and peasants"   This is a mere lawyer's trick to divert attention from the main point at issue   For it is quite evident that there is question here only of the time and manner of the transition, since two pages further back Kautsky confesses: "Production on a small scale is doomed to destruction"; nay, he even maintains that socialism hastens the absorption of small establishments by industry on a colossal scale   The truth about this general absorption of establishments will be found above (p 158 sqq).   It is interesting to note how Kautsky, in the same breath, promises the amelioration of the farmers' condition by means of socialism, and speaks of the inevitable disappearance of independent farmers.   But Kautsky must be more than naïve if he imagines that in spite of the promised improvements the peasants will gladly consent to the transition from private production to collective production on a large scale, merely on account of the attraction exercised by the higher forms of production on the lower ones   It will be a cold day when the peasant will voluntarily give up his small property in order to take out a policy in the General Socialist Happiness Insurance Company.

The platform of the *Socialist Party of the United States* also "declares its aim to be the organization of the working classes .   *for the purpose of transforming the present system of private ownership of the means of production and distribution into collective ownership by the entire people*"   And again we are told that "the same economic causes which developed capitalism

[1] In the election proclamation of April 30, 1903, signed by all the socialist members of the Reichstag, we read   "Our aim is the introduction of the socialist system of state and society based on collective ownership in the means of production and on the common duty of all to work "
[2] Das Erfurter Programm in seinem grundsätzlichen Teil erläutert, p 150.

are leading to socialism, which will *abolish both the capitalist* class and the class of wage-workers " [1]

The International Socialist convention at Paris (Sept. 1900) put up as condition for membership the admission of the "essential principles" of socialism. Among them there is in the first place "the socialization of the means of production and distribution." [2]

The *N. Y. Volkszeitung* (Jubilee ed , February 21, 1903, p. 29) presents the *Principles of Socialism* in seventeen different languages. In English they are as follows: The Socialist Party of the United States reaffirms its allegiance to the revolutionary principles of international socialism, and declares the supreme political issue in America to-day to be the contest between the working class and the capitalist class for the powers of government. We affirm our steadfast purpose to use those powers, once achieved, *to destroy the institution of private property in the means, of production and distribution, and to establish the Co-operative Commonwealth*

(*b*) Society as a whole manages production according to a uniform plan. This postulate is contained in the words, "change of private production into socialistic, i.e., for and through society." It is contained also in the reason given for this change. The Erfurt platform maintains that in consequence of economic developments "the productive forces . . . have become uncontrollable by society, and that private property in the means of production has become incompatible with their proper utilization and full development."

Therefore society at large (the state) is to regulate the proper application of the means of production and to manage and supervise the whole field of industry.

c. The national product, i.e., whatever has been produced collectively, belongs to society at large. After abstracting what is necessary for society taken

[1] Cf. above, p. 90 sqq.
[2] Cf. p. 110. Concerning Austrian socialists, cf. p. 110.

collectively, the rest of the product is to be distributed among the single members. For, according to the platform, also of American socialists, only the means of production are to become collective property. All articles of consumption are therefore to be distributed and to become private property. The Erfurt platform also makes complaint that in the present system, despite "the gigantic increase of the productiveness of human labor," the advantages of production are "monopolized." Therefore the socialist system must produce a change also in this respect, so that all may have not only equal duties but also equal rights without distinction of sex or pedigree. There will be no more distinction of classes; "the ever-increasing productiveness of social labor" will be in future "a source of the highest prosperity and of universal and harmonious perfection."

2. The plans for the future embodied in the Erfurt platform as well as in that of the Socialist Party of the United States are but repetitions of the ideas of the Grand Master of Socialism. What Marx thought about the essential features of collectivist society may be gathered from the passages quoted above (p. 54 sq.) especially from the more extensive quotation from "Capital" given in the footnote. Although Marx speaks there of collective production only by way of illustration, yet a comparison with p. 728 of the same work and with his "Criticism of the Social Democratic Platform" will prove that he had in mind the socialist system of the future.

Marx demands, in the first place, common ownership of all the means of production, systematic organization of labor, or, as he styles it, "the many individual forces are consciously expended as one social labor power." Then he continues: "The total product of the union will be a *co-operative product.* A certain part of it has to serve again as means of production and will remain common property. The other part will be for the consumption of the members. Therefore it must be *distributed.* The manner of distribution will vary according to the special organism of co-operative production and according to the corresponding degree of development in the producers. Only as a parallel to the production of merchandise do we presuppose that each producer's share will be determined by the time of his work. *The time of work will therefore play a double part.* On the one hand *its distribution on a co-operative plan will maintain the right proportion between the different functions of labor and the different requirements of the community.* On the other hand the time of work will serve *for measuring the share of the individual producer in the co-operative labor and in that part of the common product destined for individual consumption.*" A careful comparison of this passage with others quoted above, and especially with the "Criticism of the Social Democratic Platform," will show that the method of work and the manner of distributing the product here described are just what Marx assigns to the "first phase of communist society."

It is self-evident that Engels agrees on this point with his friend and mentor. Still it may not be amiss to cite some passages from his writings where the same ideas are clearly expressed.

Acording to his description of the process of evolution leading up to the new order of society, the commonwealth will abolish private production "by taking possession of the means of production." "The anarchy within collectivist production will be replaced

by a conscious organization on a well-planned system."
"The manner of production, appropriation, and exchange will be put in harmony with the collectivist
character of the means of production." "Collective
possession of the means of production will remove not
only the present artificial restraints, but also the positive squandering and destruction of productive forces
and of products. . . . Moreover, it will make available
for society at large a mass of productive forces and of
products by abolishing the senseless and wasteful
luxuries of the present ruling classes. . . . Now for
the first time there exists the possibility of assuring,
by means of collective production, to every member
of society an existence which is not only well supplied
in material respects, in ever-growing abundance, but
which also guarantees to the citizens the complete
development and utilization of their civic and intellectual gifts." [1]

In a pamphlet on the nature and aims of socialism [2]
Liebknecht expounds the socialist plans in the following manner: "Down with the wage-system! this is
the fundamental demand of socialism. . . . In place
of wage labor and class supremacy we must have social
labor (co-operative production). The instruments of
labor must cease to be monopolized by a certain class,
they must become the common property of all. No
more exploiters and no more exploited. Regulation
of the production and distribution of products on behalf
of society at large. Abolition of existing commerce,
which is no better than fraud. In the order of equality
every laborer is to take part in the work necessary for
all the members of the commonwealth. Instead of

[1] *Engels*, Dührings Umwälzung, etc., p. 270.
[2] Was die Sozialdemokraten sind und was sie wollen (1891), p. 18.

employers and their . . . wage-slaves . . . free comrades. Labor painful to no one because the duty of all (!). An existence worthy of man for every one who does his duty to society. . . . And that all this may be realized (there must be) the democratic state, . . . *a state which is a society organized on the principles of reason and justice, a general insurance company of happiness and culture, a fraternal community of freemen and equals.*" Social democracy, he explains further on, "demands order, . . . peace and harmony of interests, abolition of the classes; . . . it demands ownership for all; it demands . . . for the workingman the full product of his social labor; . . . it demands equal and the best obtainable education for each individual, . . . perfect political and social equality of women and men."

Essentially the same plans for the future are met with in the writings of all the socialists who have ever expatiated on the aims of their party. Thus Bebel,[1] J. Stern,[2] K. Kautsky,[3] who is styled by Vollmar "*the* theorist of socialism," O. Köhler, Weilgert, and others. Bebel protests indeed that he proposes no more than his own personal opinions, but considering the high regard which is paid to him in socialist circles, his views may be looked upon as the common property of the rank and file of German socialists and of many others

---

[1] Especially in his books: Unsere Ziele (6th ed., 1886), Die Frau (18th ed., 1893).

[2] Thesen über den Sozialismus, 1890

[3] "Das Erfurter Programm in seinem grundsätzlichen Teil erläutert." The official Erfurt platform was drafted by Kautsky In another work, "Grundsätze und Forderungen der Sozialdemokratie," p 26, he says "The ultimate goal of evolution . is the union of all industrial establishments into one colossal state industry, i e , the transformation of the state into one industrial society Capitalist production ceases and a new method of production is developed, based on the collective ownership of the means of production " Cf. also *Kautsky*, "The Social Revolution," Kerr & Co , Chicago.

beyond the boundaries of the empire. But as we shall have numerous occasions, in our criticism of the socialist plans, to revert to Bebel's opinions, we may spare ourselves the trouble of rehearsing them in this place.

To complete our present disquisition we might appeal to the authority of A. Schäffle,[1] Ad. Wagner, Fr. Hitze, and other prominent sociologists, who, as the result of a careful study of socialist writings, have arrived at the same conclusions as ourselves concerning the future commonwealth. But what has been said may suffice for the present.

Yet it will be necessary here to enter more fully upon one feature which is of the greatest importance for our future inquiry—*the appropriation of all means of production by the state.* It is erroneous to maintain that socialism would leave to separate communities or groups of laborers the possession of the means of labor and the organization of labor. That would be anarchism or communism, but not socialism in its genuine sense. The chief plank in the platform of modern socialism is the abolition of what it calls the anarchy of production, which it regards as the root of all social evils, and the institution of a *systematic scheme* of production. But this end can be attained only if the entire state is the proprietor of all labor materials, the distributor of labor and of its proceeds. This scheme does not necessarily exclude the existence, in the socialistic order, of guilds or labor unions, communes, districts, etc., as

[1] Quintessence of Socialism This book is advertised thus by the above-mentioned Chicago socialist publishing house

"This work is by an opponent of socialism, but an opponent who is unusually fair as well as able It is one of the best answers that can be found to the thousand and one objections to socialism that are based on nothing but ignorance or falsehood."

Later on Schäffle himself refuted the concessions made in the Quintessence in favor of socialism by publishing another work: Die Aussicht-slosigkeit des Sozialismus (Impracticability of Socialism).

members of its hierarchical order. But, in any case, a strict subordination of these various orders under one supreme state authority is regarded as essential.

If the ownership of all labor means and, consequently, of the proceeds of labor, and the organization of labor itself, would be left to separate communities, so that they could produce what they chose and as much as they pleased, our present competition would not be abolished, but only raised to a different level. Instead of the private capitalists we should then have the communities as competitors. Therefore the anarchy of production would remain in full force; and a mistake committed in the system of production would only be the more detrimental, as it would not then affect private individuals only, but entire communities. One community could in that case, by intelligence, industry, and favorable circumstances, acquire immense riches, while another might fall into a state of utter wretchedness; and if every community should be industrially independent, and if communal property should exist, would every individual of the community then be free to leave his own community and betake himself to another? And if so, is another community obliged to receive and to tolerate strangers? If such liberty and independence should not exist, we would have a condition of perfect slavery; if it did exist, then a systematic control of labor wou'd be impossible, since it could not be ascertained at any time what labor power would be at the disposal of the community. The better-conditioned communities would be deluged, while the less prosperous would be deserted.

Besides, the individual groups could not possibly each produce all its own necessaries, and would be, in consequence, obliged to enter into commercial relations with the neighboring communities or with foreign countries. Would this circumstance not lead to endless quarrels between communities, and produce a condition of universal warfare? Would not then the more powerful, that is, the richer, communities obtain political ascendency, and thus subject the democracy to their own aristocratic rule? Socialists sometimes speak of a union or *federation* of the communities as a remedy against such results. But if the several communities were industrially independent of one another, and possessed private property, such a federation would be short-lived. As in ancient Greece, the different communities would carry on a continual struggle for the supremacy; and finally the weaker communities would succumb to the stronger. And who should divide the produce among the different communities? Could such a division be made to the satisfaction of all?

We believe, therefore, that an organization in which the several communities would be industrially independent of one another, and would possess communal property, has never been seriously thought of by modern socialists. And, in fact, the great leaders of socialism do not favor such a division of the national industrial system According to their plans, the socialist state is to take the place of our modern states; and the place of monarchs and cabinets is to be occupied by a central committee, which is to direct the entire industrial system. True, Engels, Bebel, and other socialists do not wish to call this democratic magistracy a "government," nor do they wish their organization to be called a "state " They believe that this central committee need only devise the mechanism of production and set it in motion, and the entire extensive machine will move spontaneously in the most harmonious order But, though we might admit the possibility of such an improbable fact, it remains true that socialists aim at a central organization of industry, at a united, orderly, independent commonwealth of the average area of our present states, and such a commonwealth is no more nor less than a state.

Hence Schaffle [1] seems truly to have characterized socialism in the following passage: "The only system of socialism imaginable is, and will continue to be, central organization, universal and exclusive collective production by the social democracy." "It must be clearly borne in mind that socialistic production involves, as an axiomatic necessity, a single or united organization What shape this organization would take, whether centralized or federal, whether absolute or democratic, . . . need not now be considered. . . But every socialist must necessarily insist on the necessity of a social, and hence of a unified, system, i e., on the union in one management, with a definite purpose, of the process of production as such. The anarchy of individualistic competition is, according to his premises, the source of all the evils, all the swindling and disorganization, all the fluctuation, exploitation, and injustice of the present system The socialist state will not be realized till there remains only collective property in the instruments of social production " [2]

The following pen-picture of the socialistic state ready-made has been drawn by Franz Hitze: "The state is the only proprietor of all means of labor—of all lands, all manufactories, all means of transportation, all labor tools, all commerce, and perhaps also of all schools At the head of the organization stands a perfect democratic government to be chosen by the people, say every two years; this government culminates in a committee, perhaps in a president The committee has the administration of the entire state; not only the political (legislative, executive, judicial), but also the control of the entire production, of the entire distribution, of the entire consumption (at least in its more general aspect, e g , how much is to be deducted from consumption in favor of production, etc). Although labor may be entrusted to the direction of subcommittees and departments, yet there must always be one comprehensive, supreme, and decisive authority. Under this central authority are the provincial departments and communal bureaus, which discharge the same functions in behalf of their several districts as the central committee in behalf of the state; but all these must be subordinate to the supreme central board " [3]

---

[1] Aussichtslosigkeit der Socialdemocratie, p. 5
[2] Quintessence, pp 61, 62.
[3] *Hitze*, Kapital und Arbeit (1880), p 286. Cf. *Todt*, Der Radikale deutsche Socialismus (1878), p 218 *Stern*, Thesen, p 8

Similarly, Adolf Wagner: [1] "If socialists wish to be consistent, they cannot leave to the several communities communal property either in capital or in land, and must have recourse to an effective coercive control by one supreme central authority for the estimation and application of the national capital. Capital as well as land must be the property of the entire state."

Rudolf Meyer [2] characterizes as an essential feature of socialism the demand that "production established on a social basis be regulated and controlled by the state."

§ III. *Question at Issue More Accurately Determined.*

We have become acquainted with the foundations and the supporting pillars of the socialist edifice. Before we begin, however, to test their strength and solidity we must determine more accurately what we intend to prove.

1. When we call the socialistic demands impracticable or impossible, we intend to confine this statement to *modern democratic socialism.* We do not maintain that a social order, such as that devised by the socialists, involves a contradiction or is impracticable under all conditions. If men generally were entirely unselfish, industrious, obedient, filled with interest for the common weal, always ready to give everybody else the preference, and to choose for themselves the last and most disagreeable place— in short, if men were no longer men, as they are, but angels, a social order, according to the plan of the socialists, would not be impossible. But such a supposition cannot be made in favor of modern socialism.

2. Nay, we concede still more: we will not even dispute that a state organization for the regulation

---

[1] Grundlegung, p 614.
[2] Emancipationskampf des vierten Standes, p. 78.

and the distribution of all produce might be practicable under a strictly absolute government. If we could imagine an uneducated and undeveloped population blindly following the dictates of a despotic monarch, we might conceive most of the demands of the socialists as practicable. In the ancient kingdom of the Incas many of the dreams of socialists were realized. But we must bear in mind that the Inca, as the supposed offspring of the sun, enjoyed divine honor and ruled with unlimited sway. Moreover, the state of civilization in the ancient kingdom of the Incas cannot be brought into comparison with the circumstances of modern civilized countries.

Socialism on a *democratic basis*,[1] implying the absolute equality of all, is, at least in its entirety, something impossible. We say *in its entirety*, or inasmuch as it is conceived as one organized system; for whether one or a few demands taken singly may be realized or not it is not our business to investigate, since this one or these few demands do not constitute socialism. For the rest, many of the socialistic demands are essentially connected with one another, so that one cannot exist without the others. Such are, for instance, the possession of all means of production by the state, the systematic organization of production, and the distribution of produce according to some given common standard.

3. It is not our intention to maintain that socialism might not for a brief period be realized *by force*. For what a violent revolution, which sweeps over a country

---

[1] By its very nature, modern socialism implies extreme democracy, as is evident not only from the demand of perfect equality, but also from the collective ownership of the means of production. To socialize the instruments of labor, and yet to reserve their control to a certain faction would be tantamount to condemning every one else to absolute slavery.

like a hurricane, might bring about by the reign of terror goes beyond all human calculation. Even the incredible has been realized in the world's history. We need only recall the English Revolution in the seventeenth century and the French Revolution in the eighteenth. What we maintain is that a *permanent* socialistic order is impossible, because it is in direct contradiction with the unchangeable inclinations and instincts of human nature.

4. In our refutation of socialism we shall confine ourselves to that form which goes by the name of *social democracy* or *collectivism,* which terms we take to be synonymous. This form of socialism comprises the most numerous and influential opponents of the existing social order, and in the minds of its defenders has most prospects of realization because it embodies the most rational and the most systematic plan for a social revolution. If, then, we have refuted this most popular and wide-spread form of socialism, the minor systems will of themselves fall to pieces. Our attention, however, will be directed principally to its *economic aims* and to their necessary consequences. For these aims form the very marrow of socialism and differentiate it from other systems. The Erfurt platform separates the economic from the political demands, which latter are characterized as attainable already in the existing order of society. The *political demands* generally enumerated in socialist platforms are partly realized in certain states, as, e.g., the referendum in Switzerland, the initiative in Colorado, South Dakota, and some other states of the Union. Others, again, as the settlement of international disputes by arbitration, might well be adopted by non-socialist platforms.

5. In the course of this chapter we shall repeatedly have occasion to draw certain consequences from socialist demands. To guard against being reproached with useless pettifogging, we remind the reader that from the demands whose impracticability we are going to show, we draw only those consequences which follow with absolute necessity. For the best criterion of the correctness or falsity of general principles and demands lies in the consequences necessarily derived from them.[1]

Now, in all socialist writings we meet again and again the following fundamental demands which are found already in the Gotha and Erfurt platforms: (1) Socialization of all the means of production. (2) Social organization of the entire field of production to replace the existing anarchy of production, (3) on the basis of the greatest possible democratic equality, so as to remove permanently all class supremacy and class privileges. These essential demands necessarily imply (4) the distribution of the social product according to a fixed standard. For the social product is owned by society at large and must be distributed to the single members according to some standard or other. The social organization of production also involves unavoidably the distribution of work and of labor forces. Again, the transformation of society into a co-operative company is impossible without far-reaching changes in every phase of human life. It implies the abolition of private enter-

---

[1] In a review of the fourth German edition of the present work (*Neue Zeit*, 1890-1891, ii p 638) Kautsky remarks "To quarrel with them (the adversaries of socialism) about the consequences which would, might, could follow the realization of our demands appears to us entirely superfluous." Superfluous indeed! In this manner one may comfortably avoid all disagreeable discussions As if our inferences had been drawn arbitrarily and at random!

prise, of commerce, of money in the ordinary sense of the word, of banks, stock-exchanges, and financial corporations. Family life, education, etc., would take an entirely new aspect.

It is our purpose, therefore, to test the principal socialist demands by their necessary consequences and thereby prove to the thoughtful reader how utterly untenable they are.

SECTION II.

THE ORGANIZATION OF LABOR.

§ I. *Socialization of Productive Goods.*

Socialists intend to make all means of labor, the "sources of life," as Marx terms them, not only the soil, but also manufactories, machinery, raw materials, work-tools, the exclusive property of the entire community. One of their chief demands is "the conversion of all labor materials into the common property of society." [1] Only consumable articles or such as are immediately destined for use shall, as the remuneration for labor performed, become private property. But here grave misgivings at once present themselves.

1. Must the time be awaited when all proprietors will of their own accord give up their estates in behalf of society? That time will surely never come. Or will socialists make short work of it and bring about socialization by main force? "It is nonsense," Bebel said to a meeting of workingmen at Bamberg, Sept. 24, 1902, "if you are told that we wish to change present conditions by force." But let us suppose that violence is resorted to after all, will not the proprietors,

[1] Cf. above, p. 245, sqq.

especially the farmers, take up arms and repel violence by violence? "The expropriators will be expropriated." This is easily said, but not easily done. Will not the final result be a revolution that will overthrow the whole social fabric and whose clinching argument will be the guillotine?

2. Are the present owners to be indemnified? If they are not, then it will be only because private property is looked upon as unjust. But how can socialists substantiate this allegation, since many of them have abandoned Marx's theory of value as worthless? If the owners are to be indemnified, whence will be derived the immense funds necessary for that purpose? Will the new socialist society take upon itself this crushing burden although the benefits will accrue only to later generations?

3. But let us assume for the moment that the whole process is carried on smoothly and "according to programme." We are then confronted by the next question: What is meant by *productive* goods, and what are *consumable* goods? · Both these kinds of goods may well be distinguished in the mind. But as soon as we put the question in the concrete, whether this or that article is productive or only consumable, the difficulty becomes manifest. Many objects may be either productive and useful or consumable, according to the end for which the possessor wishes to employ them. A garden, for instance, is a useful object; it yields the possessor fruits, affords him the facility of taking exercise and fresh air and enjoying the beauty and fragrance of its flowers and the shade of its trees; but the fruits and vegetables which it produces may also be sent to the market either in their primitive state or prepared and preserved, and thus

rendered of still higher value. The same may be said of a house, a horse, a carriage, or of any article of furniture or of domestic use. Needles and thread and sewing-machines are articles of immediate use in a family; but they may also be used by the tailor or dressmaker to make clothes for others, and thus they become productive.[1]

Now, are all those articles of use to become common property? If so, every individual would be dependent upon the community even in the most trivial matters. Domestic life with mutual services would be a thing impossible. The only way out of the difficulty would be that such objects of use which might be also serviceable for production would be left to individuals with a legal injunction not to employ them for productive purposes, but only for their own private use.[2] Such an arrangement, however, would necessarily lead to a most extensive and minute police supervision, and give occasion to endless frauds. Let us suppose, for instance, that an orchard is given to the father of a family for his

---

[1] Cf. *Leroy-Beaulieu*, Le Collectivisme, p. 13 sqq.

[2] Paulsen (System der Ethik, vol II p 407) is of opinion that not only furniture, works of art, ornaments, and books, but also houses and gardens, might remain private property, "with all the effects peculiar to private ownership—with the right to bequeath and to donate, to consume and to preserve, to sell and to lend them." However, this would manifestly demolish the entire system of socialism This freedom would enable private individuals to acquire extensive property by the purchase, inheritance, or donation of houses, gardens, and other rentable property, and finally to come to such wealth and independence as to live on their income—which is hardly consistent with the socialistic scheme A socialist might urge in favor of Paulsen's theory that houses, gardens, etc , might be safely allowed to pass into private hands, because in a system in which all parties are daily employed in production and are forced to earn the necessaries of life no one would care for further income. However, this supposition is untrue Wealth would also in a socialistic state lead to power and influence, and would therefore not be looked upon with indifference And besides, what motives could influence a man to work if he could live on his income? Would it not be necessary, then, to use violent measures in order to make him work? But would not such force bring about the most unbearable slavery? If socialism would pretend to succeed, it cannot be satisfied with half-measures, it must remain consistent in its demands.

own use, with the strict injunction not to use the fruit for any other purpose, but to deliver the surplus to the public magazines. How much of the fruit would be delivered to the community? Would the possessor in that case deal economically with the produce of his garden? Would he keep it in good condition and endeavor to improve it? Would he not be inclined secretly to donate or to sell what he could not use for himself?

4. What is to be done with articles of value which are utterly unproductive, with objects of art, with diamonds, pearls, all kinds of ornaments? Are all women supposed to lay their jewelry upon the altars of their country, and to use the working-apron as their sole adornment? But why do we ask this? We have forgotten that vanity and love of finery will be unknown in the socialist future. Even the daughters of Eve will find their only delight in strenuous labor for the common weal!

§ II. *Mode of Determining the Social Demand.*

Let us suppose for the moment that the distinction between consumable and productive goods were sufficiently established, and that all means of production were "socialized," or placed in the possession of the community at large. Now it remains to regulate the national production. The Erfurt platform speaks plainly of the "change of private production into socialistic, i.e., production *for* and *through* society." This is quite in accordance with the ideas of K. Marx expounded above (p. 248 sqq.) and of Fr. Engels.[1]

[1] According to Engels (Die Entwicklung des Sozialismus, etc., p. 48) "social production according to a predetermined plan" becomes possible after the proletariat, by using the public powers, shall have transformed all the means of production into public property.

But such a regulation can be effected only after the average social demand has been estimated; for the satisfaction of the social demand is the object and, at the same time, the standard by which the extent of production is to be determined. The social demand must therefore be ascertained by daily, weekly, monthly, or yearly statistical estimates.

Some one may think perhaps that such estimates would be superfluous; that we might simply take the present rate of consumption as the basis of the socialistic production. But granting even that the present rate of consumption could be statistically established in detail, which, however, is hardly possible, it would by no means serve as the standard of production in a socialist state, since it is the result of the present state of property and production. It supposes, on the one hand, large incomes on the side of capital and, on the other hand, small incomes on the side of labor; it supposes particularly the wage or service system, and is based on the condition of private production. Therefore, as Adolf Wagner [1] justly remarks: "The consumption of our day is the result of the present distribution of income and property, and of private rents arising from real estate and capital. A statistic calculation, therefore, based upon the present conditions would be insufficient." Much less can we suppose that the supreme authority in the socialist state would simply fix the demand in regard to quality and quantity of the products by a peremptory *order*, and thus determine the amount and kind of production. Such an action would, absolutely speaking, be possible; but, to say nothing of the fact that it would be inconsistent with the demo-

[1] Grundlegung, 3d ed , part II, § 1*4.

cratic organization of socialism, it would be in itself unmitigated tyranny; for freedom consists, above all things, in the liberty to determine of one's self the conditions of one's life in regard to food, clothing, housing, recreation, means of mental improvement, etc. He who cannot use his free choice in these matters, but must follow the dictates of higher authority, is a slave, though he may be called a "free comrade." Freedom in the determination of one's own wants is also the necessary condition of all progress and culture.[1]

Let us suppose, then, that it was theoretically left to the choice of each to determine his own demands —we say *theoretically*, for practically this freedom would be limited by want of sufficient income. Also the factory laborer of to-day is theoretically free to determine his own wants; but practically this freedom is greatly limited by his income. This would be the case also in the socialist state; for no one would have any other income than the proceeds of his labor. Socialists, it is true, do not fail to hold out grand prospects to the laborer. J. Stern [2] assures us that in the socialist state "all would possess all things in abundance, to their heart's content," and characterizes as "Philistines" those who refuse to give him credence. However, we are not inclined to believe in such a multiplication of loaves and fishes. But we shall

[1] Also *Schäffle* (Quintessence, p. 40) remarks "Freedom of demand is a first essential of freedom in general If the means of life and culture were somehow allotted to each from without, and according to an officially drawn-up scheme, no one could live out his own individuality or develop himself according to his own ideas, the material basis of freedom would be lost. It is therefore important to determine whether or not socialism would annul individual freedom of demand If it would, it is dangerous to liberty, opposed to the growth of individuality, and hence to that of moral culture generally, and has no prospect of satisfying the most unconquerable instincts of man."

[2] Thesen, p. 28.

have occasion hereafter to submit this point to a fuller examination. Besides, the chief representatives of socialism themselves seem to entertain some misgiving in regard to such a miracle. Bebel,[1] at least, frankly confesses that "luxury will cease," but he adds, "poverty and starvation also." When all shall have nearly the same income, it is greatly to be feared that the pittance will turn out rather meagre. In another passage Bebel[2] says that the determination of the demands will be an *easy* matter, "because objects of luxury which are nowadays purchased only by the minority will come into disuse," and "the community will have to decide in how far demands are to be satisfied by new productions."

By these words is sufficiently implied, consistently with the principles of socialism, that each one will obtain only those necessaries which the community at large will agree to produce. Production, of course, depends in its quantity and quality upon the articles in demand. New demands also require new means of production. Will every one, then, be at liberty to order for his own use new objects which require new industrial arrangements, and consequently involve an increase of the common labor? But if the community at large or its representatives should have first to decide whether the wishes of individual members are to be gratified or not, the freedom of determining the demands is thereby all but destroyed.

Still more oppressive than this restriction of personal freedom would be the burden imposed upon every family—for we suppose in the mean time that in the socialist state the family would still continue to exist—to manifest all its wants in advance and

[1] Unsere Ziele, p 30   [2] *Ibid.*, p. 31.

have them registered by the officials appointed for this purpose. In order to know what and how much of every commodity should be produced, and in order to make out the plan of production, it must first be ascertained what each one needs and demands. Therefore, husband and wife, or perhaps both, must report all their wants and wishes, small as well as great, to the respective officials at the bureau of consumption, in order that they may at the specified time be able, on presenting their labor certificates, to draw the desired articles from the public magazines.

Not to make ridiculous suppositions in reference to the socialist state, we shall admit that a certain supply of the more ordinary articles of daily use is kept on hand, so that each one can, on presenting his labor certificate, draw the ordinary necessaries from the public stores. This scheme, however, could be employed only in regard to the most common articles of daily use. Now, if our present system of production, which always endeavors to be ready to meet all demands, cannot have sufficient supplies of all articles in demand, at all times and in all places, this would be all the more impossible in the socialist state; or such a state would necessarily fall into the same error of which it accuses our present system of production—that is, it would produce at haphazard a huge quantity of goods which would lie idle and unconsumed in the state or communal storehouse.

J. Stern, with surprising naïveté, is of opinion that in the socialist state there is no need of determining the demand because everything will be furnished in the most lavish profusion

The exposition of Stern is simply astonishing when he comes to describe the distribution of produce. Every one who can show that he has performed a certain amount of labor has the most unlimited right to any species of consumable goods in any quantity he may choose to fix. He draws his clothing from the public stores, he dines at the public hotel on what he pleases; or, if he prefers, he may dine at home in a highly comfortable residence, which is in communication with the public hotels (by telephone, pneumatic tube, and by whatever other inventions may be made in the mean time), whence he may in the most convenient way [per tube?] order his meals, just as he pleases; or, if he prefers, he may have them prepared at home [by whom?]; or he may prepare them himself. (Thesen, pp. 12, 13.)

Such a description may, in fact, gladden the heart of a credulous socialist. With a minimum of work-time he may enjoy himself to the full. He will see before him fountains of sack, champagne, Bavarian beer, and cognac, from which every workingman may quench his thirst at pleasure. He will sit at tables laden with the most delicate viands. With contempt he will look back upon the days of brown bread and potatoes. Having eaten and drunk to his heart's content, the workingman will go to the theatre or concert, or will drive out in a fine equipage until, late at night, tired of enjoyment, he will retire to rest upon his soft couch. Stern, however, has forgotten one thing. Who will procure and prepare all these dainties? Who will wait upon his socialistic lordship? Who will perform for him in the theatres and concerts? Who will saddle or harness his steeds, and act as his groom? Stern, it is true, revels in the prospects of great inventions in the field of electricity. But does he really imagine that electricity will be made so serviceable as finally to prepare and serve his dinner to the socialist, to fit out his residence for him, and to give him a theatrical performance? And then how can all these good things be procured and prepared in such quantities that each one with the minimum of labor may obtain the maximum of enjoyment? It is truly amazing how Stern rehearses all these foolish dreams with such a show of conviction. And yet, if any one refuses him credence, he does not hesitate to call him a Philistine—which is, to say the least, a very cheap kind of argumentation.

It remains, therefore, that every family is obliged to report all its necessities—if we except the most common objects of daily use—to the officials at the proper bureaus. Yet this cannot be supposed to be a light burden At present every one is at liberty to supply all his own wants at pleasure, either by his own labor or by purchase, when and where and from whomsoever he pleases, whether at home or abroad. Thus he is enabled to conceal the secrets of his household from the public gaze. Even business. people, laborers, physicians, druggists, etc., are bound to secrecy, at least by their own interest. In the socialist state, however, every one could, by examining the public registers, pry into the deepest secrets of every household. For in the socialist state there would be no professions bound to secrecy by their own interests as they are now, and the public registers would be open to the gaze and inspection of the sovereign people.

Besides, we cannot overlook the fact that the socialistic system would require a huge amount of clerical work to determine the demands of an extensive commonwealth. Socialists, however, point to our modern syndicates, corporations, state industries, etc., to show how easy it would be to determine the wants of a nation. But they overlook the immense difference between a single comparatively small company, established for a limited purpose, and an entire commonwealth made up of several millions of human beings. How much writing, for instance, does a single census cost? It takes years to arrange and publish its results. And yet there the conditions are comparatively simple The same schedules are to be filled out all over the country, and contain mostly simple questions which almost any member of the family can answer.

But a census is mere child's play compared with a determination of social demand. Here there is question not only of finding out the members of the family, the area of the farm, or the yearly output of the factory, but it will be necessary to inquire into the daily needs of every man or every family in the most varied circumstances. Even the smallest details in the matter of clothing, underwear, toilet articles, travelling outfits, writing materials, amusements, and luxuries would have to be ascertained and tabulated.

Add to all this the numerous articles of food which are required even in the humblest family, the supplying of the kitchen with fuel and cooking utensils, the fitting up of the drawing-rooms and bedrooms with furniture and ornamentation, the lighting and heating, the stocking of the pantry, etc., besides the necessary repairs. There must be included the mending of clothes, furniture, etc. For in the commonwealth of the future there will be absolutely no private enterprises. Since the means of production are collective property, every branch of production is to be carried on by society at large. The authorities will have to supply needle and thread to replace the missing shirt-button. All these items must be tabulated for the determination of the demand upon which the great system of production is to be based. And all this would have to be done not for one family alone, but for the millions of families which constitute a modern state and for every one of their members.

But again, how unequal the needs of different families according to their several occupations, their abode, their varying modifications! We must always bear in mind that now there is not question of families in primitive circumstances. Present society is highly civilized, and its countless exigencies were practically unknown in former times. Even a cursory glance at the immense department stores of our large cities, with their thousands of different articles, will convince any one of the great variety of modern requirements.

Moreover, the social demand is not at all constant; it varies from month to month, from week to week, even from day to day. Many requirements cannot be foreseen in the least; suddenly and unexpectedly they make their presence felt. Monthly statistics would therefore not suffice. Weekly or even daily inquiries would become necessary, or at least there would be needed numerous offices where lists of requirements could be filed.

However, it would not suffice to provide for single families; the needs of society at large, all public requirements, would also have to be satisfied. In the first place would come the arrangements for transportation: streets and roads, bridges, railways, canals, vehicles of all kinds. The care of all this would be incumbent on the paternal state. What an amount of daily exertion to supply a large city with meat, milk, fruit, vegetables, etc.! Private hotels would also be abolished. It would become the function of public officials to provide shelter, food, and service, for every comer, unless travelling is to be forbidden in the socialist commonwealth. Then, again, the whole of the building business will be in the hands of the state. Public and private edifices, dwellings, schools, hospitals, insane asylums, storerooms, theatres, museums, public halls, post and telegraph offices, railroad stations, would have to be erected and kept in repair, or enlarged as necessity required. And these buildings could not be handed over to contractors, as is generally done nowadays; the state alone could take care of drawing up the plans and specifications, of gathering the necessary materials and workmen, of directing and supervising the erection. If the state is supposed to do all this systematically, without squandering an immense amount of labor and materials, the extent and quality of the requirements in the entire commonwealth must be ascertained long beforehand by some responsible authority.

What the different city and town administrations are doing now, and as a rule through private contractors, in the matter of streets, public health, water-supply, lighting, baths, etc., would fall to the care of the state. Physicians, surgeons, druggists, nurses, midwives would have to be appointed, and it would be incumbent upon the state to provide for the professional education of a sufficient number of people for all these offices. The state would have to find ways and means to take care of education, of the press, literature, arts, theatres, museums, etc. Private enterprise would be abolished also in this respect; the editing and publishing of daily papers, magazines, and periodicals would all become official business.

Thus far we have considered the business to be transacted in the several cities. To this would have to be added the management of the farms, vineyards, vegetable gardens, cattle and stock raising, the forests and fisheries, mining, smelting, and other industrial processes. In all these departments the requirements would have to be accurately ascertained before there could be any question of a systematic regulation of production.

Finally, we must not forget the official and private relations with foreign countries. No modern state is self-sufficient. With regard to numberless products it must have recourse to other countries. At the same time due care must be taken of the export trade. As things are now, imports and exports are managed by merchants all over the country. Countless commercial travellers study the condition of the market; the most advantageous chances of buying and selling are ascertained. The transportation and distribution of commodities throughout the country is taken charge of by numerous business concerns. All this work and care, which at present is divided among thousands of different firms, would fall to the share of the socialist central government. In its hands would converge the millions of intricate threads of international relations. Can any human wisdom be equal to this stupendous task? And then consider the opportunities and temptations of embezzlement. The yearly exports and imports of Germany or the United States amount to billions of dollars. All this money would pass through the hands of officials stationed in different parts of the globe, and whom it would be impossible to control.

·It may be objected, of course, that the future commonwealth would dispense with money for its internal affairs, and that therefore this commodity could be safely entrusted to officials for whom it would have no value at home. But it suffices, if money has value at least in foreign countries, and if the officials have the chance of emigrating at the proper moment. And how could a state compete with other countries in foreign commerce, if the rate of exchange were fixed by those other countries, since in the socialist states only labor certificates would be of value? This difficulty would indeed be removed if socialism were introduced simultaneously among all civilized nations.

But this universal and simultaneous introduction of socialism is manifestly impossible.

Finally, to answer satisfactorily all the questions confronting the socialist commonwealth before it could draw up a plan of systematic production, would it not require an overwhelming amount of statistical labor, and a huge army of bureau officials? And would not such a complicated system of bureaucracy be subject to the greatest blunders, which perhaps would prove fatal to the entire system of production and to the existence of the nation? And when we consider, moreover, that these legions of officials would be bound by no private interest to the faithful administration of their office, could we expect a statistical result which might serve as a safe basis for production?

§ III. *Division of the Labor Forces.*

We suppose now that the demands have been determined by the central bureau on the basis of the statistics received from the several communities or provinces. Now comes the task of organizing the national labor, as the Erfurt platform has it, of carrying on production systematically "for and through society," or, as Marx has worded it, "of dividing the work according to a social plan." For this purpose there is required first of all a division of the labor forces, or at least an accurate knowledge of the number, ability, and strength of the labor forces of which each community or district can dispose. For it is not possible to impose upon all provinces and districts the same amount of labor without any regard to the forces at their disposal. It may not be necessary that the central committee or "council of production" distribute the labor among the individuals of the state. That task may be left to the several communities. But it must necessarily determine what and how much each district has to produce and deliver to the community. This task, however, supposes an accurate knowledge of the working forces at the disposal of the several communities.

It must be ascertained, therefore, as accurately as possible, how much each one according to his individual talents, inclinations, and strength is able and willing to do. But in an extensive community it is impossible to obtain reliable information on these points.

We shall suppose, however, that together with the statistics of demand also an accurate estimate of the number of laborers and the efficiency of the labor forces of the different districts has been furnished. But now a new difficulty arises. In order to distribute their quantity of labor to each district or community, it is not sufficient to know the forces on hand at the time the division is made. It must also be settled that all labor hands are to remain in the same place, at least for a certain time, say a year. The question then arises whether in the socialist state the present freedom of migration should be granted or not. Bebel,[1] for his part, advocates such freedom; but how is it possible to organize labor if we suppose a constantly floating population? How can a community produce a certain amount of work if perhaps within the time specified for the performance of their task a large number of the labor hands emigrate to other communities? If, therefore, a systematic plan of production is to be put in force, the population must be

[1] *Die Frau,* pp. 329, 330.

constrained to remain in a certain place, at least for a time, so that during this time the migration to another community can be effected at most with the permission of the authorities.

But even this measure does not remove the difficulty. What would be the result, if, after some time, such a migration from one place to another would be permitted? For we shall suppose that no one is constrained by law to settle in any particular place, but that each one is left free to choose the place where he wishes to settle; this is an essential requirement of freedom.

Now, what would be the result if, in the socialist state such freedom of migration were permitted? We have reason to fear that roaming propensities, and what is vulgarly called tramping, would become an epidemic. Nowadays the greater number at least of those who are not utterly bereft of property are bound *in their own interest* to choose a fixed residence, either permanently or at least for some time; and even those who have no property must choose their domicile in the place where they have a prospect of earning their living. These motives, however, would not exist in the socialist state; for each member would know full well that every part of the country, whether north, south, east, or west, would be equally his home; that he would have the same rights everywhere, and the same claims to obtain work and support.

Nor can it be answered that regard for his children, for the sick and aged, would induce the socialist citizen to choose a permanent residence; for we must bear in mind that the care of children, of the aged and infirm, would be left to the state; and consequently it could not be any impediment to emigration. Or would the love of home, perhaps, attach the socialist to his native soil? We mean the love of home in the stricter sense; for in the socialist state there would be no love of country in a wider sense, as the socialist would be alike in his own country in all places. His country is not his community, or any fixed place, but at most the entire state. Every socialist would have the same right in every community of the great commonwealth; in his birthplace he would have no more rights than in any other part. Why, then, should he feel himself permanently attached to his birthplace? The foundation of the love of our birthplace is based on the right of property. Love for the place of his birth. is generally not deeply rooted in the penniless beggar; his patriotism extends only to the confines of that place which affords him shelter and support. Not until a family has long lived and labored in the same place, until it has a part of its history connected with the place, until it has formed manifold ties of kindred and friendship, does it become attached to the place of its residence. But all this supposes private property, and, as a rule, property in land—at least the possession of a house or of a little homestead, and a roof which one may call his own. But all these elements are wanting in the collectivist state, in which every foot of the soil is equally the property of all its inhabitants. Therefore we are not surprised to hear socialists repeatedly characterizing patriotism as "prejudice" or even as "folly." [1]

---

[1] "A curse on the so-called fatherland!" Thus we read, for instance, in a socialist manifesto Cf *Meyer*, Der Emancipationskampf, vol II p 116. Already in 1848 Marx and Engels said in their "Manifesto of the Communist Party" "Communists have been reproached with endeavoring to abolish fatherland and nationality *The workingman has no fatherland* You cannot take from him what he does not possess "—But also in this respect

It may perhaps be suggested that in the socialist commonwealth there is nevertheless a way of preserving a certain freedom of migration. Let us suppose that every one is at liberty to leave his town or district and to go whithersoever he pleases. Only, the single communes are obliged to keep an exact account of all the labor forces present during the fiscal year, and at the end of the year to furnish a proportionate amount of products.

But this is a mere dodge, which will in no way safeguard the systematic production of a great commonwealth. For the requirements in the matter of coal, wheat, rye, bread, meat, wine, beer, milk, etc., are pretty well fixed. But not every district can furnish these commodities, and those which can and must furnish them must also have at hand an adequate number of capable laborers. It will be scant consolation for the commonwealth, if a district which was supposed to furnish, let us say, one thousand tons of coal, delivers only one hundred tons, but offers the excuse that the number of laborers at its disposal did not allow of more. The yearly output of different commodities should at least equal the demand. But if the socialist state allows perfect freedom of migration, it can never vouch for the eventual delivery of the required quantity of products.

This naturally leads up to another difficulty in the socialistic system. Will the future commonwealth allow the "comrades" to migrate at will from one country to another, from Germany to France, from England to North America, or vice versa? This

a transformation seems to be going on. At the party convention of Austrian socialists in Graz, Sept. 2, 1900, von Vollmar repudiated the charge that socialists are lacking in patriotism. "In the love for our nationality our commonwealth, no party or class of people can surpass us."

question is of vital importance. Socialists will no doubt answer it in the affirmative. At least we must expect so, judging from their everlasting palaver about the liberty with which they are about to bless human kind in lieu of the existing slavery. And yet at present every one is free to try his luck in some different clime. In reality it would also be impossible to prevent emigration; at least the comrades would always have it in their power to desert. The frontiers cannot be occupied by a continuous line of soldiers, and also the soldiers may tire of their job and take French leave.

It is settled, therefore, that each one may emigrate as he pleases. What will result therefrom? Unless we suppose that socialism obtains control of affairs simultaneously in all civilized countries, there will be a torrent of emigration into those countries where socialism is not established; and the first to migrate will be just the young men and the best workers. Against this fact socialism is utterly powerless. The power of free self-determination and the prospect of advancement will have more influence on a man of energy and talent than the honor of belonging to an immense industrial organization, where superiority is excluded on principle, and where every comrade of more than average excellence must necessarily be looked upon with a jealous eye.

Now, is it at all likely that socialism will be able to realize its projects simultaneously in all civilized countries? No one entertains any serious hopes or fears on this head. Even if all the different nationalities were of one mind on every subject, socialism would have no prospects of a simultaneous victory; much less so, considering the ill-feeling and jealousy entertained by one nation against the others. Socialists boast indeed of the international character of their movement; but this internationalism does not prevent, e.g., French socialists from relentlessly expelling from France Italian and Belgian laborers; the same would be done if occasion offered in England and Germany, and it would be interesting to know how many of those who clamor against foreign labor in the United States are members of the Socialist Party.

§ IV. *Distribution of Labor. Vocations.*

Engels, one of the beacon-lights of modern socialism, speaks of the transition from the anarchy of capitalistic production to the "systematic, conscious organization" of collectivist production as of the "leap of humanity from the realm of necessity into the realm of freedom." [1] Let us examine more closely the nature of this leap into the realm of freedom.

The community, or rather its representatives elected by the people, has the duty to distribute to the different workmen and workwomen, the quantum of labor determined by the central bureau. The community has to determine who is to be employed in agriculture, industry, mining; who in the distribution of produce; who is to be entrusted with its transportation, etc. It is a matter of indifference whether the communal committee determines the position which each one should occupy in the mechanism of production, or whether the position of each is to be assigned him by the authorities of the special departments of industry. In any case, the central committee must determine to which

[1] Die Entwicklung des Sozialismus, etc., p. 76.

department of industry each one is to be ascribed.[1]
Here again it must evidently be supposed that the
heads of the departments of production have at their
disposal a permanent population.

Can the distribution of the various works be brought
about on any other plan? True, some socialistic
enthusiasts would leave the choice of an occupation
to the taste of each individual: thus at the beginning
of the movement Charles Fourier, and recently Bebel,[2]
Stern,[3] Köhler,[4] and Kautsky.[5] "Each one," says
Bebel, "determines for himself in what occupation
he wishes to be employed; the great variety of the
various branches of labor will satisfy the most various
tastes. . . . The different branches and groups of
laborers will choose their own superintendents to direct
their various departments. These will not be task-
masters like most of our present labor inspectors and
foremen: they will be comrades, with this difference
only, that they exercise an administrative instead
of a productive function." The socialistic body can
at pleasure devote itself "at one season of the year
to agricultural, at another to industrial production."[6]
Not only in regard to industrial, but also in regard to
scientific and artistic studies every one will have occasion for suitable variety.[7]

We may perhaps be allowed to raise an objection.
If each one is permitted to choose his work, how

---

[1] What may be expected in this line from the representatives of the
socialist "people" is well exemplified by the resolution introduced at the
Breslau convention (Transactions, p 17) that wet-nurses should be forbidden by the state, because sterilized cow's milk is a perfect substitute for
the milk of nurses.

[2] Die Frau, pp 271 and 281

[3] Thesen, p 37 sqq

[4] Der sozialdemokratische Staat, p. 61.

[5] The Social Revolution.

[6] Die Frau, p 335

[7] *Ibid.*, p. 282.

can there still be question of a uniform, systematic organization of labor? It is a standing complaint with socialists that at present anarchy prevails in production, and yet, after all is said and done, they themselves make anarchy their ruling principle.

Or are they perhaps seriously convinced that it would suffice to draw up and publish a plan of production, and that then without further ado millions of comrades would spontaneously fall into line to take up that branch of production, in that place and at that time which is specified by the preconcerted plan? "What fools these mortals be!" If the quality of occupation is left to the choice of each, all will flock to the easiest, pleasantest, and most honorable employments. Industrial occupations are naturally very unequal, and even socialism cannot remove this inequality. To be a director or a member of the supreme council of production is easier than to be a fireman, or a collier, or a laborer in a chemical factory, who has to pass his hours in broiling heat and fetid air; the office of a committeeman would be more pleasant than that of the individual who would be deputed to clean the streets and sewers of the cities. Socialists will use much printer's ink before they can print out of the world the fact that many occupations in the socialist state would be irksome, laborious, dangerous, and repulsive. If the choice were left to individuals, certainly sufficient forces would not be found for the performance of such disagreeable work.[1]

[1] Marx is as a rule very obscure in expressing his ideas about the future; thus he maintains that in the higher phase of communism society will inscribe upon its banner Each one according to his faculties, to each one according to his needs Each one according to his faculties, probably means that each one is to serve society as best he can. But who is to judge of men's faculties? Is each one to do this for himself and to choose his occupation accordingly? This will result in anarchy Is the decision to be in the hands of a committee or something of that kind? This would

Bebel, however, tries to find a way out of the difficulty. He is of opinion that street-cleaning, washing, and other disagreeable kinds of work would in the socialist state be performed by mechanical means, so that these occupations would cease to be disagreeable.[1] But even though we should make the greatest allowances for modern and future inventions, yet it would be puerile to imagine that all the disagreeable features of labor could be removed by machinery. There would still remain much disagreeable work, which could be performed only by immediate personal action. Besides, such machines must be tended and directed. Does Bebel imagine that the socialists could bring machinery to such perfection that it would be necessary only to let a machine down a shaft in order to hoist it laden with coal? Experience teaches that industrial progress has rather multiplied than diminished disagreeable jobs. Though some kinds of distasteful work are nowadays performed by machinery, other still more loathsome ones have been created in their stead. We have only to recall the number of chemical factories which are a standing nuisance not only to the laboring men, but also to whole cities and countrysides for miles around. Besides, we must bear in mind that it is a point of the socialistic programme to utilize for the benefit of society all manner of garbage and refuse, which will certainly afford no very pleasant occupation for the laborer of the future.

Unless we admit, then, that in the state of the future unselfishness, self-devotion and thirst for self-abasement and suffering shall become general, nothing

mean intolerable slavery. It will be hard for socialists to extricate themselves from this dilemma.

[1] Cf. *Stern*, Thesen, p. 38.

else remains for us than to conclude that. finally, the influence of authority, or the vote of the majority, must force the laborer to condescend to these disagreeable and humiliating avocations. But such an interposition of authority or of the popular vote would evidently take away all freedom of choice, and be a source of endless complaint and discontent. And yet, according to the socialistic programme, there should be "equality of rights" and "equality in the conditions of life." But is it consistent with this equality, either by command of authority or by popular vote, to condemn one man rather than another to such despicable and disagreeable employments?

§ V. *Some Unsatisfactory Solutions.*

Freedom in the choice of a vocation or state of life is such an essential constituent of human liberty, that without it life is downright slavery. It is natural, therefore, that socialists and their advocates should have sought out some means of securing this freedom in the socialistic system, despite its strictly methodic arrangement. Schäffle is of opinion that by a certain regulative system, freedom in the choice of a state might be made compatible with the social organization of labor. He thinks that committees, appointed for this purpose, could by the reduction of pay stop the immoderate demand for certain professions, and, on the other hand, by raising the pay for other departments of labor attract larger numbers of aspirants to the less desirable occupations. This proposition, however, does not seem to square with the socialistic system; for it supposes that the pay for certain kinds of labor could be raised and lowered at pleasure, so far as this would be serviceable to the labor organization. By such a measure the socialistic theory of value would be thrown overboard; for the value of produce would no longer depend on the necessary time consumed in producing it, but on external circumstances—on the greater demand, or on the greater extent of social wants. But would laborers tamely submit to the reduction of their wages because perhaps in another department of industry there is a lack of labor forces? This solution of the problem would lead to the result that the lowest and most disagreeable occupation, in which the least intellectual labor is required, would be paid best of all, and that the wages would diminish in proportion as the labor would ascend in the scale of intellectuality and appreciation; for naturally the rush to the higher and more interesting kinds of labor would continue. Such treatment of the laborer would not only be unjust, but would crush every aspiration to higher culture and higher social standing.

Edward Bellamy, in the fiction entitled "Looking Backward," [1] gives a most glowing description of the future socialist state, and endeavors to represent it in all respects as practicable. He tries to meet our difficulty by the regulation of the labor-time. If the number of candidates for any one calling should be too great and too small for another, the labor-time would be lengthened for the one and shortened for the other. This, he thinks, would be a sufficient means of reducing, on the one side, the number of those who aspire to a higher calling, and, on the other side, of increasing the number of those who would be willing to be employed in less honorable

[1] Looking Backward, chap. VII.

labor or professions. But if this should prove unsuccessful, and too few laborers were found for any
department of industry, it would be sufficient, he
thinks, for the authorities to declare that such neglected
labor would be connected with special honor,
and that those who would engage in it would merit
the gratitude of the entire nation. For the youth
of such a socialist nation, he thinks, would be very
ambitious, and would not allow such an occasion
of gratifying their ambition to go unused. If, on
the other hand, the rush of laborers to any department
of industry were too great, those only should be chosen
who would distinguish themselves in that special
industry.

This theory is characteristic of Bellamy's treatment of the social question. He imagines humanity
almost free from all those passions and shortcomings
to which the children of Adam are now subject—a
generation full of zeal and devotion to the common
weal. But, we ask, are those human beings whom
we meet in daily life really such a generation of angels?
Bellamy himself shows that they are not, when he
depicts in the most exaggerated colors the egotism of
the present generation. We must deal with men as
they are and will continue to be; and for such men
Bellamy's system has no use. Does Bellamy imagine
that those who have been long employed in some
work or profession will tamely submit to have the
labor-time lengthened more and more, simply because
there are many candidates for that kind of labor?
And could a varying labor-time, suited to the different
industries, be thus established by government?
The demand for certain kinds of labor is not unchangeable, but may vary according to the varying inclina-

tions of men, or according to the circumstances of time and place. It is impossible by the regulation of the labor-time to determine the number of laborers which are required to produce the necessaries of an entire nation, without committing enormous blunders, and thus creating dissatisfaction. This policy would also have the necessary result of multiplying the number of laborers employed in the lowest and most disagreeable kinds of labor.

Let us consider the matter in the concrete. Mining, for instance, is much more irksome, disagreeable, and dangerous than the occupation of a gardener, an overseer, or an artist. In order, therefore, to obtain a sufficient number of workmen it would be necessary to reduce the labor-time of miners to a minimum. What would be the result? The number of miners would have to be increased in proportion, if raw materials, coal, etc., should be forthcoming in sufficient quantities. And what we say of miners applies also to all inferior and undesirable kinds of work—for instance, street-cleaning, stable-tending, sewer-digging. The number of laborers in all those lower employments would have to be increased considerably to make up by the increase of labor-power for the shortness of the labor-time. Thus labor forces would be withdrawn from the higher and more skilled occupations, and the entire tendency of society would be backward and downward. The more degrading and disagreeable any kind of labor would be, the more laborers it would employ. Besides, according to Bellamy, all members of the social body should have a share in the national product, so that a stable-boy by fewer hours' work could earn as much as an artist, a physician, or a lawyer, who would have to labor the livelong day.

Bebel fancies he has found another way out of the difficulty. In the first place, he has the most unlimited confidence in the self-sacrificing spirit of the laborers of the future, who at the beck of their directors will always be found ready of their own accord to fill all the breaches that may be thrown open. If this unselfish spirit, however, should not suffice, all in their turn must undertake the disagreeable jobs; for "there will be no human respect and no stupid contempt of useful labor." [1] Nay, more: he is of opinion that the superior education of future society will effect that finally every laborer, in his turn, will be able to undertake all the functions of labor. "It is not at all improbable that as organization progresses and the thorough education of all members of the social body will advance, the different functions of labor will simply become alternate—that, at stated intervals, according to a fixed rotation, all members of a certain department, without distinction of sex, shall undertake all functions." [2] Bebel maintains the possibility of such a rotation at the outset only for the various functions within the same department of production. But at a later stage of the development of his subject he gives this changing-off system a much wider application. In collectivist society the greatest regard will be had for the natural craving of man for variety; for all will have an opportunity to perfect themselves in all the branches of industry. "There will be no lack of time to acquire great facility and practice in the various branches of industry. Large, comfortable, and perfectly equipped workshops will facilitate for all, young and old, the learning of all trades, and will introduce them to their practice as it

[1] Die Frau, p. 291   [2] Ibid , p. 271.

were in play. Chemical and physical laboratories, fully answering the demands of science, will be at hand, also teachers in great abundance. Then it will be manifest what a world of force and power was suppressed by the capitalistic system of production, or how these forces and powers were at least crippled in their development." [1]

These conclusions of Bebel are most logical, and by this very fact they strikingly illustrate the absurdity of socialism. To all disagreeable employments, therefore, for which laborers do not present themselves voluntarily, every member of society will have to submit in his turn. Every one must be street-cleaner, chimney-sweep, stable-boy, etc., in regular rotation. Let us picture to ourselves Messrs. Bebel and Singer, "without any human respect," when duty calls them, submitting themselves to these disagreeable avocations, which no other member of the social body volunteers to undertake. What would the gentlemen then say of the freedom left to man in such a system? Would it not remind them of the workhouse? When Bebel assures us that in the society of the future education, and particularly technical training, would fit every member of the social body for all functions and all industries, his statement can hardly be said to deserve a refutation. Let us only imagine what such industrial and technical ability supposes. Every individual in his turn undertakes all social functions; for instance, in a factory he is director, foreman, fireman, bookkeeper, a simple laborer or hod-carrier; then he turns to some other branch of industry or social calling—becomes editor, compositor, telegrapher, painter, architect, actor, farmer, gardener, astronomer, professor, chemist,

[1] Die Frau, p. 282.

druggist. With such a programme is any thorough knowledge of anything possible?

To master a trade thoroughly, and to remain perfect in it, requires the constant application of a lifetime. This is the verdict of long experience. But now socialists are about to perfect every man in all the branches; each one is to become a first-rate engineer, architect, physician, chemist, electrician, sculptor, druggist, actor, painter, philosopher, mathematician, astronomer, teacher, agriculturist, etc. Are these braggart vaporings worthy of serious consideration?

Absurd as is the assumption that by universal development workingmen will be enabled to undertake any function of socialized production, still Marx poses as its champion. He is of opinion that " in a higher phase of communist society . . . the slavish subordination of the individual under the divisions of labor, and consequently the opposition between mental and bodily work" will disappear (cf. above p. 56). By this he cannot mean that bodily and mental occupations will become equal; this is rather too absurd. He rather wishes to assert that the communist evolution will more and more enable every worker to undertake mental as well as bodily labors and will thus remove the distinction between head-work and manual labor. Also in "Capital" [1] Marx endeavors to prove that modern evolution tends to replace the "separate individual" by the "totally developed individual," whatever that may be, and to confer upon the workingman "absolute availability," i.e. to make him fit for every kind of work.

If Marx asserted no more than the possibility of training laborers to perform many different but purely

[1] Capital, p. 453.

mechanical functions, we sh 'ld have no quarrel with him; but to maintain that also in the higher walks of knowledge and professional ability every man is to become a "totally developed individual" with "absolute availability"—this is a flight of imagination worthy of Munchausen himself. Of course, Marx appeals to the laws of social evolution, and very warily promises this universality of individual development as taking place only in "a higher phase of communist society." But shooting at long range will not avail here. Even though we make the greatest possible allowance for development, man is and remains a very limited being; and the more the circle of human activity and knowledge is widening, the greater the impossibility for the individual to become proficient in every branch of science. On this fact is based the law of the increasing division of labor keeping pace with every advance of culture and civilization. There was a time once when a man could excel in nearly every known science; at present this is manifestly impossible.

Every branch of science is continually opening up new fields of knowledge, and the greater its progress the more subdivisions it necessitates. This is the case not only in the natural sciences, but also in the arts, in medicine, history, etc. In the art of healing it has long since become impossible for a physician to be equally well versed in every branch. Therefore there are eye, ear, throat, skin, nerve, etc., specialists. Also in surgery there is required the most accurate knowledge of the minutest parts of the human organism, there is needed such skill, sureness of hand, and experience, that already nowadays the most famous surgeons confine themselves to a certain class of operations.

Therefore it is even now impossible for any one to attain even mediocrity in e ery science. This impossibility will be still more enhanced by the progress of civilization. If thus far evolution always proceeded on these lines, how can we assume that in the socialist epoch it will take a contrary direction? Therefore the assertion that in future times every individual will be an adept in every art and science is—we may be pardoned the expression—no more nor less than socialistic humbug.

Even Professor Paulsen, who is otherwise very favorable to socialism, thinks there is rather too much equalizing and levelling in the future commonwealth. He says: [1] "In the society of the future the self-same individual will be letter-carrier to-day; to-morrow he must perform the duties of a post-office clerk; on the third day he must act as postmaster-general—but why use a title?—in short, he must undertake all that business which at present the director of the national post-office has in hand—he must prepare programmes for international post-office congresses, etc ; and on the fourth day he must again return to the counter; on the fifth he condescends to be letter-carrier once more, but this time not in the metropolis, but in some out-of-the-way place; for it is but meet that the sweets of city life should fall to the lot of all in their turn   Thus it would be also in the railroad department, in the mining and in the military department, and in every common factory. To-day the member of the socialistic state descends into the bowels of the earth as a collier, or hammers at the anvil, or punches tickets; to-morrow he wields the quill, balances accounts, makes chemical experiments, draughts designs for machines, or issues general edicts on the quantity and quality of the social production, etc   In the naval department there would be a similar variety: the office of captain would fall to the lot of all in turn, as also that of steersman, of machinist, of cook, etc.   And thus also in the department of state; the various officials would exchange functions: each one would in his turn be legislator, judge, com-

[1] System der Ethik, vol. II. p. 437.

mander-in-chief of the army, and chief of police But I have forgotten where I am: in the state of the future there will be no more wars, and no more thieves, and counterfeiters and idlers and tramps; consequently there will be no more judges and soldiers necessary. Nor will there be any need of laws, or of a state at all, in the land of Utopia, in which the wolves will play with the lambs on the pasture and eat grass; when the ocean will be filled with lemonade and ships will be drawn by trusty whales; where envy, hatred, tyranny, ambition, indolence, folly, and vanity will no longer exist; where there will be only wise and good men—in the millennium, for which it will not be necessary to devise laws and ordinances In this ideal state benevolence alone shall reign supreme.

"There can be no serious thought of appointing or dismissing by ballot the directors who are to superintend the work of the community according to the necessity and according to the public opinion of the voters. Every one can easily picture to himself the results of such elections if they were to be carried out in the entire social body: the party strifes, quarrels, contentions, cheating, public denunciation, which would then ensue even in the smallest circles—even in the supposition that there would be no diversity of material interests and no ill-will—from the difference of opinion on points of mere convenience, usefulness, and possibility alone."

§ VI. *Refutation of an Objection.*

When it is objected to socialists that finally individuals will have to be constrained by the ruling of authority to perform that work which the common good demands, and that thus all freedom in the choice of employment is taken away, they raise the contrary objection that also now there is no freedom in the choice of a vocation—that most people are forced by necessity to seize upon the first employment which offers itself to them. "Social democracy," says Kautsky, the present theorist-in-chief of socialism, "cannot do away with the dependence of the laborer on the industrial machine of which he forms a cog; but instead of the dependence of the laborer on the capitalist, whose interests are clashing with his own, there will be put dependence on a society of which the laborer is a member, on a society of equal comrades with common interests." [1]

We are glad to record Kautsky's concession that after all there will be no communist "leap of humanity from the realm of slavery into the realm of freedom." But for this loss there is some compensation. In the commonwealth of the future we shall depend, not on an individual, but on a society of which we form a part. As if liberty consisted essentially in not depending on an individual! Slavery is and remains slavery; no matter whether my actions are prescribed by an individual or by a society of which I am a part, the subjection is the same. How should I be affected by the consciousness of being one of twenty or thirty million parts constituting a society which commands me to be chimney-sweep to-day, stable-boy or letter-carrier to-morrow?

As regards the assertion that also at present the laborer is not free, but depending on the conditions of production, we may concede that no absolute freedom is to be obtained. Yet there is a wide gap between absolute freedom and absolute bondage. It is not true that most people are not free to choose their vocation or employment. The great mass of the population has undoubtedly considerable freedom in this regard. There are comparatively few who are not free, on leaving school, to choose from a great variety of occupations. An unlimited freedom in the choice of a vocation does not exist, and has never

[1] Das Erfurter Programm, p. 169.

existed; nor is such freedom in the interest of society; for it is rather an advantage to society if certain callings have permanence and stability, and are generally filled by the same classes. A family in which a certain business or trade has been traditionally handed down from generation to generation has generally great advantages from a moral and industrial standpoint over a family or individual who is new in such trade or business. That at present there are many cases in which, owing to extreme poverty, the choice of a state in life is almost, illusory we shall willingly grant. But these are rare exceptions in comparison with the exigencies of the socialist state. Besides, this evil may in great part be remedied by reasonable social reforms affording energetic help to the poorer classes.

Finally—and that is the chief point—the necessity which binds men to a certain kind of work in the present state of society is only a moral one, which is independent of the will of others, while in the socialist state this necessity would emanate from the ordinations of the social authority.

In the socialist commonwealth each one's vocation would finally be decreed and forced upon him from above—let us say by a board of experts. No one will easily submit to such treatment, and necessarily, besides all dissatisfaction, every complaint about the unfitness and injustice of one's compulsory vocation would be directed against the governing body; they would be made responsible for every mistake, they would be called upon to redress every grievance.

To satisfy millions of people by allotting to each one the vocation he is to follow, would require superiors towering far above Solomon in wisdom, and inferiors endowed with an unusual share of disinterestedness.

At present, on the contrary, it is *the interest of the individual* which forces him to embrace a certain profession and to prepare himself properly for the duties connected with it. In consequence of this moral necessity the distribution of the various avocations of life is made without law or precept. Even the lowest and most disagreeable employments generally find a sufficient number of candidates, and commonly those who are employed in them are satisfied with their avocation as long as it yields them a sufficient means of subsistence. The discontent so common among laborers in our time is not with labor itself, but with excessive labor and insufficient pay. If employers would better the condition of the laborer, contentment and satisfaction with their condition would soon return to them if they were not disturbed by the visionary theories of socialist agitators. But if laborers are made to believe that all men have equal rights and should enjoy equal advantages in life, it will be found impossible to reconcile them with their condition. This same imaginary claim to absolute equality will prove the death-blow of socialism itself, for the simple reason that it aspires to an utter impossibility.

§ VII. *Impossibility of the Social Organization of Labor.*

Another flaw in the socialistic system is the tacit supposition that all kinds of work and all services for the benefit of society may be reduced to one comprehensive labor system. This supposition is erroneous. There will be always a large number of personal services, which, by their very nature, cannot be brought into any system, unless the world is to be

governed by strict military rule.   Such are, for instance
all those services which immediately regard the care
of the body—food, clothing, cleanliness, cooking,
housekeeping, washing, mending, etc.   Shall every
one bring his coat to the "social" tailor to be mended?
Must every one present himself to the state barber
and hairdresser for his toilet?   Must every one
consign his linens to the public laundries?   We
must bear in mind that the relation between masters
and servants, and, in short, the entire wage system,
is utterly repudiated by the principles of socialism.
And if in a family, to crown the difficulty, the house-
wife is sick or otherwise unfit for work, or happens to
die, do socialists imagine that her services may be
substituted in the state of the future by mechanical
means?   In answer to this difficulty they point to
our present system of boarding-houses and hotels,
where all parties at all times can be served according to their wishes, and lack no earthly comforts.
Why, then, they say, could not all such personal services be rendered in the socialistic state by means of
public kitchens and dining-halls, by public laundries
and workshops on a large scale?

To say nothing of the disintegration of family life
which would arise from such a public boarding system,
would it not be downright slavery if every one were
altogether dependent upon public institutions for the
satisfaction of his personal wants?   Besides, we can
hardly believe that such public boarding institutions,
laundries, etc., would give general satisfaction.   Our
present hotel and boarding system is conducted on
quite a different principle.   It consists of private
institutions, whose proprietors or directors have the
greatest interest to attract guests and to satisfy, as

far as possible, all their reasonable wishes; for if the guests are dissatisfied with the treatment accorded them and the prices they pay, they will go elsewhere, and thus the hotel-keeper or landlord will lose his customers, and his competitors will profit by his loss.

The socialist eating-houses, on the contrary, would be public institutions conducted by public officials, who would draw their necessaries from the public magazines, and would have no competition to fear. Would such public state cooks, butlers, waiters, etc., be as eager to satisfy their guests as the officials of our private hotels? We doubt it very much. The "comrade" cook or waiter would be independent of his guests, and if the latter were dissatisfied with his services he would have nothing to lose thereby. Nay, we fear that such socialistic institutions would be far behind our military kitchens. Let us suppose, moreover, that all these officials would have to change their offices from time to time, so that no one would understand anything thoroughly—that he who is cook to-day should be waiter to-morrow, and laundryman next day, and then butler, and finally return again to the kitchen, but only for so long a time as either his own caprice or public authority would keep him in that office. But enough of absurdity.

This difficulty did not escape the notice of Schäffle. He is of the opinion that socialists could leave such personal services to private enterprise   Such a policy, however, would open a wide gap in the principles of socialism, which intends to remove every form of wage-labor.   If socialists would leave personal services to private enterprise, they must tolerate at least the existence of paid servants.   Thus also many hands would be withdrawn from the national production; for persons who would devote themselves to the performance of such private services could not be expected at the same time to take part in the social industry. Besides, the equality of the conditions of life would be destroyed if private services were permitted, for thus it would be possible for some such servants, by superior ability, favorable circumstances, or ingenuity, to procure a large income, while another private servant would either have a miserable existence or be constrained to return to the common ranks of producers In another place, however, Schaffle [1] says that private enterprise would be altogether excluded in the socialist commonwealth, and that all those laborers who would not take an immediate part in the social production, as artists, for instance, would receive a public salary. We may readily grant that the income arising from such personal services would never attain such dimensions as that arising from the modern accumulations of capital; yet the general principle of socialism—that only public labor paid by the state is to be tolerated—would thus be subverted

SECTION III.

PROFIT AND PROGRESS IN SOCIALISM.

§ I. *Socialistic Dreams.*

The ringleaders of the socialists promise their followers a golden age. Little work and much enjoyment—that is the gist of socialism. This is manifest particularly from Bebel's published works, notably "Die Frau."

If we are to believe this popular leader, labor in the socialist state, owing to its great variety and the modern and future perfection of mechanical inventions, will be mere amusement Most kinds of labor will be performed, as it were, " in play " Besides, labor, owing to the systematic regulations and the wise utilization of all means of production, will be so productive that between two and three hours' work per day will suffice for

[1] Quintessence, p 5

the perfect satisfaction of all human wants   Egotism and the interest for the common weal will be in harmony; nay, these motives will exactly coincide with each other in the socialistic organization [1]   There will be no more idlers.   The moral atmosphere itself will incite every individual to "distinguish himself before all others." [2]   An unheard-of "world of forces and possibilities," which have been suppressed by the capitalistic system of production, will be made free.[3]   There will be no more political crimes or other violations of law.[4]   Barracks and other military institutions, court-houses, city-halls, prisons, will then be put to a better use.   The nations will no longer look upon each other as enemies, but as "brothers "   The age of "everlasting peace" will come.   The weapons of war will be stored up in the museums of antiquities   Then the nations will advance to ever higher culture and civilization.

Most particularly by means of irrigation, draining of marshes and moors, and by superior means of communication, agriculture will change the entire land into huge gardens, and thus entice the people from the cities into the country   As in the cities, so also in the country, there will be museums, theatres, concert-halls, play-houses, hotels, reading-rooms, libraries, business offices, institutions of learning, parks, promenades, public baths, scientific laboratories, hospitals, etc.[5]

In the socialist state all the faculties of man will be developed harmoniously.   There will be "scholars and artists of every description in countless numbers " [6]   Thousands of brilliant talents will be brought to their fullest development—musicians, actors, artists, philosophers, not professional, of course (for all must take part in the social production), but led on by inspiration, talent, and genius.   "An age of arts and sciences will come such as the world has never seen before; and the artistic and scientific productions will be in proportion to the general progress." [7]   Every one will also have occasion to indulge his taste for variety.   He may make "a pleasure-trip," visit foreign lands and continents; he may join scientific expeditions and colonization schemes of all kinds, which will then exist in great numbers, if he is disposed to render a corresponding service to society.[8]   In short, the human heart will lack

---

[1] Die Frau, p 274.   [2] *Ibid.*, p. 288   [3] *Ibid*, p 282.   [4] *Ibid*, p 317.
[5] *Ibid*, p. 313.   [6] *Ibid*, p. 284.   [7] *Ibid.*, p. 331.   [8] Ibid, p 335.

nothing which it can long for The golden age of Saturn will return, and all men will be happy.

Like Bebel, so also Stern [1] indulges his imagination to the fullest extent in describing the socialistic paradise of the future. Thus Bellamy's day-dreams have been seriously dreamt before by waking German scientific socialists But dreams are an easy species of production for fertile imaginations

§ II. *Industry and Economy in Socialism.*

It is a great pity that the gap between dreams and reality cannot be bridged. It is a stern fact that in thickly inhabited and civilized countries the earth is able to nourish its inhabitants only at the price of hard labor and great economy in the use of labor materials. Nor is there any lack of incentive to such economy in the modern social order, as is manifest. The interest of the individual, nay, the very necessity of self-preservation and self-advancement, urges most people to untiring and energetic labor. In the race for gain we need, therefore, a check rather than an incentive; nor is there any great extravagance to be observed in the use of labor means—raw materials, work-tools, machinery, factories, means of transportation, etc. On such economy depends to a great extent the success of all modern enterprises The great problem to be solved in every private enterprise is how to produce, with the least possible expense of labor, material, and time, the largest quantity of the best and cheapest goods. True, there will be always a number of bunglers and swindlers who will ply their trade; but such will not succeed in the long-run. Fraud will be detected in ninety-nine cases out of one hundred; and if it sometimes succeeds, it is mostly by the fault of

[1] Thesen, pp. 25, 34.

credulous or grasping purchasers, and of legislatures and governments which do not use sufficient precaution and vigilance for the prevention of deceit. But how far would diligence and economy in the use of the means of production be practised in the socialistic commonwealth?

Marx assures us that "in a higher phase of communist development, labor" will be "not only a means of sustaining life, but also a most urgent desire." Bebel is anxious to outdo his master in the matter of liberal promises. To him it is self-evident "that such an organization of labor, based on perfect freedom and equality, in which one would stand for all, and all for one, would awaken the highest consciousness of solidarity, would beget a spirit of joyous industry and emulation, such as is nowhere to be found in the industrial system of our day. . . . And this spirit would also exert its influence on the productiveness of labor and the perfection of produce.[1] Moreover, each individual and all together, since they labor for one another, have absolutely the same interest that all products should be not only as good and perfect as possible, but also should be produced with the greatest possible promptness, either to save time or to gain time to produce new articles for the satisfaction of higher claims."[2]

However, such promises are but idle talk. For what motive has the member of the socialist state to toil honestly day by day and to use the labor materials economically? Only the smallest part of the fruit of his industry belongs to himself. If we imagine a million members of a socialistic commonwealth, each one reaps one millionth of the proceeds of his labor. And if he is idle, what does it matter? Only one millionth of the production which he neglects to bring forth is lost to him.[3]

[1] Die Frau, p. 271.
[2] *Ibid.*
[3] The intensity of application to be expected in the socialist state was strikingly illustrated by the printing establishment of Werner, a noted

It is not without reason that Carring [1] maintains that the dis appearance of private interests in socialism would necessitate the introduction of other motives of action But what are they to be? Carring replies: "The ideal of socialism, the mutual co-operation of brothers, can be realized only by men whose conscience works to perfection " But only an incorrigible optimist will imagine that the socialists of the future, materialists and atheists as they are sure to be, will have a more delicate conscience than the average proletarian of to-day.

Even Schaffle, whose appreciation of socialism is rather sympathetic, says· [2] "It will not be sufficient by itself in a producing community of millions for producer A to feel My income from my social labor is conditional upon my 999,999 co-operating comrades being as industrious as I This will not suffice to awaken the necessary reciprocal control; at any rate it will not check the impulse to laziness and to dishonesty, nor hinder men from defrauding the public of their labor-time, nor render impossible a cunning or prejudiced contrivance for the unjust valuation of individual performances. Socialism would have to give the individual at least as strong an interest in the collective work as he has under the liberal system of production—it would have to secure to every sub-group a premium on extraordinary amounts of collective production, and a forfeit for collective slackness, it is as much and still more bound to bestow effective distinction for all the special success in technical development, and duly to reward great individual merit; and finally

ringleader of Berlin socialists Because socialists generally abhor piece-work as a means of exploitation, Werner engaged type-setters with a fixed weekly salary of 30 marks ($7 50) But, as Werner declared in a public meeting, the work furnished per day and man was worth sometimes no more than 35 cents All his admonitions remained unheeded. One of Werner's partners in business once requested the noisy and quarrelsome crowd to moderate their racket, which prevented him from working In reply the "comrades" shouted the socialist Marseillaise, emphasizing especially the words "Down with tyranny!" Werner was obliged to introduce piece-work again, and to dismiss two of the chief rioters This gives us an inkling of the future socialist paradise —Still more remarkable were the results of the so-called red bakery, established at Berlin by social democrats The discord among the comrades soon rose to such a pitch that they heaped reproaches on each other's heads and finally dissolved partnership (Cf *Germania*, 1892, n 154) On Nov 30, 1900, the executive board of Berlin had to intervene to stop the scandalous quarrel of the *Leipziger Volkszeitung* and its socialist employees

[1] Das Gewissen im Lichte der Geschichte sozialistischer und christlicher Weltanschauung, p 96
[2] Quintessence, pp 56, 57.

it would have to provide that all the innumerable labor forces should be directed into the channel of their most profitable use, not by the orders of an authority, but by the force of individual interest "

But in the social commonwealth there would be no private interest. If the state would, according to Schäffle's opinion, confer distinctions and premiums sufficient to urge the laborer to years of restless toil, great differences in the conditions of life would soon arise and bring envy, jealousy, and discontent in their wake. Besides, such distinctions or premiums cannot consist with the socialistic theory of value.

We have reason to believe that socialism, instead of producing abundance of all necessaries of life with little toil, would soon be forced to lengthen the present work-day in order to prevent famine. According to Engel [1] there was in Prussia in the year 1881 to a population of 26,716,701 a total income of $2,382,676,591.50. In this estimate, however, the income was set one-fourth higher than it actually was, as the real estimate was $1,972,386,965.50. Now, if this were equally divided among the population it would leave $89.25 to each person. [2]

According to Soetbeer and Böhmert's accurate calculations the average income of each person in Prussia was: [3]

In the year 1876	$79.00
" " " 1888	82.50
" " " 1890	85.50
" " " 1893–94	87 50
" " " 1897–98	97.50

[1] Der Wert des Menschen, 1883
[2] According to Richter (Die Irrlehren der Sozialdemokratie, p 16) the average income in Prussia in 1889–1890 was not quite $75
[3] Handwörterbuch der Staatswissenschaften, article Einkommen; *Böhmert*, Die Verteilung des Einkommens in Preussen und Sachsen, p. 32.

For the kingdom of Saxony Robert Meyer gives the following estimate, based upon the income-tax:[1]

In the year 1882 the average income per person was $86.36
"   " 1884 "   "   "   "   "   " 90.39
"   " 1886 "   "   "   "   "   " 96 42
"   " 1888 "   "   "   "   "   "   101.64

Böhmert himself estimates the average yearly income in Saxony at $81.85 in 1879, at $110.48 in 1892, and at $117.50 in 1896. In Great Britain and Ireland the average income amounted to $172.50 in 1886 (Soetbeer's estimate [2]), and to $180 in 1895 (M. G. Mulhall).

Such is the average income in some of the modern flourishing states, where industry and agriculture are carried on with untiring energy and assiduity. If at present the straining of every available productive force has not resulted in a higher average income, we may expect this income to dwindle down still more in the socialist commonwealth. And what is to happen if the hours of work are reduced? For socialists promise their followers a great reduction in working hours. Bebel thinks that two or three hours of work will suffice. Of course, the more liberal the promise the more easily it will find favor with the laboring classes, who would see little use in the whole emancipation movement and its grandiloquent prophecies, if in the socialist state as much work and exertion would be required as at present.

Let us suppose, therefore, that the working time of miners is reduced to four hours a day. In consequence the number of laborers will have to be practically doubled. Where formerly one hundred thousand miners were employed in a coal district there will now be need of two hundred thousand. The same will be the case in the smelting works and factories, on the farm and in the garden, in the composing-room and at the press, with the tailors, butchers, and bakers, in railroads, steamships, and cartage. Will there be labor forces at all sufficient to provide for even the most necessary means of subsistence? [1]

Of course, socialists loudly proclaim that the lazy drones encumbering present society will in future be forced to take part in the productive labor. But hence we can only conclude that collectivism precludes freedom of choice in one's avocation, not however that the quantity of work to be allotted to each one will be diminished.

Moreover, the number of idlers is not so considerable as socialists would have us believe. On this point there is a good deal of contradiction in socialist writings. Where there is question of the present distribution of property the number of owners is represented as ridiculously small—"the upper ten thousand." But since the sluggards can be found only among property owners, also their number can accordingly not be very great. How does this tally with other passages of the same writings where the number of idle drones assumes colossal proportions? Socialists may of course object that in their system many occupations, as bankers. stock-brokers, jobbers, etc , would become superfluous This is true to a certain degree. But it is not to be overlooked that much of the work done by these men would be necessary also in the socialist state Besides a number of new offices would have to be created in order to ascertain the

---

[1] Atlanticus (Ein Blick in den Zukunftsstaat) calculates in detail how great a saving will be effected by the most approved technical installations and by a systematic regulation of production. As if men would submit to this systematic regulation and be as diligent and saving of material in the service of society as they are at present in the service of self-interest! It is the old mistake of abstracting from the real nature of men and substituting some chimerical ideal And besides, the best technical appliances and the most systematic regulation obtain already in all first-class establishments How can it, then, be possible to reduce the working time and still to need fewer laborers?

demand, regulate production, issue labor certificates, transport and distribute the labor products. It is easy saying: everything is to be regulated systematically; the actual organization however, requires more men than is commonly believed, especially if, in accordance with socialist ideals, the officials are to work but a few hours a day.

Not a few socialists, and also Schäffle, build great hopes upon the *mutual supervision* and control of the laborers. But such supposition is in many cases impossible, especially if several should unite together in a league of idleness. But where such supervision would be actuated, as in workshops of limited extent, it would necessarily lead to a regular system of petty surveillance and espionage. We have striking illustrations of the truth of this statement in the case of the national workshops erected at the public expense in 1848 at the suggestion of Louis Blanc. In a tailor's shop there was introduced, instead of payment by the piece, payment by the day, in the hope that mutual supervision would incite the laborers to diligence. But soon this mutual supervision degenerated into an invidious and petty espionage, and brought about so many bitter reproaches and quarrels that it was soon found necessary to return to the old system of payment by the piece in order to restore order and harmony among the workmen.[1]

§ III. *Progress in the Socialistic State.*

If the necessary production would be impossible in the state of socialism, *progress* would be much more impossible. That private industry based on private property is conducive to progress is a fact which in our days is palpable. What wondrous progress has

[1] *Leroy-Beaulieu*, Le collectivisme, p. 354.

been made within the last century! We need only
recall the invention of steamboats, railroads, telegraphs, telephones, phonographs, and all the recent
results achieved in the field of electro-dynamics. Almost every day brings unexpected improvements; for
every one is bound by his own interest to make himself
useful to his neighbor and, if possible, to outdo his
competitors. Therefore every one is bent on invent-
ing more comfortable, useful, cheaper appliances. He
who offers the best and most useful commodities at the
lowest price finally takes the lead in the race of competition.

What will become of this progress in socialism?
Bebel, with his usual boldness, announces that in the
socialist commonwealth all will "turn their attention
to improvement, simplification, and acceleration of
the process of labor. Ambition to invent and discover
will be aroused to the highest degree; one will try to
outstrip the other in ideas and devices." [1] Such phrases
only bespeak the popular agitator. All shall be intent
upon inventions and discoveries? But suppose that
the socialistic grade of education would enable all
laborers to make inventions and discoveries—which
is very doubtful—where is the interest that could incite
them to new discoveries and inventions? And even
though there were such an interest, where would the
laborer find means to make discoveries in the production of commodities? Discoveries and inventions, at
least in the field of industry, suppose the possession of
productive goods wherewith one may experiment at
pleasure. They suppose, moreover, that one is
thoroughly trained in that one department, which he
makes the special study of a lifetime; consequently,

[1] Die Frau, pp. 271, 272.

that he is not directed at pleasure by a superintendent
or council of production, or by the vote of the people,
or by changes from one branch of industry to another,
and thus made a bungler in every branch or trade.
Schäffle [1] speaks of schools or guilds of "investigators, artists, scholars," which could be appointed by
the socialist commonwealth. But Bebel, who formerly
made the same statement himself,[2] denies the possibility of such classes. All have to take an active part
in production; but the remaining free time may be
employed by each individual in his favorite study.[3]
We have great reason to doubt that, after the social
productive labor, leisure would still remain for scientific and artistic pursuits; and we have still more reason to doubt whether the "Comrades" would employ
this time in earnest and solid study. We are inclined
rather to think that they would devote their leisure to
idleness and enjoyment.

But let that pass. We shall suppose that a socialist
has made an important discovery. Now it remains to
utilize it practically In the supposition of private
property this matter is comparatively easy. If the
inventor has capital, or if he succeeds to enlist interested capitalists, his discovery will soon make its way
into the public, if it only proves efficient. But the case
is different in the socialistic order. Here every inventor must either apply to the supreme director of production, or must bring his claim directly before the
people and try to interest the majority in his behalf.
This, however, will present no slight difficulty. It is
a difficult matter to win entire communities for any
innovation, particularly if individuals have no private
interest in the matter, but, on the contrary, thereby

[1] Quintessence, p 8   [2] Unsere Ziele, p. 32.   [3] Die Frau, p 284

only impose new labors upon themselves. If there is question, for instance, of new machineries, heating and lighting apparatus, public buildings, highways, canals, tunnels, etc., the innovation or improvement at the outset will cost a large portion of the national labor. And if such an improvement is once decided upon, it must at the same time be introduced in the entire social body, in order that the conditions of labor and life may be equal with all. But will society in all cases tamely submit to all such innovations? We fear that in the socialist state even such improvements as would certainly promise the greatest advantages from the very outset would fail to be introduced; and how much more such inventions as require repeated and costly experiments to test their efficiency?

Kleinwachter [1] makes the following just remark on the point in question: "In the socialist state, in which the entire production would be in common and systematically organized, the annual labor task of the entire population would have to be fixed and distributed among the laborers by the government. If, therefore, the government would find it desirable for the national production to introduce some innovation, and thus to increase the annual task of labor; and if the people, not being able at once to realize the advantages of such improvements, would consider the introduction of such appliances as superfluous, and would refuse to undertake the additional work—the government would in that case have no means to enforce its wishes against the majority of the population; and thus progress would be necessarily retarded. In short, in a socialist state industrial progress would be possible then only when the majority of the people would favor it; and that, as all men know, is a tedious process."

Besides, it is a circumstance not to be overlooked that in our present state of society inventions and im-

---

[1] Schönberg's Handbuch, vol 1 p 260.

provements of the same kind can be simultaneously introduced and tested, so that a thorough trial of each innovation is possible; and, finally, that improvement or invention which commends itself not only to the judgment of a few theorists, but has stood a practical test, will survive as the fittest. Thus we have a guarantee that the best and most useful appliances will finally gain the upper hand. Such a thorough testing would be impossible in the state of the future, as it would entail a considerable increase of labor, which would hardly meet with a sufficient remuneration, and of the utility of which the people at large could with difficulty be convinced.

§ IV. *Arts and Sciences in Socialism.*

If bold statements were sufficient to produce desired effects, socialism would not be opposed, but highly beneficial, to arts and sciences. But if progress on the field of industry would be, as we have seen, greatly retarded in the socialistic organization, it is natural to expect that progress in the arts and sciences would be still more restricted. According to Bebel's programme in the socialistic organization, all, without exception, shall take a direct and "physical" part in production; consequently, there shall be no professional artists and scholars. This conclusion is strictly logical, but at the same time it shows the absurdity of the socialistic system. For it is manifest that under such conditions there would be no possibility of real progress, for he who is to produce anything of considerable value in the field of art or science cannot cultivate these as a secondary object in leisure hours merely as an amateur, but must devote himself wholly to them from his very

youth. But it must be borne in mind that socialism
will introduce all, without exception, at an early
stage of youth, into all branches of production, since
production is the proper end, the only acknowledged
purpose of the socialist state. Moreover, those
disagreeable employments for which no laborers
will volunteer, must be performed by all in their
turn; and all without exception are bound for
their whole life to take an active part in production.
Can there be, under such circumstances, any higher,
scientific, and artistic aspirations and activity? Will
there be any taste and enthusiasm left for any branch
of knowledge beyond physical labor? In our present
state of society it is self-interest and necessity that
urge on the youthful student to earnest labor. Upon
his labor depends his future existence, his advancement, and his final position in society; whereas in
the socialistic order scientific and artistic abilities
can have no influence upon a man's social standing.
Remuneration will be gauged solely by the amount
of production of one's labor, and not by those occupations to which one may devote himself for his
amusement in leisure hours.

True, it sometimes happens in our day that men,
without any regard to external advantages, from
sheer love of science or art, undertake profound
studies. But this is the exception, not the rule;
and even these few have generally received the first
impulse to study from bitter necessity or from self-
interest; and they continue for their own pleasure the
studies or researches which in the course of time
have become for them a source of delight. But in
a collectivist state there would be no such incentives
for youth, since all, no matter what vocation they

may choose, shall have exactly the same conditions of life.

But let us suppose that Bebel's demand—that all should in the same manner "physically" take part in the work of production—should be dropped as impracticable by socialists; that professional scholars, artists, and scientists should be tolerated. By avoiding Charybdis they strike upon Scylla. Thus they would be forced to abandon the socialist theory of value, according to which all objects of use are to be estimated by the amount of labor consumed in their production; and by labor is here understood only such work as is either directly or indirectly productive. But there are many arts and sciences which have no value, or at least very small value, for production. What does poetry or music, for instance, contribute toward the national production? What astronomy, philosophy, comparative philology, history, etc.? And if such labors should nevertheless be remunerated by the community, what must be the standard by which they are to be estimated? But we must return to this point when we speak of the division of produce. Moreover, would not the unequal treatment of employing one as a scholar, artist, scientist, or professor, while another is forced to undergo the disagreeable labors of the mine or the factory, do away with the equal conditions of life, and give occasion to jealousy and complaints? If socialists nowadays declaim against "unproductive entities" and "drones," how much more would they do so in the commonwealth of the future, when all would be conscious of their equal rights, and have the decision of all things in their own hands? We have already drawn attention to the fact that socialism would do away with freedom in the choice of a state or profession in life. If the state would appoint philosophers and scientists and artists, the lack of this fre dom of choice would be still more keenly felt, for either it must be supposed that artists and scholars would be so placed as to enjoy respect, honor, and temporal emolument, and then all would rush to these professions, or we must suppose that they would have no distinction among their fellows, that they would have no more prestige than an ordinary shoemaker or tailor; and in this case there would be few candidates for the learned professions. In any case, the authorities would have to determine who should embrace the scientific and artistic professions. *(not much to be said.)*

§ V. *Liberty of the Press in Socialism.*

The *freedom of the press* in socialism deserves special consideration. True, we consider as objectionable that unlimited freedom of the press which allows all manner of outrage upon good morals, religion, lawful authority, marriage, property, etc., to go unpunished. But no less objectionable in our time, when different religious denominations are actually tolerated and live peaceably together, would be a censorship permitting that only to be published which would have the approval of state officials. But such a censorship would be necessary in the socialist state.

All labor materials are the exclusive property of the community; consequently, also the printing-presses would be public institutions. The community must supply the materials and the labor-hands; it is also the task of the community to decide on what is to be printed and what to be put in the waste-basket. It would

therefore depend entirely upon the majority of the respective committee, or of the entire people, whether a
literary work, be its merit great or small, should
ever see the light or not. Socialists pride themselves on this feature of their system. Bebel particularly boasts that in the state of the future much of the
"rubbish" which in our time floods the book-market
would never be published. But manifestly such a
policy would destroy the good seed together with the
cockle. True, many books, and among them much
"rubbish," would remain unpublished; but very
probably many works also of real literary merit would
be suppressed, while much would doubtless also see
the light which would fully deserve the name of "rubbish." For the question is, what is to be regarded as
rubbish? One party considers a work as worthless,
while another considers it valuable, and a third even ad-
mires it, and *vice versa.* Very often, we fear, the most
learned and scientific works would be branded as
rubbish, while frivolous and superficial productions
would find their way through the press. Let us suppose the case that a citizen of the "state of the future"
has gained the conviction that the collectivist order
of society is highly unjust and absurd, and that he
embodies and substantiates his opinion in a scientific
work, or in a series of popular essays. What will
the socialist censors judge of his lucubrations? What
we say of scientific subjects would be still more true
of religious questions. In the collectivist state a
party would have it in its power to exclude from the
press every religious opinion which it would find
inconvenient. Or could authors appeal to the liber-
ality and tolerance of the popular majority? The
masses are generally more intolerant than individuals:

the latter must regard public opinion, the former
need not.

Like the printing-press so also the foundation and
support of all kinds of scientific and artistic institutions—elementary, middle, and high schools, industrial schools, clinics, libraries, museums, etc.—would
be placed under public direction; so that new establishments could not be set up except by vote of the
majority. In the erection of such institutions the
first question which would present itself to the consideration of the community would be the increase
of the national labor, which would never, or at least
not for many years, produce any industrial fruit.

In socialism slavery would go even to greater extremes. All buildings, particularly the great public
edifices, would be the property of the entire state,
which would dispose of them by means of its officials.
. No public building could, therefore, be erected for
large assemblies, for divine worship, for public lectures, etc., except with the permission of the majority
or of the state's representatives. But let this suffice:
so much is certain from what we have said, that in
the socialist state the majority would have full power
to oppress and to enslave the minority at pleasure.
The latter would have no guarantee for their freedom except the good-will of the majority, or at the
worst revolution, to which it might claim the same
right as the socialists of to-day.

SECTION IV.

THE DIVISION OF PRODUCE.

We now come to that point of the socialistic system
of which socialists are particularly proud, and which

even commends itself to the sympathies of many who are not socialists. Is it not an undeniable fact, they say, that production is continually on the increase, and yet that the greater number of men live in extreme poverty? Whence this phencmenon? They answer: from the unjust distribution of industrial produce.

We readily grant that in our present system of distribution there is much that is defective and needs improvement. There are not a few capitalists who, for sordid gain, use the laborers unjustly; not a few who by dishonest speculation bring other men's property into their possession. What we deny is this—that socialism, in all its schemes, has devised a fairer and better method of distribution.

We shall suppose that the annual proceeds of production in the socialist state have turned out abundant—although, from our former remarks, this supposition must seem improbable; but we shall make this supposition, to put socialism in the most favorable light possible. Now the first thing will be to ascertain the total amount of the collective product. Before beginning the distribution it is necessary to know exactly how much there is to be distributed. To hand over to each one at random or at his pleasure any amount of wine or milk, poultry or venison, might exhaust the stores before long, and cause the rest to go home empty-handed. Therefore the available quantity of all products, at least of natural products which cannot be obtained at will, would have to be accurately determined. To do this even for one article only would be a difficult task, necessitating a vast amount of clerical work, and a corresponding number of officials.

The products of each kind might indeed be brought together in central warehouses, whence they would be distributed throughout the country. Thereby supervision and control would be greatly facilitated, but also an immense waste of time and labor would be the result. The grain, e.g., would first be shipped from all over to the central warehouses and then be sent back again in part to the place whence it came. To make the matter more tangible, let us suppose there is question of determining the supply of milk produced in a certain state, and how much of it can be given to each one to satisfy all reasonable demands. How can we make even an approximate estimate of the amount produced throughout the country, considering that it depends on the differences of season and fodder, and on other circumstances and contingencies varying from day to day? And yet the same trouble would arise with every one of the countless natural and artificial products of which a great commonwealth stands in need.

But, will the *total* product be distributed? Not at all. As Marx points out emphatically, there is to be subtracted first that part which is needed for the continuance of production, for the repair of machines and tools, for the improvement of factories and their equipment, for the transportation of raw material, etc. Besides, there is to be established a reserve fund as an insurance against accidents and the havoc wrought by natural calamities. Finally there are yet to be subtracted from the total product, "first, the general costs of administration outside of production . . ; secondly, whatever is required for the social gratification of public wants, as schools, sanitary appliances, etc. . . ; thirdly, funds for the disabled—

in short, for whatever belongs at present to the official bureaus of charity." [1] By this previous deduction socialism intends to abolish taxation altogether.

Only the remainder of the proceeds is to be justly divided among the individual members of the body social. Now it is evident, as we have already shown, that not all will be allowed to go to the public stores and indiscriminately, without further control, to take whatever they please. A certain clear, fixed, and practicable *standard* must be adopted; and the question is, what this standard shall be. Socialism has thus far devised not a single practicable standard. Socialists themselves are on this point, as on many other points of practical policy, somewhat reticent. Marx advocates a distribution of goods according to the amount of labor performed, at least in the primitive state of socialism; but in a more advanced phase of society, he adds, each one will draw "according to his reasonable wants." We shall now proceed to examine successively the practicability of the imaginable standards for distribution. We can imagine only five such standards that might be made the basis for the distribution of produce—the number of persons, the labor-time, the amount of labor performed, diligence, and actual wants.

§ I. *Number of Persons as a Standard.*

A distribution of produce according to the number of persons of a given section or community has not, to our knowledge, been advocated by any socialist. And naturally so; for to give the same amount of produce to each individual, whether diligent

[1] *Marx,* Zur Kritik des sozialdemokratischen Parteiprogramms, pp. 565–566

or idle, skilful or unskilful, strong or weak, whether his wants be few or many, would be evidently most unfair. Such a system would set a premium upon idleness and incapacity, and would blast all industry in the bud.

The preceding lines were written before Bellamy's novel came into our hands The American fictionist of the future has all produce equally divided among all in his socialist commonwealth Each one, according to Bellamy, receives at the beginning of the year an equal number of credit cards, on which he can at all times draw an equal value of goods from the public storehouses. In every community or ward there is such a magazine, from which each one can draw exactly what he pleases. The value of the credit cards, given to all, is so high as considerably to surpass the ordinary wants of an individual or family. If, however, in an exceptional case the value of the card is not sufficient, each one may receive credit in advance for the following year. For, as Bellamy remarks, the nation is wealthy, and does not wish its members to suffer any want Economy is no longer considered a virtue. No one is concerned for the morrow, whether for himself or for his children, for the nation guarantees nourishment, education, and comfortable support to all its citizens, from the cradle to the grave. What luxury must develop from such a state of things, in which economy is no longer considered a virtue, may be easily imagined How we are to judge of the assertion that the socialist state shall be so rich that there will be no more need of economy, and that supplies will be equal to the demands in all sections, we may easily conclude from what has been said under a previous heading

But how will Bellamy reconcile with justice the principle that no regard is had for the amount of labor performed, for capacity, and for the experience and skill of individuals; that the weakest, the most stupid, and most inexperienced receive the same remuneration as the strongest, the most skilful, and the most experienced? Bellamy, through his mouthpiece Dr Leete, replies to this difficulty that the amount of labor performed has nothing to do with the distribution of produce, since this is a question of merit; and merit is a moral idea, while the quantity of produce is material It would be a remarkable kind of logic, he thinks, to endeavor to decide a moral question by a material standard. The degree of effort alone is decisive in regard to merit; whence we do not reward a horse because he bears a heavier burden than a goat would bear But if Bellamy would compare man with a horse he must be consistent, and deny him all merit also in view of effort. We do not attribute true merit to a horse, no matter how great has been his effort; we do not feed him on account of his merits, but on account of his usefulness; and thus, too, Bellamy must treat the man of the future, if he wishes to be consistent.

But merit is a moral idea, and the quantity of labor produced is material. As to this quibble, we reply first of all that Bellamy contradicts himself; for the effort of the laborer is at least mainly material or physical, why, then, does Bellamy attribute merit to it? Or does he imagine that only the effort, but not the product of labor or the labor performed, is a rational moral activity? But when we ascribe merit to labor performed we do not understand by it the physical product of labor as such, but the performance itself, in as much as it is a valuable, creative activity We reward, not the food which the cook prepares for our use, but the labor of cooking, the value of which, it is true, we determine by the product or the food cooked

In the second place, if Bellamy asserts that merit is something moral, we must distinguish between formal merit as such—that is, in as much as it implies a right to a reward, and the title of merit—or the meritorious action The former, it is true, is something purely moral, the latter is not The title of merit is an action which is useful for another, and whenever there is not question of moral merit (with God), but of physical merit (with man), its value is determined according to the usefulness of the action performed for the benefit of our fellow men or society—always supposing, of course, that the action is free and imputable to the subject.

§ II. *Labor-time as a Standard.*

The labor-time alone cannot serve as a standard for the distribution of the proceeds of labor; for in the first place this standard is *unjust* A more skilful, better trained, more practised and diligent laborer produces more in the same time than one in whom these qualities are deficient. Let us take two carpenters both working ten hours daily. One of them is strong, experienced, skilful, and diligent, the other one lazy, stupid, and awkward. Are they to receive each evening the same labor certificates, the same title to a share of the total product? That would be unjust and demoralizing.

This difficulty cannot be avoided by taking as a standard not the actual labor-time, but "the socially required unit of labor-time"—that is, the time which is required "to produce a given value under given normal social conditions of labor, and with a given socially required grade of skill and intensity." This standard of distribution could be regarded as just only in the supposition of Marx's theory of value. If the exchange-value of useful commodities does not consist in the "crystallized" labor contained in them, as Marx would have it, but chiefly in the difference of their use-value, it is manifestly unjust not to regard the *difference of the labor-forces*, but to treat all according to the same norm. Let us suppose five laborers working side by side in a factory. How is the share of the universal produce to be determined which falls to the lot of each? According to the "average of skill and intensity of the [social] labor." But this average is a mere abstraction. Actually, perhaps, none of the five laborers has the average mean. Some have more than the average, some less. It were folly to suppose that all possessed the same skill and labored with the same intensity; for men differ greatly from one another. But why should the laborer who possesses greater skill get credit only for average skill, and why should he who possesses less than the average skill get credit for the skill which he does not possess?

German social democrats established the proposition tha useful labor—labor which produces exchange-value—is possi ble only through society, not through individuals However, though this proposition should be conceded, it would not thence follow that all the members of society produced the same amount of labor and have the same right to remuneration; but the proposition itself is untrue, and has been established only for the purpose of gaining some semblance of right to weld individuals into the machine of public production. True, useful commodities can gain exchange-value only where several persons are living together and one possesses what the other does not. But this condition supposed, exchange-value depends chiefly upon use-value; and to produce useful commodities personal ability is sufficient. Could not Robinson Crusoe produce many articles for his own use? Or would socialists only say that personal labor is in many respects dependent upon society? If so, logically speaking, labor-power is no longer private property, but must be considered the property of the community; and the community must, consequently, have the right to dispose of such common labor at pleasure, independently of the individual laborer.

The standard of the division of produce by the "necessary social unit" of labor-time is, therefore, unjust and rests upon a false assumption. But it is also *impracticable.* Here, as in similar difficulties, Bebel [1] cuts the knot and simply declares: "The labor-time which is required to produce a certain object is the standard according to which its social use-value is to be determined. Ten minutes of social labor-time in one object are exchangeable for ten minutes of social labor-time in another object—no more and no less."

Let us examine the matter practically. We wish to know how much social labor-time is contained in a bushel of wheat. To ascertain this it will not suffice to figure out how much time a farmer actually spent in ploughing, manuring, harrowing, harvesting, etc.,

[1] *Die Frau,* p. 282.

and then to divide the total number of hours by the number of bushels reaped.

One farmer is diligent and skilful, and cultivates his field in a much shorter time and in a much better manner than another. The distance of the fields from the farmers' residences, the roads, the farming implements, are different. But above all, the produce depends to a great extent upon the quality of the soil, upon the kind and quantity of manure, upon the climate and the favorable or unfavorable weather. The same soil will produce in different years very different crops. Who, then, can determine the socially required unit of labor-time contained in a bushel of wheat? With the same labor an acre of land in the fertile districts of the Rhine will produce double or three times the crop which by the same labor will be reaped on an acre in the Harz Mountains or on the sandy plains of Holland. One need only recall these difficulties to perceive that the calculation of the socially required unit of labor-time, even for a single commodity, is a thing impossible.

But this is only the beginning of the difficulty. What we say of wheat is true in like manner of all kinds of grain and vegetables, nay, of all agricultural products (meat, butter, cheese, eggs, etc.). The same may be said of the produce of mines, fisheries, etc. Who could determine the unit of labor-time for such products as change from year to year and even from month to month? We say nothing of the fact that it is altogether an erroneous process to determine the exchange-value of commodities by the unit of time required for their production.

The difficulty increases if we admit that in the society of the future there would be paid judges, physicians, surgeons, artists, scholars, etc. Schäffle [1] says: "Those who yielded services of general utility as judges, administrative officials, teachers, artists, scientific investigators, instead of producing material commodities . . . would receive a share in the commodities produced by the national labor, proportioned to the time spent by them in work useful to the community."

Proportioned to the time spent in work useful to the community! Did Schäffle consider the difficulty of calculating this proportion? How is the time spent in services useful to society to be determined in the case of the scientist, the artist, and the philosopher? Should all be treated in the same way? Would all physicians get the same salary, whether skilful or unskilful, experienced or otherwise? Are physicians to draw a higher salary than philosophers, artists, and teachers? Again, shall an elementary teacher receive the same pay as a professor of an intermediate school or of a university? It would be unjust to treat them all alike. It would be an outrage to the more gifted and industrious. But an unequal salary would be contrary to the fundamental principles of socialism, and a constant source of jealousy and contention. Nor could the present scale of payment be retained in the socialist state, for the present system, as Schäffle remarks, would on the very first day be upset by social democracy: and justly so according to socialist principles, for it is contrary to the equal rights of all; and it would of necessity lead to a social aristocracy, by whatever name we might choose to call it.

[1] Quintessence, p. 8.

§ III. *The Labor Performed as a Standard.*

The labor performed is another standard according to which, absolutely speaking, the distribution of produce might be determined. This standard is repeatedly suggested by socialist leaders. "Superior production," says Bebel,[1] "will receive higher remuneration, but only in proportion to the labor performed." This is indeed the standard which consistent socialists must needs adopt. Their chief grievance against existing society is the "revenue without work" which flows into the pockets of lazy capitalists, whilst the workingman is exploited and despoiled of a great part of his product. Socialism is to secure to every laborer the full product of his labor. Consequently the standard of distribution to be adopted must be the actual labor performed—the labor-product. But can a distribution of the total product be effected by this standard? As far as the labor performed is simply determined by the socially required unit of labor-time, we have shown it to be an impracticable standard. But if the labor performed is gauged not only by the labor-time, but also according to its intrinsic value, we must take into consideration, besides the time, also skill, strength, practice, and diligence. For upon all these elements depend the quantity and quality of the labor performed. But, particularly, the various kinds of employment in which one is engaged for the benefit of society must be compared with one another, and estimated according to their relative values. For all occupations have not, as socialists pretend, the same value for society; and, consequently, they do not deserve the same remuneration.

[1] Unsere Ziele, p 30.

No one, for instance, will consider the work of a fireman or of a stable-boy of the same value as the services of a physician or of a professor of a university. But who will pretend to have sufficient shrewdness and wisdom to determine from the consideration of the various factors the relative value of each occupation according to the demands of justice? How totally different are the opinions of men on the relative value of labor! One considers this occupation more valuable, while another attributes greater value to a different occupation. In estimating the value of labor, much depends upon subjective views. Could, therefore, a standard so complicated, so totally dependent upon subjective opinions, be employed for the distribution of produce without giving occasion to constant discontent and discord?

From what we have already said we may easily conclude the impracticability of the standard of distribution proposed by Rodbertus,[1] who suggests that the proceeds should be distributed according to the normal *day's work* [Werkarbeitstag], as distinguished from the *work-day* [Zeitarbeitstag]. First, the labor-time, or the normal working-day, must be determined —that is, the time which a workman of medium strength and with average exertion can permanently work every day in a given industry. This time is different in different branches of industry. If this normal time is once found, then it remains to determine the amount of labor to be performed—that is, that amount which an average laborer, with average skill and with medium diligence, can in a given industry produce in the normal work-time. This amount of labor Rodbertus calls the *day's work*, as

[1] Der Normalarbeitstag, 1871.

distinguished from the *work-day*, or normal labor·
time.

The normal day's work in one branch of industry,
according to Rodbertus, has the same value as the
normal day's work in another, or, to put it more
universally, the *products of the same labor-time are equal
in value.* If, for instance, a pair of shoes forms a
day's work in the shoe industry, and a table five
days' work in the joiner's trade, a table is worth five
times as much as a pair of shoes.

Attempts have been made to calculate the normal day's work
for different trades: even for the simplest labor such a calculation is most tedious and complicated, and at best only approx-
imately correct. For, as Rodbertus remarks, it is not sufficient
to calculate the labor directly employed by the shoemaker to
make a pair of shoes, but it is necessary also to reckon the wear
of the shoemaker's tools in the operation. But to make this latter calculation it is necessary to know the value of all the shoemaker's instruments, of the various materials that go to make a
pair of shoes—leather, thread, nails, hammer, awl—and, moreover, to calculate how many days' work might be performed by
every one of these instruments.

This standard of Rodbertus rests on the assumption that the value of an object is determined *solely
by the labor* consumed in its production. But this
assumption, as we have proved, is false. Good wine,
fruit, timber, cloth, grain, or land, is sold at a higher
price than the same quantity of the same object
of an inferior quality, and that independently of the
labor consumed upon it. Why are fresh articles of
food—fruit, meat, butter, etc.—sold at a higher price
than stale ones? Every child can answer this question. Should this simple question puzzle political
economists like Rodbertus? It is upon the usefulness of an object that its value chiefly depends. This

is also the case, as we have seen, with human labor; and therefore it is erroneous to make the day's work in one branch of industry equivalent to the day's work in another.

The normal day's work, moreover, is impracticable as a standard of distribution, because there are many industries and activities to which it is impossible to apply it. Who, for instance, can determine the day's work of a physician, a scientist, a teacher, an astronomer, an historian, a state official? The tailor or shoemaker can preserve the product of his labor and have it estimated by competent judges. But what has the physician, or the scientist, or the astronomer, or the magistrate, or the teacher to show? What can the husbandman present, if drought, or frost, or hail has destroyed his crops? Or what can the huntsman or fisherman exhibit, if he happens to be unsuccessful in his efforts? The standard of the day's work, moreover, is not consistent with the social democratic system. For it would necessarily bring in its wake considerable social inequalities Rodbertus himself acknowledges that the day's work standard would introduce the piece-system into the socialist state. If, for instance, he who has performed one normal day's work receives payment equivalent to one, he who in the same time performs two normal day's work receives double the amount. But he who has performed only half a day's work will receive but half the pay. Now, it is not at all impossible that a strong, healthy, skilful laborer should do twice or three times as much work as another who is weaker and less skilful. Thus considerable social inequality would soon arise, especially if the weaker laborers would, by sickness or other accidents, be for a considerable time prevented from work; for we suppose that the man who works a whole day receives better pay than he who is sick and unfit to work. Otherwise all incentives to labor would soon cease, and the rush to the public infirmaries would be universal. However feelingly the social democrats may speak of "brotherly spirit" and devotion to the common good, they cannot remove the dread of toil under which a great portion of humanity labors.

The same arguments serve also to refute the standard of division proposed by Marx In the higher phase of communism every one is to receive according to his needs. This mode of division will be discussed later on In a lower stage, however, in the transition of society from the capitalist to the collectivist system, each producer is to get back from society exactly as much as he has given. "His contribution is his individual share of labor For instance, the social working-day consists of the total of the individual hours of labor; the individual labor-time of each producer is the part of the social working-day furnished by him; it constitutes his share Society will give him a certificate that he has furnished a certain quantity of work— after deducting his work for the common fund—and by showing his certificate he will draw from society's stores an amount of provisions equivalent in value to his work. The amount of work given to society in one shape is received again in another." [1] Marx's language is rather mystifying. "Society will give him a certificate that he has furnished a certain quantity of work " If no more is meant by this than that the labor-time is to serve as a standard of distribution we need not prove again its injustice and impracticability. Marx himself confesses that the achievements of different workingmen vary greatly If, however, the amount of labor expended is to be figured out, then also the assiduity, skill, intensity, and strength of each man must be taken into consideration. Yet, in numberless cases these cannot be ascertained at all. Who can calculate the amount of labor —intensity, skill, assiduity, etc —expended by a doctor or nurse, by a scientific investigator or teacher? And even if this quan-

[1] Marx in the *Neue Zeit*, 9th year, 1. p. 566.

tity were well known, who can say how much labor is contained in a pound of bread or a quart of milk? Finally, it has been remarked already that it is unjust to consider only the quantity and not also the quality of the work. Not every kind of work is of equal value to society.

§ IV. *Diligence as a Standard.*

Much less than the amount of labor performed can *diligence* alone serve as a standard for the distribution of produce. It would be simply unjust to regard diligence as the only norm, since such a standard would put the more skilful and expert laborers on the same footing with the slowest and most awkward. Moreover, how could the diligence of each one be accurately determined? Bellamy thinks that in a socialist state each one should receive an equal share of the produce if he only makes equal endeavor, or produces that of which he is capable.[1] That is all easily said; but who shall judge whether each one does his best? How are we to form a definite judgment upon such an endeavor? At best only by an extensive system of mutual supervision and espionage. But such a system would manifestly be an unbearable yoke, which the sovereign people would on the very first day shake off with indignation. And even if such control could be permanently established, how easy would it be to deceive the over-

[1] *Bellamy* seems to look upon the men of the future as over-grown children. In the first years after entering the industrial army the young people (of 21 years and upward) will be accustomed to obedience and self-denial. Their achievements will be carefully recorded, the proficient are rewarded, the negligent are punished. Only after the lapse of these three years are they allowed to choose their profession. During their apprenticeship an exact record is kept of their proficiency and diligence and they are rewarded according to their deserts. In every branch of industry the workmen will be classed according to excellence into three categories. This classification will take place periodically, and its results will be published in the papers. Those of the first class are distinguished by a gold medal, the second by a silver, the third by an iron one. Such proposals might be realized at most in the nursery.

seers, especially if many laborers would conspire
against them? What guarantee could an overseer
give who would be elected and might be deposed at any
minute? Finally, if a laborer would be found guilty
of a lack of diligence, how much then should be deducted from his wages, and who is to judge of the
amount? We are of opinion that if such a standard
were introduced, our prisons, which socialists want to
have abolished, would soon have to be replaced by
more numerous and more capacious ones.

§ V. *The Wants of Individuals as a Standard.*

It would be still more unjust and impracticable to
distribute the produce of labor according to "the wants of
individuals," as Marx has it (as if in future there would
be no unreasonable desires), or, as the Gotha programme
more prudently puts it, "to each one according to his
reasonable demands." What are the reasonable demands? Not all have the same wants. Evidently it
would not be wise to leave to individuals themselves
the decision concerning their wants. No one is an
impartial judge in his own case; and, besides, experience teaches that demands do not exactly coincide with
real wants.

The only expedient that would be left, therefore,
would be to appoint for each district a "committee on
wants," whose task it would be to determine the real
needs of individuals—for instance, how many glasses

of beer the workman of the future would actually need,
how many new gowns and hats the socialist lady would
require every year. And as such a commission would
necessarily consist of Solons and Aristideses, who
would decide, not according to personal regards, but

only according to right and justice, and would always hit upon the right thing; and as, moreover, the socialist comrades, as Bebel loves to characterize them, would be animated by a "brotherly spirit," and would be content with little, this most delicate problem would be solved to the greatest satisfaction of all, and the social machinery would move in the greatest peace and harmony!

Section V.

OVERPOPULATION. INTERNATIONAL CHARACTER OF SOCIALISM.

§ I. *The Question of Overpopulation.*

The question of distribution discussed in the preceding pages is intimately connected with another problem affecting the very existence of socialism—we mean the problem of overpopulation. It is far easier to beget children than to feed them. This truism points to a source of great anxieties to the whole of mankind as well as individual parents, and in not the lowest degree to the future socialist commonwealth.

Even such as do not advocate strict Malthusianism [1]

---

[1] MALTHUS (1766–1834) ascribes to human society the tendency of doubling its number every 25 years, or of increasing in geometrical progression (as 1 to 2, to 4, to 8, to 16, etc), whilst the supply of victuals is increasing in arithmetical progression (as 1 to 2, to 3, to 4, etc), equal amounts being added during each period Therefore if the population were allowed to multiply freely, there would soon be a great disproportion between the population and the means of sustenance In reality population can never exceed the limits established by the supply of foodstuffs Therefore the increase is continually checked, and population is kept within the limits of the existing means of sustenance According to Malthus the causes tending to check overpopulation are partly preventive, partly positive Among the former are late marriages and celibacy, among the latter starvation, disease, war, infanticide

Cf *Malthus*, Essay on the Principles of Population, 1708

In the mathematical form given above Malthusianism is pretty generally abandoned, its fundamental idea, however, is still regarded by many as an established result of scientific research Cf *Devas*, Political Economy, pp 129 sqq , also *R von Mohl*, Geschichte und Literatur der Staatswissenschaften, vol III. p 411

are nevertheless forced to confess that population is increasing more constantly and quickly than do the provisions necessary for its sustenance. Even outside of socialist circles this fact is pretty generally acknowledged by men of science. G. Rumelin [1] says it is "an indisputable truth that, while on the one hand the human propensity to increase and multiply retains its vigor undiminished from generation to generation, and while the second million is as capable and as anxious to propagate itself as was the first, on the other hand, the same areas will allow their productiveness to be increased in continually diminishing proportions the more cultivation has been already advanced."

Therefore, political economists are even now inquiring how the growing danger of overpopulation, i.e., of an increase of population beyond the existing means of sustenance, might be averted. Of course, socialists have not the slightest anxiety on that head. According to Marx and Bebel the problem of overpopulation concerns only capitalist society and has no meaning for the future socialist commonwealth. For, in the first place the distribution of products will then be much more equalized and consequently a far greater number will be sustained, and in the second place the productivity of labor will grow in a wonderful manner, or, as Marx has it, the fountainheads of life will flow more abundantly.

To our mind, this is rank self-deception. Nay more; we maintain that in the socialist state the danger of overpopulation instead of being diminished would be far more threatening than in the existing order of society. Socialism looks upon every new-born

[1] Schönberg's Handbuch der politischen Oekonomie, vol II. p. 926.

child as a "welcome addition" (Bebel) to society, to be reared at the public expense. Moreover there is no restraint on the choice of partners. Men and women may unite whenever and as long as they please. The rearing of their offspring need not bother them; the paternal state takes the children into its care, provides them with food and clothing. This is the socialist family system, as will be explained and proved later on.

What will be the effects of this order of things, where nothing will hinder men from an unbridled indulgence of their strongest passions, since with the free choice of partners there will be combined freedom from all care for the education of the children? The answer is not far to seek. For the socialist state the Malthusian scale of progression would be too slow; the population would be doubled in much less than twenty-five years. At present many different causes restrict the increase of population. The fear of being unable to support their children prevents many people from marrying, or at least from marrying in early life. Add to this the reluctance of being troubled by too many children and the desire to keep one's offspring on the same social level and therefore to avoid splitting up the inheritance. Of course, also, in the socialist commonwealth woman would like to shirk the duties of motherhood, but notwithstanding the declarations of the socialist platform she would still be subject to man.

Socialism, however, would do away with all parental anxieties. The offspring would in no way inconvenience the parents; society would receive them as a welcome addition. There would be no more restriction on sexual intercourse. And yet the danger of overpopulation is to be less than at present?

But in the future system the productivity of labor will assume astonishing proportions; there will be an abundance of food for every one. That abundance exists indeed in the imagination of socialist prophets, not however in reality; production would be rather less remunerative, as we have shown above (p. 299 s₁q.). But, socialists tell us, the birth of every child is the birth of another laborer. True enough; but also another mouth to be fed. It is absolutely certain that the need of provisions increases with the number of births. Also in the socialist state twenty comrades will need twice as much as ten. But is it equally certain that the means of life will increase at the same rate as population? Rather the contrary. If a country is peopled at present ten times as densely as it was two or three hundred years ago, will the soil on that account yield tenfold returns? The more densely settled and highly cultivated the land, the more difficult and complicated the task is of supplying sufficient food to all its inhabitants.

Now, as long as a state is surrounded by countries less advanced in industry and more sparsely settled, it is enabled to procure the necessary means of existence by importing foodstuffs and exporting industrial products. The difficulty, however, is heightened the more the export countries advance in population and industrial development. This is the case in countries where private ownership and private industries prevail; for a socialist commonwealth in the midst of non-socialist states the difficulty would be insuperable, as will be shown to evidence in the next paragraph.

§ II. *Socialism Essentially International.*

If socialism is at all practicable, it is so only on an international basis. Already from what we have said on the division of labor forces (p. 274 sqq.) it may be concluded that a socialist organization is possible at most if it is international, if it is introduced simultaneously in all the great industrial states of Europe, America, Australia. To feel the full force of our contention it will suffice to consider how a densely settled socialist state could possibly provide sustenance for its numerous charges. Even at present densely populated districts can produce no more than a small fraction of their requirements. The rest is to be provided by importation on a large scale. To these imports there must naturally correspond exports on an equally grand scale and consequently a sufficient and reliable market. Industrial states, therefore, depend in great measure on international commerce. Now we assert a socially organized state cannot maintain its ground in competition with non-socialist states.

To prove our assertion we may refer to the testimony of socialists themselves. We have called attention in an earlier chapter (p. 302) to some co-operative companies (printing establishments, bakeries, etc.) established by socialists. Whenever socialists are confronted by the fact that in these co-operative associations wages are not higher, working facilities not better, working hours not shorter than in private establishments, they answer quite correctly that in the midst of private capitalist undertakings a perfectly socialist institution is impossible. The bankruptcy of some of these socialist companies proves indeed that the vaunted spirit of brotherly love, the cheerful desire to work, and the devotion and public zeal, the stock-in-trade of socialist agitators, are but empty vaporings. But thence we cannot prove that socialism is economically impossible, because in these co-operative concerns the prerequisite conditions of collectivist organization are wanting.

The reason why a socialist organization cannot subsist in non-socialist surroundings is not difficult to grasp. The avowed aim of socialism is the betterment of workingmen. Its programme calls for the highest possible wages, the shortest hours of work, the most comfortable and healthful shop arrangements, etc. A community organized on these principles is unable to produce merchandise as cheaply and quickly and in the same quantities as other concerns whose endeavor is to manufacture on a large scale and with the least cost. The socialist organization cannot stand the competition; either it must reduce wages or lengthen the working-hours, or else it will be bankrupt.

What we have said so far concerning small undertakings and co-operative companies applies equally to the relative position of different states. The socialist commonwealth could not compete even for one day with non-socialist countries in supplying the world's markets—much less than smaller co-operative companies. For the larger the socialist organization the clumsier also and slower is its administrative machinery.

To these difficulties would be added a host of others. The socialist state having non-socialist neighbors would have to determine for every product a twofold value based on essentially different principles. Within the country the products would be valued and divided according to the socially necessary labor contained in them; but in international commerce, prices would be regulated by supply and demand; in foreign commerce there would be required money, also negotiable papers, besides large warehouses for exports and imports. Would these immense amounts of public money and merchandise not prove occasion of colossal frauds and embezzlements?

But what if the socialist commonwealth were forced to wage war against non-socialist states? The entire system of production would shortly be thrown into complete disorder or would even be brought to a standstill, thus exposing the whole community to famine and destitution. The very fact that suddenly thousands of able-bodied men would be removed from productive labor would imply great disturbances in the administrative and productive machinery, disturbances frustrating the nicest calculations. Nay, more, if the enemy were to make an inroad into the country and sever the connection with the central bureaus, how could there still be question of systematic regulation? Under present conditions the baneful effects of war are less noticeable on account of the greater decentralization and independence of private manufactories. Again, let us suppose the socialist state takes the offensive. According to what principles shall the troops be recruited so as not infringe on the perfect equality of all? Of course Bebel tells us that then there will be no more wars, that we shall be in a period of bliss and harmony undisturbed. We submit, however, to his consideration that the making of war will depend as much on the non-socialist neighbors as on the collectivist commonwealth. Or will socialists good-naturedly bear every slight, affront, and injustice inflicted by other nations?

These are a few of the difficulties confronting a socialist commonwealth surrounded by non-socialist states.

Therefore we do not hesitate to say: If socialism can at all be realized, it must needs be introduced simultaneously in at least all the important civilized countries. But of such an international introduction of socialism there cannot be the least thought. To abstract from other reasons, an insurmountable obstacle will be offered by the national antipathies and jealousies, which in our times instead of diminishing are steadily growing. So-called jingoism was never as strong as it is at present. Consider, finally, the tremendous difficulties to be met in organizing production and distribution throughout the vast extent covered by the modern industrial states, difficulties that will be forever increasing in number, weight, and extent!

SECTION VI.

THE FAMILY IN THE SOCIALISTIC STATE.

The family is without doubt the indispensable mainstay of every well-ordered commonwealth. If socialism destroys the family it must necessarily be looked upon as the enemy of order, freedom, civilization, and Christianity itself.

§ I. *Marriage in the Socialistic State.*

We do not assert that socialism aims at the legal prohibition of marriage or at the compulsory dissolution of the family. Kautsky feigns great indignation at imputations of this sort made against social democracy. "It is a most palpable falsification," he says, "to impute to us any such intentions; only a fool can imagine that a family is created or abolished by a legislative enactment."[1] It has become a real mania with socialist writers to wax wroth at objections which no one thinks of raising. All we maintain is that the dissolution of the family is the necessary consequence of socialist principles and demands. The proof for our assertion is not far to fetch.

The destruction of the marriage bond involves the destruction of the family. Marriage is the root and foundation of the entire family. Socialism, however, by its theories of equality loosens the marriage tie, and introduces instead some amorous relation based on mere whims and passing inclinations. The truth of this statement is vouched for by the express testimony of prominent socialists. Already Marx has pointed out that modern industry, by assigning an important part in socially organized production to women, young persons, and children, and thereby removing them from the sphere of domestic life, is creating the economic basis for "a higher form of the family and of the relation of the sexes." And he adds that it is rather silly to consider the Christian Germanic form of marriage or any other form as absolute and unchangeable.[2]

What are we to understand by the higher form of sexual relations? The Erfurt platform calls for the "abolition of all laws which subordinate woman to man in public and private life." This demand implies at least the destruction of the unity of the family, which necessarily postulates one supreme head. Who is to

[1] Das Erfurter Programm, etc., p 146.
[2] Capital, vol 1 p. 455

decide the dispute, if man and wife disagree as to
their dwelling-place and similar affairs? But to make
us understand more fully what is meant by that higher
form of marriage, it will suffice to hear the evidence of
a leader, who may be said to represent the almost
universal sentiment. Bebel writes of the position of
woman in the socialist state as follows:

"In the choice of the object of her love she [woman] is no less
free than man she loves, and is loved, and enters into the marriage alliance with no other regard than that of preference. This
alliance is a *private* agreement, without the intervention of any
[public] functionary, just as marriage was a private concern till
late in the Middle Ages [1] . . Man should be free to dispose of
the strongest instinct of his nature as of every other natural
instinct. The gratification of the sexual instinct is not a whit
less the personal affair of every individual than is the satisfaction of any other natural appetite Therefore no one is obliged
to render an account of such gratification; nor is any uncalled-
for intermeddler permitted to interfere in this matter. Prudence, education, and independence will facilitate and direct
the proper choice. If disagreement, disappointment, or disaffection should arise, morality ['] demands a disruption of the
unnatural and, consequently, immoral alliance." [2]

Here we have unvarnished "free-love." What
remains of the bond of marriage if the parties, fol-

---

[1] This is a mistake The Church never looked upon marriage as a purely
private concern, beyond the limit of her jurisdiction. According to Catholic
doctrine, marriage is a sacrament instituted by Christ and entrusted to
the care of the Church Therefore marriage laws and marriage impediments were promulgated. Moreover, every marriage not celebrated according to the ecclesiastical rite (*in facie ecclesiæ*) was declared illicit. If,
nevertheless, up to the Council of Trent clandestine marriages were acknowledged as valid (that is to say, if there existed no other impediments), this
was done to prevent greater evils. But also, then, the contracting parties
were bound forever What is there in common in this institution with the
promiscuity of sexual intercourse advocated by Bebel, who permits the
utmost freedom of tying or untying the marital bond without the least
interference from any one?

[2] Die Frau, p 342 Similar ideas are propounded by *Engels* in his Origin
of the Family, by *Stern* and *Liebknecht*. Among American socialists these
views on marriage have been popularized by *Edward Carpenter's* Love's
Coming-of-Age According to Carpenter, marriage relations are raised to
a much higher plane by a continual change of partners "until a permanent
mate and equal is found " A man of ordinary common sense, however, will
characterize such proceedings as rank promiscuity.

lowing every whim and transient disaffection, are free to separate and to enter upon another alliance? However, we do not mean to confine ourselves to such explicit teaching of socialists. We shall endeavor to show that socialism *of its very nature* demolishes the family, which is the foundation of the social order.

In the first place the atheistic and materialistic tenets of socialism are incompatible with the unity and indissolubility of marriage. If man has no higher aim than to revel in earthly enjoyment, how can he be induced to bear the yoke of indissoluble monogamy? Is he to be tied for life to a partner whom he no longer loves, who is perhaps subject to loathsome diseases, who is guilty of adultery or other crimes? If even many defenders of the existing social order look upon divorce as excusable in many cases, how can socialists, with their striving after enjoyment, be brought to respect the sacredness of the marriage bond? An indissoluble marriage contract is incompatible with Epicurean principles.

The basis upon which the indissolubility of marriage, and consequently the stability of the family, chiefly rests is the education of the children. It is chiefly for this purpose that the lifelong union of man and wife is necessary; for such a lifelong union is generally required for the suitable education of their offspring. Therefore whoever wrests the education of their children from the hands of parents, and makes it a function of the state, thereby undermines the lowest foundation of the family. But socialism puts education and instruction altogether into the hands of the commonwealth. The Gotha platform demands: "Universal and equal education of the people by the state." This demand is re-stated somewhat obscurely by the Erfurt platform: "Compulsory attendance at the public schools. Instruction, use of all means of instruction, and *board* free of charge in all public elementary schools and in the higher institutions of learning for such pupils of both sexes as, on account of their talents, are judged fit for higher studies," whilst the American Socialist Party platform advocates "education of all children up to the age of *eighteen* years, and *state and municipal aid for books, clothing, and food.*"

On this point we may yet insert the words of one of the great apostles of socialism.

"Every child that comes into the world, whether male or female, is a welcome addition to society; for society beholds in every child the continuation of itself and its own further development, it, therefore, perceives from the very outset the duty, according to its power, to provide for the new-born child. And, first of all, the mother who gives birth to and nurses the child is the object of the state's concern Comfortable lodging, pleasant surroundings, and accommodations of all kinds suited to this stage of motherhood, careful treatment of herself and of her offspring, are the first requisite It is self-evident that the mother must be left to nurse the child, as long as this is possible and necessary. . .

"When the child waxes stronger his equals await him for common amusement, under public direction Here again all things are supplied which, according to the perfection of human knowledge and wisdom, for the time being, tend toward the development of soul and body Then comes the kindergarten with its playrooms; and, at a later period, the child is playfully introduced into the elements of knowledge and human activity. Mental and bodily labor, gymnastic exercises, free movement on the playground and in the gymnasium, on the ice field and in the natatorium, marching, fencing, and other exercises for both sexes, shall succeed and relieve and supplement one another in due order The introduction to the various kinds of useful labor—to manufacture, gardening, farming, and to the entire mechanism of production—follows in due succession. But the intellectual development, in the meantime, on the various fields of science, is not to be neglected. Corresponding to the high grade of social culture shall be the outfit of the lecture-halls, the educational appliances, and the means of instruction. All means of education and instruction, clothing and food, supplied by the community, will be such as to give no pupil an advantage over another. The number and the ability of the teaching body will be in proportion to the demands.

"Such will be the education of both sexes—equal and common —for the separation of the sexes can be justified only in those cases in which the distinction of sex makes it an imperative duty. And this system of education, strictly organized, under efficient control, continued to that stage of life when society shall declare its youth to be of age, will eminently qualify both sexes for all rights and duties which society grants or imposes on its full-grown members. Thus society can rest satisfied that it has educated members that are perfectly developed in every direction." [1]

This is one of the midsummer night's dreams in which Bebel's "Frau" delights to revel. How grossly immoral such dreams are needs hardly to be stated. The usurpation of education by the state, however, is quite logical according to the principles of socialism. If socialism is to effect absolute equality in the conditions of life, it must first of all remove the universal source of social inequality, i.e., unequal education; and this can be done only by making education a social concern. Such a regulation would, of course, not hinder mothers from suckling their own children and nursing them to a certain age. But mothers and children would be placed under the supervision of the body social; for there would be no servants in those days: physicians, surgeons, midwives, etc., would be

---

[1] Die Frau, pp. 322–324, 328.

in the service of the body politic; those able to work would have to contribute their share to the social production, while the care of those unable to work would devolve upon the community. The care and treatment of mothers in confinement and of their children would, of course, be the concern of the state. For if the care of the children were left to the parents, it might happen that childless husbands and wives who have never been prevented from work would attain to a much higher income than others who would have to provide for the support of a numerous family, and would thus be prevented from taking an active part in production. And if the father or mother should fall sick it might easily happen that an entire family would be exposed to starvation, while another would enjoy all comforts. And how could a mother, without the aid of servants, bring up and educate a large family, say of ten or twelve children? If, therefore, education were left to the parents themselves it would be the duty of the community at least to give an additional allowance from the public produce for their support, and to make provision for them in case of sickness. In brief, parents would have to be relieved by the state of the burden of supporting their children.

Therefore both the nourishment and the education of the children in the socialist state would be a public affair, and would be directed and controlled by the entire body social. Thus the chief duty of parents, for the sake of which marriage has been instituted as an indissoluble union, would cease to exist; for a life-long union and co-operation on the part of parents is not required for the mere propagation of children. And even though in the socialist state the indissolubility of marriage might be sanctioned by law, yet the integrity of the family would receive the death-blow. That which binds husband and wife most closely is not only the actual existence of offspring, but, above all, the consciousness that upon their united efforts and care depends the weal or woe of their children. Parents have to provide for the support and the development of their children; upon their care, in the first place, depend the life, the future position, the social standing, the honor, and the eternal welfare of their children. This consciousness urges them on to untiring activity. What they have been able to accumulate by their toil falls to the advantage of their offspring, in whom they, as it were, continue to live, and who naturally inherit the fruits of their cares and toils.

On the other hand, the consciousness that they owe to their parents, not only their life itself, but also their preservation, education, and position in society—in short, all they possess—binds the children in intimate love to their parents. They know that their own fortune is closely linked together with that of their parents. Hence there exists between them mutual sympathy in joys and sorrows. In socialism all this would cease to exist; for the entire social body would form but one family. What would become of parental authority if children knew that the state provided for their sustenance, or, at least, remunerated parents for the care bestowed upon them? Would not such a system greatly promote rash marriages and facilitate divorces, particularly as in the socialist state marriage would be a purely private concern?

§ II. *Education and Instruction.*

Let us now cast a brief glance at *education* and
instruction in the socialist state.   As we have already
stated, Bebel promises the most marvellous results
in the field of education.   But now let us imagine
children collected in large numbers, separated from
their parents, first in the spacious playrooms of the
kindergarten, then in the elementary schools, where
they are "playfully" introduced into the elements
of knowledge. Will this mass of wholesale education lead to satisfactory results?   We might consider
this possible if there were question only of a military
education for the formation of future soldiers.   But
the universal application of such a system is simply
absurd.   Nor can the socialist point to the example
of present educational institutions in which children
receive not only instruction, but also their board and
education, as in the family.   For, to say nothing of
the fact that the children are generally not confided
to such institutions before the age of ten or twelve
years, and that the pupils of such institutions form
but a small fraction of the entire youth, while socialism would have all children without exception confided to public institutions for care and instruction—
the chief difference consists in this, that our present
boarding educational institutions presuppose and are
based upon the existence of the family and of home
training   The teachers of such institutions are the
representatives of parents, and are supported by the
parents' authority; and if a pupil of such an institution
is incorrigible, he will, to his own disgrace and the
shame of his parents, be expelled from the institution.
But this would not be the case in the socialist state.

Besides, we must bear in mind that the socialist youth would be brought up without religion; that there would be no separation of the sexes. What then, would be the result? Nothing would remain but forcibly to lash the socialist youth into discipline and order. And yet how ineffectual is mere physical force in education!

However, we have not done with the difficulties arising from the socialistic principles of education. It is impossible that all children should be instructed and educated in all branches of knowledge and industry. Bebel repeatedly asserts the contrary; yet it remains simply impossible. Let us suppose that up to a certain grade the instruction and education is the same for all. Beyond this grade, however, a division would have to take place. Not all have talents for arts and sciences, and still fewer there are who have abilities to take up all studies. Not all have sufficient skill for the practice of all trades and industries. If, therefore, the socialists would not be satisfied with a very low and insufficient grade of culture, if they would not make shallowness and superficiality universal attributes of education, they must at a certain stage, say at the age of twelve or thirteen, draw a line, and then allow their pupils to devote themselves to some special branches of knowledge or industry. But who is to determine the studies to be pursued? The simplest system would be to submit the pupils to examinations; for a decision by the children themselves, or by their parents, or by the verdict of a committee, or by the vote of the majority, would be impracticable. The parents manifestly would in most cases present their children for the highest grade of education, as they themselves would not have to bear the expenses and trouble. The children, on the other hand, even the most gifted, if left to themselves, would in most cases be satisfied with little learning. If the decision were left to a committee it would lead to unjust treatment, and consequently to endless complaints on the part of those parents whose children would be slighted.

The promotion to higher studies, therefore, would have to be made dependent on the results of examinations. But even this method would be attended with serious difficulties. For either we suppose that higher grades of education would be connected with certain advantages in regard to income and social standing, or we suppose that they would not. If a higher grade of education has no advantage for future life, very few would be found to aspire to it. If, on the other hand, it should have some influence upon the future social standing of the possessor, it would result in a difference of social position, and thus there would be an end to the socialistic equality of the conditions of life. Moreover, if social position is not made altogether dependent upon the labor performed according to the logical programme of socialism, but upon other conditions, why should talent alone be taken into account? Do not also virtue, diligence, and the descent from parents who have merited well of the commonwealth, deserve consideration? Is it not harsh, nay, unjust, to make the entire future of a man's life depend upon a school examination to be undergone in his youth?

As the promotion to higher studies, so also the decision what trade or industry each one should embrace would have to depend upon examinations; for as in branches of knowledge, so also in trades and industry an equal education of all is a thing of impossibility.

If too many candidates would pass the examination for a certain branch of industry, they would have to be applied by superior authority to different industries. Therefore from the very outset the body social would have to decide the course of education and the future vocation of all and each of its members, lest there should be too great a rush to any profession, or to any particular trade or industry. Socialism and freedom, therefore, are incompatible with each other. The irreconcilable contradiction between freedom and the "universal systematic control" of the national labor is the rock upon which socialism is destined to be shipwrecked.

SECTION VII.

SOME OBJECTIONS ANSWERED.

§ I. *Communism in Religious Orders.*

It has been advanced in favor of socialism that in the religious orders of the Catholic Church perfect communism reigns. Why, then, should it not be practicable in entire nations? There is, however, an impassable gulf between the Catholic religious orders and socialism. Socialism aims at the universal introduction of a system which, of its very nature, demands the greatest detachment from earthly things and an earnest struggle for perfection, and which, consequently, in the present order of things, is suited only for the few. True, where men who have renounced all earthly goods and have devoted themselves to the service of God and of their neighbor voluntarily unite in common life, there may be community of goods without discord and contention; nay, such a

system in that case will prove most beneficial, as it
will relieve the individuals of the care of providing for
their earthly wants. But of the general run of men
few are able to rise to such a height of self-denial, and
to devote themselves entirely to the pursuit of self-
perfection and to the divine service. It is, therefore,
a vain and unreasonable attempt to force men generally to renounce all private property and to endeavor
violently to weld them together into a mechanical
organization for the purpose of production.

Socialists, it is true, plead that they demand not
the renunciation of property—that they only desire
to establish property upon the basis of justice. These
are fair words, but without meaning. He who wishes
to abolish private property in all the materials of
labor, substantially abolishes private ownership. Property in mere articles of use must of its very nature
be limited, and is not sufficient to secure to man the
necessary freedom of action and movement. If man
is deprived of private property in the materials of
labor he is thereby made an integral part of the great
public industrial machine, and thus loses all independence of action. Of this fact we believe every
one who has carefully followed our exposition will
be convinced.

Moreover, the analogy from religious orders can
afford no argument for this reason—because in them
communism is based upon celibacy. Perfect poverty
or the renouncement of all temporal goods is incompatible with married life and with the duties which
married life entails. It is utterly irreconcilable with
family life in the present state of humanity.

§ II. *Modern Industrial Organizations.*

Of greater force seems to be at first sight the objection taken by socialists from *modern industrial organizations.* In the present social order it is no rare phenomenon that eight or ten or even more thousand laborers are employed in one great industrial department; and yet the industry proceeds in the very best order. Nor do the labor materials and the machinery belong to the laborers themselves, nay, not even to the directors of such industrial establishments. Why should not such a system be extended to an entire state?

This objection unfortunately overlooks one feature, and that is the chief distinction between private industry and the socialistic organization. This modern industrial order in great manufactories and other industries is based upon the strongest moral coercion. The owner of the factory or industry, either in person or by means of his representative, confronts the laborers as proprietor and can rule them with almost absolute power. The laborer, it is true, is not forced to offer his service to such establishments, but if he wishes to obtain from them labor and support he must submit unconditionally to their ruling. The least insubordination will be the cause of his dismissal. Therefore force controls the modern system of production, but only moral force, to which each one submits for his own interest. In the socialist state, on the other hand, the directors of the various industries would confront the laborers not as proprietors, but as equals, possessing the same rights. Each one has the same right as his neighbor to consider himself a proprietor; nor can any one be dismissed;

but every one must obtain work, for the simple reason
that all private production is interdicted.

The world-famed Krupp iron and steel works have been adduced in favor of collective organization; therefore they will
form a most appropriate illustration to show the radical differences between the existing order of things and the socialist system In the Krupp works the division of labor, the system of
production, the shop regulations, the remuneration of the workingmen, are all managed with the greatest accuracy and to the
relative satisfaction of everybody.   This is due to the complete
subordination and respect paid to the orders of the directors,
who represent the owners, and who exercise quasi-monarchical
powers throughout the different departments.

But what would take place if the works were to be reorganized
on a socialist basis?   First of all they would no longer be owned
by the Krupp family, but would become the common property
of the 40,000 workingmen employed in them, all of whom would
have equal rights of ownership   The supreme management
would be taken from the hands of the permanent directors, who
thus far regulated everything uniformly and systematically, and
would be entrusted to the "Comrades" at large, who would
either have to decide matters themselves, or to depute a managing
committee elected for one or two years   Now, the first difficulty will be the division of labor.   All know that they have
equal rights, that class distinctions are abolished.   Who is to be
appointed to the coarser and who to the finer work?   Even
within the relatively limited extent of the Krupp works there is
an immense difference between various functions.   Some are as
agreeable as others are irksome, some require more skill than
others, some are honorable, others less so.   Why should one
workingman undertake disagreeable jobs rather than another,
since all have equal rights in the factory?   There will be an
accumulation of all the difficulties we have enumerated above
when speaking of the organization of labor and of vocations.
To them will be added the dilemma arising from the division of
the products.   What shall serve as a standard of division?   The
number of laborers, the time of work, or the needs of the individual?   We have seen that a division which will satisfy everybody is practically impossible.   Again, what is to be done if

some of the men play truant or go on a spree? Or if one is
reported on the sick-list? Is he to be thrown on the street
and abandoned? In the present circumstances he who is not
satisfied in the Krupp works may go elsewhere to look for a job.
If he wishes to stay, he must conform to the regulations. If he
is incorrigibly lazy, if his conduct is open to serious complaints,
he will be discharged and allowed to shift for himself These
works are ruled therefore by stringent coercion, by strict subordination Of all this there can be no question in the socialist
system. The " Comrades " are equal and free How long would
it last until order and harmony would be disturbed by fights,
party quarrels, intrigues of all kinds? And what would there
be to induce the workingman to labor diligently and to be saving
in the use of his tools and materials?

Moreover, all food and other supplies would have to be taken
from the common store rooms and eating-houses; education,
care of the sick, funerals even would be regulated according to
the decision of the majority. The same would be the case in the
administration of justice and in legislation; there would be no
appeal to any higher power Books and newspapers would be
published or not, just as it would suit the majority or its representatives.

Thereby, however, we have not yet completed the chapter of
difficulties In the Krupp works, with their 40,000 workingmen, affairs are not excessively complicated, and may be easily
controlled by a skilful and experienced manager, especially if
he has been in the business for a number of years Besides, the
operations carried on are pretty much of one kind and confined
to one establishment Socialism, however, in order to abolish
anarchy of production—and that is its boasted aim—must needs
be realized at least in the whole of a modern industrial state
Socialist leaders even dream of an international organization,
and for good reasons, as we have seen above Therefore there
would be required an appropriate division of labor forces for the
different parts of the country It would be impossible to permit
every one to change about at will, or to choose the most agreeable place of residence Also uninhabitable, rough, or swampy
districts would need a laboring population.

We need but follow up carefully those consequences, which
naturally flow from the socialization of the means of production

and from the systematic regulation of production and division
of products, and we shall arrive at the undoubted conclusion
that this system cannot be realized without entailing veritable
and universal slavery, a slavery unbearable for any length of
time and altogether impossible on a really democratic basis.

The practicability of large private industrial institutions, therefore, does not prove the possibility of extending the same system to entire states.   The arguments
taken from the *state industries* which have been
attempted by some governments, such as railroads,
mail service, telegraphs, state mines, etc., prove as
little in favor of socialism.   For in these public industries also the state or its representatives in their relation
to the laborers are considered as proprietors.   Besides,
the directors are personally interested in such establishments, and are themselves also under the influence
of the same moral coercion as the laborers.   Every
official as well as every laborer must be satisfied
with his position.   There is no alternative left him,
if he wishes to gain his livelihood.   Besides, he may
be dismissed at pleasure or his salary may be curtailed,
if he gives any occasion of complaint to his superiors.
Even a slight murmur or repugnance on his part may
suffice to deprive him of his position.   Hence it is
that in our modern state industries, wherever they
have obtained, main force is the ruling power, and
all is directed by absolute control.   But in the socialist
state of the future, in which every man is to be a
sovereign and to receive his position and his support
from the community, in which, moreover, the final
decision regarding the control of labor, the division
of produce, the appointment of officers, should be
the business of the people, the case would be quite
different.

§ III. *The Modern Military System.*

Socialists endeavor to derive an argument for the possibility of their system from the organization and direction of our huge modern armies. However, it is manifest that a strict military organization with a criminal code including, as in Germany, for instance, some thirty capital crimes, could not be extended to an entire people and brought to bear upon all phases of human life. At least socialists must lay aside their high-sounding phrases about freedom and equality if they would impose upon us such military discipline. Moreover there is no communism in the army; it does not support itself, but is supported by others. However, we have no reason to fear that such a scheme will so easily be realized. For what would become of an army if the soldiers themselves had the chief command—if they chose their own officers and generals, and deposed them at pleasure, and held court-martial over them? Our modern armies are under the strictest discipline and subordination. An army on democratic principles is chimerical. Besides, we must bear in mind that socialism undertakes to organize not only military activity, but the entire social life—production, commerce, education, instruction, the press, the arts, and sciences, etc. If, then, even an organization on socialistic principles is impracticable for military purposes, how much more so for the varied and more complex relations of social life!

§ IV.   *Stock Companies.*

Stock companies require special consideration, since they have been advanced as an argument in favor of socialism, for the reason that the capital invested in them not rarely produces large gains, although it is almost entirely alienated from the hands of the proprietors or shareholders.   Extensive enterprises in commerce, industry, mining, railroads, steamboats, etc., prove remarkably successful in companies or syndicates, although their directors have no personal interest in them.

However, the absence of personal interest is but apparent in these cases.   In regard to the subordinate officials of such companies the same rule holds good as in the case of state industries—their own personal interest binds them to their position; and the higher authorities or directors confront the laborers in the capacity of proprietors.   But the directors of these syndicates have themselves large interests in the enterprises and are, consequently, concerned for their success and prosperity; for in most cases they are among the chief shareholders, and in case the enterprises are prosperous they obtain larger dividends.   Even the subordinate officials of such companies have in many cases a share of the profit.   Since therefore, the directors have an almost absolute power over the officers appointed and the laborers employed by them, it is easy to perceive the reason why such companies, notwithstanding the apparent sequestration of the capital, should realize large profits.

For the rest, it is a well-known fact that stock companies, compared with private enterprises, are at a disadvantage in regard to economy in the use of raw materials, machinery, etc.; and, consequently, such organizations with small capital are generally unsuccessful. But in the case of large syndicates with extensive capital these disadvantages are counterbalanced by still greater advantages.[1]

Another essential difference between syndicates and the ideal socialistic organization is the circumstance that in syndicates the directors are rarely changed. The permanence of the directors is a necessary condition for the success of large enterprises. If the direction is often changed there is a lack of unity and system, as the opinions of different directors will rarely be found to coincide. What guarantee would there be for this necessary permanence in the direction of the socialist industrial organizations, since the directors would be chosen and deposed by popular vote, and the principle of the equal rights of all would admit of no permanence in the administration of the more influential offices? Would not the continual changes and experiments be a source of endless disturbances and stoppages of the industrial machinery? But if the supreme directors of industrial organizations are not entrusted with sufficient power, if their decision is made dependent upon the consent of the majority, they are thus deprived of the power necessary for the efficient administration of their offices.

[1] Cf. *Leroy-Beaulieu*, Le Collectivisme, p. 348 sqq.

CONCLUSION.

HERE we shall bring our investigation of socialism to a close. We trust that the unprejudiced reader who has patiently followed us throughout our exposition has gained the conviction that socialism, even in its most rational and scientific form, is visionary and impracticable. It is based on untenable religious, philosophical, and economic principles, and, far from leading to the glorious results held out by its advocates to the unlearned masses, would prove disastrous to that culture which Christianity has produced, and would reduce human society to a state of utter barbarism. We may, therefore, conclude in the words of Leo XIII. On the Condition of Labor: "Hence follows the untenableness of the principle of socialism, according to which the state is to appropriate all private property and convert it into common property. Such a theory can only turn out to the grave disadvantage of the laboring classes, for whose benefit it has been invented. It is opposed to the natural rights of every individual human being; it perverts the true purpose of the state, and renders the peaceful development of social life impossible." However, a permanent institution of socialism is not to be feared, since it is in open contradiction with the indestructible instincts and tendencies of human nature.

I.

If socialism is indeed a utopian dream, as we have shown it to be, then it follows that all those who listen to the words of socialist prophets and expect salvation at their hands are wofully deceived, and that the brilliant hopes held out by popular agitators are at best the fruit of ignorance and self-deception. We say "at best," because we do not care to inquire whether and in how far the doings of demagogues who make their living by propagating socialism are inspired by selfish motives.

But to one point we must call attention. Even if socialism were practicable, the great mass of farmers and artisans who are at present the objects of the most tender solicitude on the part of socialists would have nothing to gain, but everything to lose. Independent farmers, artisans, business men are out of question in the socialist system. Every man would but be a member of an immense state machinery, enjoying indeed equal rights with all the others, but utterly bereft of independence in the matter of gaining his livelihood. It were well for the independent farmer and artisan to bear this in mind.

If socialist agitators were to tell the farmer plainly: Your land and your homestead must be given up to the community; in future you will have no more right to them than any one else in the country; in return, however, you may partake of the general happiness which our endeavors will bring about; if the socialist projects were thus crudely stated, no farmer would listen to them; his land, his independent position, are too dear to his heart.

Socialist platforms and socialist lecturers may make

the most flattering promises to the farming class and
the small tradespeople. However, "Fine words butter
no parsnips." The middle classes would in no way
be benefited by the introduction of socialism. According to socialist doctrines they are doomed to destruction; the concentration of capital and the pauperization of the artisan and farmer are supposed finally to
reach a point where conditions become unbearable
and "the expropriators are expropriated." Efficient
legal protection of the independent middle classes
would be one of the strongest barriers against the
spread of socialism. Therefore it is part of the system of orthodox socialists, especially in Germany, to
oppose all efforts made for the betterment of the lower
classes. It is their policy, as Bebel has worded it, "to
retain the wounds of the body social in a festering
condition." In the German parliament most of the
legislative measures in favor of the working population were antagonized by socialists under the pretence
of their being mere palliatives which would retard
the advent of the communist paradise.

It may cause astonishment, that men who boast of
having the best interests of the people at heart should
be guilty of such conduct. But upon closer reflection
the wonder will cease. As soon as any class of people
is doing well and has something to lose, it ceases to
be socialistically inclined; it begins to fear for its
own interests and becomes conservative. Socialists
would therefore be sawing off the branch on which
they are sitting, if they were to contribute to the
passing of measures which are likely to reconcile
the lower classes with their situation. Even the
trades-unions are looked upon with a suspicious eye;
they are too liable to follow in the wake of the bour-

geois parties. And thus in the United States the Socialist Labor Party on the one hand stands completely aloof from the trades-unions "pure and simple," whilst, on the other hand, the Socialist Party is making frantic efforts to control the great labor federations, not, however, for the improvement of labor conditions, but as powerful auxiliaries in the political struggle which is to place the powers of government in the hands of social democracy. Hence also the continual carping of socialists at the existing social order. Every crime, every accident and misfortune, is ascribed to the capitalist system and furnishes a fruitful theme of tirades against our "rotten and bankrupt society."

For years we have carefully studied thousands of socialist literary productions, but not once have we come across a passage exhorting the workingman to sobriety, patience, laboriousness, thrift, contentment, etc. On the contrary, socialist agitators inveigh against "that cursed frugality and contentment." Hatred against God, against Christianity and its ministers, against the possessing classes, is the usual text of their daily sermons. But hatred and fury sown among the deluded masses are liable to produce a dangerous crop; and in the social upheaval thence resulting, these new Dantons and Robespierres may easily share the fate of their predecessors in the French Revolution.

II.

In view of the steady growth of the revolutionary parties are we to fold our arms in mute contemplation or raise them to heaven in sheer despair? Not in the least. There is no reason for giving up hope. God has ordained that also for national calamities remedies may be found. There is every expectation of averting the threatening danger, if we are serious about introducing social reforms and reviving the true spirit of Christianity.

1. *Social Reform.*—Socialist agitators endeavor to inspire the workingman with the idea that Christians, especially Catholics, wish to retain social conditions exactly as they are at present, and that they console the laborer solely by referring him to a life to come. Nothing can be further from our real intentions. We also demand social reform most energetically. We are, however, not like socialists, who find fault with every social improvement however well meant it may be; we gratefully acknowledge whatever is done to raise the laboring classes; but our demands are not all satisfied, there is much still to be reformed. At the same time we guard against falling into the other extreme of socialists; we do not flatter the workingmen with visions of impossible and unattainable happiness, merely in order to rouse for the present their dissatisfaction and to whet their appetite for luxuries far beyond their reach.

By the social reform which we advocate there may be secured for even the lowest of the laboring classes a family life worthy of a human being. For this end it is necessary not only that he receive sufficient wages, but also that sufficient regard be had for his life and health, and therefore that his strength be not overtaxed by immoderate labor. He must be treated not only with fairness, but also with love and consideration. Finally, he must have the assurance that in case of misfortune or ill health he is not abandoned or cast into the street. And since in our days personal effort and private charity are by no means sufficient *public authority must by suitable legislation take the necessary measures* for this end. Social reform should aim at such a state of things that the humblest laborer may entertain a well-founded hope by industry and economy to better his condition, and gradually to rise to a higher social standing.[1]

It may be objected that we have in this work to some extent ignored the just claims of socialism. However, if we consider what is *peculiar* to socialism as such, in contradistinction to other social reform movements—and this is precisely the point in question—socialism cannot be said to possess any just claims. If there is any justice in the claims of socialists it consists in their opposition to the extreme individualism of the liberal movement.

Man may be conceived under a twofold aspect—as a free and independent *individual,* and as a *social being,* destined to live in, and form part of, society. Liberalism—at least in former years—considered man only under the first aspect. It regarded only the individual and his independence, and almost entirely disregarded his social relations. From this standpoint liberalism tended toward the dismemberment of society, and proclaimed the maxim of *laissez faire* as the highest political wisdom. A reaction against this tendency was justified, and socialism, in as far as it can be viewed as a protest against extreme individualism, is perfectly right. But socialism, for its part, goes to the other extreme, considering only the social aspect of man, and disregarding the freedom and independence of the individual. It deprives the individual of his liberty, by making him the slave

[1] Cf our Moral philosophie, vol II, book 2, chap 4, also our article in the *Kirchenlexicon,* Die soziale Frage.

of the community—a wheel in the great and complicated mechanism of the social production—which is no less absurd.

As in most cases, here too the truth is midway between both extremes. Both aspects of man— the individual as well as the social—must be taken into consideration and brought into harmony. This is the unshaken principle from which all rational attempts at social reform must proceed. The institution and promotion of corporative associations are, as we have already noticed, the surest and best means to reconcile the claims of the individual with those of society, and thus to bring about harmony between the conflicting elements.

2. The most important and indispensable factor in the social reform, however, is the *revival of Christianity* among all classes of society. F. A. Lange, the historian of materialism, confesses that "Ideas and sacrifices can still save our civilization and change the way of devastating revolution into a way of beneficial reforms." But whence is the spirit of sacrifice to come? Legislative measures may produce the external framework of a new social order; but it is only Christianity that can give it life and efficacy. Only on the ground of Christianity can the hostile social elements be brought to a reconciliation. Let us not deceive ourselves: the wisest and most humane legislation will never appease an indolent and grasping mass of laborers. But whence is the laborer to obtain the virtues of industry and economy? Only from the ever-flowing fountain of living Christianity. How can the laborer be expected to bear the toils and hardships that are inseparable from his state, if he has been led to believe that all hopes and fears in

regard to the eternal retribution beyond the grave are childish fancies, and that with this life all shall come to an end?

This revival of Christianity, however, must not be confined to the laborer: it must also extend to the higher and more influential classes of society. Is it not bitter irony if our so-called "cultured classes" expect Christian patience and resignation from the laborer, while they themselves disregard the laws of Christianity, and publicly profess the grossest infidelity? It sounds indeed like irony if the rich preach economy and self-denial to the poor, while they themselves indulge in the most extravagant luxury and dissipation. The wealthy must begin the social reform at home. They must come to the conviction that they have not only rights but also *duties* toward the laboring man—duties of *justice* and duties of *charity*. They must bear in mind that they have been appointed by God, as it were, the administrators of their earthly possessions, which should in some way serve for the benefit of all. They should remember that the laborer is not a mere chattel, but a rational being, their brother in Christ, who, in the eyes of God, is equal to the richest and most powerful on earth. It is only this bond of Christian sentiment— of mutual love and reverence between rich and poor, high and low—that can bring about a reconciliation of the social conflicts of our times.

And since the Church is the God-appointed guardian and preserver of the Christian religion, and since she cannot fulfil this task unless she is free to exercise all her power and influence, we must demand for the solution of the social problem *the perfect freedom of the Church* in all her ministrations. Above all, we must insist on the full freedom of the Church to exercise her saving influence on the schools, from the common school to the university. Liberalism has used the schools and universities to alienate the nations from God. Socialism is beginning to adopt the same policy for the subversion of the social order; and if the Church is to exert her influence for the salvation of society in our day, she must do so chiefly in the field of education.

APPENDIX.

ENCYCLICAL LETTER OF OUR HOLY FATHER POPE LEO XIII.

ON THE

CONDITION OF LABOR.

TO OUR VENERABLE BRETHREN, ALL PATRIARCHS, PRI-
MATES, ARCHBISHOPS, AND BISHOPS OF THE CATHOLIC
WORLD, IN PEACE AND COMMUNION WITH THE APOS-
TOLIC SEE.

Venerable Brethren, Health and Apostolic Benediction.

IT is not surprising that the spirit of revolutionary change,
which has so long been predominant in the nations of the
world, should have passed beyond politics, and made its
influence felt in the cognate field of practical economy.
The elements of a conflict are unmistakable: the growth of
industry, and the surprising discoveries of science; the
changed relations of masters and workmen; the enormous
fortunes of individuals, and the poverty of the masses; the
increased self-reliance and the closer mutual combination of
the working population; and, finally, a general moral deteri-
oration. The momentous seriousness of the present state of
things just now fills every mind with painful apprehension;
wise men discuss it; practical men propose schemes; popular meetings, legislatures, and sovereign princes,—all are
occupied with it, and there is nothing which has a deeper
hold on public attention.

Therefore, Venerable Brethren, as on former occasions,
when it seemed opportune to refute false teaching, We
have addressed you in the interest of the Church and of the
common weal, and have issued Letters on Political Power,

on Human Liberty, on the Christian Constitution of the State, and on similar subjects, so now We have thought it useful to speak on the CONDITION OF LABOR. It is a matter on which We have touched once or twice already. But in this Letter the responsibility of the Apostolic office urges Us to treat the question expressly and at length, in order that there may be no mistake as to the principles which truth and justice dictate for its settlement. The discussion is not easy, nor is it free from danger. It is not easy to define the relative rights and the mutual duties of the wealthy and of the poor, of capital and of labor. And the danger lies in this, that crafty agitators constantly make use of these disputes to pervert men's judgments and to stir up the people to sedition.

But all agree, and there can be no question whatever, that some remedy must be found, and quickly found, for the misery and wretchedness which press so heavily at this moment on the large majority of the very poor. The ancient workmen's Guilds were destroyed in the last century, and no other organization took their place. Public institutions and the laws have repudiated the ancient religion. Hence by degrees it has come to pass that Working Men have been given over, isolated and defenceless, to the callousness of employers and the greed of unrestrained competition. The evil has been increased by rapacious Usury, which, although more than once condemned by the Church, is, nevertheless, under a different form, but with the same guilt, still practised by avaricious and grasping men. And to this must be added the custom of working by contract, and the concentration of so many branches of trade in the hands of a few individuals, so that a small number of very rich men have been able to lay upon the masses of the poor a yoke little better than slavery itself.

To remedy these evils the *Socialists*, working on the poor man's envy of the rich, endeavor to destroy private property, and maintain that individual possessions should become the common property of all, to be administered by the State or by municipal bodies. They hold that, by thus transferring property from private persons to the community, the present

evil state of things will be set to rights, because each citizen
will then have his equal share of whatever there is to enjoy
But their proposals are so clearly futile for all practical purposes, that if they were carried out the working man himself
would be among the first to suffer. Moreover they are emphatically unjust, because they would rob the lawful possessor,
bring the State into a sphere that is not its own, and cause
complete confusion in the community

It is surely undeniable that, when a man engages in
remunerative labor, the very reason and motive of his work
is to obtain property, and to hold it as his own private
possession. If one man hires out to another his strength or
his industry, he does this for the purpose of receiving in
return what is necessary for food and living, he thereby
expressly proposes to acquire a full and real right, not only
to the remuneration, but also to the disposal of that remuneration as he pleases. Thus, if he lives sparingly, saves
money, and invests his savings, for greater security, in land,
the land in such a case is only his wages in another form;
and, consequently, a working man's little estate thus purchased should be as completely at his own disposal as the
wages he receives for his labor. But it is precisely in this
power of disposal that ownership consists, whether the property be land or movable goods. The *Socialists*, therefore, in
endeavoring to transfer the possessions of individuals to the
community, strike at the interests of every wage-earner, for
they deprive him of the liberty of disposing of his wages, and
thus of all hope and possibility of increasing his stock and
of bettering his condition in life.

What is of still greater importance, however, is that the
remedy they propose is manifestly against justice. For every
man has by nature the right to possess property as his own.
This is one of the chief points of distinction between man
and the animal creation For the brute has no power of self-
direction, but is governed by two chief instincts, which keep
his powers alert, move him to use his strength, and determine
him to action without the power of choice. These instincts
are self-preservation and the propagation of the species.
Both can attain their purpose by means of things which are

close at hand ; beyond their surroundings the brute creation cannot go, for they are moved to action by sensibility alone, and by the things which sense perceives. But with man it is different indeed. He possesses, on the one hand, the full perfection of animal-nature, and therefore he enjoys, at least as much as the rest of the animal race, the fruition of the things of the body. But animality, however perfect, is far from being the whole of humanity, and is, indeed, humanity's humble handmaid, made to serve and obey. It is the mind, or the reason, which is the chief thing in us who are human beings ; it is this which makes a human being human, and distinguishes him essentially and completely from the brute. And on this account—viz., that man alone among animals possesses reason—it must be within his right to have things not merely for temporary and momentary use, as other living beings have them, but in stable and permanent possession ; he must have not only things which perish in the using, but also those which, though used, remain for use in the future.

This becomes still more clearly evident if we consider man's nature a little more deeply. For man, comprehending by the power of his reason things innumerable, and joining the future with the present—being, moreover, the master of his own acts—governs himself by the foresight of his counsel, under the eternal law and the power of God whose Providence governs all things. Wherefore it is in his power to exercise his choice, not only on things which regard his present welfare, but also on those which will be for his advantage in time to come. Hence man not only can possess the fruits of the earth, but also the earth itself; for of the products of the earth he can make provision for the future. Man's needs do not die out, but recur ; satisfied to-day, they demand new supplies to-morrow. Nature, therefore, owes to man a storehouse that shall never fail, the daily supply of his daily wants. And this he finds only in the inexhaustible fertility of the earth.

Nor must we, at this stage, have recourse to the State. Man is older than the State ; and he holds the right of providing for the life of his body prior to the formation of any

State. And to say that God has given the earth to the use and enjoyment of the universal human race is not to deny that there can be private property. For God has granted the earth to mankind in general; not in the sense that all without distinction can deal with it as they please, but rather that no part of it has been assigned to any one in particular, and that the limits of private possession have been left to be fixed by man's own industry and the laws of individual peoples. Moreover, the earth, though divided among private owners, ceases not thereby to minister to the needs of all ; for there is no one who does not live on what the land brings forth. Those who do not possess the soil, contribute their labor ; so that it may be truly said that all human subsistence is derived either from labor on one's own land, or from some laborious industry which is paid for either in the produce of the land itself or in that which is exchanged for what the land brings forth.

Here, again, we have another proof that private ownership is according to nature's law. For that which is required for the preservation of life, and for life's well-being, is produced in great abundance by the earth, but not until man has brought it into cultivation and lavished upon it his care and skill. Now, when man thus spends the industry of his mind and the strength of his body in procuring the fruits of nature, by that act he makes his own that portion of nature's field which he cultivates—that portion on which he leaves, as it were, the impress of his own personality ; and it cannot but be just that he should possess that portion as his own, and should have a right to keep it without molestation.

These arguments are so strong and convincing that it seems surprising that certain obsolete opinions should now be revived in opposition to what is here laid down. We are told that it is right for private persons to have the use the soil and the fruits of their land, but that it is unjust for any one to possess as owner either the land on which he has built or the estate which he has cultivated. But those who assert this do not perceive that they are robbing man of what his own labor has produced. For the soil which is tilled and cultivated with toil and skill utterly

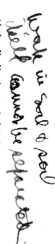

changes its condition; it was wild before, it is now fruitful; it was barren, and now it brings forth in abundance. That which has thus altered and improved it becomes so truly part of itself as to be in great measure indistinguishable and inseparable from it. Is it just that the fruit of a man's sweat and labor should be enjoyed by another? As effects follow their cause, so it is just and right that the results of labor should belong to him who has labored.

With reason, therefore, the common opinion of mankind, little affected by the few dissentients who have maintained the opposite view, has found in the study of nature, and in the law of Nature herself, the foundations of the division of property, and has consecrated by the practice of all ages the principle of private ownership, as being preëminently in conformity with human nature, and as conducing, in the most unmistakable manner, to the peace and tranquillity of human life. The same principle is confirmed and enforced by the civil laws,—laws which, as long as they are just, derive their binding force from the law of nature. The authority of the Divine Law adds its sanction, forbidding us, in the gravest terms, even to covet that which is another's: *Thou shalt not covet thy neighbor's wife; nor his house, nor his field, nor his man-servant, nor his maid-servant, nor his ox, nor his ass, nor anything which is his.*[*]

The rights here spoken of, belonging to each individual man, are seen in a much stronger light if they are considered in relation to man's social and domestic obligations.

In choosing a state of life, it is indisputable that all are at full liberty either to follow the counsel of Jesus Christ as to virginity, or to enter into the bonds of marriage. No human law can abolish the natural and primitive right of marriage, or in any way limit the chief and principal purpose of marriage, ordained by God's authority from the beginning. *Increase and multiply.*[†] Thus we have the Family; the "society" of a man's own household; a society limited, indeed, in numbers, but a true "society," anterior to every kind of State or nation, with rights and duties of its own, totally independent of the commonwealth.

　　　　* Deuteronomy v. 21.　　　　† Genesis i. 28.

That right of property, therefore, which has been proved to belong naturally to individual persons, must also belong to a man in his capacity of head of a family; nay, such a person must possess this right so much the more clearly in proportion as his position multiplies his duties. For it is a most sacred law of nature that a father must provide food and all necessaries for those whom he has begotten; and, similarly, nature dictates that a man's children, who carry on, as it were, and continue his own personality, should be provided by him with all that is needful to enable them honorably to keep themselves from want and misery in the uncertainties of this mortal life. Now, in no other way can a father effect this except by the ownership of profitable property, which he can transmit to his children by inheritance. A family, no less than a State, is, as We have said, a true society, governed by a power within itself, that is to say, by the father. Wherefore, provided the limits be not transgressed which are prescribed by the very purposes for which it exists, the Family has, at least, equal rights with the State in the choice and pursuit of those things which are needful to its preservation and its just liberty.

We say, at least, equal rights; for since the domestic household is anterior both in idea and in fact to the gathering of men into a commonwealth, the former must necessarily have rights and duties which are prior to those of the latter, and which rest more immediately on nature. If the citizens of a State—that is to say, the Families—on entering into association and fellowship, experienced at the hands of the State hindrance instead of help, and found their rights attacked instead of being protected, such association were rather to be repudiated than sought after.

The idea, then, that the civil government should, at its own discretion, penetrate and pervade the family and the household, is a great and pernicious mistake. True, if a family finds itself in great difficulty, utterly friendless, and without prospect of help, it is right that extreme necessity be met by public aid; for each family is a part of the commonwealth. In like manner, if within the walls of the household there occur grave disturbance of mutual rights, the public power must interfere to force each party to give the other what is due ; for this is not to rob citizens of their rights, but justly and properly to safeguard and strengthen them. But the rulers of the State must go no further : nature bids them stop here. Paternal authority can neither be abolished by the State, nor absorbed ; for it has the same source as human life itself. "The child belongs to the father," and is, as it were, the continuation of the father's personality ; and, to speak with strictness, the child takes its place in civil society not in its own right, but in its quality as a member of the family in which it is begotten. And it is for the very reason that "the child belongs to the father," that, as St. Thomas of Aquin says, " before it attains the use of free will, it is in the power and care of its parents."* The Socialists, therefore, in setting aside the parent and introducing the providence of the State, act *against natural justice*, and threaten the very existence of family life.

And such interference is not only unjust, but is quite certain to harass and disturb all classes of citizens, and to subject them to odious and intolerable slavery. It would open the door to envy, to evil-speaking, and to quarrelling; the sources of wealth would themselves run dry, for no one would have any interest in exerting his talents or his industry; and that ideal equality of which so much is said would, in reality, be the levelling down of all to the same condition of misery and dishonor.

Thus it is clear that the main tenet of *Socialism*, the community of goods, must be utterly rejected; for it would injure those whom it is intended to benefit, it would be contrary to the natural rights of mankind, and it would introduce confusion and disorder into the commonwealth. Our first and most fundamental principle, therefore, when we undertake to alleviate the condition of the masses, must be the inviolability of private property. This laid down, We go on to show where we must find the remedy that we seek.

We approach the subject with confidence, and in the exercise of the rights which belong to Us. For no practical solution of this question will ever be found without the

* St. Thomas, *Summa Theologica*, 2a 2æ Q. x. Art. 12.

assistance of Religion and of the Church. It is We who are the chief guardian of Religion, and the chief dispenser of what belongs to the Church, and We must not by silence neglect the duty which lies upon Us. Doubtless this most serious question demands the attention and the efforts of others besides Ourselves—of the rulers of States, of employers of labor, of the wealthy, and of the working population themselves for whom We plead. But We affirm without hesitation, that all the striving of men will be vain if they leave out the Church. It is the Church that proclaims from the Gospel those teachings by which the conflict can be put an end to, or at the least made far less bitter; the Church uses its efforts not only to enlighten the mind, but to direct by its precepts the life and conduct of men; the Church improves and ameliorates the condition of the working man by numerous useful organizations; does its best to enlist the services of all ranks in discussing and endeavoring to meet, in the most practical way, the claims of the working classes; and acts on the decided view that for these purposes recourse should be had, in due measure and degree, to the help of the law and of State authority.

Let it be laid down, in the first place, that humanity must remain as it is. It is impossible to reduce human society to a level. The *Socialists* may do their utmost, but all striving against nature is vain. There naturally exist among mankind innumerable differences of the most important kind; people differ in capability, in diligence, in health, and in strength; an unequal fortune is a necessary result of inequality in condition. Such inequality is far from being disadvantageous either to individuals or to the community; social and public life can only go on by the help of various kinds of capacity and the playing of many parts; and each man, as a rule, chooses the part which peculiarly suits his case. As regards bodily labor, even had man never fallen from *the state of innocence,* he would not have been wholly unoccupied; but that which would then have been his free choice and his delight, became afterwards compulsory, and the painful expiation of his sin. *Cursed be the earth in thy work; in thy labor thou shalt eat of it all the days of thy* *life.** In like manner, the other pains and hardships of life will have no end or cessation on this earth; for the consequences of sin are bitter and hard to bear, and they must be with man as long as life lasts. To suffer and to endure, therefore, is the lot of humanity; let men try as they may, no strength and no artifice will ever succeed in banishing from human life the ills and troubles which beset it. If any there are who pretend differently—who hold out to a hard-pressed people freedom from pain and trouble, undisturbed repose, and constant enjoyment—they cheat the people and impose upon them, and their lying promises will only make the evil worse than before. There is nothing more useful than to look at the world as it really is—and at the same time to look elsewhere for a remedy to its troubles.

The great mistake that is made in the matter now under consideration, is to possess oneself of the idea that class is naturally hostile to class; that rich and poor are intended by nature to live at war with one another. So irrational and so false is this view, that the exact contrary is the truth. Just as the symmetry of the human body is the result of the disposition of the members of the body, so in a State it is ordained by nature that these two classes should exist in harmony and agreement, and should, as it were, fit into one another, so as to maintain the equilibrium of the body politic. Each requires the other; capital cannot do without labor, nor labor without capital. Mutual agreement results in pleasantness and good order; perpetual conflict necessarily produces confusion and outrage. Now, in preventing such strife as this, and in making it impossible, the efficacy of Christianity is marvellous and manifold. First of all, there is nothing more powerful than Religion (of which the Church is the interpreter and guardian) in drawing rich and poor together, by reminding each class of its duties to the other, and especially of the duties of justice. Thus Religion teaches the laboring man and the workman to carry out honestly and well all equitable agreements freely made; never to injure capital, or to outrage the person of an employer, never to employ violence in representing his own

* Genesis iii. 17.

cause, or to engage in riot or disorder ; and to have nothing to do with men of evil principles, who work upon the people with artful promises, and raise foolish hopes which usually end in disaster and in repentance when too late. Religion teaches the rich man and the employer that their work-people are not their slaves; that they must respect in every man his dignity as a man and as a Christian, that labor is nothing to be ashamed of, if we listen to right reason, and to Christian philosophy, but is an honorable employment, enabling a man to sustain his life in an upright and creditable way ; and that it is shameful and inhuman to treat men like chattels to make money by, or to look upon them merely as so much muscle or physical power. Thus, again, Religion teaches that, as among the workman's concerns are Religion herself and things spiritual and mental, the employer is bound to see that he has time for the duties of piety; that he be not exposed to corrupting influences and dangerous occasions ; and that he be not led away to neglect his home and family or to squander his wages. Then, again, the employer must never tax his work-people beyond their strength, nor employ them in work unsuited to their sex or age. His great and principal obligation is to give to every one that which is just. Doubtless before we can decide whether wages are adequate, many things have to be considered ; but rich men and masters should remember this—that to exercise pressure for the sake of gain, upon the indigent and the destitute, and to make one's profit out of the need of another, is condemned by all laws, human and divine. To defraud any one of wages that are his due is a crime which cries to the avenging anger of heaven. *Behold the hire of the laborers . . . which by fraud hath been kept back by you, crieth ; and the cry of them hath entered into the ears of the Lord of Sabaoth* * Finally, the rich must religiously refrain from cutting down the workman's earnings, either by force, by fraud, or by usurious dealing ; and with the more reason because the poor man is weak and unprotected, and because his slender means should be sacred in proportion to their scantiness.

* St. James v. 4.

Were these precepts carefully obeyed and followed, would not strife die out and cease?

But the Church, with Jesus Christ for its Master and Guide, aims higher still. It lays down precepts yet more perfect, and tries to bind class to class in friendliness and good understanding. The things of this earth cannot be understood or valued rightly without taking into consideration the life to come, the life that will last forever. Exclude the idea of futurity, and the very notion of what is good and right would perish; nay, the whole system of the universe would become a dark and unfathomable mystery. The great truth which we learn from Nature herself is also the grand Christian dogma on which Religion rests as on its base—that when we have done with this present life, then we shall really begin to live. God has not created us for the perishable and transitory things of earth, but for things heavenly and everlasting; He has given us this world as a place of exile, and not as our true country. Money, and the other things which men call good and desirable—we may have them in abundance, or we may want them altogether; as far as eternal happiness is concerned, it is no matter; the only thing that is important is to use them aright. Jesus Christ, when He redeemed us with *plentiful redemption,* took not away the pains and sorrows which in such large proportion make up the texture of our mortal life; He transformed them into motives of virtue and occasions of merit: and no man can hope for eternal reward unless he follow in the blood-stained footprints of his Saviour. *If we suffer with Him, we shall also reign with Him* * His labors and His sufferings, accepted by His own free will, have marvellously sweetened all suffering and all labor. And not only by His example, but by His grace and by the hope of everlasting recompense, He has made pain and grief more easy to endure, *for that which is at present momentary and light of our tribulation, worketh for us above measure exceedingly an eternal weight of glory.*†

Therefore those whom fortune favors are warned that freedom from sorrow, and abundance of earthly riches, are no

---

* II. Timothy ii. 12.   † II. Corinthians iv. 17.

guarantee of the beatitude that shall never end, but rather the contrary ;* that the rich should tremble at the threatenings of Jesus Christ—threatenings so strange in the mouth of Our Lord ,† and that a most strict account must be given to the Supreme Judge for all that we possess   The chiefest and most excellent rule for the right use of money is one which the heathen philosophers indicated, but which the Church has traced out clearly, and has not only made known to men's minds but has impressed upon their lives.   It rests on the principle that it is one thing to have a right to the possession of money, and another to have a right to use money as one pleases.   Private ownership, as we have seen, is the natural right of man ; and to exercise that right, especially as members of society, is not only lawful, but absolutely necessary.   *It is lawful,* says St. Thomas of Aquin, *for a man to hold private property , and it is also necessary for the carrying on of human life.*‡   But if the question be asked, How must one's possessions be used ? the Church replies without hesitation in the words of the same holy Doctor :   *Man should not consider his outward possessions as his own, but as common to all, so as to share them without difficulty when others are in need   Whence the Apostle saith, Command the rich of this world . . . to give with ease, to communicate* §   True, no one is commanded to distribute to others that which is required for his own necessities and those of his household , nor even to give away what is reasonably required to keep up becomingly his condition in life ; *for no one ought to live unbecomingly.* ‖   But when necessity has been supplied, and one's position fairly considered, it is a duty to give to the indigent out of that which is over.   *That which remaineth, give alms.¶*   It is a duty, not of justice (except in extreme cases), but of Christian charity —a duty which is not enforced by human law.   But the laws and judgments of men must give place to the laws and judgments of Christ the true God, Who in many ways urges on His followers the practice of almsgiving—*It is more blessed to*

* St. Matthew xix. 23, 24. † St. Luke vi. 24, 25.
‡ 2a 2æ Q. lxvi. Art. 2. § *Ibid.* Q lxv. Art. 2.
‖ *Ibid.* Q. xxxii. Art. 6. ¶ St. Luke xi. 41.

give than to receive ; * and Who will count a kindness done or refused to the poor as done or refused to Himself—*as long as you did it to one of My least brethren, you did it to Me.*† Thus to sum up what has been said : Whoever has received from the Divine bounty a large share of blessings, whether they be external and corporeal or gifts of the mind, has received them for the purpose of using them for the perfecting of his own nature, and, at the same time, that he may employ them, as the minister of God's providence, for the benefit of others. *He that hath a talent,* says St. Gregory the Great, *let him see that he hide it not ; he that hath abundance, let him arouse himself to mercy and generosity ; he that hath art and skill, let him do his best to share the use and the utility thereof with his neighbor* ‡

As for those who do not possess the gifts of fortune, they are taught by the Church that in God's sight poverty is no disgrace, and that there is nothing to be ashamed of in seeking one's bread by labor. This is strengthened by what we see in Christ Himself, Who *whereas He was rich, for our sakes became poor ;*§ and Who, being the Son of God, and God Himself, chose to seem and to be considered the son of a carpenter—nay, did not disdain to spend a great part of His life as a carpenter Himself. *Is not this the carpenter, the Son of Mary ?* ‖ From the contemplation of this Divine example it is easy to understand that the true dignity and excellence of man lies in his moral qualities, that is, in virtue ; that virtue is the common inheritance of all, equally within the reach of high and low, rich and poor ; and that virtue, and virtue alone, wherever found, will be followed by the rewards of everlasting happiness. Nay, God Himself seems to incline more to those who suffer evil ; for Jesus Christ calls the poor blessed ;¶ He lovingly invites those in labor and grief to come to Him for solace,** and He displays the tender-

* Acts xx. 35. † St. Matthew xxv. 40.
‡ St. Gregory the Great. Hom, ix. *in Evangel.* n. 7.
§ II Corinthians viii 9 ‖ St. Mark vi 3
¶ St. Matthew v 3 "*Blessed are the poor in spirit* "
** *Ibid.* xi 28. "*Come to Me, all you that labor and are burdened, and I will refresh you.*"

est charity to the lowly and the oppressed. These reflections cannot fail to keep down the pride of those who are well off, and to cheer the spirit of the afflicted ; to incline the former to generosity and the latter to tranquil resignation   Thus the separation which pride would make tends to disappear, nor will it be difficult to make rich and poor join hands in friendly concord.

But if Christian precepts prevail, the two classes will not only be united in the bonds of friendship, but also in those of brotherly love   For they will understand and feel that all men are the children of the common Father, that is, of God ; that all have the same last end, which is God Himself, Who alone can make either men or angels absolutely and perfectly happy ; that all and each are redeemed by Jesus Christ and raised to the dignity of children of God, and are thus united in brotherly ties both with each other and with Jesus Christ, *the first-born among many brethren ;* that the blessings of nature and the gifts of grace belong in common to the whole human race, and that to all, except to those who are un-worthy, is promised the inheritance of the kingdom of heaven. *If sons, heirs also ; heirs indeed of God, and co-heirs of Christ.**

Such is the scheme of duties and of rights which is put forth to the world by the Gospel.   Would it not seem that strife must quickly cease were society penetrated with ideas like these ?

But the Church, not content with pointing out the rem-edy, also applies it.   For the Church does its utmost to teach and to train men, and to educate them ; and by means of its Bishops and clergy it diffuses its salutary teachings far and wide.   It strives to influence the mind and heart so that all may willingly yield themselves to be formed and guided by the commandments of God.   It is precisely in this funda-mental and principal matter, on which everything depends, that the Church has a power peculiar to itself   The agencies which it employs are given it for the very purpose of reach-ing the hearts of men, by Jesus Christ Himself, and derive their efficiency from God.   They alone can touch the inner-

* Romans viii. 17.

most heart and conscience, and bring men to act from a
motive of duty, to resist their passions and appetites, to love
God and their fellow-men with a love that is unique and
supreme, and courageously to break down every barrier
which stands in the way of a virtuous life.

On this subject We need only recall, for one moment, the
examples written down in history. Of these things there cannot be the shadow of doubt; for instance, that civil society
was renovated in every part by the teachings of Christianity;
that in the strength of that renewal the human race was lifted
up to better things,—nay, that it was brought back from
death to life, and to so excellent a life that nothing more
perfect had been known before, or will come to pass in the
ages that have yet to be. Of this beneficent transformation,
Jesus Christ was at once the first cause and the final purpose;
as from Him all came, so to Him all was to be referred. For
when, by the light of the Gospel message, the human race
came to know the grand mystery of the Incarnation of the
Word and the redemption of man, the life of Jesus Christ,
God and Man, penetrated every race and nation, and impreg-
nated them with His faith, His precepts, and His laws. And
if Society is to be cured now, in no other way can it be cured
but by a return to the Christian life and Christian institutions. When a society is perishing, the true advice to give
to those who would restore it is to recall it to the principles
from which it sprung; for the purpose and perfection of an
association is to aim at and to attain that for which it was
formed; and its operation should be put in motion and
inspired by the end and object which originally gave it its
being. So that to fall away from its primal constitution is
disease, to go back to it is recovery. And this may be
asserted with the utmost truth both of the State in general
and of that body of its citizens—by far the greater number—
who sustain life by labor.

Neither must it be supposed that the solicitude of the
Church is so occupied with the spiritual concerns of its
children as to neglect their interests temporal and earthly.
Its desire is that the poor, for example, should rise above
poverty and wretchedness, and should better their condition

in life; and for this it strives. By the very fact that it calls
men to virtue and forms them to its practice, it promotes
this in no slight degree. Christian morality, when it is ade-
quately and completely practised, conduces of itself to temporal prosperity, for it merits the blessing of that God Who
is the source of all blessings; it powerfully restrains the lust
of possession and the lust of pleasure—twin plagues, which
too often make a man without self-restraint miserable in the
midst of abundance; * it makes men supply by economy for
the want of means, teaching them to be content with frugal
living, and keeping them out of the reach of those vices
which eat up not merely small incomes, but large fortunes,
and dissipate many a goodly inheritance.

Moreover, the Church intervenes directly in the interest of
the poor, by setting on foot and keeping up many things
which it sees to be efficacious in the relief of poverty. Here,
again, it has always succeeded so well that it has even ex-
torted the praise of its enemies. Such was the ardor of
brotherly love among the earliest Christians that numbers of
those who were better off deprived themselves of their possessions in order to relieve their brethren; whence *neither
was there any one needy among them.*† To the order of
Deacons, instituted for that very purpose, was committed by
the Apostles the charge of the daily distributions; and the
Apostle Paul, though burdened with the solicitude of all the
churches, hesitated not to undertake laborious journeys in
order to carry the alms of the Faithful to the poorer Christians. Tertullian calls these contributions, given voluntarily
by Christians in their assemblies, *deposits of piety;* because,
to cite his words, they were employed *in feeding the needy,
in burying them, in the support of boys and girls destitute of
means and deprived of their parents, in the care of the aged,
and in relief of the shipwrecked.*‡

Thus by degrees came into existence the patrimony which
the Church has guarded with religious care as the inheritance of the poor. Nay, to spare them the shame of begging,

---

* "*The root of all evils is cupidity.*"—I. Tim. vi. 10.
† Acts iv. 34.   ‡ *Apologia Secunda,* xxxix.

the common Mother of rich and poor has exerted herself to gather together funds for the support of the needy. The Church has stirred up everywhere the heroism of charity, and has established Congregations of Religious and many other useful institutions for help and mercy, so that there might be hardly any kind of suffering which was not visited and relieved. At the present day there are many who, like the heathen of old, blame and condemn the Church for this beautiful charity. They would substitute in its place a system of State-organized relief. But no human methods will ever supply for the devotion and self-sacrifice of Christian charity. Charity, as a virtue, belongs to the Church; for it is no virtue unless it is drawn from the Sacred Heart of Jesus Christ; and he who turns his back on the Church cannot be near to Christ.

It cannot, however, be doubted that to attain the purpose of which We treat, not only the Church but all human means must conspire. All who are concerned in the matter must be of one mind and must act together. It is in this as in the Providence which governs the world : results do not happen save where all the causes co-operate.

Let us now, therefore, inquire what part the State should play in the work of remedy and relief.

By the State We here understand, not the particular form of government which prevails in this or that nation, but the State, as rightly understood; that is to say, any government conformable in its institutions to right reason and natural law, and to those dictates of the Divine wisdom which We have expounded in the Encyclical on the Christian Constitution of the State. The first duty, therefore, of the rulers of the State should be to make sure that the laws and institutions, the general character and administration of the commonwealth, shall be such as to produce of themselves public well-being and private prosperity. This is the proper office of wise statesmanship and the work of the heads of the State. Now a State chiefly prospers and flourishes by morality, by well-regulated family life, by respect for religion and justice, by the moderation and equal distribution of public burdens, by the progress of the arts and of trade, by the abundant yield of the land—by everything which makes the citizens better and happier. Here, then, it is in the power of a ruler to benefit every order of the State, and amongst the rest to promote in the highest degree the interests of the poor, and this by virtue of his office, and without being exposed to any suspicion of undue interference; for it is the province of the commonwealth to consult for the common good. And the more that is done for the working population by the general laws of the country, the less need will there be to seek for particular means to relieve them.

There is another and a deeper consideration which must not be lost sight of. To the State the interests of all are equal, whether high or low. The poor are members of the national community equally with the rich; they are real component parts, living parts, which make up, through the family, the living body; and it need hardly be said that they are by far the majority. It would be irrational to neglect one portion of the citizens and to favor another; and therefore the public administration must duly and solicitously provide for the welfare and the comfort of the working people, or else that law of justice will be violated which ordains that each shall have his due. To cite the wise words of St. Thomas of Aquin: *As the part and the whole are in a certain sense identical, the part may in some sense claim what belongs to the whole.** Among the many and grave duties of rulers who would do their best for the people, the first and chief is to act with strict justice—with that justice which is called in the school *distributive*—towards each and every class.

But although all citizens, without exception, can and ought to contribute to that common good in which individuals share so profitably to themselves, yet it is not to be supposed that all can contribute in the same way and to the same extent. No matter what changes may be made in forms of government, there will always be differences and inequalities of condition in the State: Society cannot exist or be conceived without them. Some there must be who dedicate themselves to the work of the commonwealth, who

* 2a 2æ Q. lxi. Art. 1 ad 2.

make the laws, who administer justice, whose advice and authority govern the nation in times of peace, and defend it in war. Such men clearly occupy the foremost place in the State, and should be held in the foremost estimation, for their work touches most nearly and effectively the general interests of the community. Those who labor at a trade or calling do not promote the general welfare in such a fashion as this; but they do in the most important way benefit the nation, though less directly. We have insisted that, since it is the end of Society to make men better, the chief good that Society can be possessed of is Virtue. Nevertheless, in all well-constituted States it is a by no means unimportant matter to provide those bodily and external commodities *the use of which is necessary to virtuous action.** And in the provision of material well-being, the labor of the poor—the exercise of their skill, and the employment of their strength in the culture of the land and the workshops of trade—is most efficacious and altogether indispensable. Indeed, their co-operation in this respect is so important that it may be truly said that it is only by the labor of the working man that States grow rich. Justice, therefore, demands that the interests of the poorer population be carefully watched over by the Administration, so that they who contribute so largely to the advantage of the community may themselves share in the benefits they create—that being housed, clothed, and enabled to support life, they may find their existence less hard and more endurable. It follows that whatever shall appear to be conducive to the well-being of those who work should receive favorable consideration. Let it not be feared that solicitude of this kind will injure any interest; on the contrary, it will be to the advantage of all; for it cannot but be good for the commonwealth to secure from misery those on whom it so largely depends.

We have said that the State must not absorb the individual or the family; both should be allowed free and untrammelled action as far as is consistent with the common good and the interests of others. Nevertheless, rulers should

---

* St. Thomas of Aquin. *De Regimine Principum*, I. cap. 15.

anxiously safeguard the community and all its parts; the community, because the conservation of the community is so emphatically the business of the supreme power, that the safety of the commonwealth is not only the first law, but it is a Government's whole reason of existence; and the parts, because both philosophy and the Gospel agree in laying down that the object of the administration of the State should be, not the advantage of the ruler, but the benefit of those over whom he rules. The gift of authority is from God, and is, as it were, a participation of the highest of all sovereignties; and it should be exercised as the power of God is exercised— with a fatherly solicitude which not only guides the whole, but reaches to details as well.

Whenever the general interest or any particular class suffers, or is threatened with, evils which can in no other way be met, the public authority must step in to meet them. Now, among the interests of the public, as of private indi- viduals, are these: that peace and good order should be maintained; that family life should be carried on in accord- ance with God's laws and those of nature; that Religion should be reverenced and obeyed; that a high standard of morality should prevail in public and private life; that the sanctity of justice should be respected, and that no one should injure another with impunity; that the members of the commonwealth should grow up to man's estate strong and robust, and capable, if need be, of guarding and defend- ing their country. If, by a strike or other combination of workmen, there should be imminent danger of disturbance to the public peace, or if circumstances were such that among the laboring population the ties of family life were re- laxed; if Religion were found to suffer through the workmen not having time and opportunity to practise it; if in work- shops and factories there were danger to morals through the mixing of the sexes or from any occasion of evil, or if em- ployers laid burdens upon the workmen which were unjust, or degraded them with conditions that were repugnant to their dignity as human beings; finally, if health were endan- gered by excessive labor, or by work unsuited to sex or age —in these cases there can be no question that, within certain limits, it would be right to call in the help and authority of the law. The limits must be determined by the nature of the occasion which calls for the law's interference—the principle being this, that the law must not undertake more, or go further, than is required for the remedy of the evil or the removal of the danger

Rights must be religiously respected wherever they are found, and it is the duty of the public authority to prevent and punish injury, and to protect each one in the possession of his own Still, when there is question of protecting the rights of individuals, the poor and helpless have a claim to special consideration. The richer population have many ways of protecting themselves, and stand less in need of help from the State, those who are badly off have no resources of their own to fall back upon, and must chiefly rely upon the assistance of the State. And it is for this reason that wage earners, who are undoubtedly among the weak and necessitous, should be specially cared for and protected by the commonwealth.

Here, however, it will be advisable to advert expressly to one or two of the more important details. It must be borne in mind that the chief thing to be secured is the safeguarding, by legal enactment and policy, of private property. Most of all is it essential, in these times of covetous greed, to keep the multitude within the line of duty; for if all may justly strive to better their condition, yet neither justice nor the common good allows any one to seize that which belongs to another, or, under the pretext of futile and ridiculous equality, to lay hands on other people's fortunes. It is most true that by far the larger part of the people who work prefer to improve themselves by honest labor rather than by doing wrong to others. But there are not a few who are imbued with bad principles and are anxious for revolutionary change, and whose great purpose it is to stir up tumult and bring about a policy of violence. The authority of the State should intervene to put restraint upon these disturbers, to save the workmen from their seditious arts, and to protect lawful owners from spoliation.

When work-people have recourse to a strike, it is frequently because the hours of labor are too long, or the work too hard, or because they consider their wages insufficient The grave inconvenience of this not uncommon occurrence should be obviated by public remedial measures, for such paralysis of labor not only affects the masters and their work-people, but is extremely injurious to trade, and to the general interests of the public, moreover, on such occasions, violence and disorder are generally not far off, and thus it frequently happens that the public peace is threatened The law should be beforehand and prevent these troubles from arising; they should lend their influence and authority to the removal in good time of the causes which lead to conflicts between masters and those whom they employ

But if the owners of property must be made secure, the Workman, too, has property and possessions in which he must be protected, and, first of all, there are his spiritual and mental interests Life on earth, however good and desirable in itself, is not the final purpose for which man is created, it is only the way and the means to that attainment' of truth, and that practice of goodness in which the full life of the soul consists. It is the soul which is made after the image and likeness of God, it is in the soul that sovereignty resides, in virtue of which man is commanded to rule the creatures below him, and to use all the earth and the ocean for his profit and advantage *Fill the earth and subdue it; and rule over the fishes of the sea, and the fowls of the air, and all living creatures which move upon the earth.** In this respect all men are equal; there is no difference between rich and poor, master and servant, ruler and ruled, *for the same is Lord over all.*† No man may outrage with impunity that human dignity which God Himself treats *with reverence,* nor stand in the way of that higher life which is the preparation for the eternal life of heaven Nay, more, a man has here no power over himself To consent to any treatment which is calculated to defeat the end and purpose of his being is beyond his right, he cannot give up his soul to servitude, for it is not man's own rights which are here in question, but the rights of God, most sacred and inviolable

* Genesis i 28. † Romans x 12.

From this follows the obligation of the cessation of work and labor on Sundays and certain festivals. This rest from labor is not to be understood as mere idleness; much less must it be an occasion of spending money and of vicious excess, as many would desire it to be, but it should be rest from labor consecrated by religion Repose united with religious observance disposes man to forget for a while the business of this daily life, and to turn his thoughts to heavenly things and to the worship which he so strictly owes to the Eternal Deity. It is this, above all, which is the reason and motive of the Sunday rest; a rest sanctioned by God's great law of the ancient covenant, *Remember thou keep holy the Sabbath day,** and taught to the world by His own mysterious "rest" after the creation of man: *He rested on the seventh day from all His work which He had done.*†

If we turn now to things exterior and corporeal, the first concern of all is to save the poor workers from the cruelty of grasping speculators, who use human beings as mere instruments for making money. It is neither justice nor humanity so to grind men down with excessive labor as to stupefy their minds and wear out their bodies. Man's powers, like his general nature, are limited, and beyond these limits he cannot go. His strength is developed and increased by use and exercise, but only on condition of due intermission and proper rest. Daily labor, therefore, must be so regulated that it may not be protracted during longer hours than strength admits How many and how long the intervals of rest should be will depend on the nature of the work, on circumstances of time and place, and on the health and strength of the workman. Those who labor in mines and quarries, and in work within the bowels of the earth, should have shorter hours in proportion as their labor is more severe and more trying to health. Then, again, the season of the year must be taken into account; for not unfrequently a kind of labor is easy at one time which at another is intolerable or very difficult. Finally, work which is suitable for a strong man cannot reasonably be required from a woman or a child. And, in regard to children, great care should be

* Exod. xx. 8   † Genesis ii. 2

taken not to place them in workshops and factories until their bodies and minds are sufficiently mature. For just as rough weather destroys the buds of spring, so too early an experience of life's hard work blights the young promise of a child's powers, and makes any real education impossible. Women, again, are not suited to certain trades; for a woman is by nature fitted for home-work, and it is that which is best adapted at once to preserve her modesty and to promote the good bringing up of children and the well-being of the family. As a general principle it may be laid down, that a workman ought to have leisure and rest in proportion to the wear and tear of his strength; for the waste of strength must be repaired by the cessation of work.

In all agreements between masters and work-people, there is always the condition, expressed or understood, that there be allowed proper rest for soul and body. To agree in any other sense would be against what is right and just, for it can never be right or just to require on the one side, or to promise on the other, the giving up of those duties which a man owes to his God and to himself.

We now approach a subject of very great importance, and one on which, if extremes are to be avoided, right ideas are absolutely necessary. Wages, we are told, are fixed by free consent; and therefore the employer, when he pays what was agreed upon, has done his part, and is not called upon for anything further. The only way, it is said, in which injustice could happen would be if the master refused to pay the whole of the wages, or the workman would not complete the work undertaken; when this happens the State should intervene, to see that each obtains his own—but not under any other circumstances.

This mode of reasoning is by no means convincing to a fair-minded man, for there are important considerations which it leaves out of view altogether. To labor is to exert one's self for the sake of procuring what is necessary for the purposes of life, and most of all for self-preservation. *In the sweat of thy brow thou shalt eat bread* * Therefore a man's labor has two notes or characters. First of all, it is

* Genesis iii 19.

personal; for the exertion of individual power belongs to
the individual who puts it forth, employing this power for
that personal profit for which it was given. Secondly, man's
labor is *necessary*, for without the results of labor a man
cannot live; and self-conservation is a law of nature which
it is wrong to disobey. Now if we were to consider labor
merely so far as it is *personal*, doubtless it would be within
the workman's right to accept any rate of wages whatever;
for in the same way as he is free to work or not, so he is free
to accept a small remuneration or even none at all. But this
is a mere abstract supposition; the labor of the working
man is not only his personal attribute, but it is *necessary;*
and this makes all the difference. The preservation of life is
the bounden duty of each and all, and to fail therein is a
crime. It follows that each one has a right to procure what
is required in order to live; and the poor can procure it in
no other way than by work and wages

Let it be granted, then, that as a rule, workman and employer should make free agreements, and in particular should
freely agree as to wages, nevertheless, there is a dictate of
nature more imperious and more ancient than any bargain
between man and man, that the remuneration must be
enough to support the wage-earner in reasonable and frugal
comfort. If through necessity or fear of a worse evil, the
workman accepts harder conditions because an employer or
a contractor will give him no better, he is the victim of force
and injustice. In these and similar questions, however—
such as, for example, the hours of labor in different trades,
the sanitary precautions to be observed in factories and
workshops, etc.—in order to supersede undue interference
on the part of the State, especially as circumstances, times,
and localities differ so widely, it is advisable that recourse be
had to Societies or Boards such as We shall mention pres-
ently, or to some other method of safe-guarding the interests of wage-earners; the State to be asked for approval and
protection.

If a workman's wages be sufficient to enable him to maintain himself, his wife, and his children in reasonable comfort,
he will not find it difficult, if he is a sensible man, to study

economy; and he will not fail, by cutting down expenses, to put by a little property, nature and reason would urge him to this. We have seen that this great Labor question cannot be solved except by assuming as a principle that private ownership must be held sacred and inviolable. The law, therefore, should favor ownership, and its policy should be to induce as many of the people as possible to become owners.

Many excellent results will follow from this; and first of all, property will certainly become more equitably divided. For the effect of civil change and revolution has been to divide society into two widely differing castes. On the one side there is the party which holds the power because it holds the wealth, which has in its grasp all labor and all trade, which manipulates for its own benefit and its own purposes all the sources of supply, and which is powerfully represented in the councils of the State itself. On the other side there is the needy and powerless multitude, sore and suffering, and always ready for disturbance. If working people can be encouraged to look forward to obtaining a share in the land, the result will be that the gulf between vast wealth and deep poverty will be bridged over, and the two orders will be brought nearer together Another consequence will be the greater abundance of the fruits of the earth Men always work harder and more readily when they work on that which is their own, nay, they learn to love the very soil which yields in response to the labor of their hands, not only food to eat, but an abundance of good things for themselves and those that are dear to them It is evident how such a spirit of willing labor would add to the produce of the earth, and to the wealth of the community. And a third advantage would arise from this, men would cling to the country in which they were born; for no one would exchange his country for a foreign land if his own afforded him the means of living a tolerable and happy life. These three important benefits, however, can only be expected on the condition that a man's means be not drained and exhausted by excessive taxation The right to possess private property is from nature, not from man, and the State has only the right to regulate its use in the interests of the public good, but by no means to abolish it altogether The State is, therefore, unjust and cruel if, in the name of taxation, it deprives the private owner of more than is just.

In the last place—employers and workmen may themselves effect much in the matter of which We treat, by means of those institutions and organizations which afford opportune assistance to those in need, and which draw the two orders more closely together. Among these may be enumerated: Societies for mutual help; various foundations established by private persons for providing for the workman, and for his widow or his orphans, in sudden calamity, in sickness, and in the event of death , and what are called "patronages," or institutions for the care of boys and girls, for young people, and also for those of more mature age.

The most important of all are Workmen's Associations; for these virtually include all the rest History attests what excellent results were effected by the Artificer's Guilds of a former day. They were the means not only of many advantages to the workmen, but in no small degree of the advancement of art, as numerous monuments remain to prove. Such associations should be adapted to the requirements of the age in which we live—an age of greater instruction, of different customs, and of more numerous requirements in daily life. It is gratifying to know that there are actually in existence not a few Societies of this nature, consisting either of workmen alone or of workmen and employers together; but it were greatly to be desired that they should multiply and become more effective We have spoken of them more than once; but it will be well to explain here how much they are needed, to show that they exist by their own right, and to enter into their organization, and their work

The experience of his own weakness urges man to call in help from without We read in the pages of Holy Writ: *It is better that two should be together than one ; for they have the advantage of their society. If one fall he shall be supported by the other Woe to him that is alone, for when he falleth he hath none to lift him up* * And further: *A brother*

* Ecclesiastes iv. 9, 10.

*that is helped by his brother is like a strong city.** It is this natural impulse which unites men in civil society; and it is this also which makes them band themselves together in associations of citizen with citizen; associations which, it is true, cannot be called societies in the complete sense of the word, but which are societies nevertheless.

These lesser societies, and the society which constitutes the State, differ in many things, because their immediate purpose and end is different Civil society exists for the common good, and, therefore, is concerned with the interests of all in general, and with individual interests in their due place and proportion Hence it is called *public* society, because by its means, as St. Thomas of St. Aquin says, *Men communicate with one another in the setting up of a commonwealth* † But the societies which are formed in the bosom of the State are called *private*, and justly so, because their immediate purpose is the private advantage of the associates *Now, a private society*, says St. Thomas again, *is one which is formed for the purpose of carrying out private business: as when two or three enter into a partnership with the view of trading in conjunction.*‡ Particular societies, then, although they exist within the State, and are each a part of the State, nevertheless cannot be prohibited by the State absolutely and as such. For to enter into "society" of this kind is the natural right of man: and the State must protect natural rights, not destroy them; and if it forbids its citizens to form associations, it contradicts the very principle of its own existence; for both they and it exist in virtue of the same principle, *viz.*: the natural propensity of man to live in society.

There are times, no doubt, when it is right that the law should interfere to prevent association; as when men join together for purposes which are evidently bad, unjust, or dangerous to the State. In such cases the public authority may justly forbid the formation of associations, and may dissolve them when they already exist But every precaution should be taken not to violate the rights of individuals, and not to make unreasonable regulations under the pretence of

* Proverbs xviii 19
† *Contra impugnantes Dei cultum et religionem*, Cap. II.   ‡ *Ibid.*

public benefit. For laws only bind when they are in accordance with right reason, and therefore with the eternal law of God.*

And here we are reminded of the Confraternities, Societies, and Religious Orders which have arisen by the Church's authority, and the piety of the Christian people. The annals of every nation down to our own times testify to what they have done for the human race. It is indisputable, on grounds of reason alone, that such associations, being perfectly blameless in their objects, have the sanction of the law of nature. On their religious side, they rightly claim to be responsible to the Church alone. The administrators of the State, therefore, have no rights over them, nor can they claim any share in their management; on the contrary, it is the State's duty to respect and cherish them, and, if necessary, to defend them from attack. It is notorious that a very different course has been followed, more especially in our own times. In many places the State has laid violent hands on these Communities, and committed manifold injustice against them; it has placed them under the civil law, taken away their rights as corporate bodies, and robbed them of their property. In such property the Church had her rights, each member of the body had his or her rights, and there were also the rights of those who had founded or endowed them for a definite purpose, and of those for whose benefit and assistance they existed. Wherefore We cannot refrain from complaining of such spoliation as unjust, and fraught with evil results; and with the more reason because, at the very time when the law proclaims that association is free to all, We see that Catholic societies, however peaceful and useful, are hindered in every way, whilst the utmost freedom is given to men whose objects are at once hurtful to Religion and dangerous to the State.

Associations of every kind, and especially those of working men, are now far more common than formerly. In re-

---

* *Human law is law only in virtue of its accordance with right reason and thus it is manifest that it flows from the eternal law. And in so far as it deviates from right reason it is called an unjust law, in such case it is not law at all, but rather a species of violence.—* St. Thomas of Aquin, *Summa Theologica,* 1 a 2æ Q xciii. Art. iii.

gard to many of these there is no need at present to inquire whence they spring, what are their objects, or what means they use. But there is a good deal of evidence which goes to prove that many of these societies are in the hands of invisable leaders, and are managed on principles far from compatible with Christianity and the public well-being, and that they do their best to get into their hands the whole field of labor, and to force workman either to join them or to starve. Under these circumstances Christian workman must do one of two things: either join associations in which their religion will be exposed to peril, or form associations among themselves—unite their forces and courageously shake off the yoke of an unjust and intolerable oppression No one who does not wish to expose man's chief good to extreme danger will hesitate to say that the second alternative must by all means be adopted.

Those Catholics are worthy of all praise—and there are not a few—who, understanding what the times require, have, by various enterprises and experiments, endeavored to better the condition of the working people without any sacrifice of principle. They have taken up the cause of the working man, and have striven to make both families and individuals better off; to infuse the spirit of justice into the mutual relations of employer and employed; to keep before the eyes of both classes the precepts of duty and the laws of the Gospel— that Gospel which, by inculcating self-restraint, keeps men within the bounds of moderation, and tends to establish harmony among the divergent interests and various classes which compose the State. It is with such ends in view that We see men of eminence meeting together for discussion, for the promotion of united action, and for practical work. Others, again, strive to unite working people of various kinds into associations, help them with their advice and their means, and enable them to obtain honest and profitable work. The Bishops, on their part, bestow their ready goodwill and support; and with their approval and guidance many members of the clergy, both secular and regular, labor assiduously on behalf of the spiritual and mental interests of the members of Associations. And there are not wanting

Catholics possessed of affluence who have, as it were, cast
in their lot with the wage-earners, and who have spent large
sums in founding and widely spreading Benefit and Insurance Societies, by means of which the working man may
without difficulty acquire by his labor not only many present
advantages, but also the certainty of honorable support in
time to come. How much this multiplied and earnest activity has benefited the community at large is too well known
to require Us to dwell upon it. We find in it the grounds
of the most cheering hope for the future : provided that the
Associations We have described continue to grow and
spread, and are well and wisely administered. Let the State
watch over these Societies of citizens united together in the
exercise of their right ; but let it not thrust itself into their
peculiar concerns and their organization, for things move
and live by the soul within them, and they may be killed by
the grasp of a hand without.

In order that an Association may be carried on with unity
of purpose and harmony of action, its organization and government must be firm and wise. All such societies, being
free to exist, have the further right to adopt such rules and
organization as may best conduce to the attainment of their
objects. We do not deem it possible to enter into definite
details on the subject of organization : this must depend on
national character, on practice and experience, on the nature
and scope of the work to be done, on the magnitude of the
various trades and employments, and on other circumstances
of fact and of time—all of which must be carefully weighed.

Speaking summarily, we may lay it down as a general and
perpetual law, that Workmen's Associations should be so
organized and governed as to furnish the best and most
suitable means for attaining what is aimed at, that is to say,
for helping each individual member to better his condition
to the utmost in body, mind, and property. It is clear that
they must pay special and principal attention to piety and
morality, and that their internal discipline must be directed
precisely by these considerations ; otherwise they entirely
lose their special character, and come to be very little better
than those societies which take no account of religion at all.

What advantage can it be to a workman to obtain by means of a society all that he requires, and to endanger his soul for want of spiritual food? *What doth it profit a man if he gain the whole world and suffer the loss of his own soul?** This, as Our Lord teaches, is the note or character that distinguishes the Christian from the heathen. *After all these things do the heathen seek . . . Seek ye first the Kingdom of God and His justice, and all these things shall be added unto you.*† Let our Associations, then, look first and before all to God; let religious instruction have therein a foremost place, each one being carefully taught what is his duty to God, what to believe, what to hope for, and how to work out his salvation; and let all be warned and fortified with especial solicitude against wrong opinions and false teaching. Let the working man be urged and led to the worship of God, to the earnest practice of religion, and, among other things, to the sanctification of Sundays and festivals. Let him learn to reverence and love Holy Church, the common Mother of us all; and so to obey the precepts, and to frequent the Sacraments of the Church, those Sacraments being the means ordained by God for obtaining forgiveness of sin and for leading a holy life.

The foundations of the organization being laid in Religion, We next go on to determine the relations of the members one to another, in order that they may live together in concord and go on prosperously and successfully. The offices and charges of the Society should be distributed for the good of the Society itself, and in such manner that difference in degree or position should not interfere with unanimity and good-will. Office-bearers should be appointed with prudence and discretion, and each one's charge should be carefully marked out; thus no member will suffer wrong. Let the common funds be administered with the strictest honesty, in such way that a member receive assistance in proportion to his necessities. The rights and duties of employers should be the subject of careful consideration as compared with the rights and duties of the employed. If it

---

* St. Matthew xvi. 26.   † St. Matthew vi. 32, 33.

should happen that either a master or a workman deemed himself injured, nothing would be more desirable than that there should be a committee composed of honest and capable men of the Association itself, whose duty it should be, by the laws of the Association, to decide the dispute. Among the purposes of a Society should be to try to arrange for a continuous supply of work at all times and seasons; and to create a fund from which the members may be helped in their necessities, not only in cases of accident, but also in sickness, old age, and misfortune.

Such rules and regulations, if obeyed willingly by all, will sufficiently ensure the well-being of poor people; while such Mutual Associations among Catholics are certain to be productive, in no small degree, of prosperity to the State. It is not rash to conjecture the future from the past. Age gives way to age, but the events of one century are wonderfully like those of another; for they are directed by the providence of God, Who overrules the course of history in accordance with His purposes in creating the race of man. We are told that it was cast as a reproach on the Christians of the early ages of the Church, that the greater number of them had to live by begging or by labor. Yet, destitute as they were of wealth and influence, they ended by winning over to their side the favor of the rich and the good-will of the powerful. They showed themselves industrious, laborious, and peaceful, men of justice, and, above all, men of brotherly love. In the presence of such a life and such an example, prejudice disappeared, the tongue of malevolence was silenced, and the lying traditions of ancient superstition yielded little by little to Christian truth.

At this moment the condition of the working population is the question of the hour, and nothing can be of higher interest to all classes of the State than that it should be rightly and reasonably decided But it will be easy for Christian working men to decide it aright if they form Associations, choose wise guides, and follow the same path which with so much advantage to themselves and the commonwealth was trod by their fathers before them. Prejudice, it is true, is mighty, and so is the love of money; but if the sense of what is just and right be not destroyed by depravity of heart, their fellow-citizens are sure to be won over to a kindly feeling towards men whom they see to be so indus- trious and so modest, who so unmistakably prefer honesty to lucre, and the sacredness of duty to all other considerations.

And another great advantage would result from the state of things We are describing; there would be so much more hope and possibility of recalling to a sense of their duty those working men who have either given up their faith altogether, or whose lives are at variance with its precepts These men, in most cases, feel that they have been fooled by empty promises and deceived by false appearances They cannot but perceive that their grasping employers too often treat them with the greatest inhumanity, and hardly care for them beyond the profit their labor brings, and if they belong to an Association, it is probably one in which there exists, in place of charity and love, that intestine strife which always accom- panies unresigned and irreligious poverty. Broken in spirit and worn down in body, how many of them would gladly free themselves from this galling slavery! But human re- spect, or the dread of starvation, makes them afraid to take the step. To such as these, Catholic Associations are of incalculable service, helping them out of their difficulties, inviting them to companionship, and receiving the repentant to a shelter in which they may securely trust.

We have now laid before you, Venerable Brethren, who are the persons, and what are the means, by which this most difficult question must be solved. Every one must put his hand to the work which falls to his share, and that at once and immediately, lest the evil which is already so great may by delay become absolutely beyond remedy. Those who rule the State must use the law and the institutions of the coun- try, masters and rich men must remember their duty, the poor, whose interests are at stake, must make every lawful and proper effort, and since Religion alone, as we said at the beginning, can destroy the evil at its root, all men must be persuaded that the primary thing needful is to return to real Christianity, in the absence of which all the plans and devices of the wisest will be of little avail.

As far as regards the Church, its assistance will 'never be wanting, be the time or the occasion what it may; and it will intervene with the greater effect in proportion as its liberty of action is the more unfettered : let this be carefully noted by those whose office it is to provide for the public welfare. Every minister of holy Religion must throw into the conflict all the energy of his mind and all the strength of his endurance; with your authority, Venerable Brethren, and by your example, they must never cease to urge upon all men of every class, upon the high as well as the lowly, the Gospel doctrines of Christian life; by every means in their power they must strive for the good of the people; and above all they must earnestly cherish in themselves, and try to arouse in others, Charity, the mistress and queen of virtues. For the happy results we all long for must be chiefly brought about by the plenteous outpouring of Charity; of that true Christian Charity which is the fulfilling of the whole Gospel law, which is always ready to sacrifice itself for others' sake, and which is man's surest antidote against wordly pride and immoderate love of self; that Charity whose office is described and whose Godlike features are drawn by the Apostle St. Paul in these words: *Charity is patient, is kind, . . . seeketh not her own, . . . suffereth all things, . . . endureth all things.**

On each one of you, Venerable Brethren, and on your Clergy and people, as an earnest of God's mercy and a mark of our affection, We lovingly in the Lord bestow the Apostolic Benediction.

Given at St. Peter's in Rome, the fifteenth day of May, 1891, the fourteenth year of Our Pontificate.

LEO XIII., POPE.

* I. Corinthians xiii. 4–7.

ENCYCLICAL LETTER OF OUR HOLY FATHER POPE LEO XIII.

CHRISTIAN DEMOCRACY.

TO OUR VENERABLE BRETHREN, ALL PATRIARCHS, PRI-
MATES, ARCHBISHOPS, BISHOPS AND OTHER ORDINARIES
IN PEACE AND COMMUNION WITH THE APOSTOLIC SEE.

Venerable Brothers, Health and Apostolic Benediction

THE grave discussions on economical questions which for some time past have disturbed the peace of several countries of the world are growing in frequency and intensity to such a degree, that the minds of thoughtful men are filled, and rightly so, with worry and alarm These discussions take their rise in the bad philosophical and ethical teaching which is now widespread among the people. The changes also which the mechanical inventions of the age have introduced, the rapidity of communication between places and the devices of every kind for diminishing labor and increasing gain all add bitterness to the strife; and lastly matters have been brought to such a pass by the struggle between capital and labor, fomented as it is by professional agitators, that the countries where these disturbances most frequently occur, find themselves confronted with ruin and disaster.

At the very beginning of Our Pontificate We clearly pointed out what the peril was which confronted Society on this head, and We deemed it Our duty to warn Catholics, in unmistakable language, how great the error was which was lurking in the utterances of Socialism, and how great the danger was that threatened not only their temporal possessions, but also their morality and religion. That was the purpose of Our Encyclical Letter *Quod Apostolici Muneris* which we published on the 18th of December in the year 1878, but as these dangers day by day threatened still greater disaster, both to individuals and the commonwealth, We strove with all the more energy to avert them. This was the object of Our Encyclical *Rerum Novarum* of the 15th May, 1891, in which We dwelt at length on the rights and duties which both classes of Society—those, namely, who control capital, and those who contribute labor—are bound in relation to each other; and at the same time, We made it evident that the remedies which are most useful to protect the cause of Religion, and to terminate the contest between the different classes of Society, were to be found in the precepts of the Gospel.

Nor, with God's grace, were Our hopes entirely frustrated. Even those who are not Catholics, moved by the power of truth, avowed that the Church must be credited with a watchful care over all classes of Society, and especially those whom fortune had least favored. Catholics of course profited abundantly by these Letters, for they not only received encouragement and strength for the admirable enterprises in which they were engaged but also obtained the light which they desired, by the help of which they were able with greater safety and with more plentiful blessings to continue the efforts which they had been making in the matter of which We are now speaking. Hence it happened that the differences of opinion which prevailed among them were either removed or their acrimony diminished and the discussion laid aside. In the work which they had undertaken this was effected, viz.: that in their efforts for the elevation of the poorer classes, especially in those places where the trouble is greatest, many new enterprises were set on foot; those which were already established were increased and all reaped the blessing of a greater stability imparted to them. Some of these works were called *Bureaus of the People*, their object being to supply information. Rural Savings Banks had been established, and various Associations, some for mutual aid, others, of relief, were organized. There were Working Men's Societies and other enterprises for work or beneficence Thus under the auspices of the Church, united action of Catholics was secured as well as wise discrimination exercised in the distribution of help for the poor, who are often as badly dealt with by chicanery and exploitation of their necessities, as they are oppressed by indigence and toil. These schemes of popular benevolence were, at first, distinguished by no particular appellation. The name of *Christian Socialism* with its derivatives which was adopted by some was very properly allowed to fall into disuse. Afterwards some asked to have it called *The Popular Christian Movement* In the countries most concerned with this matter, there are some who are known as *Christian Socialists.* Elsewhere the movement is described as *Christian Democracy*, and its partisans *Christian Democrats*, in contradistinction to those who are designated as *Socialists*, and whose system is known as *Social Democracy.* Not much exception is taken to the former, *i e.*, *Christian Socialism*, but many excellent men find the term *Christian Democracy* objectionable. They hold it to be very ambiguous and for this reason open to two objections. It seems by implication to covertly favor popular government, and to disparage other methods of political administration. Secondly, it appears to belittle religion by restricting its scope to the care of the poor, as if the other sections of Society were not of its concern. More than that, under the shadow of its name, there might easily lurk a design to attack all legitimate power either civil or sacred. Wherefore, since this discussion is now so widespread, so exaggerated and so bitter, the consciousness of duty warns Us to put a check on this controversy and to define what Catholics are to think on this matter. We also propose to describe how the movement may extend its scope and be made more useful to the commonwealth.

What *Social Democracy* is and what *Christian Democracy* ought to be. assuredly no one can doubt. The first, with due

consideration to the greater or less intemperance of its utterance, is carried to such an excess by many as to maintain
that there is really nothing existing above the natural order
of things, and that the acquirement and enjoyment of corporal and external goods constitute man's happiness. It
aims at putting all government in the hands of the people,
reducing all ranks to the same level, abolishing all distinction
of class, and finally introducing community of goods. Hence,
the right of ownership is to be abrogated, and whatever
property a man possesses, or whatever means of livelihood
he has, is to be common to all.

As against this, *Christian Democracy*, by the fact that it is
Christian, is built, and necessarily so, on the basic principles
of Divine Faith, and provides for the betterment of the
masses, with the ulterior object of availing itself of the occasion to fashion their minds for things which are everlasting.
Hence, for *Christian Democracy* justice is sacred; it must
maintain that the right of acquiring and possessing property
cannot be impugned, and it must safeguard the various distinctions and degrees which are indispensable in every well-
ordered commonwealth. Finally it must endeavor to preserve in every human society the form and the character
which God ever impresses on it. It is clear, therefore, that
there is nothing in common between *Social* and *Christian
Democracy*. They differ from each other as much as the sect
of Socialism differs from the profession of Christianity.

Moreover it would be a crime to distort this name of
Christian Democracy to politics, for although democracy,
both in its philological and philosophical significations,
implies popular government, yet in its present application it
is so to be employed that, removing from it all political significance, it is to mean nothing else than a benevolent and
Christian movement in behalf of the people. For the laws
of nature and of the Gospel, which by right are superior to
all human contingencies, are necessarily independent of all
modifications of civil government, while at the same time
they are in concord with everything that is not repugnant to
morality and justice. They are, therefore, and they must
remain absolutely free from political parties, and have noth-

ing to do with the various changes of administration which
may occur in a nation, so that Catholics may and ought to
be citizens according to the constitution of any state, guided
as they are by those laws which command them to love God
above all things, and their neighbors as themselves. This has
always been the discipline of the Church. The Roman Pon-
tiffs acted upon this principle, whenever they dealt with different countries, no matter what might be the character of
their governments. Hence, the mind and the action of Catholics who are devoted to the amelioration of the working
classes, can never be actuated with the purpose of favoring
and introducing one government in place of another.

In the same manner, from *Christian Democracy*, We must
remove another possible subject of reproach, namely, that
while looking after the advantage of the working people they
should act in such a manner as to forget the upper classes of
Society ; for they also are of the greatest use in preserving
and perfecting the commonwealth. As We have explained,
the Christian law of charity will prevent Us from so doing.
For it extends to all classes of Society, and all should be
treated as members of the same family, as children of the
same Heavenly Father, as redeemed by the same Saviour,
and called to the same eternal heritage. Hence the doctrine
of the Apostle who warns us that : " we are one body and one
spirit called to the one hope in our vocation , one Lord, one
Faith and one Baptism ; one God and the Father of all who
is above all, and through all, and in us all " Wherefore
on account of the nature of the union which exists between
the different classes of Society and which Christian brotherhood makes still closer, it follows that no matter how great
Our devotion may be in helping the people, We should all
the more keep Our hold upon the upper classes, because association with them is proper and necessary, as We shall explain later on, for the happy issue of the work in which We
are engaged.

Let there be no question of fostering under this name of
Christian Democracy any intention of diminishing the spirit
of obedience, or of withdrawing people from their lawful
rulers. Both the natural and the Christian law command

us to revere those who, in their various grades, are above us in the State, and to submit ourselves to their just commands· It is quite in keeping with our dignity as men and Christians to obey, not only exteriorly but from the heart, as the Apostle expresses it, *for conscience sake,* when he commands us to keep our soul subject to the higher powers. It is abhorrent to the profession of a Christian for any one to be unwilling to be subject and obedient to those who rule in the Church, and first of all to the bishops whom (without prejudice to the universal power of the Roman Pontiff) "the Holy Ghost has placed to rule the Church of God which Christ has purchased by His blood" (Acts xx. 28). He who thinks or acts otherwise is guilty of ignoring the grave precept of the Apostle who bids us to obey our rulers and to be subject to them, for they watch, having to give an account of our souls. Let the faithful everywhere implant these principles deep in their souls, and put them in practice in their daily life, and let the ministers of the Gospel meditate them profoundly, and incessantly labor not merely by exhortation but especially by example to make them enter into the souls of others.

We have recalled these matters which on other occasions We have made the subject of Our instructions, in the hope that all dissension about the name of *Christian Democracy* will cease and that all suspicion of any danger coming from what the name signifies will be put at rest. And with reason do We hope so; for neglecting the opinions of certain men, with regard to the power and the efficacy of this kind of *Christian Democracy,* which at times are exaggerated and are not free from error, let no one however condemn that zeal which, according to the natural and Divine law, has this for its object, viz.. to make the condition of those who toil more tolerable, to enable them to obtain, little by little, those means by which they may provide for the future; to help them to practice in public and in private the duties which morality and religion inculcate; to aid them to feel that they are not animals but men, not heathens but Christians, and so to enable them to strive more zealously and more eagerly for the one thing which is necessary, viz.: that ultimate good for which we are all born into this world. This is the intention; this is the work of those who wish that the people should be animated by Christian sentiments and should be protected from the contamination of Socialism which threatens them.

We have designedly made mention here of virtue and religion. For, it is the opinion of some, and the error is already very common, that the social question is merely an economic one, whereas in point of fact, it is above all a moral and religious matter, and for that reason must be settled by the principles of morality and according to the dictates of religion   For even though wages are doubled and the hours of labor are shortened and food is cheapened, yet if the workingman hearkens to the doctrines that are taught on this subject, as he is prone to do, and is prompted by the examples set before him to throw off respect for God and to enter upon a life of immorality, his labors and his gain will avail him naught.

Trial and experience have made it abundantly clear that many a workman lives in cramped and miserable quarters, in spite of his shorter hours and larger wages, simply because he has cast aside the restraints of morality and religion.   Take away the instinct which Christian virtue has planted and nurtured in men's hearts, take away prudence, temperance, frugality, patience and other correct natural habits, no matter how much he may strive, he will never achieve prosperity.   That is the reason why We have incessantly exhorted Catholics to enter these associations for bettering the condition of the laboring classes, and to organize other undertakings with the same object in view; but We have likewise warned them that all this should be done under the auspices of religion, with its help and under its guidance.

The zeal of Catholics on behalf of the masses is especially noteworthy by the fact that it is engaged in the very field in which, under the benign inspiration of the Church, the active industry of charity has always labored, adapting itself in all cases to the varying exigencies of the times.   For the law of mutual charity perfects, as it were, the law of justice,

not merely by giving each man his due and in not impeding
him in the exercise of his rights, but also by befriending
him in case of need, "not with the word alone, or the lips,
but in deed and in truth"; being mindful of what Christ so
lovingly said to His own· "A new commandment I give
unto you, that you love one another as I have loved you,
that you love also one another By this shall all men know
that you are My disciples, if you have love one for the other."
This zeal in coming to the rescue of Our fellowmen should,
of course, be solicitous, first for the imperishable good of
the soul, but it must not neglect what is necessary and helpful for the body.

We should remember what Christ said to the disciples of
the Baptist who asked Him. "Art Thou He that art to
come or look we for another?" He invoked, as the proof
of the mission given to Him among men, His exercise of
charity, quoting for them the text of Isaias: "The blind
see, the lame walk, the lepers are cleansed, the deaf hear,
the dead rise again, the poor have the gospel preached
to them" (Matth. xi 5). And speaking also of the last
judgment and of the rewards and punishments He will
assign, He declared that He would take special account of
the charity men exercised towards each other. And in that
discourse there is one thing that especially excites our surprise, viz.: that Christ omits those works of mercy which
comfort the soul and refers only to external works which,
although done in behalf of men, He regards as being done
to Himself "For I was hungry and you gave Me to eat; I
was thirsty and you gave Me to drink; I was a stranger and
you took Me in; naked and you covered Me; sick and you
visited Me; I was in prison and you came to Me" (Matth.
xxv. 35).

To the teachings which enjoin the twofold charity of
spiritual and corporal works, Christ adds His own example
so that no one may fail to recognize the importance which
He attaches to it In the present instance we recall the
sweet words that came from His paternal heart: "I have
pity on the multitude" (Mark vii. 2), as well as the desire He
had to assist them even if it were necessary to invoke His

miraculous power. Of His tender compassion we have the proclamation made in Holy Writ, viz.: that "He went about doing good and healing all that were oppressed by the devil " (Acts x. 38). This law of charity which He imposed upon His apostles they in the most holy and zealous way put into practice; and after them those who embraced Christianity originated that wonderful variety of institutions for alleviating all the miseries by which mankind is afflicted. And these institutions carried on and continually increased their powers of relief and were the especial glories of Christianity and of the civilization of which it was the source, so that right-minded men never fail to admire those foundations, aware as they are of the proneness of men to concern themselves about their own and neglect the needs of others.

Nor are we to eliminate from the list of good works the giving of money for charity, in pursuance of what Christ has said: "But yet that which remaineth, give alms " (Luke xi. 41). Against this, the Socialist cries out and demands its abolition as injurious to the native dignity of man. But if it is done in the manner which the Scripture enjoins (Matth. vi 2), and in conformity with the true Christian spirit, it neither connotes pride in the giver nor inflicts shame upon the one who receives. Far from being dishonorable for man it draws closer the bonds of human society by augmenting the force of the obligation of the duties which men are under with regard to each other. No one is so rich that he does not need another's help, no one so poor as not to be useful in some way to his fellowman; and the disposition to ask assistance from others with confidence, and to grant it with kindness, is part of our very nature. Thus justice and charity are so linked with each other, under the equable and sweet law of Christ, as to form an admirable cohesive power in human society and to lead all of its members to exercise a sort of providence in looking after their own and in seeking the common good as well.

As regards not merely the temporary aid given to the laboring classes, but the establishment of permanent institutions in their behalf, it is most commendable for charity to undertake them. It will thus see that more certain and more reliable means of assistance will be afforded to the necessitous. That kind of help is especially worthy of recognition which forms the minds of mechanics and laborers to thrift and foresight so that in course of time they may be able, in part at least, to look out for themselves. To aim at that is not only to dignify the duty of the rich towards the poor, but to elevate the poor themselves; for while it urges them to work for a better degree of comfort in their manner of living, it preserves them meantime from danger by checking extravagance in their desires, and acts as a spur in the practice of the virtues proper to their state. Since, therefore, this is of such great avail and so much in keeping with the spirit of the times, it is a worthy object for charity to undertake with all prudence and zeal.

Let it be understood, therefore, that this devotion of Catholics to comfort and elevate the mass of the people is in keeping with the spirit of the Church and is most conformable to the examples which the Church has always held up for imitation. It matters very little whether it goes under the name of " *The Popular Christian Movement*," or " *Christian Democracy,*" if the instructions that have been given by Us be fully carried out with the submission that is due. But it is of the greatest importance that Catholics should be one in mind, will and action in a matter of such great moment. And it is also of importance that the influence of these undertakings should be extended by the multiplication of men and means devoted to the same object.

Especially must there be appeals to the kindly assistance of those whose rank, worldly wealth and culture give them importance in the community. If their help is excluded, scarcely anything can be done which will be of any assistance for the wants which now clamor for satisfaction in this matter of the well-being of the people. Assuredly the more earnestly many of those who are prominent in the State conspire effectively to attain that object the quicker and surer will the end be reached. We wish them to understand that they are not at all free to look after or neglect those who happen to be beneath them, but that it is a strict duty which binds them. For no one lives only for his personal advantage in a community ; he lives for the common good as well, so that when, others cannot contribute their share for the general object, those who can do so are obliged to make up the deficiency. The very extent of the benefits they have received increases the burden of their responsibility, and a stricter account will have to be rendered to God who bestowed those blessings upon them   What should also urge all to the fulfilment of their duty in this regard is the widespread disaster which will eventually fall upon all classes of Society, if this assistance does not arrive in time ; and therefore is it that he who neglects the cause of the distressed poor is not doing his duty to himself or to the State.

If this social movement extends its scope far and wide in a true Christian fashion, and grows in its proper and genuine spirit, there will be no danger, as is feared, that those other institutions, which the piety of our ancestors his established and which are now flourishing, will decline or be absorbed by new foundations. Both of them spring from the same root of charity and religion, and not only do not conflict with each other, but can be made to coalesce and combine so perfectly as to provide by a union of their benevolent resources in a more efficacious manner against the graver perils and necessities of the people which confront us to-day.

The condition of things at present proclaims, and proclaims vehemently, that there is need for a union of brave minds with all the resources they can command.   The harvest of misery is before Our eyes, and the dreadful projects of the most disastrous national upheavals are threatening Us from the growing power of the socialistic movement   They have insidiously worked their way into the very heart of the State, and in the darkness of their secret gatherings, and in the open light of day, in their writings and their harangues, they are urging the masses onward to sedition ; they fling aside religious discipline, they scorn duties and clamor only for rights ; they are working incessantly on the multitudes of the needy which daily grow greater, and which, because of their poverty, are easily deluded and hurried off into ways that are evil. It is equally the concern of the State and of Religion, and all good men should deem it a sacred duty to preserve and guard both in the honor which is their due.

That this most desirable agreement of wills should be maintained, it is essential that all refrain from giving any causes of dissension in hurting and alienating the minds of others. Hence in newspapers and in speeches to the people, let them avoid subtle and useless questions which are neither easy to solve nor to understand except by minds of unusual ability and only after the most serious study. It is quite natural for people to think differently in doubtful questions, but those who address themselves to these subjects in a proper spirit will preserve their mental calm and not forget the respect which is due to those who differ from them. If minds see things in another light it is not necessary to become alienated forthwith To whatever opinion a man's judgment may incline, if the matter is yet open to discussion let him keep it, provided his mental attitude is such that he is ready to yield if the Holy See should otherwise decide.

This Catholic action, of whatever description it may be, will work with greater effect if all of the various associations, while preserving their individual rights, move together under one primary and directive force

In Italy We desire that this directive force should emanate from the Catholic Congresses and Reunions so often praised by Us, to further which Our Predecessor and We Ourselves have ordered that these meetings should be controlled and guided by the Bishops of the country. So let it be for other nations, in case there be any leading organization of this description to which this matter has been legitimately entrusted.

Now in all questions of this sort where the interests of the Church and the Christian people are so closely allied, it is evident what they who are in the sacred ministry should do, and it is clear how industrious they should be in inculcating right doctrine and in teaching the duties of prudence and charity. To go out and move among the people, to exert a healthy influence on them by adapting themselves to the present condition of things, is what more than once in addressing the clergy We have advised. More frequently also in writing to the Bishops and other dignitaries of the Church, and especially of late (to the Minister General of the Minorites, November 25, 1898) We have lauded this affectionate solicitude for the people and declared it to be the especial duty of both the secular and regular clergy. But in the fulfilment of this obligation let there be the greatest caution and prudence exerted, and let it be done after the fashion of the saints. Francis, who was poor and humble, Vincent of Paul, the Father of the afflicted classes, and very many others whom the Church keeps ever in her memory, were wont to lavish their care upon the people, but in such wise as not to be engrossed overmuch or to be unmindful of themselves or to let it prevent them from laboring with the same assiduity in the perfection of their own soul and the cultivation of virtue.

There remains one thing upon which We desire to insist very strongly, in which not only the ministers of the Gospel, but also all those who are devoting themselves to the cause of the people, can with very little difficulty bring about a most commendable result. That is to inculcate in the minds of the people, in a brotherly way and whenever the opportunity presents itself, the following principles, viz.: to keep aloof on all occasions from seditious acts and seditious men ; to guard inviolate the rights of others; to show a proper respect to superiors; to willingly perform the work in which they are employed ; not to grow weary of the restraint of family life which in many ways is so advantageous ; to keep to their religious practices above all, and in their hardships and trials to have recourse to the Church for consolation. In the furtherance of all this, it is very efficacious to propose the splendid example of the Holy Family of Nazareth, and to advise the invocation of its protection, and it also helps to remind the people of the examples of sanctity which have shone in the midst of poverty, and to hold up before them the reward that awaits them in the better life to come.

Finally We recur again to what We have already declared

and We insist upon it most solemnly, viz.: that whatever projects individuals or associations form in this matter should be done with due regard to Episcopal authority and absolutely under Episcopal guidance. Let them not be led astray by an excessive zeal in the cause of charity. If it leads them to be wanting in proper submission it is not a sincere zeal; it will not have any useful result and cannot be acceptable to God. God delights in the souls of those who put aside their own designs and obey the rulers of His Church as if they were obeying Him; He assists them even when they attempt difficult things and benignly leads them to their desired end. Let them show also examples of virtue, so as to prove that a Christian is a hater of idleness and indulgence, that he gives willingly from his goods for the help of others, and that he stands firm and unconquered in the midst of adversity. Examples of that kind have a power of moving people to dispositions of soul that make for salvation, and have all the greater force as the condition of those who give them is higher in the social scale.

We exhort you, Venerable Brethren, to provide for all this, as the necessities of men and of places may require, according to your prudence and your zeal, meeting as usual in council to combine with each other in your plans for the furtherance of these projects. Let your solicitude watch and let your authority be effective in controlling, compelling, and also in preventing, lest any one under the pretext of good should cause the rigor of sacred discipline to be relaxed or the order which Christ has established in His Church to be disturbed. Thus by the correct, concurrent, and ever-increasing labor of all Catholics, the truth will flash out more brilliantly than ever, viz.. that truth and true prosperity flourish especially among those people whom the Church controls and influences: and that she holds it as her sacred duty to admonish every one of what the law of God enjoins, to unite the rich and the poor in the bonds of fraternal charity, and to lift up and strengthen men's souls in the times when adversity presses heavily upon them.

Let Our commands and Our wishes be confirmed by the words which are so full of apostolic charity which the

Blessed Paul addressed to the Romans. "I beseech you therefore, brethren, be reformed in the newness of your mind, he that giveth, with simplicity; he that ruleth, with carefulness; he that showeth mercy, with cheerfulness. Let love be without dissimulation—hating that which is evil; clinging to that which is good; loving one another with the charity of brotherhood; with honor preventing one another; in carefulness, not slothful; rejoicing in hope; patient in tribulation; instant in prayer, communicating to the necessities of the saints; pursuing hospitality. Rejoice with them that rejoice; weep with them that weep; being of one mind to one another, to no man rendering evil for evil, providing good things not only in the sight of God but also in the sight of men."

As a pledge of these benefits receive the Apostolic Benediction which, Venerable Brethren, We grant most lovingly in the Lord to you and your clergy and people.

Given at Rome in St. Peter's, the 18th day of January 1901, in the 23d year of Our Pontificate.

Leo XIII., Pope.

ALPHABETICAL INDEX.

PRINTED BY BENZIGER BROTHERS, NEW YORK.

STANDARD CATHOLIC BOOKS

PUBLISHED BY

BENZIGER BROTHERS,

CINCINNATI: NEW YORK: CHICAGO:
343 MAIN ST.   36-38 BARCLAY ST.   211–213 MADISON ST.

Books marked *net* are such where ten per cent. must be added for postage. Thus a book advertised as *net* $1.00 will be sent postpaid on receipt of $1.10. Books not marked *net* will be sent postpaid on receipt of advertised price.

DOCTRINE, INSTRUCTION, DEVOTION.

ABANDONMENT. Caussade, S.J.	*net,* 0 50
ADORATION OF BLESSED SACRAMENT. Tesniere.	*net,* 1 25
ALPHONSUS LIGUORI, WORKS OF, ST. 22 vols. Each,	*net,* 1 50
ANECDOTES ILLUSTRATING THE CATECHISM. Spirago.	*net,* 1 50
ANGLICAN ORDINATIONS. Semple.	*net,* 0 35
ART OF PROFITING BY OUR FAULTS. Tissot.	*net,* 0 50
BIBLE HISTORY, EXPLANATION. Nash.	*net,* 1 60
BIBLE, THE HOLY.	1 00
BOOK OF THE PROFESSED. Vol. I, II & III. Each,	*net,* 0 75
BOYS' AND GIRLS' MISSION BOOK. By the Redemptorist Fathers.	0 35
BOY-SAVERS' GUIDE. Quin, S.J.	*net,* 1 35
BREAD OF LIFE, THE. Complete Communion Book.	*net,* 0 75
CATECHISM EXPLAINED, THE. Spirago-Clarke.	*net,* 2 50
CATHOLIC BELIEF. Faa di Bruno. Paper, *net,* 0.15; cloth,	*net,* 0 35
CATHOLIC CEREMONIES. Durand. Paper, *net,* 0.15; cloth,	*net,* 0 35
CATHOLIC GIRLS' GUIDE. Lasance.	1 25
CATHOLIC PRACTICE AT CHURCH AND AT HOME. Klauder.	
Paper, *net,* 0.20; cloth,	*net,* 0 40
CEREMONIAL FOR ALTAR BOYS. Britt, O.S.B.	*net,* 0 35
CHARACTERISTICS OF TRUE DEVOTION. Grou, S.J.	*net,* 0 75
CHRISTIAN APOLOGETICS. Devivier.	*net,* 2 00
CHRISTIAN DOCTRINE, SPIRAGO'S METHOD OF.	*net,* 1 50
CHRISTIAN EDUCATION. O'Connell.	*net,* 0 60
CHRISTIAN FATHER. Cramer. Paper, *net,* 0.13; cloth,	*net,* 0 25
CHRISTIAN MOTHER. Cramer. Paper, *net,* 0.13; cloth,	*net,* 0 25
CHRISTIAN SCHOOL. McFaul. Paper,	0 10
CONFESSION. Paper,	0 05
CONFESSION AND ITS BENEFITS. Girardey.	0 25
CONFIRMATION. Paper,	0 05
COUNSELS OF ST. ANGELA.	*net,* 0 25
DEFENCE OF THE SEVEN SACRAMENTS, HENRY VIII.	
O'Donovan.	*net,* 2 00
DEVOTION TO SACRED HEART OF JESUS. Noldin, S.J.	*net,* 1 25
DEVOTIONS AND PRAYERS FOR THE SICK-ROOM. Krebs,	
C.SS.R. Cloth,	*net,* 1 25
DEVOTIONS AND PRAYERS BY ST. ALPHONSUS.	*net,* 1 25
DEVOTIONS FOR FIRST FRIDAY. Huguet.	*net,* 0 40
DEVOUT CHILD, THE. A prayer-book for children.	0 10
DIGNITY AND DUTIES OF THE PRIEST. Liguori.	*net,* 1 50
DIVINE GRACE. Wirth.	*net,* 1 60
DIVINE OFFICE. Liguori.	*net,* 1 50
EDUCATION OF OUR GIRLS. Shields.	*net,* 1 00
EPISTLES AND GOSPELS. Large print.	*net,* 0 25
EUCHARISTIC CHRIST. Tesniere.	*net,* 1 25
EUCHARISTIC SOUL ELEVATIONS. Stadelman.	*net,* 0 50
EXPLANATION OF THE BALTIMORE CATECHISM. Kinkead.	*net,* 1 00
EXPLANATION OF THE GOSPELS. Lambert. Paper, *net,* 0.15;	
cloth,	*net,* 0 35

2

3

PASSION FLOWERS. Poems. HILL. *net*, 1 25
PASSION, THOUGHTS AND AFFECTIONS ON, FOR EVERY
    DAY OF THE YEAR. BERGAMO. *net*, 2 00
PEARLS FROM FABER. BRUNOWE. *net*, 0 50
PEARLS OF PRAYER. 0 35
PERFECT RELIGIOUS, THE. DE LA MOTTE. *net*, 1 00
PIOUS PREPARATION FOR FIRST HOLY COMMUNION.
    LASANCE. Cloth. *net*, 0 75
POCKET MANUAL. A Vest-Pocket Prayer-Book in very large type. 0 25
POPULAR INSTRUCTIONS ON MARRIAGE. GIRARDEY, C.SS.R.
    Paper, *net*, 0.13; cloth, *net*, 0 25
POPULAR INSTRUCTIONS ON PRAYER. GIRARDEY, C.SS.R.
    Paper, *net*, 0.13; cloth, *net*, 0 25
POPULAR INSTRUCTIONS TO PARENTS. GIRARDEY, C.SS.R.
    Paper, *net*, 0.13; cloth, *net*, 0 25
PRAYER-BOOK FOR RELIGIOUS. LASANCE. *net*, 1 50
PREACHING. Vol. XV. LIGUORI. *net*, 1 50
PREPARATION FOR DEATH. LIGUORI. *net*, 1 50
PRIVATE RETREAT FOR RELIGIOUS. GEIERMANN. *net*, 1 50
QUEEN'S FESTIVALS. 0 60
RELIGION OF SOCIALISM, THE CHARACTERISTICS AND.
    MING, S.J. *net*, 1 50
RELIGIOUS STATE, THE. LIGUORI. *net*, 0 50
ROSARY, THE CROWN OF MARY. By a Dominican Father. 0 10
ROSARY, THE. Scenes and Thoughts. GARESCHE, S.J. *net*, 0 50
ROSARY, THE MOST HOLY. Meditations. CRAMER. *net*, 0 50
RULES OF LIFE FOR THE PASTOR OF SOULS. SLATER
    RAUCH. *net*, 1 25
SACRAMENTALS. LAMBING, D.D. Paper, *net*, 0.15; cloth, *net*, 0 35
SACRAMENTALS — Prayer, etc. MÜLLER, C.SS.R. *net*, 1 00
SACRED HEART BOOK, THE. LASANCE. *net*, 0 75
SACRED HEART, DEVOTION TO, FOR FIRST FRIDAY OF
    EVERY MONTH. By PERE HUGUET. *net*, 0 40
SACRED HEART, NEW MANUAL OF. 0 50
SACRIFICE OF MASS WORTHILY CELEBRATED. CHAIGNON, S.J.
     net, 1 50
ST. ANTHONY. KELLER. *net*, 0 75
ST. FRANCIS OF ASSISI. Social Reformer. DUBOIS, S.M. *net*, 1 00
SECRET OF SANCTITY. ST. FRANCIS DE SALES. *net*, 1 00
SEEDLINGS. COLTON. *net*, 1 00
SERAPHIC GUIDE, THE. A Manual for the Members of the
    Third Order of St. Francis. By a Franciscan Father. 0 60
SHORT CONFERENCES ON THE LITTLE OFFICE OF THE
    IMMACULATE CONCEPTION. RAINER. *net*, 0 50
SHORT STORIES ON CHRISTIAN DOCTRINE. From the French
    by McMAHON. *net*, 1 00
SHORT VISITS TO THE BLESSED SACRAMENT. LASANCE. 0 25
SICK CALLS. MULLIGAN. *net*, 1/00
SOCIALISM AND CHRISTIANITY. STANG, D.D. *net*, 1 00
SOCIALISM. CATHREIN, S.J. *net*, 1 50
SODALIST'S VADE MECUM. 0 50
SPIRIT OF SACRIFICE, THE. GIRAUD. *net*, 2 00
SPIRITUAL DESPONDENCY AND TEMPTATIONS. MICHEL, S.J.
     net, 1 25
SPIRITUAL EXERCISES FOR TEN DAYS' RETREAT. SMETANA. *net*, 1 00
SPIRITUAL PEPPER AND SALT. STANG. Paper, *net*, 0.20; cloth, *net*, 0 40
STORY OF THE FRIENDS OF JESUS. 0 60
STORIES FOR FIRST COMMUNICANTS. KELLER, D.D. *net*, 0 50
STRIVING AFTER PERFECTION. BAYMA, S.J. *net*, 1 00
SUNDAY SCHOOL DIRECTOR'S GUIDE TO SUCCESS. SLOAN. *net*, 1 00
SUNDAY SCHOOL TEACHER'S GUIDE TO SUCCESS. SLOAN. *net*, 0 75
SURE WAY TO A HAPPY MARRIAGE. TAYLOR. Paper, *net*,
    0.13; cloth, *net*, 0 25
TALKS WITH LITTLE ONES ABOUT APOSTLES' CREED. 0 60
THOUGHTS ON THE RELIGIOUS LIFE. LASANCE. *net*, 1 50
TRUE POLITENESS. DEMORE. *net*, 0 75
TRUE SPOUSE OF JESUS CHRIST. LIGUORI. 2 vols. *net*, 3 00
    The same, one-volume edition. *net*, 1 25
VENERATION OF THE BLESSED VIRGIN. ROHNER, O.S.B. *net*, 1 25

VEST-POCKET GEMS OF DEVOTION. 0 20
VICTORIES OF THE MARTYRS. Liguori. *net,* 1 50
VISITS, SHORT, TO BLESSED SACRAMENT. Lasance. 0 25
VISITS TO JESUS IN THE BLESSED SACRAMENT. McAuliffe, *net,* 0 50
VISITS TO JESUS IN THE TABERNACLE. Lasance. *net,* 1 25
VISITS TO THE MOST HOLY SACRAMENT and to the Blessed
   Virgin Mary. Liguori. *net,* 0 50
VOCATIONS EXPLAINED. 0 10
WAY OF INTERIOR PEACE. De Lehen, S.J. *net,* 1 50
WAY OF SALVATION AND PERFECTION. Liguori. *net,* 1 50
WAY OF THE CROSS. Paper, 0 05
WAY OF THE CROSS. By a Jesuit Father. *net,* 0 15
WAY OF THE CROSS. According to Method of St. Francis
   Assisi. *net,* 0 15
WAY OF THE CROSS. According to Eucharistic Method. *net,* 0 15
WAY OF THE CROSS. According to Method of St. Alphonsus
   Liguori. *net,* 0 15
WHAT THE CHURCH TEACHES. Drury. Paper, *net,* 0.20;
   cloth, *net,* 0 40

JUVENILES.

ADVENTURE WITH THE APACHES. Ferry. 0 45
ARMORER OF SOLINGEN. Herchenbach. 0 45
AS TRUE AS GOLD. Mannix. 0 45
BELL FOUNDRY, THE. Von Schaching. 0 45
BERKELEYS, THE. Wight. 0 45
BEARNE, REV. DAVID, S.J.
   SHEER PLUCK. 0 85
   MELOR OF THE SILVER HAND. 0 85
   THE GUILD BOYS' PLAY AT RIDINGDALE. 0 85
   NEW BOYS AT RIDINGDALE. 0 85
   THE WITCH OF RIDINGDALE. 0 85
   RIDINGDALE FLOWER SHOW. 0 85
   CHARLIE CHITTYWICK. 0 85
BETWEEN FRIENDS. Aumerle. 0 45
BISTOURI. By A. Melandri. 0 45
BLACK LADY AND ROBIN RED BREAST. By Canon Schmid. 0 25
BLISSYLVANIA POST-OFFICE. By Marion Ames Taggart. 0 45
BOB O'LINK. Waggaman. 0 45
BOYS IN THE BLOCK. By Maurice F. Egan. 0 25
BUNT AND BILL. Clara Mulholland. 0 45
BUZZER'S CHRISTMAS. By Mary T. Waggaman. 0 25
BY BRANSCOMBE RIVER. By Marion Ames Taggart. 0 45
CAKE AND THE EASTER EGGS. By Canon Schmid. 0 25
CANARY BIRD. By Canon Schmid. 0 45
CARROLL DARE. By Mary T. Waggaman. 1 25
THE CHILDREN OF CUPA. Mannix. 0 45
CUPA REVISITED. Mannix. 0 45
COLLEGE BOY, A. By Anthony Yorke. 0 85
COPUS, REV. J. E., S.J.:
   HARRY RUSSELL. 0 85
   SHADOWS LIFTED. 0 85
   ST. CUTHBERT'S. 0 85
   TOM LOSELY: Boy. 0 85
DADDY DAN. Waggaman. 0 45
DAUGHTER OF KINGS, A. Hinkson. 1 25
DIMPLING'S SUCCESS. By Clara Mulholland. 0 45
DOLLAR HUNT, THE. Martin. 0 45
DOUBLE KNOT AND OTHER STORIES, A. Waggaman and Others. 1 25
EVERY-DAY GIRL, AN. By Mary C. Crowley. 0 45
FATAL DIAMONDS. By E. C. Donnelly. 0 25
FINN, REV. F. J., S.J.
   HIS FIRST AND LAST APPEARANCE. Illustrated. 1 00
   THE BEST FOOT FORWARD. 0 85
   THAT FOOTBALL GAME. 0 85
   ETHELRED PRESTON. 0 85
   CLAUDE LIGHTFOOT. 0 85
   HARRY DEE. 0 85
   TOM PLAYFAIR. 0 85

FINN, REV. F. J., S.J. (Cont'd.)
PERCY WYNN.   0 85
MOSTLY BOYS.   0 85
"BUT THY LOVE AND THY GRACE."   1 00
MY STRANGE FRIEND.   0 25
FIVE O'CLOCK STORIES; or, The Old Tales Told Again.   0 75
FLOWER OF THE FLOCK, THE, and the Badgers of Belmont. EGAN.   0 85
FOR THE WHITE ROSE. HINKSON.   0 45
FRED'S LITTLE DAUGHTER. SMITH.   0 45
GODFREY THE HERMIT. SCHMID.   0 25
GOLDEN LILY, THE. HINKSON.   0 45
GREAT CAPTAIN, THE. HINKSON.   0 45
HALDEMAN CHILDREN, THE. MANNIX.   0 45
HARMONY FLATS. WHITMIRE.   0 85
HEIR OF DREAMS, AN. O'MALLEY.   0 45
HOP BLOSSOMS. SCHMID.   0 25
HOSTAGE OF WAR, A. BONESTEEL.   0 45
HOW THEY WORKED THEIR WAY. EGAN.   0 75
INUNDATION, THE. SCHMID.   0 45
"JACK." By a Religious of The Society of The Holy Child Jesus.   0 45
JACK HILDRETH AMONG THE INDIANS. 2 vols., each,   0 85
JACK HILDRETH ON THE NILE. TAGGART. Cloth,   0 85
JACK O'LANTERN. WAGGAMAN.   0 45
JUVENILE ROUND TABLE. First, Second, Third Series. Each,   1 00
KLONDIKE PICNIC. DONNELLY.   0 85
LAMP OF THE SANCTUARY. WISEMAN.   0 25
LEGENDS OF THE HOLY CHILD JESUS from Many Lands. LUTZ.   0 75
LITTLE MISSY. WAGGAMAN.   0 45
LOYAL BLUE AND ROYAL SCARLET. TAGGART.   0 85
MADCAP SET AT ST. ANNE'S. BRUNOWE.   0 45
MAKING OF MORTLAKE. COPUS, S.J.   0 85
MARKS OF THE BEAR CLAWS. SPALDING, S.J.   0 85
MARY TRACY'S FORTUNE. SADLIER.   0 45
MASTER FRIDOLIN. GIEHRL.   0 25
MILLY AVELING. SMITH. Cloth,   0 85
MORE FIVE O'CLOCK STORIES. In Prose and Verse. By a Religious
  of The Society of The Holy Child Jesus.   0 75
MYSTERIOUS DOORWAY. SADLIER.   0 45
MYSTERY OF CLEVERLY. BARTON.   0 85
MYSTERY OF HORNBY HALL. SADLIER.   0 85
MY STRANGE FRIEND. FINN.   0 25
NAN NOBODY. WAGGAMAN.   0 45
NEW SCHOLAR OF ST. ANNE'S. BRUNOWE.   0 85
OLD CHARLMONT'S SEED-BED. SMITH.   0 25
OLD ROBBER'S CASTLE. SCHMID.   0 25
ONE AFTERNOON AND OTHER STORIES. TAGGART.   1 25
OUR BOYS' AND GIRLS' LIBRARY. 14 vols., each,   0 25
OVERSEER OF MAHLBOURG. SCHMID.   0 25
PANCHO AND PANCHITA. MANNIX.   0 45
PAULINE ARCHER. SADLIER.   0 45
PETRONILLA. DONNELLY.   0 85
PICKLE AND PEPPER. DORSEY.   0 85
PILGRIM FROM IRELAND. CARNOT.   0 45
PLAYWATER PLOT, THE. WAGGAMAN.   0 60
QUEEN'S PAGE. HINKSON.   0 45
RECRUIT TOMMY COLLINS. BONESTEEL.   0 45
ROSE BUSH. SCHMID.   0 25
ROUND THE WORLD. Vols. I, II, III, IV, V, VI. Each,   1 00
SEA-GULL'S ROCK. SANDEAU.   0 45
SHADOWS LIFTED. COPUS, S.J.   0 85
SPALDING, REV. H., S.J.:
    THE MARKS OF THE BEAR CLAWS.   0 85
    CAVE BY THE BEECH FORK.   0 85
    THE SHERIFF OF THE BEECH FORK.   0 85
    THE RACE FOR COPPER ISLAND.   0 85
STRONG ARM OF AVALON. WAGGAMAN.   0 85
SUMMER AT WOODVILLE. SADLIER.   0 45
TALES AND LEGENDS OF THE MIDDLE AGES. DE CAPELLA.   0 75
TALISMAN, THE. SADLIER.   0 60

TAMING OF POLLY. Dorsey.	0 85
THREE GIRLS AND ESPECIALLY ONE. Taggart.	0 45
THREE LITTLE KINGS Giehrl.	0 25
TOM'S LUCKPOT Waggaman.	0 45
TOORALLADY Walsh.	0 45
TRANSPLANTING OF TESSIE Waggaman.	0 60
TREASURE OF NUGGET MOUNTAIN. Taggart.	0 85
TWO LITTLE GIRLS Mack	0 45
VIOLIN MAKER, THE Smith	0 45
WAGER OF GERALD O'ROURKE, THE. Finn-Thiele. net, 0 35
WAYWARD WINIFRED Sadlier	0 85
WHERE THE ROAD LED AND OTHER STORIES. Sadlier and others	1 25
WINNETOU, THE APACHE KNIGHT. Taggart.	0 85
WRONGFULLY ACCUSED Herchenbach.	0 45
YOUNG COLOR GUARD, THE. Bonesteel.	0 45

NOVELS AND STORIES.

"BUT THY LOVE AND THY GRACE" Finn, S.J.	1 00
CARROLL DARE Waggaman.	1 25
CIRCUS RIDER'S DAUGHTER Brackel.	1 25
CONNOR D'ARCY'S STRUGGLES. Bertholds.	1 25
CORINNE'S VOW Waggaman	1 25
DION AND THE SIBYLS Keon.	1 25
FABIOLA. Wiseman Illustrated	0 90
FABIOLA'S SISTER Clarke.	1 25
FATAL BEACON, THE Brackel.	1 25
FORGIVE AND FORGET. Lingens.	1 50
HEARTS OF GOLD. Edhor	1 25
HEIRESS OF CRONENSTEIN, THE Countess Hahn-Hahn.	1 25
HER BLIND FOLLY Holt	1 25
HER FATHER'S DAUGHTER Hinkson. net, 1 25
IDOLS; or, The Secrets of the Rue Chaussee d'Antin. De Navery.	1 25
IN THE DAYS OF KING HAL Taggart net, 1 25
IN GOD'S GOOD TIME Ross	1 25
"KIND HEARTS AND CORONETS" Harrison.	1 25
LADY OF THE TOWER AND OTHER STORIES.	1 25
LET NO MAN PUT ASUNDER Marié.	1 00
LINKED LIVES Douglas	1 50
MARCELLA GRACE Mulholland. Illustrated Edition.	1 25
MIRROR OF SHALOTT. Benson. net, 1 25
MISS ERIN. Francis	1 25
MONK'S PARDON, THE De Navery.	1 25
MR. BILLY BUTTONS Lecky	1 25
"NOT A JUDGMENT." Keon	1 25
OTHER MISS LISLE, THE Martin.	1 25
OUT OF BONDAGE Holt.	1 25
OUTLAW OF CAMARGUE, THE. Lamothe.	1 25
PASSING SHADOWS Yorke	1 25
PERE MONNIER'S WARD Lecky	1 25
PILKINGTON HEIR, THE Sadlier	1 25
PRODIGAL'S DAUGHTER, THE By Lelia Hardin Bugg.	1 00
RED INN OF ST. LYPHAR, THE A Romance of La Vendée. Sadlier.	1 25
ROMANCE OF A PLAYWRIGHT. By Vte Henri de Bornier.	1 00
ROSE OF THE WORLD Martin	1 25
ROUND TABLE OF AMERICAN CATHOLIC NOVELISTS. Complete Stories, with Biographies, Portraits, etc	1 50
ROUND TABLE OF FRENCH CATHOLIC NOVELISTS Complete Stories, with Biographies, Portraits, etc	1 50
ROUND TABLE OF GERMAN CATHOLIC NOVELISTS. Illustrated	1 50
ROUND TABLE OF IRISH AND ENGLISH CATHOLIC NOVELISTS. Complete Stories, Biographies, Portraits, etc. Cloth,	1 50
RULER OF THE KINGDOM, THE, and other Phases of Life and Character. Keon	1 25
SECRET OF THE GREEN VASE. Cooke.	1 25
SENIOR LIEUTENANT'S WAGER.	1 25
SHADOW OF EVERSLEIGH. Lansdowne.	1 25

7

SOGGARTH AROON. Guinan, C.C.	1 25
SON OF SIRO. Copus, S.J.	1 50
THAT MAN'S DAUGHTER. Ross.	1 25
TRAIL OF THE DRAGON.	1 25
TRAINING OF SILAS, THE. Devine, S.J.	1 25
TRUE STORY OF MASTER GERARD, THE. Sadlier.	1 25
UNRAVELING OF A TANGLE, THE. Taggart.	1 25
VOCATION OF EDWARD CONWAY. Egan.	1 25
WAY THAT LED BEYOND. By J. Harrison.	1 25
WHEN LOVE IS STRONG. Keon.	1 25
WOMAN OF FORTUNE, A. By Christian Reid.	1 25
WORLD WELL LOST. By Esther Robertson.	0 75

LIVES AND HISTORIES.

AUTOBIOGRAPHY OF ST. IGNATIUS LOYOLA. Edited by O'Conor, S.J.	net, 1 25
ANGLICAN ORDINATIONS. Semple, S.J.	net, 0 35
BEGINNINGS OF CHRISTIANITY. Shahan.	net, 2 00
CHURCH HISTORY. Businger.	0 75
GOLDEN BELLS IN CONVENT TOWERS.	net, 1 00
HISTORY OF THE CATHOLIC CHURCH. Brueck. 2 vols.,	net, 3 00
HISTORY OF THE CATHOLIC CHURCH. Shea.	net, 1 50
HISTORY OF THE PROTESTANT REFORMATION. Cobbett.	net, 0 75
LIFE OF BLESSED VIRGIN. Illustrated. Rohner.	net, 1 25
LIFE OF CHRIST. Illustrated. Cochem.	net, 1 25
LIFE OF POPE PIUS X.	2 00
LIFE OF MOST REV. JOHN HUGHES. Brann.	net, 0 75
LIFE OF OUR LORD AND SAVIOUR JESUS CHRIST AND OF HIS VIRGIN MOTHER MARY. Brennan. 4to.	net, 10 00
(Easy payment plan, $1.00 down, $1.00 a month.)	
LIFE OF SISTER ANNE KATHERINE EMMERICH. Wegener, O.S.A.	net, 1 75
LIFE OF VEN. MARY CRESCENTIA HOESS. Degman, O.S.F.	net, 1 25
LITTLE LIVES OF SAINTS FOR CHILDREN. Berthold. Ill. Cloth,	0 60
LITTLE PICTORIAL LIVES OF SAINTS. New, cheap edition.	1 25
LOURDES. Clarke, S.J.	1 00
MIDDLE AGES, THE. Shahan.	net, 2 00
PATRON SAINTS FOR CATHOLIC YOUTH. 3 vols. Each,	0 60
PICTORIAL LIVES OF THE SAINTS.	net, 2 00
ST. ANTHONY, THE SAINT OF THE WHOLE WORLD. Ward. Cloth,	net, 0 75
STORY OF JESUS. Illustrated.	net, 0 60
STORY OF THE DIVINE CHILD. Lings.	0 60
VICTORIES OF THE MARTYRS. Liguori.	net, 1 50

THEOLOGY, LITURGY, SERMONS, SCIENCE, AND PHILOSOPHY.

ANGLICAN ORDINATIONS. Semple, S.J.	0 35
BENEDICENDA. Schulte.	net, 1 50
BUSINESS GUIDE FOR PRIESTS. Stang.	net, 1 00
CHRISTIAN APOLOGETICS. Devivier.	net, 2 00
CHRISTIAN PHILOSOPHY: God. Driscoll.	net, 1 50
CHRIST IN TYPE AND PROPHECY. Maas, S.J. 2 vols.,	net, 4 00
CHURCH TREASURER'S PEW COLLECTION AND RECEIPT BOOK.	net, 1 00
COMPENDIUM JURIS CANONICI. Smith.	net, 2 00
COMPENDIUM JURIS REGULARIUM. Bachofen.	net, 2 50
COMPENDIUM SACRAE LITURGIAE. Wapelhorst.	net, 2 50
CONSECRANDA. Schulte.	net, 1 50
DATA OF MODERN ETHICS EXAMINED. Ming, S.J.	2 00
ELEMENTS OF ECCLESIASTICAL LAW. Smith, D.D. 3 vols., each,	net, 2 50
GENERAL INTRODUCTION TO THE STUDY OF HOLY SCRIPTURES. Gigot, S.S.	net, 2 50

GENERAL INTRODUCTION TO THE STUDY OF HOLY
  SCRIPTURES. Abridged Edition. Gigot, S.S.   *net,* 1 50
GOD KNOWABLE AND KNOWN. Ronayne, S.J.   *net,* 1 50
GOOD CHRISTIAN, THE. Allen, D.D. 2 vols.   *net,* 5 00
HISTORY OF THE MASS AND ITS CEREMONIES IN THE
  EASTERN AND WESTERN CHURCH. O'Brien.   *net,* 1 25
HUNOLT'S SERMONS. 12 vols.   *net,* 25 00
INTRODUCTION TO STUDY OF OLD TESTAMENT. Vol. I
  and II. Gigot. Each,   *net,* 1 50
JESUS LIVING IN THE PRIEST. Millet-Byrne.   *net,* 2 00
LIBER STATUS ANIMARUM; or, Parish Census Book. *Pocket*
  Edition, net, 0.25: *Large Edition,* half-leather,   *net,* 3 00
MARRIAGE PROCESS IN THE UNITED STATES. Smith.   *net,* 2 50
MANUAL OF MORAL THEOLOGY. Vols. I and II. Slater, S.J.
  2 vols.   *net,* 5 50
MANUAL OF THEOLOGY FOR THE LAITY. Geiermann.
  Paper, *net,* 0.20; cloth,   *net,* 0 40
MEDULLA FUNDAMENTALIS THEOLOGIAE MORALIS. Stang.
                                                    net, 1 00
MORAL PRINCIPLES AND MEDICAL PRACTICE. Coppens,
  S.J.   *net,* 1 00
NATURAL LAW AND LEGAL PRACTICE. Holaind, S.J.   *net,* 2 00
NEW SERIES OF HOMILIES FOR THE WHOLE YEAR.
  Bonomelli-Byrne. 4 vols.   *net,* 5 00
OUTLINES OF DOGMATIC THEOLOGY. Hunter, S.J. 3 vols., *net,* 1 50
OUTLINES OF NEW TESTAMENT HISTORY. Gigot. Cloth,   *net,* 1 50
OUTLINES OF SERMONS. Schuen.   *net,* 2 00
PASTORAL THEOLOGY. Stang, D.D.   *net,* 1 50
PHILOSOPHIA MORALI, DE. Russo.   *net,* 2 00
POLITICAL AND MORAL ESSAYS. Rickaby, S.J.   *net,* 1 50
PRAXIS SYNODALIS.   *net,* 0 75
PRIEST IN THE PULPIT. Schuech-Luebbermann.   *net,* 1 50
REGISTRUM BAPTISMORUM.   *net,* 3 50
REGISTRUM MATRIMONIORUM.   *net,* 3 00
RELATION OF EXPERIMENTAL PSYCHOLOGY TO PHI-
  LOSOPHY. de Mercier.   *net,* 0 35
RIGHTS OF OUR LITTLE ONES. Conway, S.J. Paper,   0 10
RITUALE COMPENDIOSUM.   *net,* 0 90
SANCTUARY BOYS' ILLUSTRATED MANUAL. McCallen, S.S. *net,* 0 50
SERMONS, ABRIDGED, FOR SUNDAYS. Liguori.   *net,* 1 25
SERMONS FOR CHILDREN OF MARY. Callerio.   *net,* 1 50
SERMONS FOR CHILDREN'S MASSES. Frassinetti-Lings.   *net,* 1 50
SERMONS FOR THE SUNDAYS AND CHIEF FESTIVALS OF
  THE ECCLESIASTICAL YEAR. Pottgeisser, S.J. 2 vols. *net,* 2 50
SERMONS FROM THE LATINS. Baxter.   *net,* 2 00
SERMONS ON DEVOTION TO THE SACRED HEART.
  Bierbaum.   *net,* 0 75
SERMONS ON THE BLESSED SACRAMENT. Scheuer-
  Lasance.   *net,* 1 50
SHORT SERMONS FOR LOW MASSES. Schouppe, S.J.   *net,* 1 25
TEXTUAL CONCORDANCE OF HOLY SCRIPTURES. Williams. *net,* 3 50
THEORY AND PRACTICE OF THE CONFESSIONAL. Shieler.   3 50
VADE MECUM SACERDOTUM. Cloth, *net,* 0.25; Morocco, *net,* 0 50

MISCELLANEOUS.

ACROSS WIDEST AMERICA. Devine, S.J.   *net,* 1 50
BENZIGER'S MAGAZINE. The Popular Catholic Family Magazine.
  Subscription per year,   2 00
CATHOLIC HOME ANNUAL. Stories by Best Writers.   0 25
CORRECT THING FOR CATHOLICS. Bugg.   *net,* 0 75
GENTLEMAN, A. Egan.   *net,* 0 75
HOW TO GET ON. Feeney.   *net,* 1 00
LADY, A. Manners and Usages. Bugg.   *net,* 0 75
RECORD OF BAPTISMS. 14x10 inches, 3 styles.   3.00, 4.00, 6 00
RECORD OF MARRIAGES. 14x10 inches. 3 styles.   3.00, 4.00, 6 00
SONGS AND SONNETS. Egan.   1 00
VISIT TO EUROPE AND THE HOLY LAND. Fairbanks.   1 50
WHAT CATHOLICS HAVE DONE FOR SCIENCE. Brennan. *net,* 25

PRAYER-BOOKS.

Benziger Brothers publish the most complete line of prayer-books in this country, embracing Prayer-books for Children; Prayer-books for First Communicants; Prayer-books for Special Devotions; Prayer-books for General Use. Catalogue will be sent free on application.

SCHOOL-BOOKS.

Benziger Brothers' school text-books are considered to be the finest published. They embrace New Century Catholic Readers (Illustrations in Colors); Catholic National Readers; German-English Readers; Catechisms; History; Geographies; Grammars; Spellers; Elocution; Charts, etc.

THE BEST STORIES AND ARTICLES.

1000 ILLUSTRATIONS A YEAR.

BENZIGER'S MAGAZINE

The Popular Catholic Family Monthly

RECOMMENDED BY 70 ARCHBISHOPS AND BISHOPS

Subscription, $2.00 a Year

What Benziger's Magazine gives its Readers in a single Year.

Three complete novels of absorbing interest—equal to three books at $1.25 each.
Fifty stories by the best writers—equal to a book of 300 pages at $1.25.
One thousand beautiful illustrations.
Twenty-five large reproductions of celebrated paintings.
Twenty articles—equal to a book of 150 pages—on travel and adventure; on the manners, customs and home-life of peoples.
Twenty articles—equal to a book of 150 pages—on historic events, times, places, important industries.
Twenty articles—equal to a book of 150 pages—on the fine arts; celebrated artists and their paintings, sculpture, music, etc.
Twelve pages of games and amusements for in and out-of-doors.
Seventy-two pages of fashions, fads, and fancies, gathered at home and abroad, helpful hints for home workers, cooking recipes, etc.
"Current Events," the important happenings over the whole world.

An Easy Way of Getting Books.

Each year we publish four New Novels by the best Catholic authors. These novels are interesting beyond the ordinary; not strictly religious, but Catholic in tone and feeling.

We ask you to give us a Standing Order for these novels. The price is $1.25 a volume postpaid. The $5.00 is not to be paid at one time, but $1.25 each time a volume is published.

As a Special Inducement for giving us a standing order for these novels, we will give you *free* a subscription to Benziger's Magazine. This Magazine is recognized as the best and handsomest Catholic magazine published. The regular price of the Magazine is $2.00 a year.

Thus for $5.00 a year — paid $1.25 at a time — you will get four good books and receive in addition *free* a year's subscription to Benziger's Magazine.

Send $1.25 for the first novel and get your name placed on the subscription list of Benziger's Magazine.

10

it would introduce confusion and disorder
into the commonwealth.